C000078987

No More Buddha, Only Football

Also by Chris England

BALHAM TO BOLLYWOOD

Chris England

No More Buddha,
Only Football

Hodder & Stoughton

Copyright © 2003 by Chris England

First published in Great Britain in 2003 by Hodder and Stoughton
A division of Hodder Headline

The right of Chris England to be identified as the Author
of the Work has been asserted by him in accordance with the
Copyright, Designs and Patents Act 1988.

A Hodder and Stoughton Book

1 3 5 7 9 10 8 6 4 2

All rights reserved. No part of this publication may be
reproduced, stored in a retrieval system, or transmitted, in any form
or by any means, without the prior written permission of the publisher,
nor be otherwise circulated in any form of binding or cover other
than that in which it is published and without a similar condition
being imposed on the subsequent purchaser.

A CIP catalogue record for this title is
available from the British Library

ISBN 0 340 82547 2

Typeset in Sabon by Palimpsest Book Production Limited,
Polmont, Stirlingshire
Printed and bound in Great Britain by Clays Ltd, St Ives plc

Hodder and Stoughton
A division of Hodder Headline
338 Euston Road
London NW1 3BH

To my father and my sons

Picture Acknowledgements

Photographs are from the author's collection, except the following:

Page 1: © *The Asahi Shimbun*, Tokyo. Page 3 ©Getty Images/photos Alex Livesey below right and Ross Kinnaird above centre. Page 4: ©Action Images/photo Andrew Budd below left and ©Getty Images/photo Laurence Griffiths below right. Page 5: ©Getty Images/photo Rossm Kinnaird above centre. Page 7: ©Getty Images/photos Laurence Griffiths centre right and below left. Page 8: Getty Images/photos Alex Livesey centre, Ben Radford below left and David Cannon below right, both.

Contents

I
No More Buddha

An hour on the subway into the suburbs of Tokyo you come to the end of the line, a gleaming new station in the middle of nowhere called Urawa-Misono. This is the custom-built stop for a gleaming new football stadium in the middle of nowhere, one of ten that the Japanese have provided for the World Cup and for which the future is uncertain to say the least.

For the present, though, Saitama stadium is the centre of the sporting world's attention, since it is here, this afternoon, that England with their Swedish coach will take on Sweden with their eight English-based players in the fifth match of the tournament, which has already begun with a bang.

Hundreds of eager fans mill around outside the station, whiling away the time till kick-off. There are clusters here and there of big yellow-shirted Vikings with horned plastic helmets and fake blond pigtails, but the vast majority are wearing white England shirts with BECKHAM emblazoned across the shoulders above a big number 7. By far the lion's share of these – the three lions' share – are Japanese. Couples, children, teenagers, businessmen, all having the time of their lives at the biggest fancy-dress party in the world.

To make up for the complete lack of shops or bars or cafés of any kind here in this industrial wasteland, the organisers have constructed the International Amenities Village, a sprawling agglomeration of stalls selling World Cup merchandise, beer, and 'Foods of the World'. And bonsai trees, too, if you

I

can be bothered to cart them away in their huge earthen-ware pots.

An energetic group of youngsters, all in blue T-shirts, hover around a stall, grabbing passers-by. In front of the stall is a large sign, written on a map of Japan, which reads:

Why Don't You Enjoy Japan!! Try It!!

Since I am already in Japan, trying it, this message seems more than a little redundant, but while I look this over I am collared by one of these young chaps, who tells me that his name is Daiju.

We Love Japan! is the slogan written on his T-shirt, and Daiju explains the aim of his somewhat evangelical organ-isation.

'We want to promote Japanese culture,' he says. 'We want all our visitors to try Japanese culture. Japanese culture is very good, very exciting, so not just football, try Japanese culture, OK?'

'I see,' I say. 'Like what sort of thing, particularly?' Daiju grabs my arm and leads me over to their stall.

'Look! This machine can put your face on a badge!' Which may just be the most fantastic non sequitur I have ever heard.

Daiju's English is pretty good. He tells me that he learned it while he was living in Swansea for a short time, and I listen attentively for his conversation to be peppered with 'look you' and 'boyo', but no such luck.

Actually I find, as I have already several times in the few days I have so far been in Japan, that talking to him is a lot like talking to that oriental Benny Hill character. You know the one I mean. He has little round glasses . . . oh no, hang on, all his characters have little round glasses. Well, anyway, oriental Benny would make merry by mispronouncing a perfectly straightforward line, usually utilising the rarefied comedy of transposing the letter L with the letter R, as in the phrase: 'Then she sat down on the rhino.'

'On the rhino?' his confused sidekick – usually Henry McGee, sometimes Allan Cuthbertson – would say. This would get oriental Benny exasperated beyond belief.

'No-o-o! Not on the rhino, on the *rhino*. On the rhino in the kitchen!'

'She had a rhino in her kitchen?'

'No-o-o! Not a rhino, the *kitchen* rhino. On the froor, the rhino on the kitchen *froor*!'

'Oh, I see, the lino, she sat on the kitchen lino.'

'Yeees! That is what I said, you sirry iriot! Why you no risten?'

Hours of fun.

Daiju and his pals hope to break down our preconceptions of Japan as a closed and forbidding place, and promote his country's image as a welcoming and open society with a rich and diverse heritage. Having said that, his ambition is to work at the United Nations headquarters in New York as a translator, so he himself can't wait to get the hell out of the place.

On the subject of football he becomes very enthusiastic.

'World Cup is great!' he cries, waving his arms in the air. 'World Cup is fantastic! Many many changes here! Because of football . . . is no more Buddha!'

For a moment, I can't quite believe what I am hearing. No more Buddha? Does he mean that the Japanese have become so besotted with football that they are prepared to turn their backs on hundreds of years of enlightenment? I turn into Henry McGee.

'I'm sorry?' I say.

'Yes, yes. No more Buddha. Only football!'

'No more Buddha?'

'No-o-o!' Daiju says, exasperated. 'Not no more Buddha. No more *Buddha*! Because of football . . . is no more buddha. No more buddha between countries!'

He stops short of saying 'Sirry iriot!' or 'Why you no risten?', but it's a perfect Benny Hill routine even without the icing on the cake, and my joy is such that when he asks me to paint England flags on his face, I say: 'Why ever not?'

After all, because of football, is no more Buddha.

I decide that I will throw myself, as much as possible – I'm not eating any raw fish – into Japanese culture, and to prove it I take a few moments to try to work Daiju's admirable sentiment into a *haiku*, the ancient seventeen-syllable Japanese form of writing poetry. What is required, really, for the perfect *haiku* is a single encapsulating image, combining a strong visual evocation with a profound thought about the world and man's place in it. Or failing that, something like this:

> *Japanese couples in Beckham shirts*
> *No more Buddha, only football.*

Count 'em up. That's poetry, folks . . .

I spent five weeks at the World Cup in Japan in the summer of 2002, and this bright-eyed young lad's vision of national boundaries being rendered irrelevant by sport kept popping into my head again and again. In the beginning I scoffed, cynically, at its youthful idealism. After all, in the past the World Cup has rather drawn attention to borders rather than doing away with them. El Salvador and Honduras once started a war over a World Cup qualifier back in 1969.

As I and thousands of others were drawn into the all-absorbing joyride that was the 2002 World Cup, though, I kept seeing things, people, incidents, images, that made me think he was on to something. A young girl on a bus, for one example, with a football scarf that celebrated all the participating nations, a fan of the tournament rather than a narrow xenophobe, a citizen of the world.

The way the Japanese took to and supported the England team, for another, utterly disarmed and banished any thoughts of hooliganism or drunken rampaging. It wasn't only England, they followed all the visiting teams, and not just casually either, they went the whole hog. They literally bought the T-shirt. And this generosity of spirit eventually spread to everyone, making a major football tournament, for once, a totally civilised event in which we could all participate either in person or via the television set as citizens of the planet.

The outside world did try to burst in, with news that India and Pakistan were again rumbling towards war over Kashmir, with horrible pictures of more suicide bombings in Israel, and with threats of terrorist attacks from North Korea on the tournament itself, which happily never materialised, but all these things failed utterly to put the football into perspective. Rather the harmonious and generous atmosphere surrounding our proceedings came to shed a different light on those supposedly more important events elsewhere, showing them for the crass, stupid, pointless, ruinous, insensitive, evil, bungling, small-minded posturings they really were.

We were the ones watching history being made, out in Japan and South Korea, where there was no more Buddha. Only football.

2
Metatarsals

'Don't cry for me, England! The Empire, the Queen,
London Bridge trembles . . . once it was the hand
of Diego Armando Maradona, now it is the foot of
Aldo Duscher.'
– *Olé*, Argentina's best-selling football daily

26 MAY

When I was nine we did a project at my school. Everyone
in the class had to find out as much as they could about a
foreign country. Some, like the ostentatiously tanned son of
the local Volkswagen dealer, opted for the place they had been
on their holidays: 'Majorca is a small country with lots of sea.
I slept in a bunk bed . . .' The rest of us – having determined
that Skegness and the Isle of Man were not, in fact, foreign
countries – were left to stick a pin in the map of the world,
with the licence to go as far afield as we wanted.

I chose Japan. Not quite the furthest away in terms of miles,
but somehow more impossibly alien and exotic than Australia,
home of Skippy, Rolf, and Ian Redpath, which, as everyone
knew, was where you'd end up if you dug your way to the
other side of the world. And anyway, Australia was just a
big desert. Japan was a land of earthquakes and volcanoes,
of inscrutable and implacable comic-strip soldiers, tiny radios
and calculators, and extraordinary myths and legends.

One reason was that, as a child, I spent hours looking at
league tables. Football ones, of course, but also wherever else

6

I found them, in the atlas or the *Guinness Book of Records* or the *Dunlop Book of Facts*, and I'd noticed that Tokyo, the capital of Japan, was the World's Top City, ahead of New York (second) and London (third), with over ten million people living there.

It was so crowded, apparently, that there were people whose whole full-time job was to cram commuters into the subway trains like so much spam in a can, and there were so many cars that traffic policemen could only work twenty-minute shifts before taking a break for some oxygen. In my fascinated imagination Japan was like the planet in *Star Trek* that was so overcrowded that everyone could barely shuffle miserably around in about two square feet of space, and the president's daughter had to snog Captain Kirk in order to contract as many alien diseases as she could from him so that she could pass them on and start thinning out the population.

Another reason was the film *You Only Live Twice*, in which Sean Bond gets bathed by geisha girls, trains to be a ninja, and flies around on a miniature helicopter, and Ernst Stavro Blofeld has built a rocket launcher like Cape Canaveral inside a volcano.

And so while my classmates were drawing their pictures of kangaroos or the Eiffel Tower, I was reading about a fellow called the Kappa who had a pool of water in the top of his head, and how the way to get rid of him was to bow politely, so that he would bow in return, tip himself out, and then have to scuttle off to refill his cranium.

Ever since I was nine, then, I've had it in the back of my mind that I'd like to go to Japan. I've made a career, though, in the worlds of comedy and football, and writing comedy about football. Now the Japanese have never really looked like setting the world on fire as footballers. Their professional competition, the JLeague, has only been going since 1993 – Gary Lineker retired to go and play there for Nagoya Grampus Eight in its very first season. And if there is one other area in which Japan has never seriously threatened to make a mark in the world it's humour. So although I've managed, over the years, to get variously sent or taken to America, Australia, Israel, India, Italy, Morocco, France and Spain it did rather look as if I would never be able to wangle a work trip out to the land of the Rising Sun.

Then FIFA, in their wisdom, allocated the Japanese a World Cup – or, more specifically, half a World Cup, with the other half going to South Korea, their ancient enemies from across the Sea of Japan (or as the South Koreans like to call it, the Sea of South Korea).

England obligingly arranged to take part, via a qualification campaign positively overloaded with images burned onto the memory's retina for ever. Kevin Keegan striding off after the last game ever at Wembley with the rain pouring down and the boos ringing in his ears. The messianic arrival of the stack-heeled ice man from Sweden, Sven Goran Eriksson. The electronic scoreboard at the Olympic Stadion in Munich reading, gloriously, *Deutschland 1 England 5*. And, surpassing even that for iconic splendour, David Beckham's last-gasp free kick curving over the Greek wall and into the top corner of the Old Trafford goal.

The draw, in December 2001, dumped Eriksson's England into Group F along with Argentina (the favourites), Nigeria (the best team in Africa), and Sweden (whom we haven't beaten since 1968). This was quickly and inevitably dubbed the 'Group of Death', despite a valiant attempt by the Nigerian coach to have it nicknamed 'The Killer Zone'.

The conventional wisdom is that every tournament throws up a grouping which makes everyone else wince with gratitude at having avoided it, but I actually can't remember one anything like as difficult as this – even in Mexico 1986, when there was a 'Gruppo di Muerto' featuring Scotland, West Germany, Uruguay and Denmark. The other three teams didn't seem to regard this as a particularly challenging prospect, they simply rubbed their hands together with glee, shouting: 'Yippee! Scotland!'

Anyway, at least England were drawn to play all their matches in Japan, so I went to see my mate Jim, who works for talkSPORT, the dedicated sports-and-sports-phone-ins radio station. Jim is a stocky Geordie fixer, and something of a fancy dresser for the world of sports broadcasting. When we worked together a few years ago on a weekly comedy football show called *Who Ate All the Pies?*, I learned much from him about the world of independent radio producing, but the principal thing which has stuck with me is the desirability of wearing socks that match your shirt.

Back in 1998 we did some editions of *Who Ate All the Pies?* from the World Cup in France, which I think may have gone under the title of *Who Ate All the Baguettes?* but I'm not a hundred per cent sure of that. Our shows consisted of some comedy sketches and inserts which went alongside proper coverage of the matches. We stayed in the Camargue near Arles in a *gîte* which had once belonged to Roman Polanski and which had white horses and a swimming pool in the garden, as well as some of the biggest mosquitoes I've ever seen anywhere. Jim wangled us some tickets for matches, and all in all it was a very agreeable gig.

I proposed to him that this time I could do a sort of offbeat World Cup diary from Japan. Offbeat is a great word, and one I would only ever use in a proposal. It kind of teasingly suggests that you might do something funny, but it in no way commits you to getting any actual laughs.

Happily, Jim and talkSPORT were caught up in the euphoric post-qualification mood of the nation and had big plans for the World Cup. Obviously, as a dedicated sports-and-sports-phone-ins radio station, they couldn't ignore something like a World Cup without looking rather foolish, but it was by no means certain that they would go so far as to actually send people out to the Far East.

For Euro 2000, for example, they had baulked at paying for the rights to have their commentators actually inside the stadia, and had covered the whole tournament from off the telly. Crowd effects came from a sound effects record, volume turned up for moments of particular excitement, and this could make even the most exciting matches sound like a quiet afternoon at Hove, where Sussex are 220 for 4, meandering towards a gentle draw with Gloucestershire. Pretty soon talkSPORT were 'outed' by the press, and had to change how they described their coverage, from 'exclusive live' to '*not* exclusive, *as* live'.

talkSPORT got involved in negotiations with Kirch, the ailing German media giant who were dispensing the proper broadcasting rights for the 2002 World Cup, and Jim's initial plan was to send commentary teams to Japan and South Korea, producers, researchers, technicians, the whole kit and also not forgetting the caboodle. And there would be room on the trip for one offbeat diarist. Woo – as Homer Simpson might say – hoo!

This plan has dwindled and withered away over the last few months, until now there's just me and one other person going, and someone, somewhere, is working on a special Japanese crowd sound effects tape for Jim. Apparently a Japanese crowd sounds completely different – more little cymbals, or something. Dom, my sole colleague, is with an official FA press party and will spend the whole time in Kobe near the England team base on Awaji island covering the press conferences, injury bulletins and training sessions. I, on the other hand, am free as a bird. I start my research right away, by watching (for the umpteenth time) my video of *You Only Live Twice*.

Jim has managed to wangle me tickets for the three England games in the Group of Death, although sadly not as much actual money as it is going to cost me to go over there, but what the hell – he's still top of the list for some duty-free sake. And if England make it through to the knock-out phase, well, I'll just have to see what can be done out there.

Sven and the England squad have arrived on Awaji island, which they are making their World Cup base, via some acclimatisation training in Dubai and a friendly against Japan's co-hosts in South Korea. England looked good in the first half in Seogwipo and led through a Michael Owen goal, but then Sven made seven substitutions and they let in an equaliser while they were still trying to work out who was supposed to be marking whom.

This morning England play Cameroon in their last warm-up match. Again it is a rather disjointed performance, as Sven gives all eighteen of the twenty-three members of his squad who are fit a run out. David Seaman has a bit of a rest, poor old bloke. David Beckham is still racing against time to be fit for the Sweden match next Sunday after breaking a metatarsal bone in his foot seven weeks ago. It was a nasty foul by Deportivo la Coruna's Argentinian hatchet man Aldo Duscher that did the damage, much to the glee of *Olé*, Argentina's top sports paper.

The daily bulletins from the England camp, and from Beckingham Palace where the golden boy was sleeping in an oxygen tent with his foot in a little bouncy castle, meant we all knew a lot more about metatarsals than we did before. This was just as well because later we all knew just what the prognosis was for Gary Neville and then Danny Murphy, whose metatarsals similarly gave way. Beckham, as ever, was the trendsetter for a new designer football injury.

The other walking wounded are Ashley Cole, Nicky Butt – who has twisted his knee – and Kieron Dyer, ruled out of the World Cup immediately after being flattened in the last game of the Premiership season by Tahar El Khalej of Southampton

– whom he threatened to sue – but he has shown remarkable improvement since.

Cameroon take the lead in the fourth minute through Samuel Eto'o, and England equalise seven minutes later when Paul Scholes releases Darius Vassell in the area to bang in his third international goal. Vassell has made a late run into the reckoning, having scored with a spectacular volley on his debut against Holland in February, and he has looked strong, quick, and comfortable in every game he has played for Sven so far.

Geremi restores the African champions' lead in the second half, and Teddy Sheringham sets up Robbie Fowler for a ninetieth-minute header to make it 2–2. England's patched-up midfield emerges with some credit, Scholes plays well and so does Joe Cole, who has bagged the number 19 that Gazza wore in Italia 90. He booked his place with a sparkling performance against Paraguay in April, a game in which Dyer, suddenly and mysteriously being touted as the solution to England's problems on the left side, signally failed to impress.

Trevor Sinclair has a lively forty-five minutes after spending much of the last few days flying backwards and forwards between England and Japan, first on standby for Dyer, who was declared fit, then as a replacement for Murphy, who crocked himself while Sinclair was on his way home. Even if he doesn't get a game out here he now has enough air miles to take the rest of the lads to Disneyland Japan.

The real star today, though, as against South Korea a few days ago, is the energetic Owen Hargreaves, and at this rate the Bayern Munich youngster is playing himself into the first eleven for Saitama.

Hopefully Hargreaves' emergence will soften the blow of losing Steven Gerrard. Apparently Gerrard has needed an operation on a groin problem since about February, but Liverpool put it off in the hope of squeezing a few more half games out of him to help them to the title, and then, once that was no longer possible, into second place. Obviously the thought that this was jeopardising his participation in the World Cup never entered Houllier's thinking.

We've seen this before, of course, perhaps most memorably in 1986, when Bryan Robson badly needed an operation to pin a dislocated shoulder, but Ron Atkinson put it off, desperate for Manchester United to win the championship (they didn't), and it was England who paid the price when the skipper's arm popped out during the second match in Mexico. Mind you, with his injury record we counted ourselves lucky that his head didn't fall off.

Once the other squads were named it became clear that Sven is getting off pretty lightly. Rudi Voller has lost Scholl, Nowotny, Worns, Heinrich and Deisler, Luis Figo is struggling, and the entire Cameroon squad was five days late, stranded in Bangkok because their pilot hadn't got clearance to fly over Cambodia. Emerson, Brazil's captain, has gone home having dislocated his shoulder playing in goal in a training match, and Spain's first-choice keeper, Santiago Canizares, was ruled out after dropping a bottle of aftershave on his foot and then treading on the bits.

All these minor niggles paled into insignificance, though, alongside the Roy Keane business. The Ireland captain is in Cheshire walking his dog after coming off worst in a spat with boss Mick McCarthy, and it doesn't look as if he's coming back. Maybe the heat and humidity are getting to players already. There was another training ground bust-up in the Swedish camp, where mild-mannered Freddie Ljungberg had a pop at Olaf Mellberg after a late tackle in a practice match. Their team mates pulled them apart, both snarling in a most un-Scandinavian fashion.

So that's the preliminaries over, the end of the phoney war, and I'm flying out to Japan tomorrow for the start of the World Cup proper. I've spent the last few days trying to prepare myself, but the more guide book stuff I read, the more Japan just seems like an etiquette minefield.

Never wear the same slippers in the living room that you wear in the toilet.

Never leave your chopsticks sticking upright in your rice: this is a sign of death.

Always make sure you carry a business card – I promptly went out and got some printed with my Japanese mobile number and the London address of talkSPORT on them.

When you return a bow, remember that the angle of your bow is a statement of your status in relation to the other person . . .

I've decided that the only sensible approach is to blunder about like a hopeless foreign buffoon – a *gaijin* – and hope that the locals take pity on me and don't slice me in two with huge curved samurai swords for wearing the wrong slippers or bowing at the wrong angle. Or for stereotypically categorising them as the sort of people who might slice me in two with huge curved samurai swords.

Still, I thought I should be able to pick up a bit of working Japanese. If nothing else I should learn the phrases I will need as soon as I arrive, such as:

'It is a dark green holdall with brown handles.'

'Yes, I am sure I checked it in properly.'

'How long will it take for my bag to get from (insert foreign city here) to Tokyo?'

And of course:

'No, you see, let me explain. My name is England *and* my country is England. It's the same word. Hysterical, isn't it?'

I quickly worked out, though, that written Japanese was going to be a complete non-starter in the time I have available to me – i.e. less than about sixteen years. There are at least three distinct systems for a start, and they can all be used together, mixed in the same sentences, some of which go acrossways in which case they go left to right, and some of which go up and down in which case they are read right to left, and they all get jumbled up and the whole thing is a nightmare.

I pinned my hopes squarely on a fourth system, called *romaji*, which transliterates Japanese using our alphabet, and which at least you can read straightaway even if you don't understand anything. You get an idea of how devilishly complicated it is going to be, though, when you look at perhaps the simplest word in the English language, the first person singular. One syllable does the job for us – hell, one letter.

This is what it says for 'I' in the guide book:

I = *watashi*
I (familiar, men only) = *boku*
I (polite) = *watakushi*

'Yes' is another potential minefield. *Hai* is the word, but you shouldn't assume that because a Japanese person says *'hai'* they mean to answer in the affirmative. Often it can mean 'I understand' or 'I have heard the question and am thinking of my answer' or 'carry on' or 'can I help you'. It can also mean 'hello' – or 'hi', in fact. And you also have to take into account that they may be being polite, and saying *'hai'* when they mean *'chigaimasu'*, which is the horrible mouthful for 'no'.

The Japanese are exceedingly polite, and one word I am told to be on the lookout for everywhere is *sumimasen*, meaning 'excuse me' or 'I'm sorry'. It literally translates as 'I am inexcusable', but is such an all-purpose phrase now that it can be used as 'hello' or 'can I help you' – or *'hai'*, come to think of it – and has mostly lost that extravagant original meaning. When the Japanese really want to apologise for something they use a phrase which means something like 'I am the worthless dust beneath the wheels of your chariot' or 'please feel free to kill me now with a sharp thing'.

Daunting stuff. Yet when I look a little more closely at some of the *romaji* examples I see that it is possible to make a certain amount of headway by just pronouncing English words in a funny Japanese way. Yes, that's right, a bit like Benny Hill.

Hotel, for example. That's *hoteru*.

Suppose you want to go by cab. Why, then you will need to hail a *takeshi*.

The page with words for food looks like a minefield at first sight, but guess how you say lemon? And melon? Right both times. It's *remon*, and it's *meron*.

I note that the word for oyster and the word for persimmon is pronounced the same, *kaki*, and I hope to God that isn't going to cause me too much embarrassment. My favourite discoveries are words for fruit – *gurepufurutsu*, and *painappuru*. It seems impossible to speak about fruit in Japanese without sounding like an angry samurai. I can just imagine some sword-wielding banshee running into a village yelling '*Painappuru! Gurepufurutsu!*', whereupon everyone in the place would immediately persimmon themselves and head for the hills.

Here's another tip in the guide book. Place the sound *ka* at the end of a sentence to indicate a question. So to ask if a Japanese person is the owner of a small Ford vehicle that is either oyster-coloured or persimmon in tone, just point at them and say, with every confidence: 'Kaki Ka kaa ka?' I'll be fine . . .

3
Konnichiwa

'I go Boom!'
– Anastacia, 2002 World Cup official song

27 MAY

I'm off to the World Cup today. My flight is in the evening, so
Susan and I can pick up the boys from school and take them
with us to the airport to see me off. They are very excited. They
know that a trip to the airport means tea in a burger place and
a chance to drag me round the terminal shops at a time when
I'm just emotionally vulnerable enough to possibly buy them
a present. Peter manages to extract a kind of small beanbag
gorilla from me and John a model of Concorde to ease my guilt
at leaving them for five weeks. Michael (thirteen months) is
the only one to get into the World Cup spirit, fastening onto
a red-and-white England flag on a pointy stick, with which he
seems certain to jab someone in the eye before too long. Perhaps not the most sensible present for the baby, but what the
hell. He jabs me in the eye with it while I am paying for it.

My flight is a direct one from Heathrow to Tokyo with
All-Nippon Airways. Jim told me that their proud boast is
that all their staff have degrees, so I pay particular attention
to the stewardess attending to my side of the plane.

'I have a BA with honours in wet-wipe collection,' her cheery
smile seems to say, 'but it was my dissertation on the finer
points of UHT milk cartonette dispensing that finally swung
me my doctorate . . .'

I am on the lookout for football supporters on the plane but I can't really spot any. Usually, travelling football supporters are not shy about declaring their allegiance to the world, but I can just make out a Leeds United lapel badge on the middle-aged gent a couple of rows in front, the odd tattoo (also Leeds) and that's about it. There must be more, but maybe they are wary of identifying themselves too obviously, not knowing yet how England's travelling fans will be greeted in Japan.

Just as I am thinking this, three boisterous young lads barrel down the aisle in bright green replikit Ireland shirts, with no such concern troubling their slightly sozzled heads. A Mexican Wave of cheering and sniggering follows them to their seats, and I become a little concerned. They are planning to sit together in those shirts for eleven and a half hours – isn't there a danger that the build-up of static electricity might affect the plane's navigational instruments?

28 MAY

I arrive at Narita airport mid-afternoon, having not managed to sleep at all on the plane, as usual. On the slow shuffle to Immigration there is a disturbance up ahead, and all the zombies suddenly come back to life, craning and shoving to see what's going on.

It is the three Irish lads.

'Look!' one of them shouts. 'It's Jim Bowen!'

He and his mates are fumbling frantically in their hand luggage, trying to sort out their various cameras to capture this moment of accidental proximity to B-list celebrity. Other passengers crowd around, and there are one or two flashes as others snap a memento of the one-time tea-time darts quiz host.

The three Irish lads shove their cameras at someone to take their picture for them, and cluster round their bewildered prey. It's not Jim Bowen, of course. It's a tall, slightly stooping,

Japanese tourist, and as I sidle round the little mêlée his tor-
mentors are yelling: 'Go on! Say it! Great! Super! Smashin'!'

As they snap away at this poor bloke who looks a bit like
another bloke who used to be on the telly, a dapper little
figure in a yellow shirt, jeans pressed with a razor-sharp
crease, moccasins, and trendy narrow sunglasses slips past
unnoticed. It is Osvaldo Ardiles, a man who has actually won
the World Cup.

Heading towards Passport Control I can identify a few more
football fans. They are not wearing their club colours, or even
the national team shirt, but you can tell they are football fans
even so. They have on their courtroom suits, and are chewing
gum aggressively, walking an 'I'm hard, I am' walk, jutting
their jaws at anyone who dares to establish eye contact.

Another Irish fan is next to me in the line. A thoroughly
miserable chap in his fifties, his lugubrious features are perfectly set off by his enormous green-and-white foam top hat.
His mood is down to the fact that he reckons Ireland's chances
have been shafted by the Roy Keane fiasco – 'I'd got the tickets
by then so I thought I moight as well come anyhow,' he mutters
– and also because he has only been allowed one piece of hand
luggage (the hat).

As I head down the escalator into the open plan baggage
reclaim area, it transpires that there was yet another celebrity
on our plane. Sky TV's Chris Kamara stands at the bottom of
the escalator shouting to a journalist friend at the top.

'How you getting to Tokyo?'

'Narita Express,' his friend, who has done his homework,
calls back.

'What's that?' yells Chris, who hasn't.

'It's a train, Chris.'

'Oh . . .' Chris wanders off, clearly hoping to ponce a cab
share with someone else. Maybe someone else who hasn't
read the scare articles in the papers about how a taxi from
the airport to the centre of the capital costs 160 quid.

My bag is one of the first to emerge on the conveyor belt, and so I'm able to steal a march on everyone and hustle out into the airport terminal to begin to wrestle with the Japanese transport system. To my great relief, signs for the railway station are in both Japanese and English, and I find my way to the JR ticket office where I need to convert my voucher into a rail pass, which is the work of a minute or two.

On the platform an electronic display shows that there are only a few minutes to wait, and numbered signs on the platform show precisely where I need to stand to have the carriage with my reserved seat in it stop right in front of me. The train, the Narita Express to Tokyo, oozes into the station bang on time, the door hisses open right in front of me, and I find my seat, which is a luxurious armchair set at an angle to the slightly tinted picture window. There is a footrest, obviously intended for a much shorter person, but never mind, and on the wall by the door there is an electronic map showing the route we will be taking, on which little lights indicate our progress and count down to our arrival at Tokyo main station.

Not only that, but I find myself sitting three luxurious angled seats away from Osvaldo Ardiles. After watching the airport and its feeder roads give way to paddy fields as far as the eye can see, I dig around in my bag for the business cards I'd had printed, and proffer number one of a limited edition to the little Argentinian legend.

Ardiles spent five years coaching in Japan, latterly as manager of Shimizu S-Pulse, and says that he had a lovely time here and that it is a lovely country. I notice that the footrest is set at exactly the right distance from the seat for his tiny feet, so I'm not surprised he fitted right in, and am distracted by the memory of these very same feet doing a trick which I spent ages trying to perfect during the 1978 World Cup. He would step over the ball, and his trailing leg would then hug the ball to the heel of his other foot, which would then flick it right up over his head. He mostly did it during the warm-ups for games – I think the only time I saw him do it in open play was during *Escape to Victory* – but it still set him apart as one of the most eye-catching talents at that tournament.

He is in Japan to cover all Argentina's games for Adidas television – I am not sure what that is, a specialist cable network for all sports-shoe-related programming, perhaps – and is clearly very excited about the upcoming soccerfest. I ask him who he thinks will win it.

'Argentina have a big big chance,' he says. He is not as impressed as everyone else seems to be by France, and thinks that they have had a bit of a wobble lately which might be the start of a drop in form. Wishful thinking, I reckon. I ask him whether he thinks England will survive the Group of Death, and he goes very quiet, not wanting to upset me.

'It is a berry difficult group,' he says after a moment or two. 'Berry berry tough indeed. Sweden is strong, and Nigeria too . . .'

For a while there we are just a couple of football pundits shooting the breeze, until I blow it by asking him to sign my train ticket. Then I leave him to his own private thoughts, principally, it seems, to wonder why there was nobody waiting to meet him at Narita and why he was making his own way in on the train. Presumably he didn't fancy sharing a cab with Chris Kamara.

The view out of the window as the train heads into the city consists of a continuous series of apartment buildings, a variety of styles and colours, but all concrete, all relatively modern, and all crammed together. We pass a huge flouncy building with a sign saying 'Hearty Weddings', and then, handily nearby, a superstore called 'Babies R Us'. I imagine the same convenient complex houses the office of a divorce lawyer and the equivalent of the Child Support Agency. Everywhere the sides of the buildings are packed with giant adverts and neon signs, no surface knowingly unlogoed.

At Tokyo station I manage to negotiate the transfer to the suburban railway reasonably smoothly, with only a couple of crass misunderstandings on my part on the way. The stop I am looking for is called Yotsuya, and the first guy I approach enlightens me as to the pronunciation of my destination. Yot-*see*-ya, it should be, so I find that I've become a translated version of the joke London tourist who wants to go to Lei-*cess*-ter Square.

I walk the five minutes from Yotsuya to the hotel, which on first view seems desperately familiar for some reason. I put it down to the fact that all big international hotels look the same, as I've certainly never been here before, but there is definitely something nagging away at the back of my mind. There is a big car park at the front, and two big driveways curve up either side to the first-floor reception. I walk up the right-hand one, and am greeted by a young girl in a beige hotel concierge uniform and white gloves, who smiles, bows, and insists on powering the revolving glass door for me.

After checking in, I am shown to my twentieth-floor room by a tiny, pretty girl in a green uniform, who insists on carrying all my stuff despite visibly sagging as she slings it over her tiny shoulder. She takes me along a long carpeted walkway past a clutch of expensive-looking shops and boutiques to the main tower, and then up in the lift. It is quite a hike, and she seems even shorter when we finally reach our destination.

She points out a little checklist of features, including a kettle-which-is-always-hot and a complimentary *yukata* – a sort of tie-up dressing-gown affair for relaxing in – and then bows deeply before leaving the room backwards. I rather self-consciously venture a little bow in return, remembering at the last moment not to try to give her a tip, as they don't do that here.

Once left to my own devices I check out the room. The view is dominated, in the near distance, by a tightly packed clump of skyscrapers, all with little red lights blinking away to warn off air traffic. I spread my map of Tokyo on the single bed, and eventually decide that this must be Shinjuku, a business and entertainment district that is supposed to be one of the main hubs of the city. It looks much further away than it seems to be on the map, and I begin to get an idea of the scale of this place. It's massive. Down below, an expressway snakes off to the north. I'm on the twentieth floor and have double glazing, so I can't hear the traffic, which seems to be moving pretty freely, giving the lie to another scare story about the city being in near-constant gridlock.

The room is what's known as Western-style, which means it has swing doors, constant plinky-plonk piano music, and you can get shots of red eye on room service. Not really. It is just like any international hotel room in any major city anywhere in the world, is what it means – bed, telly, complimentary mints – until you come to the bathroom. The toilet in my room has more instructions and in more languages than your average video machine, and more computer hardware than the Apollo space capsule.

I decide I can't wait to plough through the blurb, and reckon I'll work it out as I go along. There's a control panel with buttons on it, and most seem to have little cartoon diagrams explaining their function, so I take my life in my hands and sit down. The first thing that happens when my backside touches the seat is that the toilet automatically flushes itself.

I stand up again. Quickly. Making a noise like this: 'Eyeeeoooh, now then! Eh? What?' A bit like bespectacled *Carry On* star Jack Douglas in his prime.

Perhaps I'll read the instructions first after all. Apparently Japanese ladies are so concerned that no noises should reveal what they're getting up to in the toilet that they will flush them more or less constantly. One enterprising fellow – and there's loads of them here – came up with a device which many ladies' public toilets (I'm told) now have mounted on the wall.

It makes the sound of a flushing toilet at the push of a button, thus saving gallons of water and oodles of embarrassment at one and the same time, and it's called the Melody Princess.

But what's happening in my toilet is not an automatic discretion-flush feature. My toilet has a little nozzle directing a spray up from below, it seems – the diagram by the button is unmistakably a cartoon of a jet of water hitting a bare arse, drawn exactly as it would be by an adolescent boy on his school desk – and the system flushes when you sit on it so that the cold water sitting waiting in the pipe since yesterday or whenever is replaced by lovely warm water straight from the heart of the gizmo. Very thoughtful, I'm sure, but by the time I've worked this out I've come uncomfortably close to just using the sink and to hell with it.

Later I try the spray feature, and the blow-dry feature. I find I can take it or leave it. Although in a couple of days I might wash and dry some socks in there.

I flick through the numbers on the television remote, and stumble across a variety of World Cup build-up stories on the Japanese channels. They are particularly interested in the Belgium team training session – Belgium are Japan's first opponents, a week today – and I also catch a glimpse of the Russians training, the Brazilians larking about, the Italians climbing a volcano, and Beckham risking a tentative kick with his healing metatarsal. There's Roy Keane, with a tear in his eye, saying on Irish television that he would still like to play in the World Cup, and the Irish PM Bertie Ahern sticking his oar in, saying the nation would 'sleep happier in their beds' if Keane was restored.

And on one of the two English channels, BBC World – CNN is the other – whom should I see but Osvaldo Ardiles, telling Rob Bonnet that Argentina and Nigeria would go through from the Group of Death. He obviously didn't want to upset me on the train.

29 MAY

Baffled by jet lag, I lie awake in the dark. All night. Just as I am convinced that I will not get to sleep at all and start to think about getting up for some breakfast I conk out, waking up thoroughly disorientated at about two in the afternoon.

I'd left the mobile phone charging up, and in my addled, just-awake state I think I'd better try to get the hang of it as soon as possible just in case talkSPORT are trying to get hold of me. I dial the hotel reception desk, and the phone cuts off as soon as they say '*Hai?!*' I go into a panic. I don't use a mobile phone at home, and I'm not familiar with them, and if this one doesn't work then how am I going to be able to do the offbeat reports I'm supposed to be doing? I need to try it again, so I ring Susan, thinking it's mid-afternoon, I'll catch her just before she goes to pick the boys up from school. She answers blearily, wondering what's wrong, because of course it's six in the morning in London, you idiot, and the baby hasn't even woken up yet. I begin to apologise, and the damn phone cuts off again.

I scrabble around and find the instruction booklet. It is the size of a credit card and, unlike the toilet, it has very little in the way of instructions in it. 'How to switch your phone on' is number one, and I'd managed that already. 'Dial numbers using the number keys' is next, and then, finally, comes 'How to switch your phone off'. I look for 'What to do when the bloody thing doesn't work' but can only find 'Dial numbers using the number keys' in Dutch.

Still fretting about the phone, I go out to find something to eat. My hotel is so vast that if you come out of the other end of it you find yourself at the next tube station along from Yotsuya, in a place called Akasaka. There a little bridge takes you over a waterway, with pleasure barges trolling up and down, and a little café with tables and chairs outside, the sort of thing you might see on a pleasant summer afternoon in Oxford, say. A couple of obvious England fans have set up camp there for the afternoon, with their tell-tale white knobbly knees sticking out of their Eric Morecambe shorts and pints of lager arrayed before them, and who can blame them, because the setting is quite picturesque and idyllic. Or it would be, if the sun wasn't blotted out by a huge flyover carrying an eight-lane expressway, with traffic thundering and doppler-effecting along and the fug of fumes hovering over it like cartoon anger.

Japan is an ancient country, and over the centuries innumerable events have shaped and reshaped it. One of the events that has had the most significant influence on Tokyo's transport infrastructure, it seems, was the 1964 Olympic Games. This was a chance for Japan to show the world how far it had come in the twenty years since their catastrophic defeat in the Second World War, and the last thing they wanted was for all the visiting dignitaries to be snarled up in their notorious traffic chaos. A programme of building huge arterial expressways to ferry excess cars through and around the city as quickly as possible was rapidly set up, and the quickest and easiest way to establish these huge new roads was to have them follow the routes of the waterways, hoisted above them on vast concrete-pillared flyovers. Eminently practical, but not exactly scenic.

On the far side of the bridge, under the expressway, there are at least eight more lanes of traffic, and while I'm waiting to cross these I try to phone my own hotel room. I get through – I'm not in – but just as I am leaving a message for myself, the damn phone cuts off *again*. What is wrong with it?

Amongst the shops and eateries in Akasaka is an English-style tea room. I glance in, and see it is full of Japanese customers, all taking their tea English-style, with little individual china teapots and cups and saucers, and their little individual pinkies crooked as if to the manner born. In a land which has its own elaborate and time-honoured tea ceremonies, this strikes a slightly odd note, but then many of the other establishments along this drag are big American chain franchises like McDonald's and Starbucks, so why not an English tea room too? I don't stay, but note that their menu has resolved the thorny issue of the pronunciation of the word *scone* once and for all by spelling it *scon*. So now you know.

I spot a photocopying shop advertising internet access, and nip in (sorry) to dash off a quick e-mail or two. One to Susan, apologising for waking her up just now, and one to Jim warning him that the phone may be a heap of junk.

Back in the room I try to ring the mobile monster from the room phone by the bed. It doesn't ring. I fling it over to the other side of the room and check out the latest World Cup news on the goggle box.

Sepp Blatter has been re-elected as head panjandrum of FIFA in Seoul despite a stormy six months. He was accused of rigging the FIFA presidential election in 1998, in which he surprisingly beat Lennart Johansson, by buying the votes of certain African delegates with bribes of $100,000. His enigmatic answer to this charge was: 'I often give money to people who cry.'

ISL, FIFA's marketing partner, collapsed, as did Kirch, the media company to which Blatter sold the broadcasting rights for the next two World Cups, which didn't look good. Issa Hayatou of Cameroon, the president of the Confederation of African Football, announced that he would challenge Blatter in the presidential election in Seoul, promising to be the 'Mr Transparent' of world football.

David Will, the Scottish FIFA vice-president, claimed that FIFA have in fact lost £215 million over the last four years, and have borrowed £313 million against income projected from the next two World Cups so that it looks as if they are in profit. Blatter wouldn't let him get to the microphone at the election debate this week, and Will was reduced to shouting 'FIFA is insolvent!' from the back.

Now Blatter has beaten Hayatou by 139 votes to 56, a remarkable and tearful triumph for the Swiss, who ends up being mob-hugged by many of those who voted for him, and perhaps now the true story of FIFA's financial shenanigans will never see the light of day. He's quite a piece of work, old Sepp.

I see a glimpse of an England training session. Beckham kicks a ball, and then falls over, but I can't understand whether this means he's OK for the Sweden game or has injured himself again. Freddie Ljungberg, it seems, has done himself some damage, either to his groin or a hip, and is a doubt for Sunday.

A couple of the Danish lads, larking about, have put ice in Jesper Gronkjaer's shorts, a gag which has rapidly escalated into a fist fight between the Chelsea man and Stig Tofting, who doesn't look like someone you'd want to get on the wrong side of. Maybe it's true what they say about the humid conditions not suiting the European teams. Last week it was Keane and McCarthy, then Ljungberg and Mellberg, and now the Danes, all going mad and beating each other up.

There is an article in the *Asahi Shimbun* about the so-called 'Seven Samurai', seven experienced directors of televised football coverage who have been brought in to mastermind Japan's World Cup programming from Britain, Germany, Spain and France. One of them claims to be able to predict a Zidane pass even before the Frenchman's team mates, which rather suggests he should be playing instead of working for a television company, but still . . .

I head for Ebisu early evening to meet up with Scott, a friend of a friend who works for Reuters here. This means taking the Chuo line across to Shinjuku, and then travelling a handful of stops around the Yamanote line, which is a huge loop, like the

Circle line in London only more reliable, connecting many of Tokyo's more interesting little sub-centres.

The train carriage has narrow bench seats along the sides, leaving plenty of room for standing and dangling from one of the many hand straps hanging from the ceiling. As I sway around I see that, right in front of my face, there is a television screen showing adverts. I think to myself: 'What a great place to advertise – a totally captive audience, bored out of their heads . . .' And then I look around and see that I am the only one paying any attention. This may be because I am the best part of a foot taller than everyone around me, and am the only one who can see it without cricking his neck.

As I am changing trains in Shinjuku station, I am again fiddling with the hated mobile. Suddenly I stop in my tracks, causing a stream of Tokyo commuters to break left and right at my back. Somehow I have brought up a screen which offers me the chance to 'change settings', and below the one which is flashing, the current one, presumably – no idea what it is – is one which says 'Rec Calls'. Receive Calls? That would be good, that would be a start. It might be Record Calls, but it's worth a go. I click something and manage to change things so that 'Rec Calls' is flashing. 'Now,' I think, 'I'll just leave it exactly like that, and get Scott to call the damn thing when I meet him . . .'

Immediately it starts to ring.

'Hi,' says Jim from London. 'It's working OK, then?'

We determine that the reception is probably bad in my hotel room, but I am still puzzling over what the previous setting can have been, that refused to let the phone ring and terminated any outgoing call after eight seconds. Some kind of ultra ultra economy thing?

Meeting Scott at Ebisu station is a little complicated, as the station itself seems to be an integral part of a gigantic department store, but I find him eventually, and he leads me off down a little side street.

'Where are we heading?' I ask.

'An English pub,' he says. 'It's called What The Dickens.'

I'm naturally then on the lookout for a ground-level establishment, with a sign outside showing a cheery Micawberish
fat gentleman brandishing a tankard of foaming ale. Nothing
remotely like this is in sight when Scott ducks into a doorway
and says: 'In here . . .'

It looks for all the world like a small office block, and on
a board by the lift are the names of the firms located here.
Amongst them, on the fourth floor, is written the legend *What
The Dickens*. In felt pen.

On the fourth floor you step out of the tiny lift into a perfect
reconstruction of an archetypal traditional English pub, with
weathered wooden floor, low dark-beamed ceiling, and Bass
and Boddingtons on draught. It is a shock at first, a bit like
stepping out of a time machine, or being transported onto
the planet Pub from the Starship *Enterprise*. Clearly a lot of
effort has gone into it, but how can they get any passing
trade at all?

I spend a very enjoyable evening with Scott and his mates
– Cormac, an analyst for Morgan Stanley, Jake, who works
for an Italian magazine publisher, and Sebastian, a freelance
journalist and the author of a book called *Japanese Rules*
about Japanese football which I have with me but very nearly
left behind in London, having put it to one side to try and get
my slippers into my bag.

I haven't seen many English fans here yet, and I'm hoping
that any troublemakers will stay away from this tournament
because of the expense and the distances involved, but this
seems a forlorn hope. Jake tells us that he was approached in
Shinjuku earlier this evening on account of 'looking English'
by a bloke who immediately told Jake that he, the bloke, was
a member of Combat 18. This guy was boasting about how
he had made shopkeepers understand him by threatening to
punch them, and everything he said was punctuated by waving

his fist in Jake's face. Jake felt quite fortunate that Combat 18 had decided to like him.

Combat 18 said he has seventy mates – which on the face of it seems unlikely – who are planning to dodge international security agents determined to keep them out of Japan.

'They're all waiting in Thailand,' said Combat 18.

'Really,' said Jake.

'Yeah, they're waiting for the all-clear and then they're all going to come over on inflatable boats.'

Good plan, lads.

I do my best to assimilate myself into the local culture, by drinking four and a half pints of Guinness and eating a beef and Guinness pie.

4
Swallows

'I think we are going to see a lot of surprises at this
World Cup.'
– Cesare Maldini, coach of Paraguay

30 MAY

It emerges that Niall Quinn was working behind the scenes to
try and get Keane back to Japan, even though Keane hadn't
bothered to show up for the big man's charity testimonial, and
the entrepreneur J.P. McManus had his private jet standing
by, but Keane just could not bring himself to apologise to
McCarthy.

This afternoon I am due to do my first report for talkSPORT.
I'm ready with my first impressions of Japan, and Jim and I
reckon that the phone is going to be OK as long as I am not
in my hotel room, so I set off to find a place outdoors which
will become my own personal studio.

The hotel has an enticingly quiet traditional Japanese garden, which is actually mentioned in my guide book as a tourist
attraction. It was originally designed for the lord of Kumamoto
in Kyushu over four hundred years ago, I'm told, and it is
indeed beautiful and serene, with shaded paths round ponds
full of massively well-fed koi carp, and little wooden bridges,
everything just so, but two things lead me to rule it out as a
venue for reporting back to London. One is a sign saying 'No
mobile phones', which ordinarily I would applaud. The other
is another massive flyover, with eight more lanes of cars, vans,

trucks and buses whizzing cacophonously overhead. I've only been in Tokyo a couple of days, but if I've noticed one thing about the place, it's that you're never very far away from eight lanes of traffic.

About halfway to Yotsuya station I find a spot, a bench alongside a raised and shady footpath, which seems reasonably quiet. I decide to check the phone reception by calling Susan at home, where it should be breakfast time – of course, as I'm waiting to contribute to talkSPORT's breakfast programme. I get through OK, but am suddenly bombarded with noise from all sides. A party of about ninety schoolgirls goes by, all yammering at the tops of their shrieky voices, then an ambulance with a screaming siren comes to deal with an emergency about thirty yards away, and then a gang of the largest crows I've ever seen meet for a dispute in the tree right above my seat. They look like some sort of mutant crows, straight from some terrifying movie, *Godzilla versus the Crows*, perhaps, in which the city of Tokyo disappears under a mountain of guano.

I am overlooking a football pitch, on which a training session is taking place, involving a youth team of some kind in a variety of replica strips. On the eve of the World Cup I would have expected to see the Japan national shirt well represented, but there are none. The Japanese love their foreign football, though, and I can see an Argentina, a France, two Arsenals, an AC Milan, a Fiorentina, two Inters and a Juventus. The most popular single item with these youngsters, funnily enough, is the England shirt – there are four of them in evidence.

talkSPORT come on the phone, and I am put on hold through their switchboard, which means I can hear *Parry and Brazil's Sports Breakfast* down the line. Alan Brazil is in the middle of hosting a phone-in quiz 'for a dream trip to Japan to see England play Argentina'. It takes the form of a penalty shoot-out, and it is going into sudden death. Unfortunately for Alan, most of the answers are foreign names, and I can hear Mike Parry continually correcting his pronunciation in the background.

'Which Spanish keeper starred in the 1982 World Cup?'

'Don't know, Alan.'

'It was Zubi . . . Zubi . . . retta.'

'That's Zubizareta.'

'Thanks, Mike, on we go . . .'

As the sudden-death quiz goes on and on and on, Gary from Croydon and Dave from Liverpool are proving impossible to separate, and eventually the producer comes on the line with a sigh and puts me off until tomorrow, bumping me like an edition of *Gardeners' World* when the snooker overruns. Fine by me.

Back in the hotel, contemplating an evening of Japanese television. The news is once again showing hooligan footage from Charleroi and Marseilles, frantic to build up the prospect of rampage in the streets.

The Japanese police are well prepared to deal with this, if the practice session I've seen on the news is anything to go by. They line up in full riot gear as some of their colleagues run towards them, shouting and waving their fists, and then they beat three shades of crap out of them with clubs. I've also seen them firing a 'spiderman' gun, which tangles the miscreant up in a net. The South Korean police have another tactic, which involves several of them jumping off a wall with a big net and bundling a whole crowd of hooligans up all at once, which I think they've got from *Planet of the Apes*.

I look out of the window towards Shinjuku, and between here and there I see some huge floodlights lighting up the night sky. It is obviously a sporting arena of some sort, and I decide to go and see what is going on.

I am an old hand at finding my way to sports venues in unfamiliar towns, and when you can see the floodlights as clearly as this it almost takes the fun out of it. I soon spot tell-tale patterns of pedestrian behaviour – fathers hurrying

dawdling sons along, people running across busy roads diagonally without waiting for the next zebra crossing – and pretty
soon I have found the Jingu stadium, where a pro-baseball
game is under way. It is a perfect opportunity to sample the
Japanese way of sport.

Baseball is absolutely the number one sport in Japan. I
popped into a bookshop earlier today – it was a reflex thing,
I forgot for a moment that I wouldn't be able to read anything
in there – and with one day to go before the World Cup kicks
off I expected the place to be awash with football books and
magazines. Hidetoshi Nakata, the Japanese star who plays for
Parma in Serie A, had his life story prominently positioned,
and there was a brightly coloured World Cup guide, but
what football books there were were absolutely dwarfed by
a massive promotion, hundreds of copies, of a book called
Ichiro on Ichiro. This is the life story of the biggest sports star
in Japan, who styles himself simply Ichiro, a baseball player
who turns out for the Seattle Mariners. All the Mariners'
games are on live here, and the papers are full of his feats,
as he is currently top of the US hitting rankings. World Cup?
What World Cup?

At the ticket office a girl asks me, 'Who you rike? You rike
Suarez?'

I don't know, is the answer. I wonder whether, maybe, this
Suarez is a Mexican big hitter for one of the teams, and so I
shrug. 'Sure, Suarez, why not.'

Clutching my ticket I head for the entrance, where I am
asked: 'Who you rike?'

'Um . . . I rike Suarez,' I venture, hoping this is the password.
He hasn't heard me properly, though.

'You rike Giants?'

'I've nothing against them.'

'Giants? Or Suarez?'

'Oh, Suarez, definitely, Suarez.'

I am directed to the left, where I quickly gather that the two teams in action tonight are the Giants, whose supporters are banked up to the right, and the Swallows. *Swallows*, right . . . (Why I no risten . . . ?) It's 2–2 at the start of the fourth inning, and all to play for.

Giants are the Yomiuri Giants, sponsored by a newspaper, the *Daily Yomiuri*, while the Swallows are the Yakult Swallows, backed, rather embarrassingly, by the makers of those tiny little bottles of helpful bacteria drink. Around me in the stands, families have spread out picnics, and many of these feature six-packs of the little yoggy drink, which I think is very game of their supporters, and I sympathise with them.

My football team, Oldham Athletic, were sponsored for a couple of recent unsuccessful seasons by Slumberland. Very fine beds, I've no doubt, but we suffered no end of mild ribbing in our replica shirts as a result, and I'm sure the team were demoralised too. Nowadays the logo on our shirts belongs to something called the Torex Foundation. I don't know what they do, but they sound faintly sinister, and may be dedicated to the downfall of modern civilisation. Now nobody messes with us.

The game itself seems miles away. I wander up to the back of the grandstand, where there is a wide flat concrete area. A number of family groups have set up expansive picnics here. I'm not talking a couple of fishpaste sarnies and a flask of tea – they are laying out groundsheets and sticking them down with masking tape, kicking off their shoes, and settling down to a full three courser. I find a railing to lean on, and stand at the back, reminiscing fondly to myself about the days when you could watch English football like this, before the Taylor Report made plastic bucket seating suitable for people of five feet six inches or shorter compulsory up and down the land.

Quietly, and without me noticing at first, a little group of late arrivals set up a picnic on the concrete floor right behind me. They spread out a groundsheet, and tuck into some little plastic boxes full of rice and wriggly tentacles of some kind. I feel guilty when I first spot them, because for at least three of them the baseball must be totally obscured by my backside, but then I become indignant. Why should I move? I've got a good spot, and I was here first. I turn back to the game, but now I can't concentrate. I gradually become more and more self-conscious until I finally crack and move out of their way, whereupon the whole picnicking family, mortified with embarrassment, leap to their feet to insist that I must stay blocking their view for as long as I like. They bow, they beckon, they surround, but I feel that their hearts are not in it, so I bow myself, and continue to move away. Now they are overcome with gratitude, and bow so deeply and so enthusiastically that they risk concussing themselves on the concrete.

Now I know there are those who think a whole lot of this sport, both here in Japan and over in America. To a diehard cricket fan like myself, however, it is a seriously frustrating game to watch. If they'd only let the pitcher actually pitch the ball, or let the batter use a flat-faced bat with which he could actually steer the ball where he wanted it to go, or prevent the fielders from wearing great big girl's-blouse cheat-mittens with which to nonchalantly swat the ball from the sky – well, then they'd have the beginnings of a game on their hands.

As it is, though, I soon find myself more interested in watching the crowd around me. There are whole family groups, but also great clusters of salarymen who have rushed here straight from the office without even so much as loosening their ties.

Brightly coloured drink sellers, mostly young girls, scuttle constantly up and down the aisles. They all wear the uniform of their particular brand – green and yellow for Kirin beer, luminous orange for Asahi super dry, old-fashioned baseball outfits for the Yebisu vendors, and blokes dressed as giant bottles of Coke flogging soft drinks. They each have rucksacks on their backs, and dispense beer into paper cups using a sort of mini petrol pump device, strongly reminiscent of Homer Simpson's daydream about the alcohol-powered car ('one squirt for you, one squirt for me . . .').

The crowd noise in support of the two teams is more or less constant, but as I begin to pay more attention I can see that it is very organised, even regimented. The two banks of supporters very politely take it in turns, for one thing. While the Swallows are batting, the orange-and-black clad Giants army to our right are virtually silent, and when it's their turn to make a fuss my blue-clothed neighbours are similarly considerate.

I've just been reading in Sebastian's book about *oendan*, hierarchically organised supporters' groups who attach themselves to the major baseball teams and orchestrate the crowd's responses. This approach hasn't really caught on with football crowds, because that game flows in such an unpredictable and spontaneous way. Baseball, though, is full of stops and starts and lends itself perfectly to patterns of crowd behaviour which can be manipulated by group leaders. I begin to pick these out. One guy with a whistle seems to be the main man, and his acolytes are spread out every thirty yards or so amongst the Swallows supporters. Two peeps of the whistle, and these guys stand up and bellow what the next chant will be to those around them. Then a drum marks out the beat, and everyone dutifully does as they are told.

Every now and then the guy with the whistle indicates a particular corner, where a group of supporters in blue-and-white *yukata* emblazoned with a Swallows emblem have set up a little brass band, and a tune will start up. At another signal on the whistle, hundreds of miniature plastic baseball bats appear, and bash out the rhythm of another chant.

Midway through the evening a Swallows batter whacks a home run directly into the enclosure where the Giants fans are gathered, to huge celebration all around me. From nowhere, it seems, hundreds of small luminous green umbrellas are opened, and pumped up and down in unison, and suddenly the whole place looks like a field of mutant mushrooms.

Of course, the Giants opposite have their own *oendan*, and their own rehearsed routines, but while the Swallows' brass band play tunes that I can't recognise, the Giants' band launch enthusiastically into *Go West* – or 'You're Shit, and You Know You Are', to give it its proper title. Even more unexpectedly, they later give us their rendition of the theme from *The Great Escape*. How did that happen? Surely that is an England song, first heard, I think, at the Italy v England World Cup qualifier in Rome in 1997, played by that rather irritating Sheffield Wednesday band that have attached themselves to the national side. What possible resonance does it have here? And by what process has it arrived – some sort of international supporter band telepathic osmosis . . . ?

For any fans of old Abbott and Costello routines – if you can imagine such a person – there was one particularly joyous moment, midway through the proceedings, when it appeared that a man called Hoo actually was on first.

The game ends in a Giants win, but no one seems particularly bothered on either side. After all, there'll be another game tomorrow, and the day after that, and the day after that, and for most of the crowd it seems that participating in the singing and flag waving and umbrella pumping is the main thing, rather than seeing their team actually win. How this rather bland attitude to sport watching will translate to a football World Cup remains to be seen. Starting tomorrow.

As I leave the stadium I am feeling rather peckish. I wander over to one of the food vendors to see what there might be to eat, and see a transparent plastic container with what looks like fat red noodles topped off with a hard-boiled egg. After a moment I realise that the fat red noodles are tentacles, and the hard-boiled egg is an eye. I decide to pass.

31 MAY

World Cup starts today. There is, though, it seems, a feeling that there are two separate tournaments taking place, one in South Korea and one here in Japan, and that ours does not kick off properly until tomorrow.

To fill in time before France v Senegal, and whatever ghastly multi-colour choreographed horror has been arranged as a warm-up to the main event, I decide to give Tokyo my best tourist blitz, and make for the central station.

My guide book recommends using the Yamanote line to orient yourself in Tokyo. There isn't really a centre to the capital, as such, but there are a number of small sub-centres or mini-cities which are linked together by this circular rail line. Shinjuku, for example, is approximately at nine o'clock on this circle, Shinagawa is down at six, Ikebukuro around eleven, Ueno more or less one, and at three o'clock is the massive Tokyo station.

Unlike other capital cities like London, say, or Paris, Tokyo has one single station which acts as the hub for all of the nation's mainline rail services. When you factor in a couple of major department stores and underground shopping arcades intermingled with the dozens of national and suburban platforms, not to mention the subway, you would give Tokyo station a good chance of being one of the most crowded, confusing and disorientating places on earth. I had a brief glimpse of the place when I arrived a few days ago, but then I was trying to get from one train to another, which is a piece of cake compared to finding your way out of the station altogether.

I wander the neon strip-lit warrens for about fifteen minutes, past discount shoe outlets, noodle shops, a World Cup merchandise store, the platform I arrived at (again), a bus station, more noodle shops, a Mr Donut, out of the station altogether on the opposite side to the one I was trying to find, back in again, past the platform I arrived at (again), and countless more noodle shops, before finally spotting some sunlight and breaking into the main lobby.

All over Tokyo station, Pele is doing a poster campaign for erectile dysfunction – not recommending it, you understand, but raising our awareness of it and directing us to a possible remedy for it – his thumb raised like a latter-day Fred Pontin. Pele's image as the coolest man on the planet, already damaged by his readiness to back the country of whoever he is talking to to win the World Cup, takes another bad knock.

Meanwhile Diego Maradona, his only serious rival for the crown of greatest ever player – unless Zinedine Zidane can steer France to another title – has been barred from entering Japan because of his many previous drug convictions. He has been offered entry to South Korea, however, where he would be able to watch Argentina's games on the telly. Just like at home.

England v Sweden is now only two days away, and I'm beginning to spot more and more Brits around. Outside the main station, for example, I see a fine example of international brotherhood, as two gigantic Swedish backpackers in their yellow national shirts and a Sheffield United fan in his red and white try to figure out the subway map together. After a couple of minutes the Blade's frustration gets the better of him, and he stomps off, shouting: 'Fook it, I'm walking!'

The Irish are everywhere, in Celtic shirts and 'funny' ginger wigs, barrelling up and down the passageways of the arcades, trying to find the open air.

I'm heading for the Imperial Palace, and three Irish lads have the same plan. They seem to be three generations of the same family. Dad is a ginger chap with a camcorder, Grandad is sporting a faded USA 94 T-shirt that has seen better days, and Junior is a gawky youth in gigantic trainers who is trailing around a personal ten-foot exclusion zone of adolescent body odour. I try my best to escape it, but I keep

41

getting held up by red lights on the pedestrian crossings and smell them inexorably catching up to me.

My visit to the Imperial Palace is not a blinding success. The grounds are behind a big moat, and trees mask the actual buildings from view. You can go into the imperial apartments, but only if you have made an appointment some weeks before and been checked out by the security services. You can cross the moat and stroll around the imperial gardens, but not today because it's a Friday. You can walk on the large expanse of gravel which separates the imperial park from the roaring traffic, and take forlorn snaps of the far distant corners of the occasional pagoda, so this is what I do.

I pass the Irish lads taking a photograph. Junior has the camera, and Dad and Grandad are posing in front of one of the security gates.

'All right,' says Junior. 'Say "Ireland are going to win the World Cup!"'

Dad and Grandad cheerfully oblige, and Junior clicks the shutter just as their mouths are making the P of the word 'Cup', so that'll be a great snap – both of them tightly pursed, looking as if they've just heard about something they don't quite approve of. Contraception, perhaps . . .

I can't seem to get away from a couple of Americans who are shooting a home video. One of them – whose name is Andy, I could hardly help hearing – is the star, director and producer of this opus, while his gormless mate is the cameraman. Andy is stocky, full of himself, and really rather bolshie.

'In five, four . . .' he goes, indicating impatiently that his mate should press the little red button.

'OK, now, well, here I am. I've *finally* found a gate with no security guards, so we're going to go through and see what's inside. Come with me!'

Andy turns, beckoning the viewer to follow, and sets off

towards the gate, which is maybe a hundred and fifty yards away. I am thinking that this is not going to make great watching, and Andy's mate seems to agree.

'Shall I stop filming now?' he asks plaintively, as Andy crunches off over the gravel.

'No, *Doofus*! Keep going . . . coh!' Andy decides that this shot is going to have to be redone and crunches back. This means that I reach the gate first, and find that it leads not into the Imperial Palace but actually out onto an eight-lane expressway.

Later I stop for a drink on a park bench next to a large but undistinguished statue of a samurai warrior on horseback. After a minute or two Andy and Doofus turn up. Doofus is tired and demoralised, and it looks as though he has been sacked from the project. Andy loves the samurai, and begins to shoot some footage of it. After about half a minute I start to time him. How long is he going to shoot moving pictures of a statue for, exactly?

After two minutes, two whole minutes, he begins to walk slowly round the statue, still filming. After three minutes the futility of this strikes even Doofus, and he moans: 'Andy, you're filming a statue, man, it's not going anywhere . . .'

'Shut *up*, Doofus!'

Four and a half minutes, and he's round the back, shooting the samurai warrior's horse's arse. Just past the six-minute mark, and Andy is back round the front where he started, and finally figures he has enough footage of this completely static non-event.

Imagine going round to his house to see his holiday films – that's an invitation you'd only accept once, isn't it?

'And here's a statue of a samurai on a horse . . .'

'Yeah, Andy, that's great . . .'

'Sssh! In a minute I start walking round it . . .'

(coughs, looks at watch)'An-y . . . way . . .'

'Look! Look! Here I go . . . I'm walking round it now . . . Doofus, get them some more nuts . . .'

I head up through Kitanomaru park and have some lunch in the canteen of the Science Museum. I am thinking to myself that all the buildings I have seen today are very modern – not having been able to see any of the Imperial Palace, of course – registering that this is down to the rebuilding frenzy of the sixties, and the destruction wrought by Allied bombing during the war, not to mention the great earthquake of 1923 . . . Suddenly there is a tremendous shaking, and a horrible wrenching noise like that of a whole building twisting and preparing to collapse. All around me people grab the trays with their lunches on, and our eyes dart around wondering which way to run . . . and then it is over as soon as it had begun. Just a tiny tremor, nothing to worry about.

About an hour later, my heart rate returns to something like normal, and I carry on through the park and find myself looking at a massive grey steel *torii*, supposedly the largest anywhere. The *torii*, a simple square arch, marks the entrance to a shrine, and this shrine I have come to is possibly the most emotive and significant one in Japan. It is the Yasukini *jinja*, dedicated to the divine spirits of the war dead of Japan, both military and civilian, going back to the Meiji restoration of 1869. The dead are all respectfully listed here by name, along with the dates and localities of their deaths, somewhere in the region of two and a half million of them, and they are all considered deified for their sacrifice.

There was an angry reaction in South Korea to Japanese PM Koizumi's controversial visits to Yasukini last August and again in April, which came close to derailing the World Cup co-hosting arrangement. One nation's war dead, you see, being another's class A war criminals.

It is said that during the Second World War kamikaze pilots would shout, 'See you at Yasukini!' to one another, before running to their flimsy planes to embrace their fate. Their actions are commemorated in a small military museum within the grounds of the shrine, with personal belongings and letters on display, and photographs of groups of young men, strikingly young, and strikingly happy, gathering round a small pet kitten just before taking off on their last flights. A *kaiten* is on display here, the naval equivalent of the kamikaze glider, a sort of long black torpedo steered directly to its target by a volunteer submariner, and an evil-looking monster it is too. It is all but impossible to imagine myself into the shoes of these young Japanese airmen and sailors, but maybe the thought of being worshipped here was a part of what drove them on. It is a peaceful place – indeed Yasukini means 'peaceful country' – but a chilling one, and I don't think I'll be finding any material here for my humorous report for talkSPORT this afternoon.

Speaking of which, I make it back to my 'studio' – the log bench on the path near the hotel – in time for the call from London. This time I find myself listening to a long story about some treatment that Alan Brazil had in the far distant past when an American doctor injected sugar water into his spine. It seems to go on for ever, and I can almost feel my timeslot dwindling away, but mercifully Mike Parry manages to change the subject and I get to do my piece.

Then I get an e-mail from home, which Susan has entitled 'From the House of Plague'. John is throwing up, Peter has diarrhoea, and Michael is throwing up and has diarrhoea. Sounds as if she's coping admirably without me.

5
Openers

'I've never even heard of Senegal.'
– Paul Gascoigne

31 MAY (STILL)

At this point, I should perhaps say that there is in fact another reason why I was so keen to come to Japan. Apart from the school project thing, I mean. I want nothing more nor less than to reignite my passion for the game.

I have followed football for as long as I can remember, and have seen my team, Oldham Athletic, play on ninety-three different grounds over the years. I play, too, a little bit. My occasional team, Les Raymonds Célèbres FC – named on a tour of Paris after a question category on French TV's version of *Going for Gold* – won our second-ever trophy in May despite being shorn of our midfield playmakers at the last minute, which I am taking to be a good omen for the World Cup.

And yet, despite having made football such a large part of my life for so many years, I have been finding, recently, that a certain amount of disillusionment is setting in. The television schedules are bloated with so many inconsequential live matches that I hardly ever bother to sit through a whole one any more. Even the real life article has started to lose its edge for me, for some reason. I still go to games, and Oldham will be winning or they'll be losing, and I'll be sitting there, feeling almost detached from proceedings, interested certainly

46

but not particularly bothered, where once I would have been biting my nails, and unable to sit still, and finding it impossible not to just shout some instruction or some warning to men who would never hear me and would never do what I said even if they did.

Back in 1990 Oldham got to the semi-final of the FA Cup and took Manchester United to a replay at Maine Road after a thrilling three-all draw (still the best game I have ever seen). United went one up and seemed to be coasting to a miserable 1–0 win, but then with ten minutes or so left Andy Ritchie banged in an equaliser, and I leapt up so fast that I actually blacked out. The football was so exciting that I lost consciousness for a moment or two. The reason I have come to the World Cup is that I want that feeling back, I want to see some football that is just so absolutely fucking important that I feel as if my heart is going to stop.

Part of it is age, of course. The football fan passes through several watersheds in his watching life. At first, as a boy, all the players seem like impossibly heroic titans. Then one day he realises that there is a player younger than himself, and the dream of playing for the club dies a little. Soon, too soon, he realises that all the players on both teams are younger than he is, and then, with a jolt, he suddenly one day notices that both the managers are younger than him. I interviewed Graeme Sharp, once, when he was manager at Boundary Park, and for a while I was schoolboy-thrilled at being given this chance, but then I met him, and he was a perfectly agreeable and charming fellow . . . who is a few months younger than I am. I think when you get there, to that point, it can – it does, trust me – start to feel more than a little foolish to invest so much time and emotional commitment into living vicariously through the sporting adventures of a bunch of idiot boys half your age.

And then, of course, football itself has changed. It began, I think, with Italia 90.

Before that, if you recall, football was pure poison. It was unmarketable, unpromotable, it was a ghetto. As far as the media were concerned it was Heysel, it was Hillsborough, it was Millwall v Luton and plastic seats raining down on the pitch, it was Ken Bates putting electric fences around Stamford Bridge, it was David Evans of Luton – remember him? – and his ID card scheme, it was theatre but it was theatre of hate.

Back then if you met someone who was similarly in thrall to the beautiful game it was as if you shared a dark, guilty secret. The football friends I made and kept from school and college all supported similarly under-achieving outfits, like Sheffield Wednesday, Rotherham, Stoke, Heart of Midlothian, and of course Oldham, and you wear your love for a club like these as a badge of courage. You have to. You are saying that, in the words of Kipling, you will meet with 'triumph and disaster, and treat those two impostors just the same', except you probably won't be seeing quite so much of triumph.

Football trundled along for the people who liked it, clubs hovered just above the extinction line but somehow never fell under it entirely, and the rest of the world kind of left it to one side.

Gazza's tears changed all that – and I dare say the funny plastic breasts played their part too. When 25 million people watched the semi-final game between England and West Germany in Turin, it was a national event of a major sort. People who had never watched a game in their life watched that one. People who had drifted away from the game, put off by its image, remembered how exciting it could be to be involved. Marketing men, money men, advertising men quickly fastened on to this, and an unstoppable bandwagon of trendification began.

There was *Fever Pitch*, and *An Evening with Gary Lineker* – OK, so I carry the burden of half of a small amount of the blame – and *FourFourTwo* magazine. There was the Taylor Report, and all at once all those atmospheric and crumbly old grounds had to be all-seater and family-friendly and safe, when somehow them not being those things was part of the point. Suddenly it was impossible to be a celebrity of any kind without announcing to the world that you were a lifelong West Brom fan, or an Arsenal fan, or a Middlesbrough fan. Lifelong – i.e. for the rest of my life, starting now. Every second advert featured football, a footballer, a football fan.

And, most of all, there was the Premiership. Dreamed up by greedy chairmen of top clubs so they wouldn't have to share out television money with the rest of the league, and driven by Sky's desperate need to establish itself in the largest possible number of homes as quickly as possible, everything about it leaves a nasty taste in the mouth. And not just because Oldham aren't in it (we were, remember, to start with).

The history of the Premiership, that's all you hear now. So-and-so has scored the fastest goal 'in the history of the Premiership', or the most goals 'in the history of the Premiership', or has got the most points, or reached the highest position, or has made simply the most *money* 'in the history of the Premiership'.

Every time I hear something like this: 'Manchester United have never finished lower than second in the history of the Premiership . . .' I feel a little bit more foolish for having invested so much time and interest in watching Manchester United never finishing higher than second between 1968 and 1993.

If you erase all football history before 1992 – well, not erase exactly, but downsize to virtual irrelevance – then you end up with a football product that has been going precisely one year longer than Japan's JLeague. And look how snooty we are about that.

When I started being interested in football, back in the early seventies, it seemed like a different team won the league every year – Everton, Leeds, Arsenal, Derby, Liverpool, Forest – and more than that it actually felt possible that teams like Tottenham, Chelsea, Man City, Wolves, West Brom, QPR, and – although a distant possibility in those days – Manchester United could even tap up and win it.

Nowadays you can tell before the season has even started what the top six is going to be, and only the order might change slightly from Premiership year to Premiership year. It used to be a truism, a cliché, that nobody has a divine right to win things, but the big clubs are doing everything they can to make it something they can reasonably expect on a regular basis. For the rest of the football world, unless you can get bankrolled by an Al-Fayed or a Jack Walker, it is a smug closed shop moving ever further out of reach, the dream of 'doing a Wimbledon' becoming ever more preposterous. And how exciting is that?

And players are making money that is not just good money, not just enough to make them so rich they don't know where to stick it all, but amounts of money that are absolutely fucking obscene. Amounts of money which, if earned by Ken Dodd, would mean the buck-toothed funnyman sleeping with his nose pressed to the ceiling. That a character like Roy Keane is earning three times the national average annual wage every single week – I think that takes the edge off. I think that takes the edge off the pleasure of watching him assaulting whichever poor sod has looked at him in a slightly funny way this week.

It makes me laugh when the FA hauls up Keane or Wise or some other yobbo in a disastrously silly modern suit and 'charges' them with bringing the game into disrepute. For me the game lives in a permanent state of disrepute, surrendered utterly to short-termism and greed. And this is a bubble that will burst. In trying to appeal to the widest possible constituency football has made itself into a fad, and the one thing that fads all have in common is built-in obsolescence.

But if the Premiership – even the word is a horrible history-free committee-of-marketing-men concoction – is an off-putting confection, then the Champions' League is ten times worse. A competition devised, it seems to me, so that the richest teams on the continent can interminably play as many not-quite-crucial money-spinning games as possible on Europe-wide live television without anybody ever getting knocked out. Even the teams who perform spectacularly badly can wind up in the UEFA Cup to soothe their pride and their cashflow.

The systematic easification of the Champions-plus-three-runners-up League means that nowadays the UEFA Cup is so far a distant second best that clubs like Chelsea are actually disappointed to find themselves stuck in it, their sulking megastars being annually shown up by the detritus of European football.

So what is there left to get the pulse racing? The FA Cup? A mere bauble now, which Manchester United opted out of entirely a couple of years back, and which, since the demise of the European Cup Winners' Cup, dumps the winner into the UEFA Cup, despised by all the big boys. The Worthington Cup? Don't make me laugh.

The World Cup, though, is the one thing the game's administrators haven't managed to spoil. Oh they've tried, don't get me wrong. There's the horrible aberration that is golden goal extra time, for a start. Undeniably exciting, but still an utterly crap American-style idea. If we'd had it in 1970 we'd have been denied one of the all-time great games, the semi-final between Italy and West Germany – 1–1 at full time, 4–3 after extra time. England would have won the Cup 3–2 in 1966, and Tofik Bakhramov's controversial intervention would have immediately brought the final whistle. And would two-goal Hursty now be Sir Geoff without ever having completed his epoch-making hat-trick? Granted, his later contributions to the worlds of after-dinner speaking and motor insurance have been impressive, but still . . .

The players play for pride and not for money, that's an important aspect of it. Of course there is always paper talk

about 'bonuses' for doing such and such or getting so far –
the Russians can win a Mercedes each, or something, usually
– but the amounts involved are mere pocket money for these
lads, although naturally it would be a life-changing windfall
for most of us watching. And of course anyone can greatly
improve their market value and earning power by shining on
this stage, but, well, I don't resent that – good luck to them.

No, the World Cup, it seems to me, is the last remaining
jewel of the sport. It has provided the mileposts of my adult
life, from Mexico 1970 onwards – yes, I am of that cursed
generation that was too young (just) to enjoy 1966 – images
burned onto my memory for ever. The Banks save, the Moore
tackle, the Pele header from Mexico. The Cruyff turn and the
Muller goal from 1974. Wee Archie dancing through to put
Scotland in dreamland, Ossie Ardiles and his overhead flick,
and the showers of confetti in 1978. Keegan missing an open
goal, and Tardelli's open-mouthed roar of celebration in the
final of 1982. The Hand of God and the godlike second goal
in 1986, as well as all those Lineker goals. Platt, Gazza,
Roger Milla dancing with the corner flag, Pearce, Waddle
and Lineker again in 90. Ray Houghton's goal, and then
that arid sunlit shoot-out final in USA 94. The two-footed
ball-grasping Blanco hop, the Beckham free kick, the Owen
goal against Argentina, that red card, and Zinedine Zidane
from last time.

Surely here in Japan, and over in South Korea, some real,
bright-burning football history will be made. Not just 'history
of the Premiership' history, but something to set the blood
boiling in the veins.

The early signs are good. I have already rediscovered the
childish pleasure of scouring international squad lists for funny
names. I remember last time hoping that Germany would play
Holland, in the hope of seeing Cocu and Kuntz together on the
same field. Or at Euro 96, in an uncanny echo of the history
of superband Genesis, the Czechs removing Petr Gabriel and

substituting him with Fukall. This time I am looking out for Arce of Paraguay, and wondering whether Utaka the attacker will come up against Bak the defender. I note, with a literary eye, that the Mexico squad has, at numbers 2, 3 and 4, Gabriel, Garcia, and Marquez. Always acknowledging, of course, that we have names that seem amusing to the outsider in our squad. Butt, for a start, and Fowler who, if he is not careful when and if we play Belgium, could find himself in de Boeck.

I am hoping that this World Cup will rekindle the flame for me, will get the juices going once again, will remind me what it feels like when your heart and your Adam's apple are just much closer together than they are meant to be. And that, with a bit of luck, I will rediscover what I liked about the damn game in the first place.

This evening I settle down in my hotel room to watch the opening ceremony broadcast on Japanese television. The show is presented by a venerable senior broadcaster (think Des Lynam) accompanied by a young man with dyed hair and a trendy jacket (think well-known current player inexplicably overlooked by Phillippe Troussier) and an older chap with glasses whose awkwardness on-screen suggests that he is a former player attempting to forge himself a media career (think maybe Nigel Spackman). There is also a young lady on the panel, but as the programme goes on she makes very little contribution, and it looks as though it may be her job to look after the mascots.

One thing they really do love here is a mascot, a cute, brightly coloured little cartoon character to brighten up your business or your anything really. The airport has two little cartoon planes, and even the police come with a cute and cuddly sidekick. It's no surprise, then, to find that where every other World Cup has made do with a single merchandising gimmick, sometimes designed by a competition-winning local child – Pibe™, World Cup Willie™, Footix™ – this one has three. Nik, Ato and Kaz, they are called, and they're . . . well, I don't really know what the hell they are. The literature describes them as 'energy forms' who live in the Atmozone and have come to earth to make 2002 the best World Cup ever. So there.

There is the usual kind of performance, involving lots of schoolchildren making patterns on the pitch in brightly coloured clothes, a bit with flags in it, and some lovely but inexplicable music and movement by some bald monks – in short the kind of thing I can't stand at any price, and my itchy remote control finger shows me that Japanese sports fans are so into the World Cup that baseball is only on two of the other channels when usually it's on at least five. I flick back to see what's going on, and after a few minutes discover that I have been watching the Fiftieth Annual Yokohama Masquerade Parade on the wrong channel – easy mistake to make.

Sepp Blatter makes a little speech, sending out his message to the world. I don't catch what he actually says as it is drowned out by near-simultaneous translation and open booing from some FIFA representatives, but I gather it's something along the lines of: 'I did it! The money is all hidden away in a Swiss bank account, suckers! Ha ha ha ha ha!'

Then, at eight thirty in the evening here in Japan, the 2002 World Cup gets under way. My inveterate fiddling with the remote control leads me to a button marked 'Bilingual', which has had no effect before, but now suddenly it brings me the familiar tones of the BBC's John Motson, saying: 'Here in Seoul we're barely forty kilometres from the border with North Korea, but when an event of this magnitude is launched, and in a brand-new 65,000-capacity stadium, there are no borders in football . . .'

I switch back to the Japanese commentary.

France against Senegal has a couple of unusual statistical quirks, which I am sure the Japanese Motty is unbuckling even now. For a start, the Senegal team are not exactly the plucky African outsiders they perhaps seem at first sight. Although they have never played in the World Cup finals before – and actually forgot to enter the 1994 competition altogether – all of their starting line-up earn their living playing professional football in France, which only Frank Leboeuf of the French team does. And Senegal has produced one acknowledged world-class footballer. Unfortunately for them his name is Patrick Vieira, and he's playing for France.

Roger Lemerre sticks to the 4–2–3–1 formation which he has been constructing around balding superstar Zinedine Zidane. He's out, though, having pulled a thigh muscle in their last warm-up match against South Korea, and his place is filled by Youri Djorkaeff, whose name is giving the Japanese commentators a kind of tongue paroxysm every time they attempt it. As well as a back four whose average age is thirty-three, Lemerre can call on three outstanding forwards in Henry, Wiltord and Trezeguet. Oddly he is using two of them as wide midfielders, Henry on the left and Wiltord on the right, but they are the World Champions so they must know what they are doing.

Three of Senegal's stars have been in the news all week, Salif Diao and El Hadji Diouf being strongly linked with moves to Liverpool, and Khalilou Fadiga because of his arrest for allegedly stealing jewellery from a store – shades of Bobby Moore in Bogotá.

France begin with a languid arrogance, stroking the ball around, while Senegal try to hurry and harry them. Ferdinand Coly, the right back with a big mop of hair, and the pacy Diouf catch the eye in the early exchanges. The French seem remarkably unconcerned, though, and soon create a smooth passing movement which culminates in a neat ball from Henry through to Trezeguet inside the penalty area. The Juventus man turns and strikes the ball against the right-hand post. The Japanese commentator shouts out 'Bigga chance-o!' but Trezeguet's smile as play continues is not the expression of a man who is worried that he might not get another such opportunity. France are absolutely certain that they are going to win this game by a street.

That confidence is dented on the half hour. Petit and Vieira stroll forward casually, and then Djorkaeff has the ball nicked off his toe and pushed forward to Diouf, who skips past the floundering Leboeuf leaving him on his backside. He reaches the bye-line, looks up, and plays a low cross towards Pape Bouba Diop. The ball deflects slightly off the stumbling Desailly's heel, and Petit's interception rebounds off Barthez to Bouba Diop two yards out and he pokes it in for the World Cup's opening goal.

Bouba Diop beckons his team mates to the corner flag, where he removes his number 19 shirt and lays it on the ground for the Senegal players to dance around in a well-rehearsed celebration routine. It's good, but it's not Roger Milla.

Bruno Metsu, with his trendy-teacher white T-shirt and grey jacket combo, anxiously flicks his curls from his eyes as France come back at his African team. Djorkaeff plays Trezeguet in, but Sylva gallops out to clear. Henry lifts in another ball to the Juventus striker, but again Senegal hack it away. Zidane comes to the touchline to encourage his team, but he doesn't look desperately concerned, not yet anyway. Wiltord manages a duff shot, Petit gets booked, and Senegal make it to half time a goal to the good.

In the second half France develop a little more urgency, but Senegal continue to stifle their attacks and cut off the supply to Trezeguet with some ferocious closing down in midfield. Henry's header from two yards out goes high and wide. There are no casual smiles this time, and Fabien Barthez holds his head in dismay. Footballers, like fans, get a sense sometimes that it's just not going to be their day.

On the breakaway Fadiga hits the bar. Then Henry's curling shot, less than a minute later, clips the bar at the other end with the keeper stranded.

'Ca-rossa-bar!' screams Japanese Motty, and then starts talking about something which sounds awfully like 'open gayness' . . .

In the last minute a mistake by Daf lets Henry in for the sort of chance he snaps up week in week out for Arsenal, but he snatches at it and fires it straight at Sylva, when a square ball would have left Trezeguet a tap in. And then, in injury time, Leboeuf has a chance, unmarked at a corner, but he doesn't get hold of it and Sylva plucks it out of the air.

Full time, 1–0 to Senegal, and it is the biggest shock since Cameroon beat Argentina in the opening game of Italia 90. This dogged and well-organised Senegal team look capable of emulating the success of their African counterparts that year, and in El Hadji Diouf they have the man of the match, a pacy and skilful forward who could light up this tournament. The champions, meanwhile, are left shaking their heads with disbelief. This France team was meant to be even stronger than the one which took the trophy last time, given that it now has an actual strike force where in '98 they had Stephane Guivarc'h, but they couldn't manage to score a single goal.

Desailly, harking back to *Jeux Sans Frontières* but not remembering the rules properly, says: 'We have now used our joker.'

It could be just the result the World Cup needs, though, because suddenly any result seems possible.

In the ferociously expensive hotel bar I meet up with Nick and Paul. Nick is a friend I have known for years, since we appeared in a student production of *Zigger Zagger* together. For a large part of the late eighties we shared a flat, if you count him sleeping on the floor of my living room 'just until I find myself somewhere else' for three and a half years sharing a flat. We don't go to football together that often, but when his team (Stoke) and mine (Oldham) are in the same division those fixtures are always the ones I look forward to the most.

Earlier this year Nick did some work for one of the companies who are allowed to call themselves 'Official Partners of the World Cup', and managed to negotiate to be paid in World Cup tickets rather than money.

He thought he was sorted all the way to the final, but just a couple of weeks ago he got a call from a representative of the company in question, advising him that he should 'downsize his expectations ticketwise'. All he could really say in return was that they should downsize their expectations him-working-for-them-again-wise, and so, like me, he will be on the lookout for second-phase tickets should England get through.

Nick has tried to conquer jet lag by taking sleeping tablets and sleeping for the entire flight. As a result he is wide awake and looks like being so for at least another twenty-four hours.

Paul is an old friend of Nick's whom I have also known for ages. Nick has decided that Paul's face has become cube-shaped, and has begun to call him The Cube. I decide to join in – I don't want him to turn on me, not with my pentagonal features.

In his days as a travelling salesman, specialising in a line of decorative ceramic telephones covered in pictures of fruit, The Cube spent many a night at our flat, using it as a base to hit the major department stores of south London. Nowadays he works for a mobile phone company. Their phones are not covered in pictures of fruit, but I'm sure The Cube could fix that for you if it was something you really wanted.

The Cube is always very jolly whenever I see him, but he has a great capacity for letting things get him down and then slagging them off at great length, which makes him very good company. Tonight – and I am with him on this one – he is muttering about all the Irish people in the bar.

'We're the friendliest supporters at the World Cup!' one ginger-headed loon butts in, insisting on shaking us all by the hand and thumping us between the shoulder blades, before moving off to another table.

'How does he know? The World Cup only started three hours ago. There might be hundreds of really friendly Poles who haven't even set off yet . . .'

On the evidence so far, the Irish are making a determined early bid to fill the gap left by the non-qualifying Scots as the most sanctimonious fans at the tournament. Some years ago – and it's not clear how or when this happened – Scotland fans underwent a sea change. One moment they were terrorising Wembley, sitting on the crossbars until they splintered, galloping drunkenly about the place looking for trouble. Then, all of a sudden, they were the most ostentatiously well-behaved supporters in international football, helping old ladies across the road, carrying people's shopping, giving blood. It made you sick. Host countries loved them, they were never any trouble, they spent loads on beer, and they were so happy and colourful in their tartan get-ups and their funny bonnets that you just had to love them.

I remember heading to the opening game of France 98 with my Scottish friend Rob – we didn't get in – surrounded by jolly kilted blokes singing their heads off, watched indulgently by smiling Parisian locals and police alike, who couldn't quite make out through the thick accents that what they were singing was this:

> *There's only one Ronaldo,*
> *One Ronaldo,*
> *With a packet o' sweets,*
> *And a cheeky wee smile,*
> *Ronaldo is a fuckin' paedophile.*

Despite the fact that I enjoy going to Scotland games, and feel much safer there than at England matches, something about New Scotland sticks in my craw. I think it's because it is so obviously a reaction to the hooligan stories that have traditionally surrounded England fans abroad, a deliberate bid to go to the other extreme. It's sad that England are still followed around by an element who are looking for trouble, youths like Combat 18 in Shinjuku, waiting for his seventy mates to come over from Thailand on inflatable boats, but there is something synthetic and self-conscious about the Scots proclaiming themselves 'the best-behaved supporters in the world'. It's taking the piss, that's what it is, and now the Irish are doing it too.

'We don't care if we win or lose, we're only here for the craic!' burbles a man with an RTE pass slung round his neck, who seems to have forgotten that he's also here to work.

I ask Nick and The Cube whether they came into Tokyo on the Narita Express, but it appears they made other arrangements. During a brief period of consciousness, Nick got talking to his neighbour on the plane, a Japanese man who makes fishing nets. Nick is an enthusiastic angler, and some international fishy kinship developed between them. They chatted about the World Cup, and Nick, getting into the spirit of the host nation where gift-giving is an ancient and honourable tradition, handed his new pal his spare ticket for England v Sweden at Saitama on Sunday.

Fishing-net man, desperate to give something in return, offered to drive Nick and Cube from the airport to the hotel, and they cheerfully accepted. When they got to Narita, they found Fishing-net man's son waiting to meet his dad with, sadly for him, a very compact little car. His dad handed over his luggage, took the car key, and packed the lad off on the train, so that he could fit Nick and Paul and their bags into the tiny motor. They last saw the son glumly shuffling off to the railway station as they sped off. In his car.

Eventually Nick decides to call it a night, despite having slept for most of the day, leaving Cube and me alone with the Irish.

'I thought I recognised yer man there,' says one, as Nick heads for his room.

'Really?' I say.

'I think I know him from the old country,' he says, scratching his beer-fuddled head.

'Whatever makes you think that?' says Cube, nice as pie. 'He didn't have a pig under his arm . . .'

1 JUNE

I read in the paper that dozens of football fans from around the world are sleeping rough in Ueno Park, in a sort of impromptu international campsite. I need something to do a bit on the radio about, so I head off to take a look for myself.

Disappointingly, when I get to Ueno this turns out not to be true. The report seemed to suggest that Argentinian fans had gathered here in particularly large numbers, with the desperate state of their country's economy meaning that they had less disposable income than their counterparts from more prosperous countries. All I can see, though, are families strolling in the sunshine or heading for the zoo. I leave the main pathways and make for the trees, where I do start to find little encampments of people. Ropes have been slung between the trees, and tents made from large sheets of blue tarpaulin. A little further, and I realise that there are literally hundreds of these tents, and literally hundreds of people living in them. They are not football fans sleeping rough for the duration of the World Cup, though, they are whole families living here permanently.

A peek under the edge of some of the tarpaulins reveals trolleys and carts piled up with bundles of personal belongings, furniture and clothes, and for homeless people they all seem to have an awful lot of stuff.

In another part of Ueno Park I come across an eye-catching ritual taking place, and stop to take a look. On a large open space of tarmac in front of a large museum, about three hundred people are being corralled like sheep and bossed around by some very busy young men, who shout to one another constantly. The three hundred are subdued and silent, and I think at first that this is some nightmarish museum trip and they are all queueing for admission, but no, they are all clutching bits of cardboard box or carrier bags full of stuff they've found, and it's clear that these are the serious homeless.

Shouting '*Hai! Hai! Hai!*' to one another, two of the bossy young men pull out a length of rope, for all the world like they are about to do some fiendishly clever magic trick. What they actually do is lay it on the ground in a straight line, and then herd twenty of the vagrants into a row behind it. They snap an order, and the bums all sit down at once. The rope is lifted over them, and twenty more unfortunates are seated in a row behind. It is fascinating to watch, horribly efficient and totally inexplicable.

The moment the corral of unfortunates has been arranged into a tidy little audience, two minivans speed up and squeal to a halt in front of them. A dozen bright-faced young things in matching yellow shirts leap out, and begin unloading boxes of food, bananas, plastic bowls, big vats of rice. Three hundred homeless heads follow the food noiselessly, apart from the faint drip-dripping of their drool. A man next to me spits on the floor.

'Christians!' he hisses.

On the yellow T-shirt of the young enthusiast nearest me I can read the message 'Jump Right In!' His pals have similar slogans – 'Make a Better World!' and 'Show Our Goodness!'

Once the three hundred have seen the food and registered what it is, it is just left to one side, almost daring them to rush over and start tucking in. Instead of doling it out, the yellow T-shirts start setting up a lectern with a microphone on it, and handing out hymn sheets. When this is all done, a dapper little chap in a sharp suit with a pink tie and a huge toothy smile bounds out of the minivan where he has been waiting for his acolytes to do their good work, and springs up to the mike. He speaks in Japanese, but I don't need a translator.

'Hello, everybody!' he is clearly saying. 'I want to talk to you about Jesus . . . !'

The bums' shoulders sag slightly, and their eyes flick to the rice and bananas, but they all sit patiently and clutch their hymn sheets as they are force-fed the good news.

The man next to me feels sorry for them. He says that in Japan there is no provision for the unemployed, no benefits, and so if you lose your job and can't find another you quickly find you are out of options apart from loading your stuff onto a cart and pitching a tent in Ueno Park. This handout by the Christians happens three times a week, he says, and in between times the homeless are going through the garbage bins outside restaurants. He manages to make this seem like quite an agreeable way to feed yourself, compared to sitting on the tarmac listening to the good news.

It occurs to me that I am looking at one of the reasons why people here are so conscientious and provide such good service, even without the Western incentive of the tip. The alternative to having a job, any job, is just too unpleasant to contemplate.

Our World Cup – the Japanese one as opposed to the South Korean one – kicks off this afternoon, with the match between Ireland and Cameroon in Niigata. Back at the hotel I hook up with Nick and also David, a friend of ours who has come over to cover the World Cup for the London *Evening Standard*. We set off in search of an Irish pub to watch the game in, and head for a place called The Dubliners that Scott told me about the other day.

It takes a little bit of finding. As with What The Dickens, The Dubliners doesn't really look much like a pub from the outside.

It is on the second floor of a building in a busy shopping street, and we are right underneath it before we notice it. We go up, and it is absolutely heaving – full of English fans, of course, as all the Irish have decamped to Niigata. We can barely get through the door, let alone see the television or reach the bar, so we head downstairs into a restaurant. This has a huge and impressive plasma television mounted on the far wall, and David is confident he can get the waiter to switch over from the golf to the football – 'it's the World Cup, for God's sake!' – and so we get a table and order food.

The waiter has no English at all, but the menu has photographs so we think we have managed to get our choices across. When it comes to changing the channel on the big television, however, communication becomes a little stickier.

David points at the television. The waiter nods and smiles. David does a using-the-remote-control mime. The waiter smiles and nods. David says, 'Football. World Cup. OK?' The waiter nods, smiles, and leaves.

'See?' says David. 'That's sorted then.'

In Niigata, Cameroon and Ireland kick off. In the restaurant beneath The Dubliners, we are watching a recording of Phil Mickelson missing a putt.

Our waiter returns with some beers. David tries again to make him understand that we would like him to switch over to the football. He nods, as if the light has dawned finally, and disappears again.

Five minutes pass. Still no sign of the football. Or the waiter.

Eventually another waiter comes close enough for us to attract his attention. We have begun to suspect that the first waiter has gone into hiding rather than face having to disappoint us. David runs through his pointing, remote control miming and 'Football!' pleading again.

'Ah! Foot-a-ball!' says the second waiter.

'Yes!' we all reply, desperately.

'*Hai* . . .' He scuttles off. When he returns he has clearly been practising. 'Foot-a-ball,' he says, then points energetically at the ceiling, in the direction of The Dubliners. 'Here . . .' he then adds, pointing at the floor. 'Gorruf!'

David refuses to give up. 'But look,' he says plaintively, 'nobody's even watching the gorruf . . .'

Just then, ten elderly Japanese gentlemen come in and sit at a table between us and the television. They are all wearing pastel-coloured jumpers and golfing hats, and loud-checked golfing slacks. One of them is removing a pale leather glove, as though he has just walked in from the eighteenth green. 'Ah,' they murmur approvingly to one another. 'Gorruf . . .'

We concede defeat.

Food bolted, we make for The Dubliners. Cameroon are having much the better of things, in their white shirts with the black sleeves, specially designed to look like the basketball singlets they wore during the African Nations Cup in February and which have been banned by FIFA for some unknown reason. Holland and Kinsella are trying manfully to fill the gap left by the absent Roy Keane, while Robbie Keane is making a nuisance of himself up front.

In the thirty-ninth minute Cameroon work the ball across the middle to Geremi on the right. The Real Madrid man finds Samuel Eto'o down the line, and he skips past Steve Staunton, who is winning his ninety-ninth cap today. Staunton doesn't give up the chase, and catches Eto'o on the bye-line, but finds himself being nutmegged as the Cameroon forward sets up his strike partner Patrick Mboma. The big man takes a touch, and then slides the ball under Shay Given and past the despairing lunges of Matt Holland and Gary Kelly to give the African Champions the lead, to the delight of boss Winfried Shafer, who if anything has even more eye-catching hair than Senegal's Bruno Metsu.

The almost entirely English crowd in the room seems split

more or less half and half. Some are subdued, wanting the Irish to do well, others enjoy the footballing *schadenfreude* of seeing them fall behind.

At half time we can stand the crush no longer. We've given the Irish experience a go, but there weren't actually any Irish people in the place, and we couldn't get near enough to the bar to get a Guinness. We get in a cab and go back to the hotel bar for the second half.

We are just in time to see Harte slip on the edge of his area and let Geremi in for a snap shot which fairly whistles past Given's right-hand post. The Cameroon defender slaps the turf in frustration, and is out of position as Given's long goal kick floats over his head to Kevin Kilbane. The Sunderland winger strides forward and sends a low innocuous-looking cross into the box, where Kalla, falling, heads it out. Matt Holland, twenty-five yards out, strides onto it and hits it first time, low and hard into the bottom left-hand corner for a brilliant equaliser.

After this Ireland look the more likely to nick a winner. Robbie Keane slaps a twenty-yard drive against the post, Kinsella has a shot charged down, and young Millwall sub Steven Reid hits a powerful free kick too straight and Alioum tips it over.

Both sides will be content with a draw, and Cameroon look a skilful muscular side who could do well. I hope they both go through to the next stage, because that will mean the Germans go out.

Even though the hotel bar is very expensive, it is comfortable and not too crowded, and so Nick, David and I decide to stay there for the next game, which is Uruguay v Denmark in Group A. There is no sign of Cube, who was supposed to meet us at The Dubliners, and may still be wandering around Shinjuku looking for the place. As kick-off time approaches an awful truth begins to dawn. The game isn't on.

The bar staff are convinced that it is going to be on, and flick through the channels for us, but there are no tell-tale signs of big match build-up – no talking heads, no painted faces outside space age new stadia, no brightly coloured aliens from the Atmozone – and even their confidence finally begins to wane. I have a brainwave, and go into the hotel lobby, where there is a World Cup information desk. There I get some information, but it isn't what we want to hear.

It seems that many of the matches have been sold exclusively to a satellite channel called Sky PerfecTV. This is an issue of mild controversy locally, but in point of fact any Japanese football fan worthy of the description will be a Sky PerfecTV subscriber, and will be a regular consumer of its diet of European and South American football. For the thousands of foreign visitors like us, however, this is a disaster. Only the evening games will be shown live on free-to-view channels, like the ones we can get in our hotel rooms. In order to see the others, we will have to roam the streets looking for sports bars that subscribe to Sky PerfecTV, which will, in all probability, be as crowded and unpleasant as The Dubliners this afternoon.

As this development sinks in, jet lag catches up with David and he begins to fall asleep, so we go our separate ways.

In the evening I go out to send some e-mail and pick up some food, and I get back to my room about twenty minutes into Germany v Saudi Arabia. It's still o–o; excellent. I switch on the English commentary to hear Tony Gubba saying that the Saudi keeper is 'a great shot-stopper'. That's what I want to hear – I have high hopes that the Saudis might pull off an upset here. This is such a tight group that the result against the outsiders might just be crucial.

I've barely taken a bite, though, before Miroslav Klose scores, an easy free header from a left-wing cross, and a big blob of mustard and ketchup falls out of my takeaway burger and onto my hotel *yukata*. I still haven't finished wiping it up when the Germans score another identical goal, Ballack crossing from the left, and Klose, unmarked, heading in. Ten minutes later they do exactly the same thing again, this time Ziege crossing for Ballack to head the ball into virtually the same square foot of the goal. This keeper may be a great shot-stopper, Tony, but he's rubbish at headers.

Just before half time the Saudis compound their embarrassment by allowing Carthorse Jancker to score a tap-in. In the second half Klose (unmarked) completes his hat-trick with another header, Linke (unmarked) does a remarkably accurate impression of Klose and nets a sixth, Oliver Bierhoff (marked, but not particularly well) takes the keeper by surprise by shooting from twenty-five yards rather than heading the ball past him and sneaks a seventh, and Schneider finds the top corner with a last-minute free kick to make it eight.

Then highlights of Denmark 1 Uruguay 2. Jesper Gronkjaer and Jon Dahl Tomasson play a one-two – actually two one-twos, or a one-two-one, strictly speaking – which pulls the Uruguay defence apart for Tomasson's opener just on half time. Then, early in the second half, Alvaro Recoba of Inter Milan takes a corner, which is headed clear by Henriksen as far as Garcia on the edge of the area. He juggles it once, twice, and then lifts it square to Dario Rodriguez, who bangs an unstoppable volley past Sorensen with his left shin. The ball doesn't touch the ground from the moment Recoba takes the corner until it hits the back of the net.

Gronkjaer and Rommedahl continue to torment the Uruguayan full backs in the second half, and on eighty-three minutes Jorgensen flicks a right-foot cross from the left wing onto the head of Tomasson, who nods his second off the underside of the bar.

Bad news for France, who would have preferred a draw in this game, and Denmark look a good solid side with dangerous attacking players.

6
Saitama

'We've sold our birthright down the fjord to a nation of
seven million skiers and hammer throwers who spend
half their lives in darkness . . .'
– Jeff Powell, *Daily Mail*, on the appointment of
Sven Goran Eriksson

2 JUNE

The word *dasai*, meaning 'from Saitama', is slang for dull or
boring, and the place's main claim to fame is that it is the
bonsai tree capital of the world, so I'm not going to argue
with that.

Saitama prefecture is to the north of Tokyo, near enough
for its main cities to be at the outer reaches of the tube map.
A bit like Watford. Saitama City is a brand-new idea, formed
by merging the existing suburban centres of Urawa, Omiya
and Yono. Before the war this was an agricultural area, then
an industrial one, and nowadays Saitama is trying to reinvent
itself as a bright spanking-new financial and business centre.
It doesn't attract much in the way of tourist traffic, so, on
the face of it, it seems an odd place for Yoko Ono to locate
her John Lennon museum, as she did a couple of years ago.
Presumably the feeling was that Liverpool would be just too
obvious – far better to do it in *her* home town.

The football stadium is very much in keeping with Saitama's
self-image as a modern centre, a futuristic 63,000-seater, open
at the ends, with the main stands along either touchline

69

covered by matching triangular roofs that look like a pair of giant napkins. And, unlike Tokyo, Saitama is actually a bona fide football hotbed, as the Urawa Red Diamonds are one of the JLeague's best-supported sides.

I head up to Saitama ridiculously early. I have to meet Dom, the other talkSPORT reporter, who was in Urawa last night, having come up from Awaji island with the official FA press party. I am keen to meet him, to get some inside guff on team selection, and to use his superior satellite telephone equipment to do my piece for the breakfast show. He is keen to meet me, because I have his match tickets.

I suggested, when we spoke on the phone last night, that the best way for us to find one another was for him to stand outside the stadium holding a big flag with my name on it. What can possibly go wrong?

Outside Urawa-Misono station, at the end of the Namboku line, the landscape is kind of empty-industrial. The former city of Urawa, home of the Urawa Reds, is a little way off, and this stadium has been built in the middle of nowhere. There is a factory, and plenty of overhead cabling, but precious little else in the way of scenery.

The weather is cloudy and warm, and shouldn't be too difficult for either side to deal with. When the draw was made back in December, Steve McClaren said he thought the conditions would be the most difficult opponents out here, which just goes to show he hadn't been paying attention. Actually, if anyone in the Group of Death is going to have an advantage when it comes to acclimatising it'll be the Swedes, who are already well used to paying five pounds for a pint of beer where they come from.

At the bottom of the escalators are dozens of highly optimistic Japanese youths, boys and girls, holding up cardboard hitch-hiker signs which read 'I Need Ticket' or sometimes 'I Need 2 Ticket'. A couple of unmistakably cockney youths, wiry and also shifty (those may not have been their actual names), stroll amongst them, murmuring, 'Tickets? Any tickets? Buying and selling...' Interested in what the current going rate is, I stop one and ask how much he's selling for.

'I haven't got any to sell,' he says. 'That's just what we say.'

I wonder how ticket touts ever get away with it, as any serious clampdown would surely wipe them out as a species. Can there be a group of people in any other walk of life that more closely correspond to their own stereotype? You can spot them a country mile off.

A month or so ago, when Jim was having trouble getting our tickets, he spoke to one archetypal fixer, an absolute ringer for Arthur Daly.

'What we do, Jim, is this. You organise a competition on the radio, and the prize is World Cup tickets, right? You get the tickets from some sponsor somewhere, right, and then what happens is – your man wins the competition. And Bob is then very much your uncle.'

Jim protested that this was, not to put too fine a point on it, illegal, and that he would end up in jail, but Arthur Daly was not in the least put off.

'Nonsense,' he said. 'I've already done the exact same thing for (insert name of popular tabloid paper here) and also (insert name of large satellite television news provider here)...'

Hundreds of fans are milling around in the sunshine, with dozens of police looking on. I am impressed by how many England shirts there are on display – the whites and reds are outnumbering the yellows by about twenty to one, I'd say – given the stories in the press at home about how many fans would be giving this expensive and too-distant World Cup a miss.

Then I start to notice just how many of these England shirts are being worn by Japanese people. There are dozens of them, young lads, couples holding hands, whole families, many of them with the cross of St George already painted onto their smiling faces, all playing at being England fans for the day. The England fans – the ones from England, I mean – seem thoroughly enchanted by this, and the atmosphere is very jolly.

It seems a million miles away from Charleroi, and the possibility of the Japanese authorities getting to use their Spiderman guns is looking extremely remote.

Or is it?

One English chap, mid-thirties, is swaggering around with BEKCHAM emblazoned across his back. I circle round him, trying to snap a surreptitious photo with him legibly in it, and overhear him talking to a mate.

'I bought this in Thailand . . .' he's saying. Uh-oh . . .

To make up for the lack of any town, shops, or other signs of life between the purpose-built station and the purpose-built stadium, the organisers have constructed something called the International Amenities Village. This is a bunch of tents, stalls, and semi-permanent displays which large numbers of fans are already wandering curiously around by the time I arrive, a good four hours before kick-off.

Tiny little schoolgirls greet us, handing out home-made cards welcoming us all to Saitama and little origami cranes, tokens of propitious fortune.

The food stall is called 'World Gourmet Shop' and boasts a wide range of international cuisines including 'Chicken Carry', 'Couscous', 'Viande de boeuf', 'Risotto' and 'Borschch'. The English contribution to this global smorgasbord is 'Fish and Chip', of course, but before we become too self-deprecating about our standing in the world of fine cuisine, I note that I can see no Swedish offering whatsoever. Not so much as a bowl of muesli or a single herring. Hang on, though, what the hell is 'Kryddiga Kottbuller' . . . ? Maybe I noted too soon . . .

There is a stage, with speakers on either side, and when I first get there a local school band is giving a display of Kodo drumming, which supporters from both sides are watching with interest. The atmosphere is very relaxed, much more so than at other England games I have been to – against Tunisia in Marseilles four years ago, for example, where I thought I was going to get stoned, and not in a good way.

A big fat bloke in an England shirt sits on the floor, beaming seraphically around him. Unlike nearly everyone else, whose shirts have BECKHAM written on the back, the fat bloke's shirt has FUCKFACE written on it, and he clearly feels this is comedy from the very top drawer.

Of course there is plenty of merchandise to buy, but not all of it is what you might expect outside a football match. There are replica shirts for sale, with crowds of Japanese supporters lashing out for their BECKHAMS. There are woollen scarves, with both England and Sweden written on them, despite the fact that it is so warm that many men are not bothering with shirts.

And there is a stall selling bonsai trees. Some as much as seven or eight feet tall, in huge heavy earthenware pots. If you dropped one of these off the top tier of the grandstand you would certainly kill someone. Actually, there is a little sign, reading:

The commodity here cannot be brought into the stadium.

The busiest stall of all is the one offering face painting. The queue is several dozen long, almost all Japanese people in England shirts, wanting to go the whole fancy-dress hog.

Up on the stage the drummers give way to a demonstration of keepy-uppies by a fat Japanese bloke and a runty little chap in a filthy Argentinian number 10 shirt – not an outfit calculated to make him King Popular with this audience. After a couple of minutes the reason why he is so dirty becomes apparent, as he spends most of his act rolling about on the floor like a break dancer, bouncing the ball off various parts of his runty anatomy. His ball control is undeniably impressive, but I find myself wondering whether he'd be able to play a square pass to keep possession with his team under pressure, or hoof the ball onto the roof of the stand with the clock ticking down . . .

I make my way along the wide path to the stadium. It looks imposing but odd stuck out there in no man's land all by itself, with only the various display stands set up by the World Cup's corporate sponsors for company. The Hyundai one has a strongman fairground machine, which seems to suggest that you can win a car by bashing the gizmo with a big hammer, but I see several people light it up all the way to the top and then get shuffled away with just a carrier bag with a T-shirt in it.

The gates are not open yet, but already hundreds of Japanese fans are queueing up in orderly lines, seated cross-legged on the concrete piazza outside the gates. At 3.30 on the dot, still three hours before kick-off, all the entrances open at once, and they start eagerly filing in. Why do they want to get in so early? Unless they want to stick up those big Union Jacks with 'Grimsby Town', 'Bristol Rovers' or 'Woking' scrawled across them in white paint, and I can hardly believe they do.

Jim has got Prestige Silver tickets for the Group of Death games for me and for Dom, which means we are entitled to go to a reception in a marquee alongside the stadium. I meet Dom outside, with his satellite phone equipment in a couple of cases. He's having a rather fraught afternoon, because FIFA jobsworths won't let him set up and broadcast on the precincts of the stadium since talkSPORT haven't forked out for the full accreditation, so he's having to do his reports on the run before security move him on like some sort of independent radio guerrilla.

Dom is a very pleasant, curly headed lad, and we hit it off right away when we met up briefly in London the week before last. He is a big Manchester United fan, which might have been

74

a problem once upon a time except my attitude has softened slightly in recent years. This is solely due to the presence of Paul Scholes in the United side, as he has been my favourite England player for four years now. Since, in fact, he did a press conference after his great goal against Tunisia in Marseilles. He was asked who his favourite player of all time was, with the assembled press pack all having their biros poised to scribble Bryan Robson or Eric Cantona, but Scholesy said:

'Andy Ritchie, Roger Palmer and Frankie Bunn.'

Which, more or less, is what I might have said myself. Turned out he was a Latics fan, and what's more had gone to the 1994 FA Cup semi-final against United at Wembley, whilst a United apprentice, and sat with the Oldham fans. I could wish he'd decided to play for us as well as support us, but in every other respect Scholes is the top man.

Dom has been living with the national press big boys, and the word is that Vassell will start alongside Owen, with Heskey wide on the left, and Hargreaves keeping his place in the centre with Scholes after his fine showing in the warm-up games. And Beckham definitely starts, which will be a relief to the shirt sellers in the International Amenities Village if not – hopefully – to Sweden. Mills has got the nod at right back, alongside Ferdinand, Campbell and Cole, with Seaman between the sticks.

The two of us swan into the Prestige Silver reception and help ourselves to some free beer. On television sets inside the marquee the Group of Death is under way. It's well into the second half of Argentina v Nigeria, and still 0–0, which suits us just fine. I watch for a few minutes, and both teams look worryingly capable.

Dom is due to do a report for the *Breakfast Show*, so I can go on at the same time. Yesterday Parry and Brazil were doing the show from Dublin, and everyone went out on the most enormous piss-up after Ireland v Cameroon. They've all only just made it back to London in time for today's edition.

Dom beckons me over, and we sneak to the far end of a not-too-busy car park, unpack all his satellite equipment and point it at the sky.

He dials up London, we both quickly slap on some headphones and chat a bit with Mike and Alan about what a great stadium it is and how all the Japanese have dressed up as England supporters, all the while swivelling our eyes around shiftily to check for security jobsworths wanting to eject us.

That done we pack up and head back to the marquee. There have been two developments while we were away. A load of free food has appeared, and Argentina have scored.

A Veron corner has floated over everyone in the packed Nigerian penalty area, and Gabriel Batistuta has nodded it back just inside the post. Nigeria are coming back at the South Americans, but Batigol and his mates look composed, and it looks very much like this will be the final score. Twenty minutes later it is. We could have done without that, really, and I drown my disappointment in more free beer.

Dom introduces me to some of the people who are staying in his hotel. There are a couple of lads who work for Nationwide, and who are involved in the sponsorship of not only the England team but also the Football League. They are also responsible for carting round a board covered in Nationwide logos and shoving it into the background of as many television interviews as they can. Very genial, especially when they ascertain that I support a Nationwide League club, rather than one of the spawn of Satan that form the Premiership.

Also a couple of national newspaper journalists, professional footy pundits who make their living writing opinionated pieces about the England matches. I try to earwig, partly at least because I am fascinated to know whether they use the words 'bid', 'dubbed' and 'goalden' in conversation as often as they do in print. I ask them what they think will happen later, and they both shrug. Wait and see. We don't know any more than you do . . .

Dom has disappeared into the car park again. I grab one last piece of orange roulade and garlic sausage and go into the stadium. I'll see him inside.

There is a moment just before the start when a big shot of Sven Goran Eriksson sitting in the dugout, smiling serenely, appears on the screen just above the clutch of Sweden supporters with their yellow shirts and banners. It is a great photo opportunity, but by the time I have fumbled my disposable camera out of my pocket the moment has passed. I notice, though, now that the Swedish fans have caught my eye, that there is a big Swedish flag draped over the railings with 'PEKING' written across it. Once again – no more Buddha . . .

Beckham lines up with the team, sporting his already much-copied faux-mohican hairstyle, a little moustache, and a bizarre beard which is a kind of stripe underlining his jaw.

The Japanese band plays the national anthem, and then unexpectedly launches into a second verse. Not many of the team sing even the first verse, let alone the stuff about confounding her majesty's enemies – not particularly encouraging for her on the day of her golden jubilee.

Sweden are playing in blue, following a row over their first strip, which is said by FIFA to be 'too yellow'. They turn out in blue as a protest, even though blue is supposedly bad luck in Sweden.

Ljungberg is in their starting eleven, despite stories all week about him having some kind of hip problem, along with the shaven-headed Celtic star Henrik Larsson, who has been inundated with cards from well-wishers in Glasgow.

The game gets under way. Everyone is watching Beckham, to see if he's moving freely, wanting reassurance that all will be well. His first touch of the ball brings a dazzling light show of flashbulbs going off all around the stadium, and at first the game is all about him.

He has a run with the ball down the right-hand side. The

Swedish midfield, looking nervous, backs away from him, and he sends Danny Mills bombing past him on an overlap. Then to a huge cheer, he robs Ljungberg in the centre circle, and he's clearly sending the message that he's going to be prepared to put his foot into the tackle.

With a fabulous lack of feeling for context, the Sheffield Wednesday band strike up the theme from *The Great Escape*.

Hargreaves finds Beckham wide on the right, and the captain whips in his first cross, in another cascade of flashes. England are starting well, and it rather looks as though the Swedish team have pinned all their hopes on Beckham not being fit for this match. Now that he's here, he's intimidating them by his sheer presence.

As Sweden settle a bit, though, there are one or two less encouraging signs. Sol Campbell, for a start, seems to have forgotten how to head the ball. One clearance skims off the top of his head and falls to the ground, with backspin, about four feet away. Another goes straight to Larsson, and Sol fouls him trying to win it back, getting booked into the bargain. Another, from a corner, should be a regulation nod-out under no pressure from anyone, but it somehow skews off the side of his head right across the six-yard line to where Seaman just manages to nick it off Larsson's head.

And then there's Heskey on the left wing. Scholes pinches the ball in the centre circle and sets the big Liverpool forward free, but instead of charging for the bye-line he runs up to the full back, dithers, gets blocked, turns, and plays Hargreaves into trouble.

Mills is finding lots of space on the right side, but his balls into the area are not reaching the heavily marked Owen and Vassell, and long balls through to the strikers are also being easily snuffed out by much taller men who are better at heading.

But then England score. Beckham takes a corner from down in front of all the Swedish supporters. It is a beauty, swinging into the centre of the goal. Campbell leaps to meet it. Possibly Hedman is distracted by all the flashbulbs reflecting dazzlingly off big Sol's gleaming bonce. Certainly he is blocked by his own player, Allback, who is marking Michael Owen. He flaps, falling, and Sol thumps the ball into the back of the net with the first decent header he's managed in the match.

Now we can start to breathe a little more easily. Now we can start to say to one another that Sweden look a poor side, dejected and demoralised, who have relied on a player who is half fit. Ljungberg is wandering infield, trying to get into the game, allowing Beckham and Mills to double up on the left back, Lucic.

England are having a lot of possession in midfield, but Scholes and Hargreaves seem to be under instructions to pump the ball forward as quickly as possible to Owen, and Mjallby is still winning all their aerial battles, as you'd expect. It seems a baffling tactic, especially when Heskey is in the side, albeit hugging the left touchline rather than putting himself about trying to nod down these high balls.

In the last few minutes of the half Sweden start to get it together a little bit. Ferdinand is keeping Larsson quiet, but Allback is wriggling away from Campbell, and works three half chances for himself.

And there is another frenzy of flashbulbs as it looks as if Beckham has started limping. Half time comes, and Sven looks thoughtful. We look comfortable enough, I suppose, but surely he's going to tell them to hold on to the ball a bit more in midfield – we're just inviting Sweden to come at us.

The second half begins with Paul Scholes dominating the game, and he coordinates a couple of decent moves, with the ball being passed along the ground instead of just hoofed upfield as quickly as possible. After a few minutes, though, England seem to go back into their shell. Beckham and Heskey are hugging the touchlines, and England find themselves in a spread-out 4–2–4 formation too much of the time. Gradually

Sweden's more compact midfield four begins to outnumber and overwhelm Scholes and Hargreaves, who are chasing shadows.

I am getting very wound up at this point, shouting at Dom that Ferdinand and Campbell are dropping too deep, and surrendering the ground at the edge of the penalty area. This is how England have been conceding goals for the last couple of years, to Figo, to van Bommel, to Gattuso, and Sweden are getting far too much of the ball twenty yards from Seaman's goal.

Anders Svensson comes on for Sweden, and straightaway he backheels the ball into space around the D of England's area. England's backline are defending so deep that it looks as if Sweden's midfielders are queueing up to have a shot, and only a last-minute dash by Hargreaves snuffs out the danger.

Next time we are not so lucky. A long ball into the England area finds Ferdinand, Campbell and Mills all marking Larsson. Mills chests the ball down, and it skids away from him, so that he has to lunge to clear it from the Celtic striker. The ball is picked up twenty-five yards out by Alexandersson, who is allowed to stride towards the D unmolested. I am yelling for someone to come out and close him down, but Cole makes half a move and then gives up, Campbell inexplicably turns his back, and Ferdinand stands stock still in the middle of the goal, unsighting David Seaman, who gets his fingertips to Alexandersson's shot but can't prevent Sweden from equalising.

On the big screen, Mills is shouting 'Fuck!' to himself. I'm sure he will carry the can for this one, but I blame Campbell for not closing down. Where is Martin Keown when you need him?

Beckham, invisible since half time, is replaced by Kieron Dyer, another man who doesn't have ninety minutes in him just yet, and a game which England should have sewn up before half time begins to slip-slide away.

Lucic and Linderoth are given the freedom of Saitama to take pot shots from the edge of the area, then Larsson threads the ball through the backpedalling defence and frees Lucic one on one with Seaman, and the keeper makes a crucial save with his enormous chest.

Darius Vassell has a little purple patch, running at the Swedish defence. Sven then takes him off, strangely, and on comes Joe Cole. Vassell has been the one player who has tried to get the ball on the ground and play – perhaps he's off for ignoring team orders. Young Joe comes out to the left of midfield, allowing Heskey to play as an out-and-out centre forward. Suddenly we see what the big Liverpool man can do, as he starts putting himself about, winning headers. On seventy minutes Michael Owen gets his first shot of the game away, which skids the wrong side of the post and into the side netting.

England's shape does actually look a bit better now, and the movement of Dyer and Joe Cole is finally giving the England midfield some threat, but as the game peters out towards a draw it is Sweden who have the best late chance, a crossfield ball slipping under Ashley Cole's foot to Larsson, who drags his shot wide.

Full time – and it's 1–1. The Swedish fans wave their giant cardboard Eriksson cut-out, and the England band play *Rule Britannia*, again capturing the essence of the moment with uncanny sensitivity.

'I fucking hate that band,' the bloke next to me mutters. 'If they ever sit behind me I'll stick their fucking tuba up their arse . . .'

I hope I'm sitting nearby if that happens. I'd like a picture of that.

Dom and I trudge heavily out onto the forecourt of the stadium, where the biggest imaginable bottleneck is building up. The literature from the organising committee boasts that access in and out of this ground will be impeccable, as there are no fewer than twenty-seven exits. That's all very well, but all twenty-seven of them lead to the one path to the station, the coach park, and the car parks, so all 63,000 spectators are trying to leave the same way all at once. Dom has to rescue his recording equipment from the security people, who took it off him on the way in, and so we split up and I head into the crush inching slowly away from the ground.

I need to talk to someone, so I ring David on the mobile, saying, as is my wont: 'England here . . .'

'What, the whole team?' he says. 'Have you rung up to apologise?'

'Yes,' I reply. 'We've rung to say we're really really sorry for letting an Everton player score. Sol says he's really sorry that he only managed one decent header in the entire match, even though that was a goal. Danny is sorry for fannying around in his own area, Emile begs your forgiveness for not really being international class, David apologises for not telling the truth about how fit he was, and Sven is here too, he wants us to mention that he's really sorry that he turned out not to be as clever as everyone thought, and says you all just assumed he was smart because he wears specs.'

David says he has got his hotel to video Spain v Slovenia, which is just kicking off, if I want to go back and watch it. I can't really imagine I'll be in the mood.

Back at our hotel I meet up with Nick and Cube, who have got back from Saitama much earlier than me. One reason for this is that Nick, it seems, has left the game at half time.

Some halfwits behind him started trying to get a Mexican Wave going towards the end of the first half, and Nick, who hates this, got himself into a row with them and stomped off. Before he could cool off he found himself outside the stadium and halfway to the station, leaving Cube on his own with

Fishing-net Man's son. The youngster had found the sacrifice of his ride home from the airport ultimately worthwhile, as his dad ended up giving him the precious match ticket, and as the second half got under way he started asking Paul: 'Where is Mr Nick?'

'He's . . . gone to the toilet.'

'Ah . . . OK.'

Five minutes later, he asked again.

'Where is Mr Nick?'

'Still in the toilet.'

'Ah . . . OK.'

And so on, every five minutes throughout the second half.

'Where is Mr Nick?'

'Still in the toilet.'

'Ah . . . OK.'

The Cube could not concentrate on the game, becoming oppressed by the prospect of having to leave the stadium at full time with the young man still under the impression that Nick was in the toilet, engaged in some cataclysmic bowel-emptying episode. A few minutes before the end he stood up.

'Where you going?'

'Toilet,' said Cube, and legged it out of the ground.

At about this very moment, Nick was arriving back in Tokyo, still unaware of the final score. A Japanese gentleman spotted him in the station, and said, 'Ah! Enguran win?!'

'Did they?' said Nick. 'What was the score?'

'Ah! Enguran win! What score?'

'Yes, what was the score?'

'Enguran win 2–1?'

'Two-one? It was 2–1?'

'Ah! Enguran win 2–1!'

And then they went their separate ways, each convinced that the other had told him that the result was 2–1 to England.

In the hotel bar I find Nick and The Cube talking to a pair

of English lads, Darren from Manchester and his mate John, a Grimsby Town fan. Darren is very talkative, and John, it seems, has got used to just listening and smiling. They have made a last-minute decision to come over to Japan for the weekend, determined to enjoy themselves, and their glorious rambling conversation is the perfect antidote to the disappointment of the football.

At one point, Darren gets on to the subject of philosophy. 'Have you heard of Itchy?' he asks.

And of course I have. He's the insanely violent cartoon mouse in *The Simpsons*.

'No, the philosopher Itchy . . .'

I start thinking there must be a Japanese philosopher, or perhaps Chinese, called Ichi . . .

'You know, wrote about the *ubermensch* . . . ?' Oh, that would be Nietzsche. I remember first coming across that name in the stories of P.G. Wodehouse. Young women were always trying to improve the mind of Bertie Wooster by force-feeding him Nietzsche, and in my head, never having heard it pronounced, I always used to think of him as Nee-yetsh. In my life, I must admit, I have read an awful lot more P.G. Wodehouse than Nee-yetsh. Nonetheless, I gear myself up for faking a discussion about German philosophers, but Darren has moved on to an anecdote about the time he landed in a helicopter on the centre circle at Boundary Park. With Denis Law.

Time for bed.

7
Oh, Mr Ambassador

'We are all looking forward to seeing Totti.'
— Jamie Redknapp

3 JUNE

It looks as though I've missed out on the two events that have been most preoccupying the people of Great Britain this week, namely the Queen's Jubilee, and the contest for the number one slot between Will Young, the ghastly Pop Idol winner with his cash register chin and his drippy version of *Light My Fire*, and Ant 'n' also of course not forgetting Dec. The FA – again with its finger on the pulse of the nation's footy fans – chose this pair of chirruping *Byker Grove* child stars to put on sheepskin car coats and unconvincing old-man make-up in order to deliver the Official World Cup Song. Its lyrics, along the lines of:

Rio to Gerrard, Gerrard to Scholesy, Scholesy to Beckham, Beckham to Owen . . .

and so on ad infinitum through a prolonged spell of imaginary England possession, have been rather taken over by events, not only the injury to Steven Gerrard (although in fairness these may not even be the exact right words, I could barely stay awake long enough to jot these rough ones down) but also Sven's tactics against Sweden. I bet the lovable Geordie rogues are wishing they'd plumped for:

*Rio to Hedman, Scholesy to Mjallby, Millsy to the group
of Swedish supporters behind the goal with the big
cardboard cut-out of Sven . . .*

Then they'd not only be top of the pops, they'd also be topical.
Of the popical.

Catch up with the rest of yesterday's games on CNN.
Paraguay took a two-goal lead against South Africa, through
a Roque Santa Cruz header and a swinging free kick from the
marvellously monikered Francisco Arce. I'm sure he'd want
you to know that it's pronounced Ar-chay (not in my house,
it isn't). Maldini's Paraguayans looked to have this game well
under control, even after Teboho Mokoena pulled one back,
but then the Bafana Bafana managed to grab a last-minute
equaliser – a penalty by Quinton Fortune after a clumsy foul
by the keeper Tavarelli, who was standing in for the suspended
comedian Jose Luis Chilavert.

Both teams are chasing Spain in Group B, after they
beat Slovenia 3–1, with goals from Raul, Valeron, and
Hierro (a penalty). Slovenia's consolation effort came from
Cimirotic, but the real story is of a fist fight between
the manager, Srecko Katanec, and his star player, Zlatko
Zahovic.

The Benfica striker, who was one of the stars of Euro 2000,
did not take kindly to being substituted after an hour or so,
and reportedly said to his boss: 'I can buy you, I can buy your
house, and your family. You were a dickhead player and you're
the same as a coach. You motherfucker from Ljubljana, you're
only substituting players from Styria.'

He's a sort of Balkan Roy Keane, by the sound of things.
Presumably he hasn't heard that because of football, is no
more Buddha . . .

Argentina look strong and fluent in the highlights. There
is one piece of encouraging news, though, as their captain
and defensive linchpin, Roberto Ayala, picked up an injury

in the warm-up, and may not be fit in time for the England game.

I meet up with David for lunch. He loves sushi, and is determined to make me try some, even though I hate fish. We walk up and down Akasaka looking for a sushi place, deciding against Bar Stockholm for a number of quite obvious reasons, and eventually David spots a restaurant with a big octopus painted on the front and drags me up an alley alongside it until we find an entrance.

We find ourselves in a dark, tiny little room. Only one other pair of customers are eating here, which ordinarily isn't a good sign. Here, though, it's quite good news, because there are only two tables in the place, and any more diners would have filled it up.

The waitress who greets us makes a token show of looking around to see where to put us, and then shows us to the only possible table. She gets us water, and chopsticks, and napkins, and then raises her eyebrow as if to ask what we would like to eat. We mime a menu, with surprising success as a menu appears. It is, though, entirely in Japanese, and doesn't have any helpful pictures of the food, as we have seen in other establishments. There aren't even, as there are in almost every eating place I've seen, plastic versions of the food on display that we can point to.

David plonks the menu down on the table. 'Sushi?' he says.

The waitress shakes her head, and points to what the people at the other table are having, which seems to be a big slab of beef and a load of noodles. Her meaning is quite clear. 'This is what we do,' she is saying. 'Take it or leave it.'

A disappointment for David, and a narrow escape for me, as we seem to have found ourselves a specialist slab-of-beef restaurant. With, it has to be said, a big octopus painted on the front. We could leave, of course, but we've been napkinned, and watered, and chopsticked, and we're English, so we stay.

Still trying to absorb the disappointment of last night's result, David and I use the salt and pepper pots in time-honoured fashion to talk through how Ferdinand and Campbell are too similar to defend as a pair because neither of them wants to attack the ball on the edge of our area. And how Beckham and Heskey played too wide, leaving Scholes and Hargreaves trying to do the job of four men in midfield. And how Owen and Vassell are too similar to attack as a pair, and how playing the long ball up to them, however quick they are, was just too predictable and easy to cut out.

When the food arrives, it comes with two little dishes of warm water. I have read in a guide book somewhere that in Japanese restaurants they will sometimes bring you the water that the noodles have been cooked in, and you can mix it with the sauce to make a sort of soup. Which is how we come to drink the finger bowls.

David has been in touch with an acquaintance of his, Derek, who as it happens is his local MP, and has been invited to a reception at the British Embassy this evening. I can tag along if I want, as long as I dress up smart. But who brings a tie to the World Cup? Sven Goran Eriksson, obviously, and Sepp Blatter, but not me.

On the way back to the hotel to do my thing for talkSPORT, I pass a local landmark which is on my tourist map. Hie Jinja, it's called, and it's most likely a shrine of some kind, although it sounds like a knocking shop specialising in an Irish clientele.

My own personal studio – the path from the hotel to Yotsuya station – is happily free of gigantic noisy crows. I have some diverting and amusing observations prepared, but when I get to talk to Mike and Alan on the air the programme is still digesting yesterday's game, and I just get asked the question all their callers are getting asked.

'. . . Thank you very much, Ian from Leatherhead, and now we've got Chris on the line from Japan. Chris, what did you think of the game yesterday . . . ?'

I tell them about the miserable walk to Urawa-Misono station after the game. It took ages, everybody shuffling along, their noses pressed into the shoulder blades of the person in front, but it was eerily quiet. The English weren't in the mood for singing, and neither were the guys in the plastic Viking helmets, while the locals who had turned up dressed in England shirts didn't realise that they were supposed to. Everyone was really subdued, and I think fans of both England and Sweden reckoned that their teams had just missed out on their best chance of picking up three points.

Mike and Alan think the same.

Once I'm done, I call Nick to see if he's brought a tie with him, but of course he hasn't. He suggests I ask at the hotel reception. When I explain to them that I am going to the British Embassy this evening, I am taken very seriously. A senior manager, bowing more or less constantly, guides me to the lifts and down into the basement of the hotel. I am expecting to be shown a tie rack in the boiler room with a couple of the manager's spare ties on it, but find myself instead in a vast costumier complex.

Chic ladies bustle to and fro, taking measurements and offering cups of tea, and maybe twenty businessmen are waiting to be kitted out for some event or other in the hotel this evening. Sleek black jackets, crisp white shirts, and fancy little waistcoats are whisked to and fro, gleaming hankies are tucked into front top pockets, and it's like being behind the scenes of a multi-million yen movie about a really high-class Japanese wedding. Next door, an equally busy establishment is hiring out party frocks for the ladies.

I'm thinking this is all a little bit much for what I require, and anyway it looks as if I'll have to wait for several hours for my turn, but my bowing manager mate leads me up to the boss lady, and mutters something which clearly includes the phrase 'British Embassy'. Suddenly, and rather embarrassingly, I've jumped the queue, past the conference riff-raff and the wedding hangers-on, and four smiling and perfectly groomed ladies are measuring me and relieving me of my own rather shabby clothes. In no time at all I am a penguin-suited, dicky-bowed vision, and I can see my stubbly face reflected in my black shiny shoes. I *shall* go to the ball . . .

Of course it's absurd. If I turn up dressed like this I'll spend the rest of the evening serving drinks. The clincher, for me, comes when I discover that to hire the whole outfit for the evening will cost me three hundred and fifty quid.

'Any chance I could just borrow a tie?' I venture, but this simply does not compute. I scramble back into my own clothes and leave, having struck yet another death blow to the image of the dapper English gent abroad.

Upstairs in the bar I find Nick with Darren and John, the guys we met last night. They, it appears, haven't been to bed at all, and Darren's throat is rasping raw with God knows how many hours of constant talking. Nick insists that of course I can go to the embassy without a tie, but not without a large box of Ferrero Rocher, so he's been out and bought me one.

Later I head down to Roppongi for the first time. This is the self-styled 'entertainment district' of Tokyo, and I'm meeting David to hunt out a bar in which we can watch Brazil v Turkey before going to the embassy – another good reason not to hire the full penguin regalia. Our enthusiasm for the World Cup has been dimmed ever so slightly – we haven't put ourselves out to see Croatia play Mexico this afternoon, a poor game won by a single Cuahtemoc Blanco penalty – but we feel we really ought to check out the Brazilians.

Roppongi-dori is a wide and busy thoroughfare, and, like many wide and busy thoroughfares here in Tokyo, it has a wide and busy expressway flying overhead which covers exactly the same route. It is heaving, with hundreds of people out on the streets looking for a venue to start off an evening's drinking. It is perhaps the most obvious place for foreign football fans to gather and get tanked up prior to it all going off, and so last night there were hundreds of police in this area, all nervously fingering their Spiderman guns and their water cannon, but the England army were all very subdued and there were no arrests.

A couple of the city's largest and most popular sports bars are nearby, and, given that the Brazil game is on Sky PerfecTV rather than on the ordinary telly, they are packed to the rafters. There is a significant Brazilian émigré population here in Tokyo, and many Brazilian footballers have plied their trade in the JLeague – most famously the great Zico. There was much disappointment when Brazil were drawn to play their group games in South Korea, but it is difficult to see Turkey, China and Costa Rica denying them a place in the second phase, and for that they would definitely be here in Japan.

David and I meet up, eventually, after a number of brief mobile phone conversations along the lines of:

'I'm standing next to the thing. The thing, by the big thing . . .'

'Can you see the Hyundai garage? Next door to a sort of sex shop?'

'No, I'm by a sort of crossroads, and there's a building with a big telly on the front.'

'Have you got a brown jacket on?'

'Yeah . . .'

'OK, I'm about eight feet away, to your left . . .'

We find ourselves, a moment or two later, in a place called Geronimo's. It is small, dark, not too busy, and the Brazil v Turkey game is on. The decor has, as you might expect from the name, a native American theme, with pictures of lads in feathery headdresses and the odd bow and arrow. We grab two glasses of firewater and a couple of seats.

Brazil have Ronaldo at centre forward. His last World Cup finals appearance, in France 98, ended in baffling illness on the day of the final, and he has spent most of the intervening four years injured, in the sporting shadow of his twenty-two-year-old wife, Milene, who is a famous footballer in her own right. She is known as Rainha de Embaixadinhas – The Queen of Keepy-Uppies – for keeping a football in the air for 9 hours 6 minutes (55,187 touches). And that, as Norris and Roy would have said, is a record. And even outside football that could be quite a desirable nickname, I would imagine . . .

As the game progresses, I notice that Red Indian isn't the only decorative theme here at Geronimo's. All around the picture rail, near the ceiling, they have hung ties. Ties, a wide variety of colours and patterns, each with a little paper label pinned to it with a name on it – Colin, Kazuki, Dave, Neil, Muji. The sheer serendipity of this is breathtaking, and I start eyeing the bar staff, waiting for them to turn away so I can climb up on a chair and half-inch one. I quite like the look of Muji's, actually . . .

Then there is the 'Shot Wall of Fame'. This is covered with hundreds of little metal plaques, with personal messages on them and dates going back five or six years. To qualify for a plaque on this wall presumably you have to pull off some fearsome drinking feat. It doesn't say here what that is, but whatever it is it has the effect of scrambling the brains of the participants, if their chosen legends are anything to go by.

Stuff like:

Vivian: Is this Saturday? 17 Aug 96.

Anton The Wog – But New Zealand.

Necakov – Yeah I Want Cheesy Poofs. 3 July 1998.

Carla-Maria – Been There Once With Jonny Ham. Oct 97.

The Octopus – Don't You Wish You Had Eight Arms? 12.10.97.

Each one tells a story. A deeply confusing and very short story that reeks of alcohol. But I do find myself wondering: what was Anton The Wog going to go on to say about New Zealand? Or is 'But' the name of his home town? But, New Zealand, like, say, Butte, Montana? Nestling somewhere up

Conjunction Cove alongside the neighbouring townships of If, And, and However, New Zealand.

Did Necakov ever get his cheesy poofs? And was it this very plaque on this very wall that finally blew his cover as a Soviet agent and meant he had to return to the motherland in a diplomatic bag?

And did Carla-Maria ever go there again with Jonny Ham? There's no evidence here that Jonny Ham ever warranted a plaque of his own. Maybe he frowned on her excessive drinking, which is why they only went there once. Or maybe, just maybe, Jonny Ham is the Octopus . . .

Well. We've been misinformed. Brazil are supposed to be a dour, defensive outfit, aren't they? They're meant to have struggled to qualify, didn't I hear? Isn't their coach, Big Phil Scolari, on record as having declared that 'the beautiful game is dead'?

But here we are watching Ronaldo, stepping over the ball this way and that, sending Alpay chasing his own shadow. Here's Cafu nutmegging the Turkish left back, not once but twice, and Roberto Carlos bombing down the left wing as though defending was somebody else's job entirely. Rivaldo, the leggy genius, has a thunderous shot well saved by Rustu, and a header grabbed almost on the line. Ronaldinho, the third of the 'Three Rs', whom I've not seen before, is relatively quiet, but even he is jinking his way through the defence to bring a save out of Rustu.

The Turks give almost as good as they get, even though Hasan Sukur looks isolated and slow up front for them. And then, in injury time, a spectacular goal. For Turkey. Yildiray Basturk, who has had a great season for Bayer Leverkusen, picks out a glorious angled ball to the left of the penalty area which catches the Brazilian defence flat. Hasan Sas lets it bounce once and then lashes it past Marcos with his left foot. Little bald Sas jogs away towards the corner, looking more like a man who has run over his cat than one who has scored for his country against the mighty Brazil, but almost immediately it's half time, and I expect they get a smile out of him in the changing room during the break.

Turkey start the second half well, but Rivaldo and Ronaldo both carve out chances to equalise, and Brazil are pressing, far from dourly, for an equaliser, when my mobile phone rings.

'Hi, Chris, it's Gary from talkSPORT . . .'

I can hardly hear him above the noise from the bar, and anyway I don't want to be the man who shouts 'I'M IN A BAR!' thus spoiling being in a bar for everyone else in the bar, so I scuttle out into the stairwell.

At the exact instant that I remove myself from the room with the telly in it, Gary says, 'Oh that's a *great* goal!'

Shit! I turn to go back, but someone else is coming out and swings the door onto my nose. Ow! Fuck it, I'll see the goal later. Once I've dealt with these stars and cartoon tweeting birds . . .

'So Gary, what can I do for you?'

'Yeah, we were wondering if you could inject a bit more humour into your pieces?'

'A bit more humour?'

'Yeah, we like what you've been doing but we want it to be more . . .'

'Funny.'

'Exactly. More funny. Bye . . .'

All in all a great call to get. Massaging my nose and my ego I return to Geronimo's. Once both have stopped throbbing I indignantly remember that I didn't even manage to do any of the stuff I'd prepared for this afternoon, as Mike and Alan had just wanted to talk about the England v Sweden game. The answer, clearly, is just to make sure that I actually do the material I've thought of. All the same, I could do with something funny happening to me before tomorrow afternoon . . .

Gary was right about one thing – Brazil's goal was a beauty. Rivaldo floated it in from the left wing, and Ronaldo surged through the Turkish back line and flew to meet it horizontally, two-footed, like a giant yellow buck-toothed clothes peg.

With a couple of minutes left, Luizao runs through the middle. Alpay has hold of his shirt, and the Brazilian forward, on as a sub for Ronaldo, strains and struggles with all his might, trying to reach the penalty area before going down. It's clearly a red card for the Villa defender, but there's no way it should be a penalty. The Korean ref points to the spot, though, and Rivaldo slots the kick home hard and low to Rustu's left. 2–1 to Brazil.

There's time for two more noteworthy incidents. First Turkey's wild boy sub Ilhan Mansiz makes a bid for immortality – or at the very least the title sequence of World Cup *Match of the Day* – by flicking the ball up and over Roberto Carlos with his heel, Ardiles-style. And in a competitive match, too, not just in the warm-up or in a work of fiction . . .

Then at the other end of both the pitch and the scale of footballing glory, Hakan Unsal boots the ball at the time-wasting Rivaldo, hitting him on the thigh. The Brazilian, though, holds his face and rolls on the floor in feigned agony, succeeding in reducing the Turks to nine. It is a disgraceful display, and amazingly stupid too, as he must know that there are at least half a dozen cameras on him. Despite the nasty aftertaste of this, it has been the best game of the tournament so far.

Outside Geronimo's we jump into a cab and say to the driver, 'British Embassy.'

He looks blankly back at us. David and I are a little perplexed, as we have no more address to go on than this, and years of experience of watching old spy movies has led us to believe that cab drivers everywhere will know where the nearest British Embassy is. We try the only other thing we can think of, which is to pronounce it '*Blitish* Embassy?'

No joy. This guy clearly hasn't done the Knowredge.

Then David has a brainwave. The *Evening Standard* have hired a photographer to go around with him, a local girl called Tomoko. We are meeting her at the embassy, so David calls her up, and asks her to tell the cab driver how to get there. Bingo.

Once we arrive, though, we need more help, as we don't seem to be on any sort of guest list for this do, and have turned up like inept gatecrashers mumbling, 'Um . . . friends of Derek . . . Derek said it would be OK . . .'

We might as well have had a Watneys Party Seven. And I still don't have a tie, as Gary's phone call has driven my scheme to grab one from the wall of Geronimo's clean out of my head. Perhaps just as well.

Derek himself appears to sort it out, and we are let in. He is a larger-than-life and very jolly host, and he ushers us into the building saying, 'We've run out of beer, I'm afraid, so you'll have to have gin and tonic.' By the half pint, apparently, and not much tonic, to judge by the glass he thrusts into my hand. Not surprising, then, that most of the people in the beautifully decorated, high-ceilinged reception room seem to be rolling around drunk. Many of them are dressed the same, in dark blazers and identical red ties.

'We're the UK Parliamentary Football Club,' Derek says proudly. 'We're over here playing some football matches. We've just beaten the Japanese Diet.'

'That must have been a tough match,' I say. 'The Japanese Diet is mostly fish, isn't it?'

Actually, looking round, I would say that most of them could do with a diet of some nationality. Derek, for one, has the most Santa-esque physique of anyone I've ever met. Most of the chaps in red ties – the members of the UK Parliamentary Football Club – are British Members of Parliament. I meet Ivan, the stocky and boisterous member for Harwich, and a tall, athletic young man whom I take to be a ringer, brought in to do the running for the senior members of the squad. He assures me, though, with a shy smile, that he genuinely is the MP for Gloucester.

A healthy sprinkling of the socerati has found its way here this evening. Over there, look, it's Nancy dell'Olio, Sven's svelte Italian girlfriend. She, it must be said, has stood up incredibly well to the media blitzkrieg that went off around her when the mind-boggling story emerged that Sven had been secretly knocking off Ulrika Jonsson, formerly of TV's *The Weather*. The pair were said to have been introduced by Labour Party PR guru Alastair Campbell, who apparently said something along the lines of: 'Hey! You two are both Swedish . . .' and then wandered off to see if he could pair up a couple of stray Finns elsewhere in the room.

Nancy dug her long nails in, and gave him a damn good talking to at their £2 million Regents' Park home. She refused to oblige the tabloids by storming out, and the papers had a bit of fun with jokes about 'tricky selection problems' and 'games of two halves'. A couple of days later it was all over.

I was a little concerned, at the time, about whether this would affect Eriksson's credibility amongst the players. One of the tales that appeared in the tabloids told of Sven and Ulrika being caught in mid-romp by Ulrika's nanny, after which Sven always left his shoes outside the bedroom as a sign for the nanny not to burst in and take photographs or anything. The thing was – his shoes were the stack-heeled props of the self-consciously tinier gentleman. How would the players react to this? Knowing that the manager was not all he appeared to be? We'd had short managers before – Kevin Keegan, Graham Taylor – and frankly it hadn't been a great success.

Derek cheerfully introduces me to a few people. I can see David Platt, England hero of the nineties and England under-21 coach, amongst the many interesting people I could be talking to. How then do I end up on the terrace outside with the Sheffield Wednesday band?

Or the England band, as I must apparently call them now. They are a very jovial bunch, having a whale of a time, blissfully unaware of the teeth grinding all round the stadium every time they crank out their *Great Escape* and their *England Till I Die*. John, the ringleader, tells me that the FA – as usual judging the mood of the ordinary football fan to perfection – makes sure that the band get tickets for every single England game nowadays. I suspect this to be part of a master plan by the Scots infiltrator Adam Crozier to break our spirit before reintroducing the Home Internationals.

It's an expensive old hobby for the band, though, and they were delighted when it seemed as if they had got their whole trip sponsored by a mobile phone company. It was, however, a different mobile phone company to the FA's official mobile phone company, and so they were given an ultimatum: drop the sponsorship or forget the tickets. They chose the tickets, naturally enough, and the status of Official England Band, which means that each of them is now several grand out of pocket. Shame. Join the club.

The town where I was brought up, Worksop in Nottinghamshire, is only seventeen miles from Sheffield, and as we chat I discover that the degrees of separation between myself and the members of the band are distressingly few. One of them knows the father of one of my best friends from school and university, and another is very friendly with my former maths teacher. I don't quite know how to deal with this.

Tomoko, David's photographer colleague, turns up. She is a very friendly, attractive young lady, who smiles at absolutely everything. She met Nick and Cube yesterday at Saitama, and I know Nick was worried that they had upset her somehow, because he has given me a bottle of wine to pass on to her by way of apology for whatever it was they said or did. Meeting her now myself, though, I can't see how they could possibly have offended her, or have noticed if they had, because her face looks as if it only knows how to smile.

Just before half past eight the whole party moves en masse to another part of the embassy compound, where there is a bar. One whole wall is taken up with a projection screen, and we are going to watch Italy play Ecuador. There are empty seats at the front, and when we sit in them we see why they are empty. The screen is so big that watching a perfectly ordinary passage of play from this close involves cranking your head around from side to side as if you were watching a particularly spectacular rally at Wimbledon.

More MPs and embassy staff spill in through the door and elbow their way to the bar. Amongst them is a familiar face. I grab Derek's arm.

'Derek? Isn't that Lawrie McMenemy? What's he doing here?'

'Lawrie? He's our manager. Here, say hello to Ann, she's one of our star players . . .'

Derek drifts away. I say hello to Ann, the member for Dewsbury if I'm not mistaken, and she immediately glazes over and moves away too. Charming.

Italy are all over Ecuador. After seven minutes Totti gets to the bye-line and pulls the ball back for Christian Vieri, who sidefoots thunderously into the roof of the net to open the scoring. The Italians' tight blue shirts have a kind of plain round-necked sixties-style retro-chic, which has the unnerving effect of accentuating their man breasts. No wonder Ecuador look rattled. Vieri looks like Batman.

I introduce myself to Lawrie McMenemy. Actually, we have met before. We did a sketch together for Comic Relief in 1989 which, bless him, he remembers. I was one of a bunch of footballers, and Lawrie, as 'The Gaffer', brought in Timothy West, playing against type as a hammy old thesp, to show us all how to do play-acting properly.

Lawrie lights up briefly as we reminisce about that day, and I dread to think what sort of locker-room banter he's been enduring on this trip.

'If you pass the ball to me, then I'll support you on the broadcasting sub-committee in October . . .'

'You might very well say that was a bad back pass, but the fact is – no, let me finish – that circumstances beyond my control intervened between the decision being taken to give the back pass the go ahead and the execution of the back pass itself . . .'

'I refer my right honourable friend to the pass I gave some moments ago . . .'

On the big screen and in the Sapporo Dome Christian Vieri muscles his way past the flimsy Ulises de la Cruz and bangs in another goal to put the Italians two up. He's already had a couple more near misses, and looks very good indeed. His nickname is Bobo – 'stupid' – because he starts every utterance with a long 'Errrrm . . .'

At half time I get out the box of Ferrero Rocher that Nick gave me, and go around the room handing them out. My deadpan impression of an embassy butler would have been improved, no doubt, by the three hundred and fifty quid penguin outfit, but even without I get plenty of laughs – or rather Nick does. I'm pleased for him, as the only previous time he attempted this joke was at an Iranian embassy, and the advert had never played in the Middle East. Here one or two people go the whole hog, and simper 'Oh, Mr Ambassador, you are spoiling us!' and the whole thing is a palpable hit.

John, from the Sheffield Wednesday band, pulls out a rather grubby England scarf. It is a photo scarf, with a picture of an England team and a Northern Ireland team lining up before a Home International, and a big Admiral logo on it.

'We call this the Tebbit test,' he says. 'How many can you name? I'll give you a clue. It's from the Home Internationals of 1973.'

I pick off the easy ones – Ball, Bell, Clemence, MacDonald . . .

'There's just two we can't get,' John prompts.

'So you'd all fail your own Tebbit test then, is that what

you're saying? And how difficult is it just to check the line-up in a book?'

But he just grins. Either he doesn't notice that I am taking the piss out of him, or he doesn't care. Now let's see . . . Keegan, Todd, Watson, Hughes . . . who's that ginger youth? Whitworth, of course. Now for the two they don't know. Well, one of them is Dennis Tueart, obviously, but the other . . . ? Must be a midfielder . . .

In the end we ask Lawrie McMenemy, who identifies the last man as Colin Viljoen of Ipswich Town, a two-cap wonder.

In the second half, typically, the Italians ease up, knowing that with their defence – Panucci, Nesta, Cannavaro, Maldini – they have already done enough to shut Ecuador out of this game. Trapattoni, usually one of the more dour members of the international management community, feels comfortable enough to have a wink and a grin at the touchline camera. Ecuador's manager, Dario Gomez, on the other hand, recently survived an assassination attempt. His team, who beat Brazil in qualifying and finished a point ahead of them in the South American table, seem riddled with nerves on their World Cup finals debut, and have little to offer. They are fulfilling the role usually taken on by Colombia, and are even wearing their kit.

Some of the MPs, a little the worse for wear, start singing at the tops of their voices. The tune is recognisably the old Andy Williams hit *Can't Take My Eyes off of You*. The lyrics are recorded here for posterity.

We love you Lawrie
Because you've got grey hair
We love you Lawrie
Because you're everywhere
We love you Lawrie
You're Eng-er-lund through and through . . . (repeat over
and over again)

Lawrie shoots us a look in the middle of this display, and I can almost hear him thinking: 'I won the FA Cup, you know, in 1976 . . .'

Actually, I'm impressed by the big man's determination to get to the World Cup, by hook or by crook. He tried for USA 94 as Graham Taylor's right-hand man, but that was something of a long shot. He had a stint as boss of Northern Ireland, which was on the face of it only slightly more likely to succeed. Now he's finally made it, as the manager of a team whose star player is the middle-aged lady MP for Dewsbury.

> *We love you Lawrie*
> *Because you've got grey hair*
> *We love you Lawrie*
> *Because you're everywhere*
> *We love you Lawrie*
> *You're Eng-er-lund through and through . . .*

I'm sure if they'd had a little bit more time and they hadn't been quite so wasted they'd have come up with a further lyric, to the effect that although they love Lawrie for being Eng-er-lund through and through, that doesn't mean to say that they aren't constantly and equally aware of the needs and electoral significance of Scotland, Wales and Northern Ireland.

This is by no means the first time that I've found myself in a bar surrounded by a load of drunken yobs making a mindless racket, but usually you can console yourself with the thought that at least they're not running the country.

David tells me that Derek is concerned because the MPs are getting a lot of stick in the press at home for coming out here on a jolly at the taxpayers' expense.

'What is his answer to that, then?'

'Not really sure . . .'

I decide to go and ask Derek, who slings his arm around

me and says, 'Hey! Do you want to play for us? We've got a game lined up on Wednesday against Nomura, they're our sponsors.'

Well, tempting as that sounds . . .

'None of us is going to be there, you see, we're all going to Ibaraki to watch Ireland v Germany.'

That puts the tin lid on it. I get out one of my limited-edition business cards with my mobile phone number on it and hand it to him, saying, 'Call me if you have any spare tickets, I wouldn't mind going to that one.'

Derek glances at it and it's obvious that the word 'talkSPORT' positively leaps out at him. In a trice he has strong-armed Ann away from another conversation, and the two of them are giving me the full press release about the charity they are apparently promoting out here. Truce International, it's called, and Sven Goran Eriksson is its patron. The aim is to provide football facilities in war-torn areas around the world – Afghanistan, the Balkans, and, any day now by the sound of things, India and Pakistan. There is some soundbite humbuggery about transforming killing fields into playing fields, bombs into balls, and uniting the world's youth, linking peoples across conflict to make the world a better place, and football, it seems, has the power to do this.

I'm impressed. Essentially what this boils down to is a vision of a world in which, because of football, no more Buddha.

Derek says they've raised at least ten thousand pounds towards laying a new astroturf pitch in Kabul, which is obviously fine as far as it goes, but seems an oddly puny return on carting thirty members of the UK Parliamentary Football Club out to the most expensive country in the world. Maybe I didn't hear him properly. I promise to try to give them a mention on the radio tomorrow. Derek taps the side of his nose and says, 'I've got a spare ticket for the Ireland game. Call me.'

Who's using who, here, I wonder . . . ?

Once Italy v Ecuador has finished the bar closes and the MPs begin to drift away. David, Tomoko and I decide to find somewhere to eat. The helpful information leaflet provided for the MPs' stay in Tokyo includes the remark: 'Shinjuku at night is *not* recommended.'

So we go there in the hope that we won't run into any of them.

After a very hot Thai meal Tomoko takes us for a walk to have a bit of a look round. Shinjuku at night is a dazzling, buzzing mix of skyscrapers covered in hi-tech neon signs and blokes selling stuff off wooden barrows.

As we stroll along I say to Tomoko, 'I believe this place was the inspiration for the design of *Blade Runner*.'

'I'm sorry?' she says.

'Shinjuku is supposed to have inspired the look of *Blade Runner*,' I say. She smiles, but she clearly doesn't understand. David butts in.

'Brade Runner,' he says. Tomoko beams.

'Oh yes, *Brade Runner*, I know this film.'

I can't believe that worked.

We find ourselves in a district where it seems every building has a sex club on every floor. Seven or eight of them piled on top of one another, their neon signs twinkling pinkly and competitively, trying to attract you to their sex club of the seventy on offer.

'Excitement Sex Bar!' flashes one.

'Angel Kiss!' shines another one, and in case that doesn't give you enough of a feeling for what is on offer, another smaller sign below it reads: 'Talent in Pub.'

Even though the signs are in English, many of these establishments are not open to foreigners. Gaudily dressed hostesses stand in the street outside handing out vouchers to Japanese businessmen, studiously avoiding the likes of me. Even when I walk backwards and forwards in front of them several times.

David looks along a back street absolutely jam-packed with these joints and rival sex paraphernalia emporia, and remarks, 'How does a new sex shop ever get established here? Does a bloke walk down the street and think: "I'll tell you what this place really needs . . ."?'

It dawns on me that this is why the MPs have been warned off this part of town. I bet some of them are wandering around here, even so. One thing's for sure, though, they're not kerb crawling, nobody is. We walk past a crossroads, two narrow streets packed solid with traffic in absolute gridlock in every direction. Bizarrely, every single car is a taxi. Each one, somewhat optimistically, has its 'For Hire' light on. Imagine coming out of a sex club halfway along one of these streets, looking for a taxi home. 'Yippee! There's one right outside! It must be my lucky night . . . !'

8
Mickey

'We are Lego. Many bricks that fit together to make a
smooth wall.'
– Jerzy Engel, Poland manager, before their first game
against South Korea

4 JUNE

Nick and The Cube are naturally curious about the do at the
embassy. I tell them about the Tebbit test scarf episode, and
they are most indignant. Cube, as it happens, knows exactly
which scarf I'm talking about.

'It's from 1975 not 1973,' he says. 'It's an Admiral scarf,
isn't it, and Admiral didn't do England kit till the Revie era.'

And Colin Viljoen is such a Revie pick, and of course Tueart
didn't play for England until he was at City, not straight after
the Sunderland Cup final in '73, and if it's '73 then where's
Bobby Moore, where's Martin Peters? I'm very annoyed with
myself for not picking up on this. Nick wants me to ring the
bloke from the England band and put him straight. Maybe I
will . . .

In the lounge bar overlooking the traditional Japanese garden a group of Argentina fans are sitting contemplating a
menu. They all wear shirts with CRESPO written across
the shoulders, some Argentina, some Lazio. I hear that the
families of the Argentina players are staying in this hotel, so
these might actually be Hernan Crespo's relatives. They might
even be his shirts.

On the far side of the Japanese garden is an outdoor pool. It is closed, out of season, but this hasn't stopped two skinny old Irish gits from sitting by it with knotted hankies on their heads. There is an indoor pool for guests to use, but it costs thirty-five quid a time.

A couple of days ago there was an article in the *Japan Times* about the phenomenon of young Japanese men in their twenties and thirties, still living with their parents, who disappear into their bedrooms and don't come out for months, sometimes years on end. One lad stayed in his room for twelve years, another tricked a nine-year-old girl into visiting him and didn't let her out until she was eighteen. The parents in these cases just endure the situation, it seems, feeling a tremendous burden of guilt for not having equipped their offspring better to cope with the outside world.

This story has had a profound effect on The Cube, who went into his hotel room after the England v Sweden match and stayed there for twenty-three hours.

Today the Asian World Cup begins in earnest. For the first time, three Asian teams are in the World Cup finals, and all three of them are playing today.

Japan v Belgium in Saitama has been sold out for months. I've been thinking it would be interesting to watch the game with a really serious Japanese fan, and so have been trying to get in touch with a chap called Mickey Watanabe. I got his e-mail address from my friend Annie, whose son Louis is best friends with my son Peter. She told me that Mickey's built like a sumo wrestler, has long hair, rides a motorbike, and is a professional photographer. Apparently he stayed with Annie in London during France 98, nipping over (sorry) to France to see all of Japan's games. He sounds perfect, but sadly when I finally managed to speak to him a couple of days ago he wasn't very well.

'I have big pain ass hall,' he said plaintively. 'I must stay in house all time.'

'Oh dear,' I said.

'I'm working Thailand three years. Maybe my ass hall big surprised by Japanese food. I send e-mail when I'm OK.'

Come the morning of the game, however, it seems Mickey's health has been vastly improved by big match buzz, and he rings me up.

'Hello, Chris. I am Watanabe. This evening I go to National Stadium,' he says. 'My country is on big screen. I have ticket. You can get ticket, you can go too.'

I look into this, and find that there is indeed a big screen showing of the Japan v Belgium game at the National Stadium in Tokyo. Thousands of tickets have been sold already, but three thousand more go on sale at half past three.

I get there an hour before the ticket office opens, and am dismayed to find two enormous queues heading off into the distance already. My shoulders sag, and I set off to find the end of one of them, resigning myself to being here for two or three hours at least, and hopefully longer if I can actually manage to get in. Finally I find the end of the line, where a couple of young lads have laid out a groundsheet and are just starting in on lunch.

I plonk my bag down beside them, feeling hungry myself now, and just realising that I'm going to have to speak to talkSPORT – injecting, you will recall, more humour into my contribution – from this very bit of pavement. I get my notebook out, but I'm not feeling funny just at the moment. I'm not even feeling offbeat.

One of my neighbours offers me a rice cake, wrapped in leaves, which is very nice of him, and we embark on the best conversation we can manage given that he has no English at all and I have no Japanese. We establish that we are both looking forward to the game, and we both hope Japan will win. He shows me his ticket, and with a sudden sinking feeling I realise that I am in the wrong queue, I'm not queueing up for tickets at all, I'm just queueing up to get into the stadium stupidly early.

I shove my notebook in my bag and get to my feet, where-upon my friend shows me that he has a spare ticket, and he sells it to me for 2,000 yen, even though the price on it, I notice later, is 2,300. Top man.

This means I have four hours to kill, and can get back to my 'studio' in time to speak to talkSPORT. I thank my friend profusely, wishing Japan great good fortune this evening, and head to Shinanomachi station. There I catch sight of the same food vendor that I saw the other night after the baseball, selling his plastic dish of fat tentacles garnished with an eye that looks like a hard-boiled egg. This delicacy plays a major part, shortly afterwards, in my on-air conversation with Alan Brazil, and I get a satisfying 'Bleurgh!' noise out of him and a few decent laughs to boot. Phew.

China, this afternoon, make a dispiriting start to their World Cup finals career. Much of the preview material I have seen has concentrated on the size of the country's population, which, apparently, could sink the Isle of Wight if they all jumped up and down on it at once. Why they would want to do such a thing is not entirely clear – boredom, possibly. There may be the best part of a billion of them, but only eleven can play at any one time.

Two second-half goals from Ronald Gomez and Mauricio Wright take care of business for the Ticos. Paolo Wanchope spurns a couple of chances to impress his new Manchester City team mate Sun Jihai, and Bora Milutinovic, enjoying his fifth consecutive finals coaching his fifth different national side, seems able to sport a cheerful smile despite the disappointment. Perhaps the knowledge that he will face no criticism from bolshie Chinese pundits is contributing to his sense of well-being – an instruction from the Chinese Communist Party to the press over there reads: 'The Publicity Department advises you not to criticise the national team, even if there has been a bitter defeat or when the play has not been that flashy.'

After the usual rigmarole with the mobile phones, which seems to be how everybody deals with directions in this country, Mickey and I find ourselves face to face under the main grandstand at the National Stadium at about five o'clock. I wonder how strangers ever found each other before this technology became available. Street signs here are rare and incomprehensible, and taxi drivers haven't a clue where anything is.

Mickey is shorter than me, and well built, certainly, but either he's lost a lot of weight in the last four years or Annie hasn't seen the same sumo wrestlers that I've seen. His long hair is dyed light brown, and it is common here for young people to dye their hair blonds and browns, to stand out from the crowd and to copy the much-prized Western look. Most of them have started out with jet-black hair, and their new artificial shades do look a little odd with the natural tones of their oriental skin, not to mention their jet-black eyebrows.

Mickey leads me into the arena to where his friends are saving us seats, and my jaw simply drops open. There are thousands and thousands of people here. I know the actual match in Saitama is a 63,000 sell-out, but there must be at least as many here, if not more.

The National Stadium is slap in the middle of Tokyo. Even though Japan have been playing their international home matches here for years, the decision was taken to use only purpose-built new stadia for the World Cup, so this grand old place has missed out. It is an oval-shaped, open-air bowl, with a perfect green football pitch surrounded by an athletics track. The screen on which the match will be shown is a permanent fixture at the back of the seating behind the goal to our right, and all the seats, naturally enough, face the pitch, so there'll be some cricked necks in the morning.

Mickey introduces me to his friends, who are sitting behind us. One of them has a lucky gonk, which looks disturbingly like the ITV Digital monkey. I can't see that being particularly lucky, somehow. They are all fans of Shimizu S-Pulse, while Mickey himself follows Kawasaki Frontale, a J2 outfit who sound like a Japanese equivalent of Oldham Athletic. Like almost everyone else, Mickey and his mates are sporting the blue Japanese national shirt. Mickey has topped them, however, by adding a fancy blue *yukata* to his ensemble.

Whereas at the England game the vast majority of the replica shirts were emblazoned with the same name and number – BECKHAM and 7, of course – amongst the Japanese supporters here there is a wide range. NAKATA, 7, is prominent, but considering that Hidetoshi Nakata of Parma is the biggest star in the Japanese squad, he doesn't rule the roost to quite the extent you might expect. ONO, 18, a UEFA Cup winner with Feyenoord, is well represented, as is ALEX, 14, a naturalised Brazilian who turns out for Shimizu S-Pulse in the JLeague. Strikers NAKAYAMA, number 10, and YANAGISAWA, number 13, have plenty of support near where we are sitting, and TODA, MORISHIMA, INAMOTO – the Arsenal bench warmer – and MIYAMOTO are not far behind.

In the D formed by the running track and the goal line to our right a stage has been set up, with some big stacks of speakers. After a couple of pop acts strut their stuff a DJ takes over and starts to lead the crowd in a vast singing practice, launching them into a rendition of a song which goes:

Nippon! Nippon! Nippon Nippon Nippon!

Everyone joins in, thousands of us. Flags wave, banners are unfurled, and there is wholesale bouncing up and down at the far end. At the finish, despite the fact that it could have been heard in South Korea, the DJ embarks on that old panto staple of: 'Call that singing? You can do better than that! We're going to do it one more time . . .'

And we do, and even though it scarcely seemed possible, it is even louder than the first time. We move on to *Allez! Japan!*, their 1998 World Cup song, and then a performance in which the words of *There's No Limit* are replaced by the surname of the Japanese number 18.

It suddenly strikes me as a bit mental, all this. First of all, everyone getting here early for crowd practice. Clearly participation is a big part of the sporting experience for the Japanese sports fan, and it is obviously important to avoid the potential embarrassment of singing the wrong thing at the wrong moment, or not knowing when to open your little green umbrella and pump it up and down, but even so. Crowd practice. It's not exactly spontaneous, is it, lads? But everyone does it. There are no shirkers, no slackers off.

Then there's the fact that the crowd here are singing purely for themselves. They aren't going to encourage the players on to greater efforts, are they, because they're all in Saitama, which is over an hour away on the subway train. Still, perhaps it's just as well, as everyone in the place is now singing:

Ono! Ono Ono! Ono Ono! Ono Ono Ono . . . !

Which sounds a little apprehensive, to say the least.

There is a nasty shock, when the teams appear on the screen, for all of the blue-shirted throng here in the National Stadium. Over the last few days, when I've popped into a convenience store or gone to a vending machine for a drink, I've taken to picking up a bottle of iced white coffee, partly because I liked the name – Blendy. And this is exactly the colour of the shirts the Japanese team are wearing. The colour of Blendy.

Why they have had to change is beyond me. Their blue against the Belgian red – it's the classic encounter, red against blue, United against City, Liverpool v Everton, AC and Inter, but no, FIFA just can't leave well alone. Trust Sepp Blatter and his boys; if there's something they can tinker with and spoil, they'll be in there, a-tinkerin' and a-spoilin'.

The camera pans along the line, and there's not a single member of the Japan team with black hair. Bright red, blond, blond, brown, silver blond, honey blond, brown, bald . . . Not a single one of these dye jobs looks convincing. They look like . . . well, have you ever seen one of those videos you can get of old black-and-white Laurel and Hardy movies which have been 'colorised' by computer? At best it looks like a team of blokes in bad wigs. Junichi Inamoto looks as if he's wearing a hat. It is the most startling World Cup hairstyle collection since the entire Romania squad bleached their heads for their third group game in France 98.

The atmosphere as the game starts is tremendous. I try to say this to Mickey, but we can't hear each other let alone make ourselves understood. Japan, roared on in Saitama as well as here in Tokyo, make a frantic start. Toda, in particular, is kicking everything that moves, and the Belgians, canny and more experienced, try to slow things down and take the heat out of the crowd's massive expectations.

This is supposed to be the World Cup at which 'simulation' will be stamped down on by the referees, but the Belgians, especially Gert Verheyen up front, are going to ground at every opportunity, holding their fraudulent injuries and howling their fake agony. Before long the rather poor first half has resolved itself into a struggle between the goodies, the abundantly honest and somewhat naïve Japanese, who are trying to create, attack, and play an open game, and the baddies, the evil, cynical Belgians, faking, diving, tapping ankles and already time wasting.

Japan have been coached for this, their second World Cup finals campaign, by the Frenchman Phillippe Troussier. Troussier is an emotional man, who is not afraid to show his feelings. After one surging Inamoto run is halted by an abrupt

Belgian foul, the screen is full of Troussier expleting in French and waving his arms around.

The crowd at the National Stadium are not sympathetic. Like Mickey beside me, almost to a man they point at the image of Troussier and laugh their heads off. In a country where reserve and control are prized, the demonstrative Frenchman is nothing less than a comedy turn.

Half time arrives, and it's been something of an anti-climax. Mickey grins and exhales slowly. I know that exhale – it means 'at least we're not losing yet'.

The second half is like a different match – thrilling, exciting, surging from end to end. Belgium strike first. Toda, instantly recognisable with his striking red coxcomb, seems to be spoiling for a card to match his hair, and he clatters a Belgian thirty yards out. Japan can't clear the free kick, and a bit of head tennis works it to the edge of the area, where Van Meyer lifts it hopefully forwards towards Marc Wilmots. It's not a particularly promising situation, but Wilmots suddenly upends himself and sends a stunning bicycle kick under Narazaki and into the net.

The silence is eerie. At Saitama there are a few Belgian supporters – we see them on the screen dressed in fancy-dress devil costumes – and their tinny celebration is issuing from the loudspeakers here, but inside the National Stadium sixty thousand people are standing with their mouths open and their hands clasped to their heads in dismay.

There is no noise at all for about two minutes. Then Verheyen, the chief villain, loses the ball to Koji Nakata, and for once the Belgian forward forgets to collapse in a heap on the floor. Shinji Ono, shaven-headed like a youthful Buddhist monk, plays a long, long ball through the centre of the Belgian defence. Van Buyten leaves it to the keeper, but Takayuki Suzuki slips between the two of them and at full stretch toe-pokes it past De Vlieger for the equaliser.

Instantly there is an astonishing bang, and I jump out of my skin. Dozens of the most extremely percussive fireworks I've ever heard are let off all at once all around the running track, there's smoke everywhere, people jumping, dancing, waving huge flags, careering up the aisles. I take my hands from my ringing ears for a moment to clap Mickey on the back as he leaps onto his seat, and I know I'm shouting but I can't hear myself above the sheer noise of it all.

The game has kicked off again. Inamoto, who is having a fantastic match, wins the ball on the halfway line. It breaks to Toda, who plays it back into Inamoto's path. He runs straight past the last defender into the area and smashes an unstoppable shot into the net for 2–1.

Again the fireworks go off with a 'Whump!' that I can feel in the very centre of my chest, and the party goes up another gear. Japan have been looking forward to this for four years, and they've never won a single World Cup finals match. Now they lead Belgium – not exactly a superpower, but still a very decent scalp – with twenty-three minutes left on the clock, and they deserve it too.

Ryuzo Morioka, the captain, has to go off, and Tsuneyasu Miyamoto comes on, wearing a black Batman mask to protect his broken nose. Then, after eight heady minutes of unfettered joy, Peter Van der Heyden beats a rather shambolic offside trap and lobs Narazaki to equalise. Ecstasy turns to panic in a heartbeat, and fingernails find their way into mouths all around the National Stadium.

Troussier's Japan aren't done, though, and they have the better of the closing minutes, until, with time almost up, Inamoto leaps into the area through two Belgian defenders, turns, nicks the ball off one of them, beats another, and slips the ball into the net from about six yards out.

The fireworks go off again, there's smoke all over the place, and the party has begun again. Mickey is pointing, though, and Inamoto is not celebrating, and it seems the goal has been disallowed. Why is not clear. What is clear, though, is that –

what with all the smoke, and the fireworks, and the music, and the jumping – at least half the people here think it's 3–2.

It doesn't help that the big screen is two and a half times as wide as it is high, and so a director has been constantly bobbing a letterbox up and down the television picture to keep the ball in vision for us. This means that the captions in the top corner have rarely been visible, if at all, and the scoreline along the bottom reading 'Japan 2 – 2 Belgium' which would have cleared it up for everyone winks into view for maybe half a second.

At the far end of the National Stadium a huge celebration is now in full swing. The final whistle is greeted by yet more fireworks, a hell of a lot more smoke, and a lot of people are going to get a nasty shock when they check the paper tomorrow morning.

Outside, Mickey is beaming. His team have done him proud. I am very impressed, I tell him. Nakata was great, Ono too, Toda a monster, and Inamoto just fantastic. What a side that Arsenal must be if they can't find room for this lad. The defence could be better in the air, but it seems a little unfair to expect them all to grow six inches. I remember Gary Lineker saying that when he played here they expected him to come back for corners, because he was the big one.

This is just what the World Cup needs to really take off here in Japan. Top that, South Korea . . .

As it happens, they do. In front of a rapturous full house in Pusan, and many thousands more watching on a big outdoor screen in Seoul, Guus Hiddink's well-organised and athletic Korean side run Poland ragged. They make Jerzy Dudek of Liverpool look a very ordinary keeper, and the much-touted Emmanuel Olisadebe doesn't get a kick.

Midway through the first half Eul Yong Lee is given lots of time and space on the left, and he squares it to the equally unmarked Hwang Sun Hong, who sweeps it past Dudek on the turn. Early in the second half Yoo Sang Chul rides a challenge outside the area and wallops a shot at what I've heard pundits call 'a nice height for the keeper'. Dudek doesn't think so, and the ball slaps against his floppy hands and flies into the corner of the net. The crowd go frantic, and their high-pitched squealing is too much for the effects mikes to deal with without distorting.

In the stand, the South Korean president waves a red baseball cap and smiles a strange humourless fixed smile, like someone who has had faulty plastic surgery and is thinking about suing.

Ahn Jung Hwan, the long-haired pin-up boy of Korean football who's been playing – though not that often – for Perugia in Italy, is a second-half sub and looks fantastic. He creates at least four brilliant chances for himself and others, and comes very close to scoring. It finishes 2–0. The Koreans could have had five.

And they all have jet-black hair except, funnily enough, the goalscorer Yoo Sang Chul who has gone for a Japanese brown dye job. I look him up, and sure enough he plays for Kashima Reysol in the JLeague.

We've seen all but four of the teams in action now, and with both the co-hosts having kicked off in thrilling and optimistic style, the World Cup is coming alive.

5 JUNE

Tonight is the Ireland v Germany game in Ibaraki. I give Derek, the MP for Sittingbourne and Sheppey – and don't try saying that unless you've got your teeth in properly – a ring about this spare ticket he reckoned he had. That was the other night, though, in a bar, when he was my best mate.

'Ah, yes,' he says. 'I'm afraid that has to go to a member of the embassy staff as a matter of policy. Sorry.'

Neglecting to mention that this is a completely spurious rule he has just made up himself on the spot.

It seems that each of us has misled the other. I was under the impression that he could wangle me a ticket for the Ireland v Germany game. He seemed to be under the impression that I was going to go on talkSPORT yesterday afternoon and chat in a lovely positive way about the MPs who are over here and their many good works, whereas in fact I haven't done it yet, and I go on later and talk about them all being pissed up in a bar and serenading Lawrie McMenemy in an embarrassing fashion. Mike Parry, bless him, has a bee in his bonnet already about this story and we have a bit of fun at their – rather than the taxpayers' – expense. Ha!

I should say that even though he'd been playing me in a rather obvious manner, I found Derek immensely like-able. I'd vote for him (if only I could afford a house in his constituency).

In the afternoon Russia and Tunisia begin their campaigns in Group H. Many pundits have Russia down as the favourites to top this rather soft group, and expect them to reach the last eight. This match gets a lot of attention in the Japanese press, as these are Japan's next two opponents, and watching this rather mediocre game it's possible to imagine the hosts going through. Egor Titov pounces on an error by keeper Ali Boumnijel in the 59th minute, and Valery Karpin of Celta Vigo converts a penalty five minutes later.

Nick, Cube and I head out to find a bar to watch USA v Portugal, and come across an Irish bar just around the corner from the hotel, near Yotsuya station. It is called Morrigan's, and you can just imagine the Irish owner, a Mr Mulligan, coming back from his holidays, slapping his own forehead, and saying, 'I knew I shouldn't have ordered that new sign over the phone . . .'

Morrigan's is quite a big bar, with plenty of seats and tables. It's almost empty but there's nowhere to sit, because everywhere you look the tables have been reserved. Several of the articles I've read preparing English people for the experience of visiting Japan have described the Japanese people as 'reserved' – they certainly never go out to a pub or a restaurant without ringing ahead. In the end we settle at a table and resign ourselves to moving once the people who've phoned ahead arrive.

Portugal are one of the handful of teams being given a genuine chance of winning the trophy. They haven't been in the finals since 1986, but their current side contains a clutch of top-class players known as the 'Golden Generation'. There's Luis Figo, Nuno Gomez, Rui Costa, Joao Pinto, all of whom are capable of turning a game with a flash of brilliance.

The USA team has improved in leaps and bounds in recent years, but their world ranking of 13 seems mostly to be based on easy qualification wins over the likes of Barbados. Four years ago in France the Americans' love of sporting statistics was tested to the full as someone worked out that they had finished last of the thirty-two teams in the finals. Nick and I saw that side lose to Iran, and the next day overheard one frustrated supporter saying, 'I can't *believe* we lost that game! We had four pole shots!'

Just before the game kicks off a group of young Americans mills around a table between where we are sitting and the television. The ringleader is a young lad who is the absolute spitting image of Ian Ormondroyd, the enormous gangly winger whom you may remember playing for Aston Villa, or in two subsequent spells of gawky ineffectiveness at Oldham. This American's resemblance to the Latics' former stick insect is so striking that for a moment or two I wonder if it might not actually be the man himself. Then he walks from the bar to his table without bumping into any furniture or spilling anything so I realise it can't be.

In the fourth minute of the match the USA have a corner from the left, which Ernie Stewart takes. Brian McBride gets up above three flat-footed Portuguese defenders and powers a header downwards, which the veteran Porto keeper Vitor Baia parries away. Behind him two more defenders fall over on the goal line and John O'Brien is able to lift the loose ball over their tumbling bodies to give the States a surprise early lead.

At our table we break into applause, but the American table seem hardly to have noticed.

'What happened?' Ormondroyd says, blinking round at the telly. 'We score . . . ?'

'I think so,' says one of his mates.

'Woah! Excellent! U-S-A! U-S-A . . . !'

Portugal are casual, complacent, and slow, moving the ball around at walking pace and playing fancy little flicks to one another. Whenever the Americans get it off them the whole game suddenly moves up a gear, and, on the half hour, the ball breaks to Landon Donovan on the USA right. Jorge Costa ambles over, but doesn't get within six yards of closing the danger down properly. Donovan looks up and tries to pick out McBride, but his attempted cross cannons off Costa's shoulder, wrong-footing Baia and squeezing inside the near post.

You can see it dawn on Portugal that they've got a game on their hands, but before they can get themselves going a good American passing move works the ball out to Anthony Sanneh on the right wing, and his perfect cross finds Brian McBride barrelling in between two defenders and thumping a header in for 3–0.

It's a stunning scoreline. Ormondroyd pauses in mid-anecdote to punch the air, and then carries on.

'Woah! Anyway, as I was saying . . .'

Suddenly Portugal are galloping after every loose ball, and they win a corner. Beto's header is half cleared back to him and he sticks it in, and the guys in dark red slope into their dressing room 3–1 down for what must be a fearful bollocking.

I have been telling Nick and Cube about Mickey, who has been desperately trying to get tickets for matches, any matches. Actually, the ticket story is, as usual, not all that impressive:

150,000 World Cup match tickets that were being printed by a firm in Manchester called Byrom were delivered too late to be distributed, and fans had to travel without them and trust that they would be able to collect them at the stadia, which is far from ideal.

A spokesman for the FIFA ticketing operation appeared on Sky News just before I left England, and the gist of what he had to say as he held up a sample ticket was: 'Well, I've got mine, look . . .'

Now the spare tickets which have come back from all the participating associations are on sale via a FIFA hotline, which no one can get through to, and a FIFA website, which is jammed. Mickey spent twenty hours trying to connect and stay connected the other day. He's managed to get his hands on one ticket for Croatia v Ecuador in Yokohama, but the game he really wants to see – as well, obviously, as Japan's sell-out fixtures – is England v Argentina, which is shaping up to be the biggest game in the first phase by a mile.

Nick has a spare ticket for the Sapporo game – as another friend of ours who was due to be here was forbidden from making the trip at the last minute by his girlfriend – and he decides that Mickey sounds a worthy recipient. I give him a call at home in Kawasaki to say that if he's interested he should come up to Morrigan's, and . . . There is a bang as the phone hits the floor, and then cartoon sound effects of feet running away, a door opening and slamming, and the muffled roar of a motorbike starting up. I guess he must be on his way over.

In the second half in Suwon Luis Figo starts to get involved at last, and it is his probing and prompting around the edge of the area that makes the space for Pauleta to cross in the seventy-first minute. The unfortunate Jeff Agoos manages to shin it past Friedel, and this becomes the first-ever World Cup finals match to feature two own goals. Portugal try to engineer a stirring finish, but Bruce Arena's side hold out for a 3–2 win, which is probably an even bigger surprise than Senegal beating

France on the opening day. It's been a fantastic game, one of the best so far. Ormondroyd and his table barely notice that the final whistle has gone – it's enough to make you despair, really.

The Cube spots the breathless arrival of Mickey, which is good going considering he's only got my description – 'a sort of sumo-biker' – to go by, and we decide to leave Morrigan's and head back to the hotel. I'd like to be able to say that the Americans are tearing the place up with wild celebrations and chattering excitedly about what they will need to get through to the second phase, but they really aren't.

Mickey, on the other hand, is beside himself with excitement at the prospect of making the trip to Sapporo. We head into one of the ludicrously expensive restaurants in the hotel – there are thirty-four of them – to watch Ireland play Germany, and he is debating whether to ride his bike up to Hokkaido, or get a train, or try to get a flight, and how to find somewhere to stay, and it's fun to watch his nervous excitement. There was, I think, some apprehension in the footballing superpower countries that Japan wasn't really an appropriate place to hold a World Cup, but there is tremendous enthusiasm here and a far from negligible genuine bedrock of proper football fans, and I think it's a much better idea to bring the tournament – or at least half of it – here than it was to take it to America.

After the thrilling encounter between Portugal and the USA, Ireland v Germany is just as good. Damien Duff plays on the left wing for Blackburn Rovers, but Mick McCarthy is using him as an out and out forward, and he torments the lumbering giants of the German defence. Nonetheless, it is the Germans who take the lead on eighteen minutes. Michael Ballack floats a high ball into the Irish penalty area, and Miroslav Klose runs through ahead of the dozing Harte to nod his fourth scoring header of the tournament past Shay Given, followed by his fourth knee-crunching celebratory somersault.

The Irish then carry the game to Germany, and there is a

great upsurge of noisy encouragement whenever they break forwards. Every shot of the crowd in Ibaraki shows dozens of green shirts, orange wigs, leprechaun beards, and big green foam top hats.

'Look at that lot,' mutters The Miserable Cube, shaking his head scornfully.

For the rest of the half Ireland have the better of it. Oliver Kahn has to race out of his goal to flatten Duff, Holland sends a carbon copy of his Cameroon shot just the wrong side of the post, and Robbie Keane tries a bicycle kick when all alone in the six-yard box.

In the second half the Germans have a couple of decent chances to put a bit of daylight between them and the Irish, but happily they fall to the hopelessly out of form Jancker. Ireland are causing consternation in the German defence with long high balls from Steve Finnan at right back. One of these is nodded down by Kevin Kilbane, sending Duff racing through one on one with Kahn. It looks a certain equaliser, but somehow the big keeper blocks it with his arse.

A quarter of an hour from the end McCarthy decides to really give it a go. He takes off the full backs Kelly and Harte, and brings on Steven Reid, the youngest player in the squad, and Niall Quinn, the oldest. Almost immediately the changes begin to pay off. One clever Quinn touch sends Keane through, but Kahn smothers, and another strong aerial challenge gives big Niall a sight of goal, but he fluffs his kick. The Germans are clearly rattled, as two of them go down in the box and stay down to waste time getting treatment.

It is looking as though Germany are going to hold on for a win they hardly deserve, Jeremies comes on to shore things up, and Paul is rubbing his hands together with glee. He is planning to stay up to see all the Irish fans who are staying in the hotel dribbling miserably back into the bar at about one in the morning with their floppy top hats.

Then, with time almost up, Finnan pumps another long

diagonal ball up the middle. Quinn outjumps Metzelder and flicks it on into the area, where Robbie Keane gathers the ball with his belly and races past Ramelow's despairing attempt to bring him down. Kahn rushes out to meet the threat, but without breaking stride Keane lashes the ball in off the keeper's hand and the inside of the post.

Without a word, The Cube gets up and goes to his room, and we don't see him again.

On the screen, Keane is cartwheeling into a forward roll, coming up firing two imaginary guns. It's not as gymnastic as Klose's somersault, but it's a lot more satisfying to watch. Best of all, though, is McCarthy's reaction. In slow motion, we see his jaw drop open in amazement as Quinn's flick finds Keane, and then his pop-eyed, mouth-wide glee at the goal is fantastic. Mickey thinks it is one of the funniest things he has ever seen. For myself I enjoy Rudi Voller's reaction almost as much. Even the most amateurish bit of bilingual lipreading can spot him spitting out the single word 'Scheisse!'

9
Sapporo

China lost, Japan drew.
What about us?
We won,
We won!
– blank verse poem by the ruling Millennium Democratic
Party of South Korea, no less

6 JUNE

Imagine Tony Blair writing a poem about England beating Germany in Munich – he'd never be able to show his face at St James's Park again.

The only thing which prevents The Cube from spending another twenty-three hours in his room after the thwarting of his plans to taunt the Irish last night is the need to get to Haneda airport to catch our flights to Sapporo.

At the check-in desks the soccerati are gathering. Motson, Rosenthal, Brooking, Barnes, Zico and Atkinson are variously spotted carting their fancy hand luggage about the place. At the best of times more passengers travel the Tokyo to Sapporo route than any other in world aviation, but today, with the biggest game of the World Cup scheduled for the northern city tomorrow, the bulging manifests are swelled by football fans, press, former players and dignitaries, and there is quite a queue for cappuccino in the coffee bar.

Ron Atkinson is very sprightly, relieved to be heading somewhere, anywhere, after his spell at what he calls the

'Hanoi Hilton' – I think he means the Saitama Hilton – which he describes as 'like spending three days in Bromsgrove'. He makes his own contribution to international relations by pinching a football from an advertising display and starting up an impromptu kick-about on the concourse with a bunch of Argentinian lads.

While I am waiting, I hear a rumour that ticket prices for the Argentina game have soared from £850 to £1,300 since Saitama, as fans want to see England before their anticipated early return home. There were heated scenes in Tokyo at the International Forum where fans tried to buy the remaining tickets, and were told to go upstairs to an internet café and buy tickets through the FIFA tickets website, and then come back to the JAWOC office to pick them up. 'If they have tickets why can't they just sell them over the counter,' said one frustrated fan, after spending ten hours failing to access the ticket site.

I spot a couple of 'No more Buddha' stories in today's *Asahi Shimbun* – first a picture of two middle-aged ladies going to Japan v Belgium wearing blue Japan shirts and red-and-yellow Belgium scarves. They travelled up from Kumamoto, where Belgium are based, to support both sides.

And apparently tapes of four first-round games have so far been smuggled into Pyongyang and broadcast on North Korean television. Incredibly, FIFA bigwigs are trying to put a stop to these broadcasts on the grounds that they have not been properly paid for. How typical that these people should allow financial concerns to get in the way of a chance, however small, that football could reach across the Demilitarised Zone, the most inhumane barrier in Asia. Surely an exception could be made, in the hope of drawing the North Koreans back into the community of world football . . . ? Oh well . . .

I join the line shuffling towards the plane. Two short and smiley Japanese airline stewardesses greet everyone, and they are handing out photocopied sheets of paper. Not to everyone, though. They are picking out those of us who look English.

I draw level with them, and they both bow and beam at me.

'Hoorigan?' they ask.

'Um . . .' I say.

'Fank you have a nice fly!' they chirp, and hand me my sheet of paper.

Then to the chap behind me: 'Hoorigan?'

'Well, not . . .' he starts, but he gets a sheet anyway.

'Fank you have a nice fly!'

'Hoorigan?' the ladies chirrup at Jim Rosenthal and John Barnes.

'No, no, I don't think you . . .' They both get a sheet.

'Fank you have a nice fly!'

The sheet of paper contains a plea, in many languages, from the airline. They tell us that, as well as ourselves, there will be many non-hoorigan passengers on this flight, and they would be obliged if we would not disturb these valued customers by 'shouting, singing loudly, especially by group'.

This message is reinforced by a little cartoon which is shown on board the plane before take-off. It shows a variety of examples of unacceptable behaviour. A cartoon parrot uses a mobile phone, a big fat cartoon dog smokes a cigar in the toilet, an abusive and aggressive gorilla stands on his chair and thumps his own chest, and a seriously intoxicated tiger wobbles up and down the aisle and bores the other animals with lengthy and incomprehensible anecdotes about plane crashes. After this, the word 'NO!' flashes over and over again, in bright red, like some subliminal sixties brainwashing technique they've picked up from *The Ipcress File*.

Over the last couple of days the Japanese news programmes have featured more and more items about the hoorigan problem. Heavily padded police chiefs demonstrate the various techniques that will be employed to subdue the anticipated hoorigan threat. There's the familiar-looking riot equipment, and also the much-vaunted Spiderman gun – which no one seems prepared to fire at the newsmen, just to show what it does – but they seem to be setting a lot of store by simply outnumbering the England support.

There's a feeling that the Sweden game in Saitama was just a blip of calm, and that Argentina tomorrow is where the hoorigans will show themselves. I hope that many of them are still drifting between here and Thailand on their inflatable boats.

Watching the Tokyo suburbs sliding away, mile after mile, out of the window of the plane, I begin to realise just how big the place is. I have spent ten days there and was beginning to feel I'd got the measure of the centre of it at least, but the residential sprawl of suburbia is enormous. Gradually it gives way to green carpeted hills, covered in forest, with flat valleys in between, and plains spreading to the coast. Every square inch of the flatlands is taken up, it seems, with housing or rice fields, and the hills are very distinctive, like the ones James Bond flies over in *Little Nellie* in *You Only Live Twice* . . .

Of course! The Osato Corporation. That's why the hotel in Tokyo looked so familiar. It was the headquarters of the Osato Corporation in *You Only Live Twice*. Bond is taken there after the killing of Dikko Henderson, and then returns the next day pretending to be a businessman interested in buying chemicals. Osato has an X-ray machine in his desk and sees Bond's gun, and when Bond leaves Osato says to his female assistant: 'Kirr him!'

Bond, blissfully unaware that his cover is blown, then strolls out of the front of our hotel, where some assassins in a black car creep up behind and are about to shoot him when the lovely Aki speeds up in an open-top white sports car and whisks him away. There is a chase around the car park, and then the bad guys are removed from Bond's tail by a big helicopter with an electromagnet dangling underneath it, which picks up the black car and drops it unceremoniously in Yokohama harbour.

Well. I wish I'd remembered that while I was still staying there.

As we fly, quite low, across the channel between Honshu and Hokkaido the view is nice and clear, and with the land mostly forested and dark green and the sea bright blue it looks exactly as it does on the map. Not far away, a little, perfectly conical volcano pops up above the scenery.

John and Richard, the two guys sitting beside me, are Birmingham City supporters. They're members of *englandfans* – the FA's trendy lower-case rebranding of the England Supporters Travel Club – but decided months ago that Japan was too far away and too costly to make the trip, and they planned to save up for the European Championships in Portugal in 2004. Once the show started, however, and with their faith in football rekindled by City's play-off win, they changed their minds, and simply had to be here. They've dropped everything and flown out. They've got no tickets, hardly any money, and John has left his passport somewhere in Tokyo, and they're visibly trembling with the excitement of it all (or possibly the air conditioning is a little fierce).

John asks me what I think he should do about his passport, and, as it happens, I have the phone number of the British Embassy on me. I tell him: 'Just say that you know the Ferrero Rocher man and I'm sure they'll sort you out.'

Sapporo is a pleasant change after the packed streets and skyscrapers of Tokyo. It feels a very spacious, airy and light little city, and ancient trams rattle scenically along the middle of its wide boulevards. In the winter it is a centre for all kinds of winter sports, and it was the host for the 1972 Winter Olympic Games. Sven was a decent ski-jumper in his youth – better than Eddie the Eagle, at any rate, but then so is a sack of spuds in a bobble hat – so hopefully he'll feel at home here.

For the Japanese, the northern island of Hokkaido is seen as an idyllic, unspoiled place. Three-quarters of the island is covered by forest, and its huge national parks, snow-capped mountains, active volcanoes and rocky coastline attract millions of back-to-nature visitors every year.

Hokkaido was only colonised by Japan from the 1860s onwards, when the Japanese began booting the local aboriginal people – the Ainu – off their lands, destroying the forests where they hunted, introducing them to some interesting new diseases and outlawing their culture. Sapporo, the main city, was designed to a grid system by a team of European and American architects in 1870, and – unlike many other Japanese cities which have been pulled down, burned down, bombed and rebuilt haphazardly over many centuries – it is a piece of cake to find your way around here.

A long thin park called Odori-koen sits east-west across the middle, and streets number north and south from there. At the east end of Odori-koen is a rather ugly red Blackpool Tower-shaped television transmitter, and streets number east and west from this point. The address of my hotel, for example, is S4 W5, i.e. four blocks south of the park, and five blocks west of the TV tower.

The advantage of this grid system is that you can find your way around really easily. The disadvantage, I found doing it on foot, is that it means that at every corner you come to you have to wait an age for the pedestrian crossings to change from red man to green man, and if you are walking to somewhere that is on a diagonal from where you start you can quickly lose the will to live.

I find a hotel in the Susukino district of the city, which is supposedly where all the action is come nightfall. Outside my window I can see a sex club called Two Melons and a pachinko parlour called Big Carrot City. A sign out-side reads:

INFORMATION
Entering in the foreigner will hold back while
holding the World Cup for the following reasons.

Speaking as a foreigner, if someone tried to enter in me while holding the World Cup I would be able to think of one or two reasons why they should hold back . . .

The afternoon match in Daegu between Denmark and Senegal is one of the first where the conditions play a big part in the outcome. The sun is dazzling, carving sharp shadows across the bright green pitch, and it is very hot and very humid. Denmark start strongly, and take the lead through Jon Dahl Tomasson from the penalty spot after a quarter of an hour. Denmark dominate the first half, but in the second half the game changes. Bruno Metsu brings on 'the paparazzi', Henri and Souleymane Camara, and suddenly Senegal are much more of an attacking force. The Danes tire in the heat, but the Africans thrive, and seven minutes after the break they score the goal of the tournament so far. Henri Camara robs Martin Jorgensen to the left of the Senegal area and plays it down the line to Diouf. He backheels it first time infield to Diao, who whips it crossfield to Khalilou Fadiga. Diao then gallops forward with tremendous pace as the Danish defence seem to be running in treacle. Fadiga plays a perfectly weighted ball into the middle which Diao runs onto, bursts between two shattered Danes, and slots it in with the outside of his foot.

For the rest of the half Senegal rip the tired Danes to shreds, but can't get a winner. Salif Diao is sent off for an ugly over-the-ball challenge on a Danish shin, and he's had an interesting match. And one thing's for sure: you wouldn't want to be a European side playing this Senegal team in the middle of the afternoon.

Cameroon beat a rejuvenated Saudi Arabia by a single goal, scored by Samuel Eto'o running onto a long through ball from Geremi. The African champions are complacent, strolling around, clearly expecting to thrash the group's whipping boys, and the narrow victory is a nasty shock for them, as it means they now have to beat Germany to be sure of qualifying. It's a great result for Ireland, though, as a two-goal win over the Saudis will see them through whatever happens in the other game.

Nick goes to his room to have a kip, and Cube and I head out to have a look around. We find our way to Odori-koen, the park in the centre of the city, and find it is chock-a-block with football fans just hanging out. England flags are draped around on bushes, on railings, fans sit on the grass and on the edge of the ornamental fountains, and Argentinian supporters stroll amongst them without any concern.

The only thing which is disturbing the peace, particularly for the face-painted, funny-wigged, fancy-dress brigade which always seems to attach itself to these occasions in the hope of getting on the telly, is a constant stream of giggling Japanese locals requesting them to pose for photographs.

The Cube and I stroll amongst the crowds, but there is no sense of the coiled spring, or the blue touch paper about to be lit, that I have felt on other days at other tournaments. At the foot of the big red television tower there is a café with dozens of white plastic seats set out in the evening sun, and this area looks a prime candidate for a later appearance on news bulletins. The Sapporo police clearly think so, as they are here in visible force.

In fact the whole town is on 'hoorigan watch'. There are rumours that all the bars and restaurants will be closed tomorrow, and that the town will be virtually boarded up. The Sapporo folk out walking in the park this evening, though, seem remarkably unconcerned, and view the visiting 'hoorigans' as a cute, amusing, even vaguely titillating tourist attraction. They are certainly making it as easy as they can – the tourist map shows a place in the shopping precinct marked BIG OFF.

We take the subway a couple of stops down to Susukino, the entertainment district, which is where my hotel is. A rangy youth sits alone in a surly cloud at the other end of the carriage. He is wearing a tweedy sort of jacket, and a matching cap like a sort of deerstalker. He stands out a mile. Cube gives me a nudge and nods in his direction.

'Burberry,' he says.

'You what?'

'Burberry, that's what that is. It's what they wear nowadays. Remember once it used to be all Pringle sweaters? Now it's Burberry.'

So this actually is a hoorigan? He looks like Sherlock Holmes.

'Watson! Bring your service revolver and have Mrs Hudson call for a hansom cab, there's a good fellow. Moriarty and his mob are hanging about down at the shopping precinct and I want to get over there before it all goes off . . .'

Cube and I find a bar, order some Sapporo Beer, and watch France and Uruguay play out a thrilling goalless draw in Busan. In the build up there were optimistic noises from the French camp that Zinedine Zidane might be fit for this one but in the event he isn't even ready to sit on the bench in his kit.

The first half is a niggly affair, with both sides looking apprehensive, knowing that a defeat would see them eliminated from the competition. Trezeguet has the ball in the net, but is ruled offside, and at the other end Alvaro Recoba brings an excellent save out of Fabien Barthez when his low shot from the edge of the area is deflected, and the French keeper sticks out a desperate foot to clear.

The key moment of the match comes from a Uruguayan free kick in a dangerous position on the left wing. Recoba feints to cross but then pulls it back towards the middle. Thierry Henry intercepts it and looks to break quickly, but the ball runs away from him, and in trying to retrieve it he does a horrible two-footed forward's challenge on Marcelo Romero which draws one of the fastest red cards I've ever seen from the Mexican ref.

The second half is real edge-of-the-seat stuff. Trezeguet has a good shot saved, Micoud comes close with a free kick, and Candela has a good shot tipped over. In between these chances, the baby-faced Ronaldo-toothed Alvaro Recoba could have won the game several times over, on one occasion missing an empty net vacated by Barthez, who galloped past him and seemed to be on his way to the dugout to fetch something.

Both teams are desperate for the goal that will give them a fighting chance of progressing, and terrified of conceding one that will have them on the plane home, and in the last minute Wiltord squanders a great chance at one end, Magallanes an even better one at the other. Vieira has been immense, and Recoba a star, but both teams now need to win their last game to go through. France will need to beat the impressive Denmark by two to have any chance.

Cube and I drift away, and shortly afterwards find ourselves in the Sapporo Soccer Bar, a cramped little joint with almost as many television sets as customers. The walls are decorated with pennants and shirts from Consadole Sapporo, the local JLeague outfit, along with the ubiquitous posters of Ono and Nakata. Half the people in there are Brits, stripped to the waist and standing on the tables singing *Rule Britannia*. The other half are Japanese newsmen taking pictures of them.

The atmosphere of good cheer still pervades the place, though, even into the small pissed hours, and the only scrap of any kind that I see is between two rival Japanese television crews, frustrated and blaming each other because there are no hoorigans to film.

7 JUNE

Mickey arrives in the morning, having left his place in Kawasaki at about five o'clock to catch an early shuttle flight. He seems very relieved not to have had to ride his motorbike all the way up here – I haven't enquired about his illness of last week, his 'big pain ass hall', as I don't like to pry, but if he didn't have a sore backside to begin with then he would have had after twelve hours in the saddle.

I haven't really slept much, partly thanks to Sapporo Beer and partly due to the sheer big match buzz about tonight. I have been lying awake, watching the neon flashes from Two Melons over the road on my ceiling, going through the permutations of the Group of Death in my head. Best would be a draw in the Sweden v Nigeria encounter this afternoon; then a draw for England tonight – which in my heart of hearts is the best I am expecting – would leave us with a chance of qualifying if we beat Nigeria in Osaka. Worst scenario, I reckon, is a win for Sweden, because then a draw tonight would mean that they and Argentina would both qualify if their match next week is also drawn.

With a day to kill, Mickey and I get on a bus to the city's main attraction, the Sapporo Beer Museum. It was either that or the Miyabe Hall, 'with its intriguing displays of letters and journals belonging to Professor Miyabe Kingo, the first director of Hokkaido University, who established the botanical gardens in 1886 . . .' Tough call.

I ask Mickey about BIG OFF. He explains, 'In my country, economy very bad. People want buy very cheap things.'

So BIG OFF is a discount store. There have been stories in the Japanese press over the last few days of politicians indignantly complaining about some strange new statistic which gives Japan the same credit rating as a third world economy, which seems a bit off the mark for the land of the rising Nissan, but there's no doubting the slowdown in consumerism here. Mickey points out a vast second-hand bookshop – called, gloriously, BOOK OFF – and another place called UniQlo, which sells very cheap clothes from China. These shops are part of big nationwide chains that have sprung up, and yet the idea of buying second-hand books or cheap Chinese clothes would have been unthinkable here even five years ago.

Everywhere you go in Japan the restaurants have plates of food in the window, so that you can forestall any menu queries by the simple expedient of dragging the waitress out of the front door and pointing at something a bit like what you fancy eating. For the first few days I was in Tokyo I would peer at these dishes closely, unable to tell for certain whether these were fake or genuine food covered in some sort of preservative glaze.

Walking along with Mickey, I ask him and he is quite definite on the subject.

'Prastic, all prastic,' he says.

'They're very good, aren't they?' I say admiringly.

'Oh yes. My uncle invent this. My uncle, big prastic food factory. He very rich.'

'Really?'

'*Very* rich.'

I'm not surprised. Prastic food is everywhere, and some of it looks good enough to eat (which would be the point of it).

At the Beer Museum we can either have lunch or see how beer is made.

'We can go biking,' Mickey says.

'Don't you want to have lunch?' I ask.

'You know biking? With helmet?'

'I suppose so . . .' I say, miming hands on handlebars, but

evidently I've got hold of stick A end B, as Mickey juts his fingers up like cow horns on either side of his head.

'Biking helmet? Like bikings.'

Vikings. To 'go Viking' is a phrase meaning 'all you can eat', apparently, and the restaurant here offers as much barbecued lamb or beef as you can sling down your neck in a hundred minutes for a set price.

We make our way into the large and busy dining hall, and as soon as we appear all the waiters, wherever they are, whatever they're doing, turn and bellow a short Japanese phrase at the top of their voices. I am ready to turn and run out, but Mickey reassures me that they are shouting 'Welcome!' rather than 'You! Where do you think you're going?!'

Our table is dominated by a large, black, shallow, dome-shaped metal griddle, from which a gas pipe snakes down a table leg and into a hole in the wooden floor. Our waiter flicks it on, and it begins to hiss slightly.

'This *jingisukan*,' Mickey says.

I try the word out myself. '*Jingisukan* . . .'

'Like . . . you know Genghiz-o Khan?'

The great Irish-Mongol leader, of course. Now he mentions it, if you look at the griddle from above it does have something of the look of an ancient central Asian war helmet, with various ornamental metal flaps and horns jutting out from underneath.

A piled trough of sliced red lamb and vegetables arrives, and Mickey begins slapping slices onto the helmet, where it sizzles and spits impressively. While we wait for the meat to brown, which doesn't take more than half a minute, we are provided with big plastic bibs, as though they know we are going to make absolute pigs of ourselves. And we do.

There is something incredibly satisfying about cooking your food right in front of yourself at just exactly the speed you can eat it. Whenever I've been involved in a barbecue of any kind before – usually in a standing-nearby-saying- 'you want to put more lighter fluid on, mate, that'd get it going' capacity – it has seemed to take forever to do a couple of sausages and a burger, and then you turn your back for half a second and the food instantly becomes indistinguishable from the charcoal. Here, though, you slap a bit of meat on, it goes brown, you take it off, dip it in the special sauce, eat it, and by the time you've finished chewing it's time to grab the next bit. It's great fun, and I've barbecued quite a lot of lettuce as well, just for the hell of it, by the time we sit back for a breather.

The seductive thing about the 'all you can eat' offer is that you feel absolutely duty-bound to stuff yourself till your eyeballs bulge, and by the time we've burrowed and barbied through our second trough Mickey and I have each put on about a stone and are not thinking about eating again until after the weekend.

Then, as if I didn't feel enough like Homer Simpson already, I drag Mickey round the Beer Museum. With many bars and restaurants in the centre of Sapporo closed for the day, this is just about the only place in town to get a beer this afternoon. I'm by no means the only one who's clocked this, and with Sapporo's finest on ever-more-vigilant hoorigan watch, I can safely say that this is the most heavily policed museum tour I've ever been on.

It begins with a dark passageway which has large portholes set into the wall, and through them all I can see is bubbling amber liquid. We have a Japanese guide, and I have been given a little Walkman tape machine which is giving me an English translation.

'This is Tunnel of Foam,' my tape guide is saying. 'This is where you would feel if you were at bottom of a sea of beer . . .'

Also on the tour are a group of young England supporters. They are so eager to get to the end of the tour that they missed being given the little free Walkman at the beginning, and so they are traipsing around not knowing what the hell is being said. Our guide shows us a machine for putting beer in cans, and they press their noses up against the window like penniless kids outside a sweet shop.

'Look, cans . . .' one of them murmurs.

They are not really interested in 'Barley and Hops Corner', or the huge German Wort Kettle, or the display of Sapporo Beer labels, or the exhibition of seventeenth and eighteenth century beer tankards collected by former president of Sapporo Beer, Mr Kurando Uchida. They desperately want our guide to hurry up.

'What's it say, mate?' one of them says, pointing at the Walkman. 'Does it say anything about where we get to drink any?'

'Not yet,' I have to say. 'We need to know more about mashing.'

There is one kind of unusual display. It's a three-dimensional holographic cartoon, which purports to tell you 'the secret of delicious beer'. Unfortunately it tells me in Japanese, but the little holograms are extremely clever. The story involves fairies and demons, and the holographic acting is a touch on the hammy side, but it is amazing to be able to see right round the little projected figures.

The England lads aren't interested, though. Now they have their noses pressed up against a cabinet with bottles of beer in it.

The tour ends, eventually, at a bar where a tasting is laid on, and a barman is reverently pouring some halves of Sapporo. Our guide is thanking us most graciously for attending the tour, and learning how 'beer is created from the blessings of nature and human ingenuity', but the lads have galloped off to the bar and are already asking for seconds. There are dozens of England fans in here, all of whom have trudged through the forty-minute lecture on hops and barley to finally make it through to the promised land. Which just goes to show – there's no point in closing all the bars and restaurants in town if there's a beer museum where you can get free beer.

I think to myself: 'While I'm here, in the brewery, I should perhaps try to get together some kind of drink-related social event . . .' but the whole thing proves beyond my organisational capacity.

Mid-afternoon I take Mickey to Nick and The Cube's hotel and leave him with them while I nip back across town to where I'm staying to do my piece for talkSPORT.

I'm walking along the street minding my own business when a wiry youth crosses the road diagonally and falls into step with me. He is wearing only shorts and training shoes, has his shirt bunched up tightly in one hand, and he is very very cheesed off indeed.

'Fookin' hell!' he cries, as an opening conversational gambit. 'In't life shit, eh?!'

'Hey, come on, cheer up,' I say to him. 'We haven't lost yet . . .'

The lad barrels along as though he hasn't even heard me.

'I won a fookin' competition to come here, you know. Supposed to be trip of a fookin' lifetime. Naah they tell me, those fookers from— *(here he spits out the name of one of our top razor manufacturers. Suffice it to say they claim to provide the optimum item in the field that it is possible for a male person to obtain)* that me ticket for t'match is still back in Manchestoh!'

'Really?' I say to him. 'That's bad luck. But surely there's something they can . . .'

'I'm goin' straight to t'fookin' airport an' gettin' the fust fookin' plane home. Those FOOKERS!'

And off he goes, the most furious man in the world. Thinking about it, it defies belief that a firm as big as the one he was talking about would allow such a PR disaster to be loosed upon the world at large. I bet he just didn't let them finish explaining before he put his fist through the door and set off for the airport.

As it happens I don't get a call from talkSPORT at the appointed hour – I guess it must be frantic at home building up to the Argentina game – and so I make my way back across town to meet up with the others. At least it's given me the opportunity to walk off some of that barbecued lamb.

I find them in a restaurant on the top floor of their hotel with a panoramic view of Sapporo and the surrounding hills. Nick is ready to eat, but Mickey and I politely decline, as I've a feeling we'll still be doing tomorrow.

Theo, a friend of Nick's, has arrived and joins us. He's a tall, enthusiastic chap who works in advertising, and he's somehow managed to swing it to come over here even though his wife has only just had a baby a couple of days ago.

'Yeah, it's lucky really,' he says. 'If she'd hung on for another twenty-four hours I'd never have been able to get away.'

The chef is cooking a meal for Nick and Theo right in front of us, deftly flipping meat and vegetables around on a smooth flat metal surface, and it is quite a show. He is constantly on the move, stirring, prodding, wiping, squirting, all his actions assured and confident, and the whole cooking area somehow remains spotlessly clean throughout, with not a drop or a drip astray. Mickey is transfixed.

'I can't believe you're thinking of eating,' I say to him.

'I just watch. He is an artist.'

Theo has a palm pilot, a little hand-held computer, and he shows me a program on it that updates all the group tables as soon as you type in the latest results. We try out all the various permutations of the Group of Death, and then suddenly realise that Sweden v Nigeria must be almost over. It has been on Sky PerfecTV, of course, and all the bars in which we could have seen it have been closed all afternoon.

Just then I get a call from talkSPORT, and Giles the researcher tells us that I'm on in five minutes and that Sweden have won 2–1. Damn.

Theo taps that into his palm pilot with his special little

pencil, and I head down to the car park opposite to get better reception on the phone. On the way I'm working out the doomsday scenario – can we still qualify if we lose tonight? (We can, if Argentina go on to beat Sweden as well . . .) One thing is certain. Nigeria are out of the running, which might make them all free and easy next week and that much more difficult to beat.

I chat to Mike and Alan from the car park, and their show is positively humming with excitement. What must it be like back in England? Everyone just getting up, looking forward to a lunchtime kick-off. Nobody will get anything done today.

I go on about the 'hoorigan' fascination here, and the beer museum – Mike says: 'Remind me never to go on a day out with you' – and then I have to do a prediction, because everyone else is doing one. I take a deep breath and go for 1–1, with my fingers crossed.

Mickey wants to get to the ground early to take some photos, and so we head for the subway, leaving Nick and Theo to continue to marvel at their chef's handiwork.

The station and the train are already busy, with plenty of England shirts in evidence, and, as in Saitama, many of them being worn by enthusiastic Japanese. The genuine English supporters are being watched hungrily and with wide-eyed amusement by the locals, in the way that people generally watch celebrities.

I overhear a snatch of conversation from some England lads hanging from the handstraps a few feet away.

'We just started havin' a kick-about,' says one. 'In that park, the long thin park wi' all the fountains in. There's about eight of us, so we're four a side, like, but then people start joinin' in from everywhere, till we're ten, eleven a side, and it's turned into us against the Argies. And it's great, and we get a bit of a crowd, and there's telly cameras there, and it's all very friendly . . .'

Aha, I think to myself, no more Buddha . . .

'Anyway, in the end it's a draw, so we decide we'll have a penalty shoot-out. One of the Argies goes first, and his kick gets saved, but he wants to take it again, so there's a bit of pushin' an' shovin', and this Argie's giving someone a right spankin', an' I'm saying "Calm down", like, because the telly's there, and we don't want no trouble. Suddenly out of nowhere this Burberry bloke comes running over and gets stuck in, he's going fuckin' mental, kicking and punching, and we're all going "Who the fuck are you?" . . .'

Sherlock.

Out of the tube station and up onto the street. The atmosphere is very tense, much more so than in Saitama. The kerb is lined by police, urging everyone to keep moving by waving their red light-up wands.

'All right, Darth Vader . . .' someone mutters.

Some England fans have dressed up as though this were some kind of medical students rag parade. There are blokes dressed as nurses, a couple of Vikings who presumably did some sort of costume-swap deal in Saitama (unless they are 'all you can eat' enthusiasts, of course), and many many lads in *yukatas* borrowed from their hotel rooms.

The Japanese football fans in their BECKHAM shirts are all grinning as the police urge them along, as though the little frisson of being on the edge of the law is all part of the experience for them.

The buildings to our right come to an end and we turn into an open space where we get our first look at the Sapporo Dome. It is startling, and a number of people actually stop in their tracks to take it in before drifting down into the mob milling around outside the first security checkpoint. It looks as if a huge silver alien spaceship has landed on the outskirts of the city, and on the web of walkways and staircases leading up to it you can just make out a steady stream of puny humans, brainwashed like zombies, trudging up into its belly to be whisked off who knows where.

Two brash youths – the sort who will jump onto a stranger's shoulders like Neil Ruddock defending a corner – get their first sight of the Dome, and shout out so everyone around us can hear.

'We made it! We're here! We're on the fucking banned list, but we came through Thailand and we got in anyway! Yayyy . . . !'

And they do a little jig of celebration. I'm just thinking that this is a bit of a blow for the international intelligence operation, and wondering whether they came on inflatable boats, when these two are suddenly and efficiently surrounded by at least a dozen armed policemen and hauled off kicking and wailing. I bet they're not on the banned list, either, I bet it was just bravado. Silly buggers.

Mickey, like the many Japanese fans already heading in, wants to get inside as early as possible and he scuttles off. As important as the match is, I know there will be England lads still back in the centre of Sapporo, determined, as a point of pride, not to arrive at the ground until five minutes before kick-off at the absolute earliest. Nick and The Cube, for a start. I hang around for a while, watching the bloke dressed as David Seaman and the bloke dressed as Elvis doing interviews for the television cameras.

Then I make my way up to the mother ship. The Sapporo Dome is a year old, and the very latest in high-tech sporting venues. It has a grass pitch which slides in and out, the subject of innumerable tedious articles over the last six months. With the grass pitch in, this is the home of JLeague outfit Consadole Sapporo – the name, incredibly, comes from the syllables of the word *dosanko* (meaning 'native of Hokkaido') pronounced backwards with the Spanish word '*olé*' tagged on the end – and with the pitch out, an astroturf surface exposed and the seats reconfigured, it is a baseball stadium.

As I make my way in I pass a handful of groin-clutching, beered-up youths queueing for a single Portaloo. The entrance is less than fifty feet away, and there's nothing so certain as that there will be a hundred pristine and gleaming bogs inside that they could have their pick of, so why are they tormenting themselves like this? Perhaps they are homesick for somewhere like The Abbey Stadium or Millmoor.

But even in the UK stadia have reached a certain standard of hygiene these days. Years ago I went to an Edinburgh derby at Easter Road with my Hearts fan friend Rob, and as we got into the ground I asked him where the bogs were.

'Look around you,' Rob said. 'The whole place is a toilet.' And sure enough, dozens of blokes as far as the eye could see were just blithely pissing where they stood.

Inside I find my seat, in front and to the left of the vast video screen, which is showing highlights of previous England v Argentina encounters. Not something I want to dwell on, particularly. The place is a fantastic setting for a game of football, the sight lines are terrific, there's just something a little odd about the acoustics. With the roof bouncing all the noise back, you can hear individual shouts from the far side of the ground very clearly, and it sounds as if we are waiting for the start of school assembly rather than a World Cup classic, but still, well done everybody, I say.

Dom hasn't arrived yet, but to my right some of the soccerati are already settling in. Jeff Stelling, the estimable host of the excellent *Soccer Saturday* programme, and Chris Kamara, who does those odd match reports with his back to the action for the same show, are standing together in front of the big video screen. Kamara is good-naturedly fielding requests for photographs – 'Course you can, yeah!' – from people who have recognised him easily, being so used to seeing his face obscuring their view of football going on in the background.

A curly-headed chap stops in the aisle next to me, studying his ticket with a puzzled expression, trying to make sense of the seat numbering. I watch him for a while, and then say:

'Hello, Dom.'

He jumps – 'Ah, there you are!' – and scrambles past me into his place, already imparting the latest team gossip. 'Butt's in for Vassell, Joey Cole's got a groin strain, not even on the bench. They've brought in Kily Gonzalez for Lopez.'

'Is that good?'

'Dunno . . . Whew, this is something, isn't it?'

The two seats directly in front of us are occupied by a young Japanese couple. They are very much into one another, holding hands, and gazing into each other's eyes, which you don't see much at football (perhaps if we did, the world would be a better place). This lovey-doveyness is the more remarkable because he is wearing a white England top, while she sports its pale-blue-and-white Argentinian counterpart. Hey, no more Buddha . . .

The Argentinian national anthem is obliterated by whistling and catcalls, and from what I can hear of it music lovers may be responsible. Again we get two verses of our national anthem, wrongfooting the crowd, who go for the big 'Come On!' cheer far too early, and have to go back to mumbling about sending her victorious all over again.

Pierluigi Collina, old Nosferatu himself, surely the world's best referee, blows his whistle and we're off. England in red, Argentina in blue-and-white stripes.

Generally I watch football matches with a sort of quiet reserve, however much I am churning inside. Suddenly I surprise myself by shouting out, 'Come on! It's our turn! It's our fucking turn!' so loudly that my throat hurts for the rest of the half.

Gabriel Batistuta is well pumped up for this game, and right from our kick-off he hunts the ball down from England player to England player, finally clattering into Sol Campbell and leaving him in a heap.

In the early minutes it's clear that England have a much better shape than against Sweden. The midfield four is much more compact, and Heskey up front wins a couple of good headers and flicks them on to Michael Owen. The reds are doubling up on the opposition, harrying and hustling them. Hargreaves loses the ball to Pocchettino on the far side, and immediately Beckham and then Owen pounce to help him win it back, which is good to see. Although in the end they get in each other's way, and Hargreaves is injured in a collision with the Liverpool striker.

Argentina are strolling it in midfield, with Juan Sebastian Veron and Diego Simeone looking to take control. Juan Sorin backheels into the path of Kily Gonzales for the first shot on goal – Nicky Butt does just enough to put him off and it flashes wide.

Batistuta is charging round like a mad thing. First he clatters Ashley Cole, and the Argentinian's 'he dived, ref' mime doesn't save him from a booking. Then, barely two minutes later, the long-haired Roma star jumps at David Beckham elbow first and should have been sent off.

Beckham takes the free kick himself, forty yards out. It's too far to shoot, really, but he does anyway, having been deprived of any sight of goal in Saitama, and hits it into a crowd of defenders.

Owen Hargreaves plays a nice ball through, and for the first time Michael Owen gets to run at the Argentine defence. They crap themselves, remembering what he did to them in France 98, and scramble it out for a corner. Hargreaves, though, is limping badly, and Sven has to bring him off and send on Trevor Sinclair.

'What a story that is,' Dom murmurs, preparing in his head to tell that same story to the nation a little later on.

The England midfield still looks in good shape after this

change. Paul Scholes moves into the middle alongside Nicky Butt, and Beckham and Sinclair tuck in close on either side, not getting too stretched.

Time and again the Argentine midfield knock the ball square across the face of this compact foursome, and then Emile Heskey drops deep and pinches the ball off them. England aren't playing the long ball so much tonight, but when they do, Emile is winning everything, and he's having a blinder.

In the twenty-fourth minute Heskey again nicks the ball brilliantly and lays it off to Butt, who strikes a perfect low, long, rapier pass through the Argentinian defence to Owen on the right of the box. He finds Samuel facing him, and seems momentarily undecided about which way to go past him, but then he realises that the defender is so terrified of his pace that he's standing too far off and just shoots from where he is. The ball nutmegs Samuel, and skates along the deck with Cavallero utterly stranded. It would have been a great goal, but it comes out off the far post and is booted gratefully out for a corner.

Even though we are only a quarter of the way through the game, I can see in my mind's eye this miss being replayed over and over at the end of the match, with pundits shaking their heads sadly and saying that this was the moment, this was the chance, if only . . .

Then Argentina go close. Gonzales whips a ball into the area, and Batistuta slips free behind Campbell but his diving header is straight at Seaman.

Sinclair turns Pocchettino inside out, but then the ball runs away from him in the area. Next time he tries it Pocchettino stamps down on him, nowhere near the ball, but Collina doesn't see it.

As the half develops, England are getting on top. Veron's passing goes to pieces, and he starts whacking hopeful crossfield balls straight into touch to whistles of derision. Rio Ferdinand and Sol Campbell are snuffing out any threat that makes it as far as our area, and Nicky Butt is playing out of his skin.

Just before the break England find themselves camped outside the Argentine area, probing. Scholes lays a ball smoothly
out to Sinclair, Sinclair nicks it in to Owen. Owen thinks about
taking the defence on, but then squares to Butt, who lays it
back to Scholes to have a shot. This is charged down, and
Beckham and Heskey scrap to win it back. Beckham is sent
flying, but Collina waves play on. Scholes carves it out left to
Owen, who half steps over and then cuts inside Pocchettino.
The defender, hopelessly drawn in, sticks out a leg, and Owen
goes down over it.

Pierluigi Collina has given the penalty before Owen has
landed.

Cheering and wild celebration erupt all around, but I can't
understand this, never can. We haven't scored yet. Enough of
this fate tempting, please . . .

Beckham is putting the ball on the spot.

Dom, the journalist to his fingertips, can't help saying, again:
'What a story this is . . .'

Four years ago, in St Etienne, England lost on penalties to
Argentina. We'll never know if Beckham would have scored
his, because he didn't take one. He'd been sent off for a
petulant flick at Simeone, who had just, let us not forget,
assaulted him.

Somewhere in the stadium, I know, Nick has turned his
back on the game. He never watches penalties. Cube will be
explaining this to Mickey. Mickey will be grinning.

Cavallero is standing right next to the England skipper, in
his face, talking to him, telling him to kick it to his favourite
side. Beckham walks away.

Simeone, his old nemesis, follows him to the end of his run
up, offering to shake hands in a gesture of fake sportsmanship,
trying to mess up his concentration. Beckham ignores him,
shuts him out, and Scholes and Butt, his United muckers,
ride shotgun for him and drive the Argentina captain away
to mind his own business.

This is taking for ever. Blue-and-white shirts keep creeping into the area to hold things up. Finally Collina is satisfied.

Beckham looks down, breathes out, starts his run.

An ecstasy of flashbulbs decorates this short moment.

The little red-shirted figure at the far end of the ground from me sprints forward and blasts the ball as hard as he can. All the disappointment of four years ago, all the subsequent pain, the effigy burning, the abuse, the name calling, all of this goes into the fierceness with which he propels the ball towards the goal.

Cavallero starts to move to his right. The ball flashes past him to his left.

All around the mother ship the carpet of fans gets three feet taller as thousands of pairs of fists thrust into the air, and we all choose the same single word to say.

'Ye-e-e-ah!'

Beckham, beside himself, has carried on his run to the far corner, and is pulling his shirt out from his torso to show to the supporters as his team mates catch up with him.

I spot David in the next block, and run quickly up one aisle and down the next to commune.

'Fantastic!' I manage to splutter.

'Nicky Butt is having the game of his life,' he shouts.

The game kicks off, and suddenly an icy dread settles on me. I look at David, and I know he feels it too.

'What is the matter?' asks Tomoko, smiling her head off. 'You should be happy!'

'Yeah, but now we've got to hold on to it.'

For some reason, it is infinitely more nerve-racking to be a goal up than it was to be level. The final minutes of injury time seem to go on for ever. Only another forty-five to go.

On the replay on the big screen we can see that the penalty went almost straight down the middle. How strange that Beckham, one of the great placers of a dead ball in the modern game, should rely on power. The chatter around us is saying that he nearly fucked it up, but I think he sent the keeper. I think he knew exactly what he was doing.

Just along from David is Nancy, Sven's other half, chatting away, looking remarkably unconcerned. David has met her a couple of times, and earlier this evening she gave him a hug of greeting, during the course of which David accidentally elbowed the wife of the vice chairman of one of our most prominent Premiership clubs in the face. She took it badly, and this is preying on David's mind. At least it's giving him something else to think about.

We are mightily apprehensive. England have played extremely well, but the memory of the disastrous second half in Saitama is still fresh, and we agree that England need to hold firm in the next fifteen when Argentina are bound to come at us strongly.

For the second half Pablo Aimar comes on for the misfiring Juan Sebastian Veron. Veron is a pirate, Aimar is a little tousle-headed cabin boy, and within a minute he's unleashed a shot on goal from thirty yards. It is England, though, who look like scoring. Heskey flicks a long ball on to Owen, who brilliantly spins round Placente and races into the area, only to drag his shot across the keeper and wide.

Then Mills charges clear down the right and crosses to Owen who loses his footing in the box. Heskey thumps the loose ball against a defender, and it rebounds to Scholes, who sends a swerving dipping volley goalwards that Cavallero punches out.

A few minutes later, Sinclair sends Beckham into the box. Placente should be favourite, but the skipper strong-arms his way past him and toe-pokes the ball just wide.

The hobbling Heskey leaves to a tremendous ovation – he has surely had his best game for England – and Teddy Sheringham comes on. Scholes sends a gorgeous volleyed pass more than half the length of the field to set Owen free, but the Liverpool lad is muscled off the ball.

England are keeping the ball, and the Argentines don't know what to do about it. An amazing period of possession leads up to a beautiful diagonal ball from Scholes to Sheringham. Teddy watches it all the way, and volleys it perfectly, van Basten-style, towards goal. It is creeping under the bar until Cavallero tips it over at full stretch, and it would have been the goal of this or any World Cup if he hadn't.

Chances, chances, chances, but still it's only 1–0 . . .

Batistuta leaves to a chorus of catcalls, and Hernan Crespo comes on. Then Kily Gonzales too is withdrawn and replaced by Claudio Lopez.

A Beckham free kick is deftly backheaded on by Sheringham, but it floats just wide. This, with twenty minutes to go, is England's last chance. After this it is all Argentine possession. Ortega is trying everything in his box of tricks to find a way through, but Ferdinand and Campbell are getting everything away.

From a corner Pocchettino gets in a good downward header, which Seaman, squatting, blocks with his arm and his chest. It is their best chance of the match, and after it I sit with my head in my hands for quite some time before I recover my composure, such as it is.

Sven tries to shore things up by bringing Wayne Bridge on for Owen, and this means that Beckham and Butt will have to go the full distance.

I can barely look at the action now, and I am more or less constantly on the move up and down the aisles, switching between the seat next to Dom and the one next to David one block over. I do, though, catch sight of one Aimar shot fizzing over the bar and on over the unusual high wall behind the goal, which is more used, I suspect, to having home runs hit over it. This is where all the Argentine flags are, including one that reads: '*Pele sera rey, Diego es dios*'. I persuade myself that if I read all of them then when I look back at the game it will be over.

Two minutes of added time feel like about twenty. I am glaring at my watch, willing the second hand round, and the clock inside the stadium seems to have stopped altogether.

And then it's over. The moment of release, of abandon, of joy, is the best thing I have experienced watching football. I just watch, my arms raised, unable to speak or do anything for the longest time. This is it. This is what I've come out here for.

Dom grabs David for a voxpop on the way out.

'How far do you think England can go now?' he asks.

'We've just beaten the favourites. Doesn't that make us the favourites now?'

10
Onsen Every Lifetime

'As soon as I hit the ball it just sort of went blank . . .'
– David Beckham

8 JUNE

When I wake up on Saturday morning after the emotional roller-coaster of the night before, I find I am in the mood for a complete break from the World Cup. I have also had two weeks of Japanese big city dwelling and fancy a break from that too, so I get on a bus and head out into the countryside, looking for some of the idyllic unspoiled wilderness that Hokkaido is famous for.

About an hour out of Sapporo I come to a little place called Jozankei. Obviously it's not going to be all that unspoiled, given that it has a bus stop, but once I walk down into the village from the main road it is at least quiet.

There is one cobbled street, which crosses a picturesque river burbling its way down a scenic valley, and at the far end a small Buddhist temple. Set back from the road are a number of large hotels, and this is clearly some kind of resort, but it's deserted just now. Water trickles down the face of the rock wall alongside the road, and it is steaming hot, and suddenly it clicks. Jozankei is a volcanic spa, an *onsen*, where people come to bathe in the natural hot springs that bubble up from the ground.

Maybe I'll give it a try later in the day, but what I want just now is to get some fresh air into my lungs and clear my head, which is feeling furred up inside like an old kettle after the celebrations in Sapporo last night. I get off the road, scramble down to the bank of the river, and head off upstream.

I follow a well-worn path, up some moss-covered steps cut into the rocky river bank, and into the cool canopy of a wood. I can still catch glimpses of the river to my right, picked out in the sunshine, and after about half an hour the path is less trodden down, and I begin to think to myself that I'm getting out into the proper countryside now, a bit of wilderness. Just then I round a bend, and find a clearing with a pristine public toilet which seems to have materialised there like a Tardis. I press on.

Much as I hoped to leave the World Cup behind for a few hours, it's not *I Love to Go a-Wandering* that's playing in my head as I tramp along, it's a different routine, that goes along these lines:

'If France beat Denmark and Uruguay beat Senegal then they'll all have four points . . .'

or:

'If Argentina thrash Sweden then England can still qualify even if we lose to Nigeria . . .'

I've come to a small wooden footbridge over the river. I stop, and – I think for the first time since I arrived in Japan – I can't hear any traffic. Excellent. On the other bank a large hill – or small mountain, depending on how you look at it – covered in dark green forest slopes up into the sky. I decide to get to the top of it and see what I can see.

Once across the bridge the path turns back towards Jozankei, so I strike off into the trees, crunching pine needles underfoot.

It takes about an hour to reach the top, accompanied by the constant screeching of cicadas as I go. I can also hear some birds smashing around in the branches overhead, but don't see any, and every now and again there is a loud crashing noise not too far off, which I take to be a dead branch coming down. The thick forest doesn't thin out at all at the peak of the hill, and so it is difficult to find a vantage point with any sort of view, but finally I find a gap and can see Jozankei, satisfyingly small and distant down in the gorge below.

I sit on a fallen tree and get out the guide book. There's nothing in there about this place, which I find rather pleasing, as though I am exploring unknown territory, but then a particular phrase catches my eye.

You are advised not to head off alone into the woods. Locals are careful to warn you of the potential dangers of an encounter with *ezo higuma*, the Hokkaido brown bear . . .

Well, no one was careful to say a word to me. Suddenly the crashes I've been hearing take on a more sinister cast. And that shadow – is it moving . . . ? I get down the mountain a hell of a lot faster than I got up it, and not just because it's downhill all the way.

Back in Jozankei I stick my feet in a free hot foot spa outside the Buddhist temple – man, that's hot – and contemplate my *onsen* options. The big white hotel overlooking the river seems a good bet, and so once I can feel my toes again I head up there.

First of all I am politely asked to take off my shoes before entering the hotel reception. The desk clerk's eyes widen at the sight of my enormous plates, and he scuttles off into a store cupboard to find the biggest possible slippers for me to wear. These barely cover the balls of my feet and I can't get all of my toes in, so I teeter after him on tiptoe over to reception to hire towels.

He gives me one big towel and one small one.

'This one,' he says, holding the small one back before letting me take it, 'is for face.'

'For face, I see,' I say.

'No, no,' he says, looking me meaningfully straight in the eye. 'For *face*.'

Yeah, face, I got it.

I go through into the gentlemen's public bath, and find myself in a small disrobing area. There are baskets for you to put your clothes in – not lockers, the idea of ransacking someone's pockets and nicking their watch is anathema here – and through a window I can see the large bathing pool. I undress, wrap the big towel around myself, and go on in.

The pool itself is large and a sort of bent oval shape. The room has been built around the part of the rocky river bank where the hot spring comes out of the ground, so there's kind of an outdoor look to indoors here. Around the side of the pool there are a number of low dressing tables, each with large mirrors and an impressive array of soaps and shampoos. Each also has a hand-held shower attachment, a little stool, and a bucket. I am very anxious not to get this wrong and make some bathing faux pas, so I have a look at what everyone else is doing. There are a couple of Japanese gentlemen in here soaping themselves down, and I quickly realise that watching them for etiquette tips is broadly similar to just standing here and looking at their bare arses, so I take myself over to a little stool, hang up my towels, and squat down to inspect the equipment (the shower attachment, I'm talking about).

The thing about public bathing, I discover, is that you are duty-bound to make yourself as clean as possible before you get in. My Japanese neighbour, I can see out of the corner of my eye, is a veritable fiesta of lather, and he fills the bucket with cold water and tips it over his head, before wandering over to the hot spa bath and sinking slowly into it.

I follow suit. Birthday suit.

As I'm finishing the rinsing-off part, half a dozen American guys come in. One of them takes the stool next to me.

'OK,' he says, clapping his hands together. 'What we got here, how does this work, eh?'

I – already an old hand – talk him through it, and go over to the hot bath. The water, blisteringly hot and with a low swirling fug of steam hovering just above the surface, spills out over the rocks, which are decorated by years of no doubt extremely healthy mineral deposits, and down into the pool. I can hardly bear to be in it at first, and stand on a step, hot water up to just below my knees. After about half a minute I look as if I'm wearing Liverpool FC socks.

The Americans finish lathering and rinsing, and come over to the hot bath. They all clamber straight in up to their necks, each making an 'Aaaaaaaaah!' noise. Maybe I imagine the faint sizzling of cooking flesh. Anyway, I can't stand on the edge any longer without looking faintly odd, so I grit my teeth and lower myself in too. An involuntary 'Aaaaaaaah!' escapes from my mouth, and I have the unusual impression that all my hair has stood on end. Maybe it has.

This is blinking hot. If a passing lobster fell in it would be lunch in about five minutes. (Not lunch for me, I don't actually like lobster, but I thought it more likely that one would be passing by than a poached egg.)

Now when you are in a communal bath with eight other naked men, a certain amount of surreptitious locker-room-style sizing up is bound to occur. It's inevitable. It's a man thing.

It happens in the showers after a football match, as I'm sure you are aware, and the award for Best Tackle at many a football club annual end-of-season dinner will have nothing to do with anything that happened on the pitch. I find – although I'm aware that I'm bleating somewhat here – that I'm never at my best after ninety minutes' hard exercise in wintry weather. Today it seems that this is also the case when being lightly broiled.

The Americans are letting it all hang out, entirely untroubled by concerns such as modesty. The two Japanese gentlemen, however, when they get out of the bath and leave, deftly cover themselves with the small face towels and so escape being entered into the unofficial competition. It is at this point that I realise what the man upstairs was trying to tell me. The small towels are for face – not for wiping it but for saving it. If I'd known that was what he was on about I'd have said to him: 'You may as well just give me two of the big ones, mate . . .'

When I get out and follow the Americans into the next room I make sure I have grabbed my save-face towel from its peg.

Actually, through the door it is not another room, but a staircase down to another pool, which I hope won't be quite so hot. The second pool is an outdoor one, and halfway down the stairs I realise that there is a spectacular view down into the valley, and I can see people out for a walk on the other side of the river. After a moment or two I realise that they can see me. And I'm stark naked. I scuttle on down.

The outdoor *onsen* is smaller, and a little more habitable. I get chatting to the Americans – it's difficult to be shy when everyone is bare – who are discussing property prices in Dallas, not a subject I know a great deal about.

'Did you see the Portugal game?' I ask them, knowing that by starting a World Cup conversation with a group of Americans I run the risk of getting the reply: 'What is a World Cup, exactly?' Not with these guys, though.

'Oh yeah, we were there. It was unbelievable!'

We have been talking about the game for a couple of minutes before I remember that the USA are actually playing in the other World Cup, the one in South Korea.

'Yeah, we didn't want to stay in South Korea. It's right next to North Korea, and they're part of the Axis of Evil, so we're staying here and just flying over for the matches and then flying straight back. We're just there for a couple hours. In and out, like a surgical strike.'

When they find out I'm from England, they all say: 'Congratulations!' Not just for living in England, you understand, but because of the result yesterday evening. I'm always at a loss when this happens, when people congratulate me for the result of a football match that I wasn't playing in. It feels rather fraudulent, somehow, to accept congratulations when I was just a spectator, but still . . .

'Sensational. It was a sensation. You guys played so well . . .'

Um, thanks, yeah . . .

One of these guys plays for a top indoor league side in the States, and another is a big cheese in Major League Soccer, and so they do actually know what they are talking about. The MLS chap reckons soccer is still a tough sell at home, simply because baseball and gridiron are so firmly entrenched in the American psyche and feel like 'their' sports, while football feels like something the rest of the world does, and why should they bother. Still, not as hard a job as the one he was headhunted from, which was trying to establish American football in Holland.

'I had thirty footballers we took over to live in Amsterdam, and do you know what the biggest problem I had to deal with was?'

Surprise me.

'Every couple days some teenage girl would turn up in my office claiming one of these guys had knocked her up. I couldn't control them. They were like animals.'

I have to leave them as I am in serious danger of overheating. I feel as if I'm at the side of a road with my bonnet up and my driver is standing with his hands on his hips looking out for the AA man. Upstairs I try to cool off with a cold shower, but as I make my way back into the room where my clothes are I feel things beginning to slip away. I half stumble, half fall onto a bench and actually pass out.

The next thing I know all the Americans are there, fully dressed, combing their hair, talking, wandering around while I am lying naked on a bench in the middle of the room like some sort of modern art exhibit. I can't tell whether I managed to position the face-saving modesty towel before blacking out, but reaching down to my groin to check doesn't feel like a stylish option somehow. I decide to sit up as though nothing has happened, and – phew, there is a towel down there, that's a relief.

As long as it was me who put it there . . .

A little later I am at the bus stop trying to make sense of the timetable. At exactly the moment the Sapporo bus is due to appear, here it is. What a country.

Back at their hotel, Nick and Cube have also had a traditional Japanese experience. They haven't left their rooms all day. Evening room service hasn't started yet, and the only food Nick has been able to acquire without getting dressed is some little tubs of ice cream from a vending machine in the corridor. The tubs didn't have spoons in, so Nick has been eating the ice cream with his toothbrush. This kind of oversight seems so unlikely in the land that can make a country bus appear precisely on time that I go and have a look at the vending machine, and sure enough there is a little spoon-dispensing compartment with about two hundred plastic spoons in it.

Refreshed by my short break from the football, I catch up with the goals and games from yesterday, when I was too absorbed in England v Argentina to notice the rest of the World Cup.

Sweden beat Nigeria 2–1 as we know already. Julius Aghahowa gave Nigeria the lead, which meant a first World Cup airing for the acrobatic flick-flack somersaulting celebration with which he illuminated the African Nations tournament in Mali earlier in the year. The goal was a flicked header from a glorious cross by the Nigerian number 2, so that on a day when the expected hoorigan problem in Sapporo failed to materialise, at least one Yobo was making the headlines.

Freddie Ljungberg was much closer to his best form, terrorising the full backs and threading a killer pass through to Henrik Larsson, who wrong-footed West and Okoronwo and slotted the ball past Ike Shorunmu as easily as if he was playing against Dunfermline. He got the second, too, a 63rd minute penalty.

Nigeria had chances to equalise. Yobo hit the post, and the twinkling Jay-Jay Okocha brilliantly set up the player with one of the best names in the whole tournament – Utaka the attacker – but he scuffed his shot. Sweden held on and they are top of the Group of Death while Nigeria are its first fatality.

The first team to go through to the knock-out phase were Spain yesterday evening. They beat Paraguay 3–1, recovering from an awful first half which saw them trailing to a Puyol own goal. Jose Luis Chilavert, the archetypal bit-of-a-character goalie, was back between the sticks for Paraguay, who were sporting a really nasty peach-coloured strip. His route uno free kick into the box from near halfway fell to Arce, and Casillas punched the save against the hapless Puyol's shins and in.

In the second half, though, things rather got away from Chilavert. He was rooted to his line as sub Fernando Morientes thumped in a header from a corner, and he flapped helplessly at De Pedro's cross to gift Morientes a tap in for the second. The clincher was another late Hierro penalty, which the veteran stopper slotted home as Chilavert flung himself about as far from the line of the ball as was humanly possible.

In the same group, South Africa beat Slovenia this afternoon in a poor game. The only goal was a fourth-minute mis-hit, as Siyabonga Nomvethe somehow bundled Quinton Fortune's free kick in with his knee while clearly trying to head it. The highlight was the celebration of Jomo Sono, the big fat Bafana Bafana coach, flapping his arms like a great chicken.

His counterpart, Srecko Katanec, had a bad day. He was sent from the dugout for abusing the referee, and without their star, Zlatko Zahovic, now back in Slovenia after a row with the coach, his team had little to offer, and were eliminated from the tournament. And their shirts have the Slovenian national anthem painstakingly woven into the design for luck as well. At least Katanec knows he has only one more game in the job, and Sono can cluck his head off, peck up some grit, and celebrate South Africa's first-ever World Cup finals win.

The highlights programme on Japanese television has pop music playing throughout, behind all the match action, and behind all the presenter-pundit chatter as well. Difficult to imagine Jimmy Hill standing for that. During today's round-up I realise that the music I can half hear is *Enola Gay* by Orchestral Manoeuvres in the Dark, which seems a deeply peculiar song to be listening to here in Japan.

There is a little Brit interest in this evening's first match, Italy v Croatia, as the referee is Graham Poll, who has been speaking openly about his ambitions to ref the final. This almost represents a conflict of interest, as Poll's best chance of getting the gig seems to lie with Italy reaching at least the semis, which would disqualify his main rival, Pierluigi Collina.

Italy were impressive in their first game, and Croatia, third in France 98, disappointing, but it is the Croatians who have much the better of the first half. Milan Rapaic and Davor Vugrinec create a number of good chances before the break, while Italy lose Alessandro Nesta injured on twenty-three minutes and this seems to rob their defence of its usual calm control.

Croatia, well organised and threatening going forward, have a lucky escape shortly after the interval. Cristiano Doni swings a cross in from the left-hand side, Gianluca Zambrotta touches it on, and Christian Vieri swoops to head the ball home. The Danish linesman flags for offside, though, and Poll disallows the goal – wrongly as it turns out, as replays show that neither Zambrotta nor Vieri was offside, or even close.

Two minutes later this mistake is all but forgotten, however, as Vieri rises above his marker, Josip Simunic, to loop Doni's cross into the corner of the net to give Italy a lead they hardly deserve.

Croatia come back hard, and the Italian defence seems oddly languid and disorganised. With seventeen minutes left, Robert Jarni puts in a low hard cross past a half-hearted Christian Panucci challenge. The ball bounces between the Italian back line and the keeper, and while they all watch it Ivica Olic bursts through them and taps it in. Three minutes later Rapaic and Marco Materazzi both swing a boot at a bouncing ball, and it slices crazily up and over Buffon. Croatia are 2–1 in front.

Italy, not surprisingly, finally rouse themselves. A Francesco Totti free kick slaps the inside of the left-hand post, and then, right on time, Materazzi punts a long hopeful ball upfield. It clears a clutch of players and falls to sub Filippo Inzaghi, who makes to nudge the ball past Pletikosa, but makes no contact. The keeper is fooled and the ball trickles into the net. Cue wild celebrations amongst the Azzurri, but the same Danish linesman is again flagging, indicating that Inzaghi has pulled the shirt of a Croatian defender, and Poll has to disallow the goal. Again it is a wretched decision. If anything Inzaghi was being fouled, and at full time the English referee, flustered and flanked by his errant assistant, faces a barrage of abuse from the Italian striker.

You have to feel sorry for Graham Poll. He could hardly overrule the linesman, Jens Larsen, but the wheels have certainly come off his campaign to ref the final.

And now Italy, France, Argentina and Portugal – four of the tournament favourites – have each lost one of their first two games. It's getting interesting, this World Cup . . .

And those surprise early results have left Felipe Scolari's once-derided Brazil as the new favourites. Their second game, tonight's 8.30 kick-off in Seogwipo, is a routine 4–0 win over World Cup new boys China, who are seriously out of their depth. There are some points of interest, though. I particularly enjoy Brazil lining up for their *Mouse That Roared* national anthem with their little mascot children in front of them. Someone with a sense of humour has ensured that the tiny

Juninho has been allocated a child that is almost as big as him, and almost twice the size of all the others.*

Roberto Carlos bangs in his first free-kick goal in international football for five years, and there is not the slightest hint of swerve on the shot as it screams past the defensive line-up – you'd have to say, not a great wall, China.

Then the 'Three Rs' take over. Ronaldinho sets up Rivaldo for the second, Ronaldo is hauled to the deck and Ronaldinho slots the penalty, and then in the second half Ronaldo gets a tap-in after a great run by Cafu, sent on his way by Rivaldo.

* Later, in Tokyo, I met a man who was in charge of these little mascot kids, and he told me that they were all McDonald's competition winners aged seven or eight, apart from Juninho's companion, who was twelve – and a *big* twelve – and the son of the president of McDonald's Israel. Juninho was his favourite player.

11
Under the Sea

'Suzuki's got a great engine.'
– Mark Lawrenson

9 JUNE

I have a few days on my own now, as Nick and Cube are flying down to Osaka while I am making my way south by train. This is my first experience of the much-vaunted Shinkansen bullet train, and I am not disappointed.

The Shinkansens all have names which make them sound even more impressive than they already are. Hikari, Nozomi, Super-Hatsukari, Max-Asahi, Hitachi – actually that one sounds more like a sound system. Imagine if Connex South Central trains had names. Oh, hang on, they do. The Delayed, the Cancelled, the We Regret To Announce . . . Platform 5 for the Virgin Hopeless to Manchester Piccadilly . . .

I am aboard the Hokuto Shinkansen from Sapporo to Hakodate, which is a small port on the south tip of Hokkaido. Mickey tells me that it is a very beautiful little town, so I'm going to break my journey there for a couple of hours. I have a reserved seat, very comfy, and a big picture window through which I watch Sapporo sliding away. The Hokuto is already going quite fast, by my reckoning, when it changes gear. I feel a definite thump in the back as it picks up speed. Now we are really moving. Then another thump, and again, and all of a sudden Japan is becoming a blur. This is travelling in style – I could get used to this.

Hokkaido whizzes by – pine-wooded slopes, with rice fields covering all the valleys in between them, houses that are chalet-style, in keeping with the region's identity as a winter sports destination, with steeply sloping roofs to deal with the five months a year of snowfall. No two neighbouring houses are the same colour, not even the roofs. A green house with a white roof sits next to a blue house with a brown roof, right by a red house with a yellow roof – it's like Legoland out there.

We run swiftly along the coast of Uchiuri-wan, a bay which faces out to the Pacific Ocean, and the Hokuto slows down, as if to let us have a look at the nice seaside view. I think nothing of this, so am very surprised when a guard comes into the carriage, bows deeply and informs us, with deepest regret and most humble apologies, that the train will be fourteen minutes late arriving at Hakodate.

This seems to trigger an automatic grumble reflex amongst the English passengers, who know from years of bitter experience the proper way to react to information of this kind. Never mind that the guard is explaining to them how they can get out one station early, at Goryokoku, and make their connection on to Aomori without a second's delay to their overall journey. It simply isn't good enough. When did we learn to have such high expectations of our rail service, I wonder? Oh yes, before it was privatised, I remember.

At Hakodate I get off, sling my bags into a coin locker, and go and have a look around. Mickey's description of this as a beautiful little town certainly doesn't seem to be borne out by the bit near the railway station, where there is a large and ugly container port and a ferry terminal. Everything's relative, though, and Mickey does live in a suburb of Tokyo, which is one of the ugliest cities, all in all, that I've ever seen, so maybe that explains his fondness for this hole.

There is a market, but its speciality is fresh seafood, which is not something I am at all partial to. Hundreds of stalls are crammed into a couple of blocks here, some outside on the side of the road, many more packed into a large indoor hall. I gather as I stroll around, peering at the squid in a tank (really fresh, in fact still very much with us), that the market's busy time has passed, and that by eleven o'clock on a Sunday morning, which is what it now is, these stallholders have more or less shifted all the eels and big red crabs and lobsters that they are going to shift. Not many other people are browsing, and I'm getting plenty of beady looks, which make me quite self-conscious, because there is not a chance that I am going to buy anything. Not in this squirming, wriggling, slippery, fishy, stinking hell-hole . . .

A happy chap with a huge glass vat full of simply enormous brown crabs calls me over.

'Hey, where you from?'

'England.'

'Ah, Enguran, very good. Beckham very good.'

'Yes, as you say.'

'Hey, I give you, you want to try?'

'Um, no, no thanks, I—'

But he has hold of my arm and is pulling me over to his stall with a vice-like grip.

'You try very good. I give you very special Japanese snack.'

'Snack?'

'Yes, *Japanese* snack.'

All along the row the other stallholders have no customers, nothing to do except watch us. I give them a wan smile: they stare back, miserably, and yes, inscrutably. I become oppressed suddenly by thinking about etiquette. I have read that the Japanese are very hot on the whole notion of giving gifts to guests, and where in another country I would probably be doing a runner, here I feel there is a pressure on me to be as polite as I can. This gentleman is offering me the chance to sample his wares. The very least I can do is have a taste, and even though I cannot abide seafood at any price it seems to me that the only way I can get out of here without losing face, with my – and my nation's – dignity intact, is to have a bit of a nibble. And if I absolutely have to buy something I can go straight over to the sea with it and give it its freedom, because there's precious little chance of it being dead, I'll tell you that. I take a deep breath.

'OK, matey,' I say. 'Japanese snack. Bring it on.'

He reaches behind him and lifts a lid, then he turns and suddenly thrusts something right in my face. It's huge, it's red, it's wriggling, it has tentacles the size of a baby's leg, with suckers all along it, it stinks, it's heavy, it's alive, and oh God, it's disgusting . . . !

'Yeaaaarghhh!' I shout, giving up all thought of the nation's dignity, and leaping backwards out of reach of the thing.

The bloke absolutely pisses himself laughing. He can hardly stand up. All his mates are laughing, and the whole hall is echoing with their fishy derision. I can see now that it is a single octopus tentacle, and although it's big it's no longer actually connected to an octopus. Laughing boy drops it back into an ice tray with a slippery plop, and I am on my merry way, having inadvertently continued my life's work, which is to bring joy and laughter to the world.

And they say the Japanese haven't got a sense of humour. It may be a cruel sense of humour which makes fun of foreigners, but they've definitely got one. Oh yes.

The Seikan Tunnel carries the rail link which joins Hokkaido and Honshu. The whole project took forty years to complete, and it is the longest tunnel anywhere in the world. The Japanese are like the Americans in this – they love to have the 'biggest/longest/tallest/oldest/fastest anywhere in the world'. Of anything.

It's all but 54 kilometres long, and until the Channel Tunnel was opened (at 49 kilometres) it was well over twice as long as the second longest. Where it scores over the Chunnel – apart from the fact that it's not crawling with Eastern Europeans trying to make their way towards a better life in the land of Boddingtons and Ant 'n' Dec – is that it has a station in it. A railway station under the sea. I've decided to get out when the train stops there and have a bit of a look.

At Hakodate station I retrieve my bags and make my way to the train for Aomori via Yoshioka Kaitei, the station under the sea. The engine, unexpectedly, is decorated with a huge picture of a thing called Doraemon, and there are dozens of kids everywhere, running around and having their photo taken with a man in a foam-rubber Doraemon suit.

Doraemon is a very popular and long-running cartoon character. I think he is a big blue cat, though he walks on his back legs, has no ears, and seems to be able to make a helicopter rotor come out of his head. He does also have a pet cat, which is another thing that real cats tend not to go for.

Inside the train, too, there are pictures of Doraemon and his small boy pals Nobita, Jaya and Tsnail (I had to ask about these, and they may not be spelled like this, or pronounced like this, in fact the small child I spoke to may have been telling me what he was having for his dinner). Doraemon's tinkly theme music plays the whole time, and I have to say I'm not sure what the hell is going on. Some sort of Doraemon festival in Aomori, perhaps. Kids scramble excitedly all over the carriage, and begin ripping into their flat square cardboard lunch *bento* boxes, which typically contain rice cakes wrapped in dark green leaves, some cold meat and vegetables, and some chopsticks to eat them with.

As the Doraemon train nears the entrance to the tunnel I must admit to becoming a little apprehensive. I'm beginning to doubt the wisdom of spending a moment longer than absolutely necessary under the sea in a part of the world this seismically active. The train rattles past a concrete works, and I catch sight of the name of the company.

It's OOPS! (their exclamation mark, not mine). 'OOPS! Concrete basics for life' their sign says, and over the door it says that they are the OOPS! Corporation. I fervently hope that they were not sub-contractors for the tunnel.

Now that I've started to contemplate the possibility of disaster, the rest of the passengers in the carriage become eerily reminiscent of characters in something like *The Poseidon Adventure*. The cutesy children, for instance, tucking into their lunch boxes while their parents refuse to discuss their marital problems.

'Look, let's just enjoy the day out – we can talk about it later . . .' But they never get the chance.

The old guard on the train: 'Hi, kids. This is my last trip under the sea, you know. I retire tomorrow . . .' A goner, for sure, just like that elderly couple on the trip of a lifetime after finding love again late in life.

And the nervy woman in therapy: 'Don't you understand? I've *got* to make this journey, it's the only way I'll ever conquer my claustrophobia . . .'

With one last glimpse of the slate-grey clouds louring over the angry – and decidedly heavy-looking – sea, we plunge into the tunnel, and Doraemon's train heads quite steeply downhill.

Then, without any warning – at least not one that I under-stand – we stop. There is definitely tunnel wall right outside the windows on both sides, but everyone in the carriage is heading for the door so I follow, and sure enough we have arrived at Yoshioka Kaitei. The station under the sea doesn't have a platform. One door only opens and leads straight into a service tunnel. The kids skip and chatter off down the slight incline away from the track, and behind me the single door hisses shut, and the train continues its journey to Aomori.

The small tunnel opens into a wider one running parallel to the track, and we spill out into it. We are greeted, silently, by four ancient gentlemen in sitcom stationmaster costumes, which last saw service during the unlamented *Oh, Doctor Beeching!* series. They are very grey, not just their hair, but their skin, their hands, their eyes. They give the impression that they haven't been to the surface for many many years, and wouldn't quite know what to do if they ever did. They are Morlocks.

The first Morlock manages to subdue the children's excitement by standing perfectly still in front of them until they shut up. He doesn't say a word. It's rather eerie, in fact, to hear their little echoing voices fade away, stifled by nothing more than a grey half smile. The Morlock slowly waves his arm, indicating a large cage with forbidding-looking padlocks on it. Another Morlock swings open the gate and beckons slowly, spookily. For a moment I think he is going to usher all the children in there and lock them up. The children think this too, and draw closer to their parents. But the Morlocks only want us to put our luggage in here, so we're not carting it all around the station.

We do as we are told – well, mime told – and then the Morlocks point slowly down the long tunnel in front of us. At the far end we can just make out another Morlock, beckoning, beckoning, and we dutifully, silently, head down the sloping pipe into the bowels of the earth.

This is one of the weirdest places I've ever seen, and the thought occurs to me that this is exactly what it might be like immediately after dying. 'Walk towards the far distant light, don't be afraid . . .' the Morlocks seem to be saying, their faces benign yet curiously lifeless. As we walk, I see that the walls are covered with faded black-and-white photographs, and tiles on which people have written in *haiku*, the ancient, seventeen-syllable poem form. Those that have gone before . . .

The tunnel goes down, and then turns right so that we are now standing in a large open space underneath the railway track. Here the head Morlock makes a little speech of welcome, punctuated with achingly slow bowing. Not understanding, I have time to ponder again the extraordinary greyness of the Morlocks. They look as if they have been made up to look old for a production by a bad amateur dramatic society.

When he finishes there is a little 'toot toot' sound, and a nightmarish vision appears around the bend of the tunnel. A little green car, a bit like a golf cart, chugs towards us, and sitting in it are two nine-foot giants, waving their enormous floppy hands at us. Rather than running for their lives, however, the children cheer, and these seem to be characters from the Doraemon cartoon – which is to say, insufficiently employed actors in big foam-rubber costumes.

A friend of mine used to eke out a living in this way, as Postman Pat in shopping centres up and down the country. They never knew where they were going from one day to the next. The back doors of the transit van would swing open, and out would jump Pat, Bart Simpson, a generic moose and the Pink Panther to spread joy and merriment amongst the shoppers of Anytown. Alan didn't like being Postman Pat. Kids would kick his shins, and he wouldn't be able to see them coming because of Pat's big nose. He dreamed of being the Pink Panther, because the Pink Panther was cool, and what's more he had a particular walk that needed mimicking so he felt his acting abilities would be challenged, however tinily. Tragically, though, he was too short for the costume, and whenever he tried it on the head would flop down on his chest and he wouldn't be able to see out.

The giants in the golf cart reverse away, and the children and their parents skip off in its wake. I don't know what to do now – should I follow? I take half a step, but a young fellow with a rucksack catches my eye and shakes his head. I stop.

Tentatively, unsure of his English, the young chap asks, 'You are . . . friend of Doraemon?'

Now there's a euphemism if ever I heard one.

'No,' I say firmly. 'I'm not.'

We stand still and wait. The boy with the rucksack, the head Morlock and me. The tinkly little Doraemon music is fading, and an eerie silence descends. I think I can just make out the sound of running water, which is not something you want to hear in a station under the sea, in the dark.

The tunnel down which the children were led swings back into view about a hundred yards away, and we briefly see them skipping along, Pied Piper-style, behind the golf cart. The music and their chatter echo along the tunnels, distorting nightmarishly. They turn another corner and they are gone. Where to, I just don't know. Under the sea somewhere.

Now I don't know quite what I thought would happen at a station under the sea. Maybe I thought there'd be a bookshop – Waterstone's – or a café – Starfishbucks, perhaps – but no such luck. I certainly wasn't expecting twenty children to be led away by nine-foot-high, foam-rubber men in a golf cart and swallowed up in darkness. And now this stranger and I have been left alone with the head Morlock – what horrible fate is in store for me?

Actually it seems I am going to get a guided tour, but the head Morlock doesn't speak English and I don't speak Japanese. The young chap with the rucksack – his name is Shu, I discover – speaks a little English, but not much.

When the head Morlock comprehends the situation, he summons up another Morlock, who seems to cringe slightly as he listens to his instructions – 'Ah. *Hai, hai . . .*' He shuffles off into a nearby tunnel, and re-emerges moments later astride an ancient black bicycle, which he rides off like a sitcom old man, wobbling about all over the place. Imagine Clive Dunn going for help in *Dad's Army*.

While he is gone we do nothing, we just stand there. The head Morlock says nothing. Shu says nothing. I stand there wondering what would have happened to this guided tour if there had only been me, and trying to work out what Shu's interest is. I come to the conclusion that he is a train-spotter.

Actually, though, that's something you don't see here in

Japan. Little clutches of train-spotters at the end of the platforms, with their flasks of green tea and their rice cakes. What
would be the point?

Sheeeeeewwwwww!

'Did you get the number?'

'No, too fast, too fast. I think it was a white one . . .'

The cycling Morlock teeters back into view with an explanatory brochure in English, which I can refer to as we go along,
and the guided tour of the facility begins.

Much of what the head Morlock appears to be telling us
concerns the safety features of the Seikan tunnel – rather too
much, actually. There are sprinkler systems for extinguishing
fire, five separate electric power sources in case one or more
gets cut off, and in case of my chief concern here this afternoon
– which is the Tsugaru Straits 140 metres above our heads
suddenly rushing in through a big crack in the roof – it is
reassuring to learn that the service tunnels are all sloped so
as to allow water to drain away quickly and efficiently. At
least it would be reassuring if we weren't standing in a service
tunnel.

Then there is some description, I gather, of the forty years
it took to construct the Seikan. Because it was so much larger
than any other previous project, many of the engineering
problems seem to have been solved by trial and error, such
as the drilling of small pilot tunnels just to see what would
happen. Shu helps out with the occasional English phrase,
such as:

'Many killed . . .'

We pass a curious display featuring some extremely pale, in
fact virtually transparent, fish mounted in a glass case. The
description, in Japanese and English, reads: 'These fish were
discovered during the excavation of the tunnel.'

Now I'm no engineer, but I reckon if you're discovering
fish in a tunnel that you're excavating under the sea, then
you haven't dug it far enough down.

Another feature which I would perhaps have considered doing differently is the one whereby all trains in the tunnel would stop immediately if there was an earthquake. I'm not sure, but the head Morlock seemed to be describing a device whereby big spikes would come up from beneath the tracks to help stop the trains as quickly as possible. Now my approach, in the event of an earthquake, would have been to devise a system whereby the trains go as fast as they possibly can until they are out of the tunnel, but hey, that's just me.

A Morlock appears on a bicycle from another tunnel. As he passes, ever so slowly, he catches my eye and opens his mouth as if to speak. Then he glances at the head Morlock, who shakes his head sharply, and the cycling Morlock pedals on by without stopping.

What was it that he wanted to say to me?

'Help me, please, for the love of God take me with you . . .'

'What is it like up there, is it day or night? Is it winter or summer . . . ?'

'Is the war over yet? Did we win . . . ?'

The highlight of the tour is actually a tremendous *coup de théâtre*. The head Morlock leads us through a big double metal fire door, and we find ourselves in a pitch-dark steeply sloping tunnel with a railway in the middle of it. In between the tracks – we can just see from the light spilling through the fire doors – is a track with teeth, like you might see on a funicular railway up the side of a mountain. This tunnel, we are told, is used for bringing equipment to and from the surface, and also goes down much deeper, well below the railway tunnel.

Shu and I shrug. OK, fine, what next? Then the head Morlock throws a switch, and suddenly we can see lights coming on along the whole length of the tunnel, racing away from us in both directions. It is a horrible vertiginous optical illusion. In an instant we see how very very far away the surface is, and also that we are perched precariously in a concrete pipe that leads to the very bowels of the earth. Your eyes try to

flatten it, telling your mind that the tunnel is horizontal, but
the spirit level in your ears and your knees and your feet are
telling you that it's steeper than forty-five degrees, and to hold
onto something or you'll fall, fall away and never ever stop.
The head Morlock flicks a switch and plunges us back into
darkness, which actually comes as quite a relief.

Not all the trains that barrel through the tunnel stop at
Yoshioka Kaitei, and the ones that don't cause tremendous
gusts of wind in the service tunnel. At the end of the tour
an express whooshes through, and the blast of air plucks the
head Morlock's ancient stationmaster hat off his grey head
and sends it swirling off down the tunnel. He creaks off after
it, catches it, dusts it off, and pops it back on, and I realise
that he must know that was going to happen, it must happen
every time, it's a little bit of slapstick to make the tour go
with a swing. And they say the Japanese don't have a sense
of humour – this is my second out-and-out joker of the day.

Then we find out where all the children went to. One of the
side tunnels has been made into a play area which is hired out
for kids' parties. Doraemon and his friends are there, and a big
black steam train for the kids to clamber over, there's a ball
pit and a soft climbing area, somewhere to watch cartoons,
and various other Doraemon-related activities. Like the other
tunnels, the purely functional ones, it is quite dimly lit and
miserable, and it is probably one of the very last places on
earth I would ever consider holding a children's party.

There are a few minutes to wait before the train on to
Aomori, and I find myself in front of a display of the history
of Doraemon. He began appearing in cartoons in 1969, at first
educational ones, but latterly just knock-about humour for the
kids. He seems to have something in common with Felix the
Cat, in that he can make ladders appear out of a little door in
his stomach, and Felix had that magic bag, didn't he, but even
so his appeal continues to escape me. Mind you, if he'd had a
successful thirty-three-year run like this in the States he'd have

been made into a live action movie by now. There would have been plenty of stories in the press about how Mike Myers was going to be in it, along with the girl out of *Buffy the Vampire Slayer* and perhaps Jim Carrey, but when the film actually appeared it would have had Joe Schmoe and Bindy Drama School instead.

And then the train to Aomori – where I will change for Morioka – arrives. The Morlocks gather to wave us all off, and we pile up the little slopey tunnel to the only door on the only carriage we can see. As we trundle off into the darkness I am left to ponder the curious little community that lives at Yoshioka Kaitei, the station under the sea. Four ancient grey gentlemen who look as if they haven't seen the light of day since the Seikan tunnel opened for business fourteen years ago and who ride silently around the service tunnels on their vintage black bicycles. And four far from successful actors in giant foam-rubber costumes, who are probably, even now, kicking off their outsized floppy boots and massaging their bruised shins, going: 'Little bastards! I tell you, as soon as I've got my Equity card I'm out of here . . .'

At which point one of the Morlocks will sidle up and whisper mournfully: 'Help me, please, take me with you. I want to feel the sun on my face again . . .'

This afternoon in Miyagi, a little way south of where I am, Mexico take on Ecuador in Group G. Agustin Delgado heads in a cross from Ulises de la Cruz in the fifth minute to give the South Americans the lead, but Mexico's talented midfielders gradually take over the game, with Gerardo Torrado and Cuahtemoc Blanco outstanding. On twenty-eight minutes Torrado sends Ramon Morales away down the left, and his low near-post cross is cleverly angled home by Jared Borgetti. Then midway through the second half Torrado himself scores the winner with a classy left-foot shot after Ecuador give him the freedom of the midfield. Blanco has a couple more chances

Chris England

– although we don't see the Blanco hop, perhaps because he is never faced by two Ecuadoreans at once – and Mexico could have won by more than the 2–1 final score.

Now they are top of the group with six points, but strangely still third favourites to qualify from this group. Defeat by Italy and a win for Croatia over Ecuador could see them miss out on goal difference, and both those results seem rather likely.

Meanwhile, in the other World Cup over in South Korea, Costa Rica and Turkey scrape together a nervy one-all draw. The Turks know that defeat will mean the end of their campaign, and in the second half a sustained spell of pressure brings the opening goal. Hasan Sas chests the ball down for Emre Belozoglu, whose first shot is blocked by a diving Costa Rican. Emre then manages to spin through 360 degrees to slot the loose ball just inside the post. Costa Rica come back strongly, with Winston Parks ramming home with four minutes left, thus saving the referee from having to make a decision on how Hernan Medford came to be flattened four yards out as the ball came over. Turkey are furious with themselves for letting the lead slip through their hands, and Emre gets booked for a fracas with a Costa Rican official who won't give him the ball back quickly enough for a throw-in.

In Morioka, early evening, I check into a hotel by the station, and go for a walk around. I'm on the lookout for things to mention on talkSPORT, as ever, and I don't know quite how I'll be able to describe the odd afternoon I've had under the sea. My guide book mentions that this medium-sized city in northern Honshu is famous for its *wanko* contests, and that sounds perfect, so I set out in search of one.

So what sort of image does that conjure up for you?

'Lay-deeez . . . and gentlemen! Tonight Jeremy Spake off of *Airport* against Roy Keane . . . !!!'

Actually *wanko soba* is Morioka's speciality food, named after the little bowls that the thin flat buckwheat noodles are

179

traditionally served in, and the *wanko* contest is an eating competition. Apron-toting contestants try to shovel down as many bowls as possible while a super-attentive waitress is on hand to continually dish up more. The object is to be the first to finish, and you do this by getting the lid onto your empty bowl, but if you're not quick enough you get lumbered with another helping. The record, apparently, is something like 350 bowls at a sitting, and they're little bowls but they're not so little that that isn't an enormous amount of scoff.

I'm out of luck, though, as the town is absolutely deserted. Pedestrian crossings bleep and tinkle away to themselves, there's virtually no traffic on the street, shops are closed up, there's not even anyone in McDonald's. A couple pass me, the girl's heels clacking on the pavement as they hurry off to get home in time for the kick-off. The *wanko* contest restaurant is one of many establishments not open for business tonight. Actually, it looks rather like a bank, so maybe it went bust.

There is a bookshop open, and the display at the front is laden with football books, books by Phillippe Troussier, Arsene Wenger, Hidetoshi Nakata, and a whole range of magazines all featuring the grinning face of young Junichi Inamoto straight after his wonder goal against Belgium. The boy's a star. I am pleased to see that *Ichiro on Ichiro*, the baseball star's biog, has been shunted to one side in the current mounting frenzy for football. And they are learning the finer points of the game too. Mickey told me that France v Uruguay was the first time Japanese football fans appreciated that a nil-nil draw could be exciting, so they're ahead of the Americans already.

Near the station I find a small restaurant. Japan v Russia is showing on a small portable telly on top of the fridge, but actually the Japanese clientele doesn't seem that bothered about it, they're just tucking into their meals. A group of English lads, like me on their way down to Osaka a bit at a time, are much more into it.

I manage to fulfil one small ambition by saying to the wait-ress: '*Wanko*, please . . .' and she doesn't slap me, or redirect me to another establishment down a nearby back alley.

Japan have Miyamoto and his Batman mask in for the injured captain Morioka, thus depriving me of the chance to watch him play while sitting in a place with the same name. And if you think there's an edge between England and Argentina because of the Falklands, bear in mind that Japan and Russia are still disputing the sovereignty of a group of islands off north-eastern Hokkaido – Kunashiri, Etorofu, Shikotan and the Habomai group – since they were occupied by the old Soviet Union at the end of the Second World War.

Troussier's men give a committed, high-energy performance, harrying the rather languid Russians out of their stride. After a quiet first match, their star player Hidetoshi Nakata of Parma shows what he can do. He and Inamoto control the middle of the field and are a constant threat with their quick breaks out of defence, the Arsenal man creating the best chance of the first half for himself with a powerful driving charge.

Early in the second half Japan suddenly create a goal out of nothing. A rather scuffed low cross from the left into a crowded Russian penalty area is met by a gorgeous cushioned touch by Nakata, which instantly, shockingly almost, sets Inamoto absolutely free in front of goal. The number 5 takes a touch, and fires an unstoppable close-range shot into the roof of the net.

In the restaurant the Japanese diners break into applause, but these aren't football fans and I think they got the idea from the English. There just doesn't seem to be the same habit, here, of watching big football matches communally in bars and cafés – people are doing their own thing at home.

After this Nakata hits the bar with a fantastic strike from outside the area, and Vladimir Bestchastnykh should equalise, but having beaten the keeper he fires wide of an empty net.

His name, apparently, means 'unlucky' in Russian, which must take a bit of getting used to, like being called Micky Misfortune or Bobby Curse.

At full time Japan have won 1–0 (anything South Korea can do . . .) and are top of the Group H table, with Tunisia to come.

12
Au Revoir, Au Revoir, Au Revoir . . .

———————

'For the third goal I blame the ball. During the shots the
shape becomes completely different.'
– Mohammed Al Daeyea, Saudi Arabia

10 JUNE

Last night the Japanese World Cup round-up show featured
Arsene Wenger, with a little Japanese translator tucked behind
his shoulder, sitting next to Junichi Inamoto, the man of the
moment. Wenger was giving his replies in English, so in his
spell here managing Grampus Eight he doesn't seem to have
picked up that much Japanese.

Wenger rather woodenly compliments his young star, saying, 'Congratulations, Ina. I told you you would have a strong
World Cup and you are having it.'

At which Inamoto looks distinctly unimpressed, shrugs,
wrinkles his nose, as if to say: 'So why aren't you picking me?'

This morning there is a story in the *Daily Yomiuri* that
Arsenal have in fact released Inamoto on a free transfer,
despite his two man-of-the-match awards out here, so perhaps
his shrug at Wenger's remark meant: 'Yeah? What's it got to
do with you?'

Lennox Lewis beat Mike Tyson in Las Vegas, an eighth-
round KO, and immediately sent his best wishes to 'the British
soccer team'. Bless . . .

I'm catching a lunchtime Shinkansen down to Tokyo and

183

then Yokohama, so I have the morning to wander around Morioka, which is a pleasant enough little city just a little light on tourist attractions. To give you an idea of what I mean – the main highlight is a big rock that has been split in half by a cherry tree that has grown up through a crack in the middle.

There are one or two curiosities here, though. I go into a bank to change some money, and can't help noticing that the bank staff are not quite as sharp and efficient as Japanese service personnel I have seen elsewhere. It is a nice bank, actually, a beautiful ornate old building, hushed like a library, and a lot of the transactions seem to be taking place on paper and in ledgers rather than on the computer, so it seems a relatively relaxing place to work, but the cashiers all seem a touch tense for some reason. I hand over my traveller's cheques and sit down on a comfy leather bench to wait. And then I hear it.

I've noticed on my way through the town that the pedestrian crossings don't just beep when the little green man appears, they play a little tune, and the tune they play is that old Scottish ditty that goes:

If a body meet a body coming through the r-r-rye . . .

The thing is, it is incredibly loud and piercing and electronic, and there's a busy junction right outside the window of this bank. As the music starts up for what must be the umpteenth time that day a collective flinch shivers through the room, eyes close, temples are massaged, pens hit the desktop in despair. It takes several minutes for the poor zombie behind the counter to complete my transaction, with much scribbling out and starting again, and after a while I myself am ready to kill someone, preferably Kenneth McKellar. What it must be like to work there, enduring that ghastly tune every minute or so for eight, nine hours a day, I dread to think.

And then walking along the street – actually looking for the big rock that has been split in half by a cherry tree that has grown up through a crack in the middle – I pass a huge outdoor press conference-cum-photo opportunity of some kind. A handful of rather sober-looking Japanese fellows – maybe businessmen, maybe local politicians – in dark suits, each wearing a diagonal beauty queen-style sash, are standing having their pictures taken in front of a large pile of clocks, all shapes and sizes, just dumped higgledy-piggledy on the pavement. They look very pleased with themselves, these lads, and I imagine they are wittily illustrating how the current administration is wasting time, or something of that kind. Or possibly clocks have been outlawed, although this is probably the least likely country in the world to come up with such a measure, except maybe Switzerland.

The calm and quiet comfort of my lightning-fast rail journey south is abruptly disturbed when the Shinkansen stops at Sendai. This is the mainline station closest to Miyagi stadium, the venue of yesterday's Mexico v Ecuador match, and I suddenly find myself surrounded by Mexicans. Not just any old ordinary Mexicans, either, but a large posse of parody Mexicans. Sombreros are tossed gleefully into the luggage racks, along with a gigantic feathery Aztec headdress, ponchos are hung over the backs of seats, and each of them seems to be carting around enough luggage for a six-month round-the-world trip. They could hardly be more Mexican if they started calling me 'gringo'. And then they do.

'Hey, gringo, I sit here?'

I find myself in the middle of a long and mostly shouted conversation about their decisive game against Italy next Thursday, in which Mexico need a draw. These lads reckon they'll get it, of course, and if they do it's off to South Korea for them. If they don't, though, they plan to stay in Japan and follow Brazil. I wonder if any England fans have contingency plans to support somebody else. Germany, perhaps . . .

Then at Omiya a Japanese businessman who has reserved

the seat next to me turns up and is about as thrilled to find a big muchacho sitting there picking dirt from under his toenails with the corner of the complimentary magazine as I have been. The ousted Mexican stands near by for the rest of the ride to Tokyo, right under the sensor which opens and shuts the sliding door of the carriage, so that it opens and shuts every eight or nine seconds for about forty-five minutes. This is only just preferable to sitting in the bank listening to the pedestrian crossings.

In Tokyo I am only about half an hour away from Yokohama, which is where I am headed, but if I go straight there I will be on a train when talkSPORT are due to ring (not ideal), so I bung my bags into a locker and leave the station to look for some open space. I am also, incidentally, hoping to meet up with a friend of a friend who has a spare ticket for Ireland v Saudi Arabia tomorrow. I find the perfect spot – a quiet little square with a small and distinctive clocktower in it where I can arrange to meet the guy with the ticket, and also speak to London without interference.

I am expecting the call any moment, just going through my offbeat notes injecting some more humour, when suddenly a young Japanese man in a short-sleeved smart shirt and a tie comes and stands right next to me. This is mildly annoying, but what the hell, I'm not going to move, he'll just have to listen to me while I do my stuff. Then he whips out a megaphone and starts screaming at the top of his voice, trying, it appears, to drum up trade for his nearby Blood Donor van.

I jump out of my skin, clamp my hands over my ears, and right then my mobile phone goes off. I can't hear it, obviously, I can't hear anything except this maniac with the megaphone shouting about blood, but I can feel it buzzing away in my trouser pocket. Hell! I dart into a department store to get away from him, and moments later I am trying to deliver comedy World Cup material as unobtrusively as possible while walking up and down the aisles of a crockery department.

Outside Yokohama station there is a large red neon digital sign, counting down to the final – '20 Days To Go' – which will be here in Japan's third-largest city. A small and temporary impromptu market has sprung up on the pavement, three or four large stalls, selling exclusively World Cup memorabilia. After Japan's first-ever finals victory yesterday the country has suddenly woken up to the tournament. The crush surrounding these stalls is several bodies thick all the way round, and blue Japan replica shirts at eighty quid a time are flying out as fast as the local Del Boys can flog them.

At this rate, the blue hysteria here will soon match the crimson frenzy at the other World Cup, where the hosts, South Korea, took on the United States in front of an almost totally red-clad crowd in Daegu this afternoon.

Guus Hiddink's athletic and well-organised side dominated the match and created plenty of chances, but it was the Americans who scored first on twenty-four minutes. Bayer Leverkusen's Frankie Hejduk chipped a through ball down the middle, and Clint Mathis chested it down brilliantly and tucked it away with his left foot. Mathis was sporting a startling mohican hairdo not unlike Christian Ziege's, which is the sort of thing you might ordinarily expect to see between the legs of a porn model.

The NY/NJ Metrostars striker was played onside by Lee Eul Yong, who had an up and down sort of a game. When South Korea were awarded a penalty shortly afterwards, it was Lee Eul Yong who planted the kick too close to the excellent Brad Friedel, but then in the second half it was his free kick that was glanced in by the substitute Ahn Jung Hwan for the equaliser.

Ahn, of Perugia in Serie A, celebrated his goal by impersonating a speed skater, a reference to a controversial incident at the Winter Olympics in the US earlier in the year. South Korea's Kim Dong-Sung was disqualified after a protest by the Americans, and the gold medal which his countrymen clearly believed should rightly have been his was handed to the runner-up, Apolo Anton Ohno. Of the United States.

Afterwards Hiddink was disappointed with the draw, as Seol Ki Hyeon and Choi Yong Soo had glorious chances brilliantly saved by the outstanding Friedel, and it leaves South Korea in serious danger of being dumped out by group favourite Portugal next Friday.

Now, Tunisia against Belgium would not ordinarily be one of the most interesting of World Cup clashes, but with Japan poised to qualify from Group H if they can avoid defeat by the African side this match was dissected in great detail on Japanese television.

The news for the home fans was not that great, as Tunisia greatly improved on their showing against Russia and should really have won. The venue was the Big Eye Stadium in Oita, which is the most southerly of all the World Cup grounds, and the early evening heat was stifling. At least Belgian protests caused the organisers to open the roof. 'It was like hell in there,' Jacky Peeters said.

The Belgians took an early lead through captain Marc Wilmots, who turned in a clever knock-down by van der Heyden from close range, but Tunisia were quickly level. Slim Ben Achour was brought down by Gert Verheyen twenty-five yards from goal, and Khaled Badra lashed the loose ball into the top corner with keeper De Vlieger a helpless spectator. Unfortunately Australian referee Marc Shields was too quick with his whistle and Tunisia had to settle for a free kick, which Raouf Bouzaine swerved in brilliantly with his left foot.

The heat clearly sapped the Europeans, who were at walking pace for much of the second half, and Kaies Ghodbane had two marvellous shots which could have won the game for the Africans.

After catching up on these games, and before this evening's

live match, I check out the area and find a Kinko's – one of the handy chain of twenty-four-hour photocopying and internet shops – to check through some e-mail from home. There is one from Susan saying she is running out of money for things like the mortgage and food, while I am spending the family fortune hand over fist out here. I have left her a blank cheque, but it's not much use unless I have some funds in my account, so I send Jim an e-mail to see if he can give talkSPORT a nudge into paying me.

Later, I am in my hotel with a Japanese McDonald's salt beef with lemon burger watching Poland v Portugal from Korea. Without realising it I have the bilingual feature switched on, and so the Japanese studio discussion suddenly becomes the English BBC commentary just before kick-off, and the first thing I hear is junior mikeman Steve Wilson saying: 'Fank you velly much, Missa Rineker!' in a funny Benny Hill voice. He should go far.

Pauleta of Bordeaux opens the scoring after a quarter of an hour. He pulls away from his marker, Tomasz Hajto, in the area and controls a crossfield ball on his thighs. Hajto lumbers after him, but Pauleta takes a touch inside and whacks it past a rather floppy-wristed Jerzy Dudek inside the near post.

Midway through the first half it starts to absolutely tank it down, and suddenly there's surface water everywhere and the players are sliding around all over the place, as if it were the Baseball Ground in an early seventies February. Scottish whistle man Hugh Dallas always looks like a little boy who is about to cry after being bullied by bigger boys. In the pouring rain he looks as though the tears have started in earnest.

Luis Figo is clearly not fully fit, but Poland's defence is slow enough for him to be able to impose himself nonetheless and show glimpses of what he is capable of. His low right-wing cross is touched in by Pauleta for 2–0, and then he himself smashes a right-foot curler against the post with Dudek beaten.

Portugal coach Antonio Oliveira, who resembles a fatter older brother of Martin O'Neill, waves his crutches in the air to celebrate Pauleta's second, having done his bit for team morale by falling down stairs at his hotel earlier in the day and breaking his ankle. Poland's manager, Jerzy Engel, is still in one piece, but looks like a depressed walrus, as well he might.

Pauleta again easily pulls away from his marker, this time Tomasz Waldoch, to make space to receive a crossfield pass from Rui Costa, and turns him right and left before tucking it in off Dudek's shin for his hat-trick. As the ball hits the inside of the side netting Waldoch is still recovering from Pauleta's first shimmy, with all the turning speed of an oil tanker.

The demoralised – and now eliminated – Poles cannot live with the Portuguese forwards, and the white boots of Rui Costa slide in to nudge home a fourth from a Nuno Capucho cross with two minutes left.

11 JUNE

I'm on the sixty-ninth floor of Japan's tallest building, the Landmark Tower, which is part of the futuristic Minato Mirai 21 development in Yokohama. I got up here in the world's fastest lift – they love their world's fastests in Japan – and I can safely say it is the only lift I've ever been in that has a speedometer. Top speed is 750 metres per second, and it whisks you up 69 floors in about 40 seconds. If you've ever been in a lift you know exactly what it's like. They've tried to make it more exciting by having stewardesses in uniforms as if it was an airline journey, and by having an illuminated skyscape on the ceiling, and by plunging the passengers into darkness on the way up, but there's no getting away from the fact that a ride in a fast lift, even the world's fastest, is very much like a ride in a slow lift.

You do get a pretty good view of things from up here, though. Tokyo's skyscrapers – all smaller than this one – are clumped together a little way off to the north, there's Yokohama harbour, where Tiger Tanaka's helicopter dumped the black sedan that chased Bond and Aki away from the Osato Corporation, and my first view of Mount Fuji. It's covered in cloud, pretty much, but I can see the bottom half of it.

Suddenly I get a brief, mad, musical phone call from Nick in Osaka.

'Can you hear me?' he's shouting, and I can, but only just, over some tinny electronic music and a constant clattering noise. 'I've just won the jackpot at pachinko, it's going fucking mad!'

'What have you won?' I ask him.

'About eight large buckets of ball bearings so far. It hasn't stopped paying out yet.'

Nick says he saw the top half of Mount Fuji sticking up above the cloud from the plane when he flew down to Osaka, so between us we've seen the whole thing.

In the afternoon I ask around the bellboys at the hotel until I find one who is into the World Cup, because I need somewhere to watch the crucial France v Denmark decider, which is only on Sky PerfecTV. He tells me about a sports bar called Yankees by the station to which he sneaks out to watch baseball, and he's pretty sure they'll have the football on. Get there early, though, he says, because it gets packed long before the games start, and if you are late, then 'view very bad'.

I go an hour before kick-off and, like all the bars I've had to find in Japan since I've been here, it's not easy to pin down. I eventually discover it on the sixth floor of the Cial building, in a sort of multi-storey shopping arcade. Already there's only one seat left in the entire place, which is packed with Irishmen in their green shirts drinking lager. I plonk myself down, and get chatting to Gary, a Niall Quinn look-and-sound-alike who's in there on his own, and we go through all the various permutations in the various groups. This is where the World Cup starts to get really interesting, the last round of games in the group stage, and the teams that go through from this group, group A, will play against the teams who survive the Group of Death.

Gary says that he's met Damien Duff's dad out here, and that Damien had told his dad that at half time in the Cameroon game, a 3.30 kick-off, he'd found the heat so debilitating that he felt he couldn't carry on. He was persuaded to give it a try, and then a cloud came over in the second half and the Irish all felt a lot more comfortable, hence their much improved performance.

Just before the kick-off, when it's far too late to find anywhere else, and there's already quite a crowd outside the bar looking in through the windows, the manager comes over and tells us that the table where we are sitting is reserved. I begin to give the man a hard time over this, because there's no sign, no way we could have known, but as it happens our table for four has been booked by just two girls who are happy to squeeze up and the whole thing sorts itself out amicably, which is just as well because when the manager's gone Gary shows me where he'd hidden the little 'Reserved' sign under the condiments.

A handful of very boisterous Frenchmen burst in. One is draped in a French flag, another is on roller skates, and a third has a tray of cigarette lighters which seem to be for sale. The Irish break into loud choruses of '*Au revoir, au revoir, au revoir!*', and the lead Frenchman plays up good-naturedly. Like all Frenchmen, he seems to have the knack of being sarcastic using just body language. When it is time for the national anthems he leaps to his feet, claps his hand to his heart, and bellows the *Marseillaise* at the top of his lungs, so loudly that he loses track of the band on the telly and finishes way too early, while the players are still mouthing '*Marchons, marchons* . . .' over in Inchon. For this he gets a ribald round of ironic applause, and he bows splendidly, full of himself.

About twenty minutes into the game I have to do a spot for talkSPORT. I can hardly leave the restaurant, as there is a heaving, hungry crowd outside in the arcade, pressing against the windows and trying to watch the telly through the lace curtains, and if I get out I'll never get back in. The phone goes right on schedule, and I have to crouch down by the door of the toilets so I don't get in anybody's sight line. I manage to hear Alan Brazil saying that Senegal have taken the lead against Uruguay in the other match, then that they will be coming to me after the break, and then the phone's reception abruptly packs in. I can't get them back, and they can't get me . . . Hell – I'll have to try again at half time.

Senegal's goal is a penalty by Khalilou Fadiga, given after a suspiciously theatrical-looking fall by El-Hadji Diouf. It puts them top of the group, but only for a couple of minutes. I have just regained my seat when the Bolton bulldog, Stig Tofting, lobs a long throw into the box. Patrick Vieira heads it straight up in the air, and then Marcel Desailly does no better with his header. Vieira scuffs it half clear, and the loose ball comes back to Tofting, who scoops it over to the back post where Dennis Rommedahl prods it in on the half volley with the outside of his right boot. The French defenders turn to start blaming each other, and Denmark are one up.

Zidane, even though barely fit to play, is still France's best player, and he almost grabs a spectacular equaliser. He nicks the ball outside the area, turns, and curls a tremendous shot inches wide of the top corner with Sorensen stranded.

Meanwhile in Daejeon a classic counter-attack by Senegal ends with an emphatic strike from the edge of the area by Pape Bouba Diop to put them two up, and he gets a third off the underside of the bar before half time to make the rampant Africans clear group leaders on goal difference.

France can still go through, but they need to score three goals in the second half, and they seem to have used up all their luck in winning their previous two tournaments. Desailly heads a Zidane corner against the bar, and pounds the turf in frustration, and Wiltord tries to plough a lone furrow through the packed Danish defence before looking round in despair to ask who was supposed to be supporting him.

Then on sixty-seventh minutes Denmark rip the French defence apart. A clinical ball down the left wing splits Vincent Candela and Lilian Thuram, who raise their arms in a half-hearted appeal for an offside decision they know is not coming, and lets in Jesper Gronkjaer. The Chelsea man has time to pick out a cross for Jon Dahl Tomasson, and Desailly's stumble leaves him with all the time he needs to slide his shot under Fabien Barthez for 2–0.

Some of the Irish guys try to talk to the flamboyant Frenchman, who is not in the mood.

'You need four now, you know?'

'Hmmmph!'

'Four goals, to go through.'

'Hmmmmph!'

'And you haven't scored any goals in the tournament at all yet.'

'Shurrrooop!'

'I'm just saying, that now you need four goals and up till now you haven't scored a single one . . .'

'Shurrrooop!! Fook off!! You all fook off!!'

'But . . .'

'You speak again and I will do you 'arm!! Now fook off!'

On screen, Desailly tweaks Kasper Bogelund by the ear. The French are not great losers – mind you, they're a bit out of practice. If they need further confirmation that this is not to be their tournament, then watching Djibril Cisse's thunderous volley squirming out of Sorensen's grasp but wide of the post, or Trezeguet's close-in shot crashing down off the bar and out to safety will have provided it. The most telling image of France's campaign is probably Zidane's desperate attempt to control the ball in the Denmark area, clutching his damaged thigh as he runs.

Long before the final whistle our Frenchman has got up and left the bar, waving his arms at the screen, chuntering to himself, with a reprise of the earlier prophetic '*Au revoir, au revoir, au revoir . . .*' ringing in his ears.

Amazingly, Denmark's 2–0 win puts them top of the group, as the news of a thrilling second half in Daejeon comes through. Victor Pua, the Uruguay coach, threw caution to the winds and brought on two more strikers after half time – Richard Morales and Diego Forlan.

Forlan's first touch was a hopeless left-foot shot from way out that was going miles wide. It cannoned off a defender, however, and fell to Dario Silva, whose shot was much more accurate and the Senegal keeper could only beat it out to Morales who tucked it home. The Nacional attacker ripped off his pale blue number 18 shirt in jubilation, to reveal another one exactly like it underneath.

I saw a number of articles before the World Cup started about new shirt technology, about special extra-thin fabrics and aerated panels at the small of the back, to allow the players to function in the heat and the humidity. Morales clearly felt it was just a little parky out there.

On sixty-nine minutes an Alvaro Recoba free kick was headed clear to Forlan on the edge of the area, and he confounded critics of his poor – indeed, non-existent – scoring record at Manchester United by chesting the ball down and volleying a sensational goal to make it 3–2. Coach Victor Pua's assistant was caught on camera using a mobile phone when the Forlan goal went in, perhaps arranging a post-match press conference.

'Si, Señor Pua is going to resign . . . no, wait a minute, maybe not . . . !'

Senegal switched to abject panic mode, but held on until two minutes from time, when Morales flung himself to the deck to win an outrageous penalty. The unshaven Recoba of Inter Milan, reputedly the best-paid player on the planet, licked his lips nervously then slammed the equalising kick home, and now another goal would put Uruguay through ahead of Senegal, whose last-sixteen slot seemed done and dusted just forty-five minutes ago.

In a full injury-time flap, keeper Sylva galloped miles out of his goal in a doomed attempt to gather a throw-in. Gustavo Varela lashed a thirty-yard shot towards the empty net, and Lamine Diatta stooped desperately to head the ball up in the air. As it dropped towards the unmarked Morales three yards out Sylva and Diatta were sprawled helplessly on the floor, scrambling to their feet. Uruguay were all but in the next round, but incredibly Morales put his free header wide of the post.

So Denmark, with seven points, and Senegal, with five, are through, and Uruguay and France – the world champions – go out.

I wish Gary luck for this evening and pleasingly, when I ask what he plans to do between now and the kick-off, he doesn't give me any of this sanctimonious crap about only being here for the craic.

'I'm going up to the ground really early and then I'm going to walk about nervously for a couple of hours.'

I try to reassure him. 'You only need to win by two to be sure.'

'Yeah, two to be sure, to be sure . . .' he says.

Back to the room for a couple of hours, and on the way in I find that the Ireland team are also staying in the same Yokohama hotel as I am, and the official team bus is waiting at the back entrance. It has been decorated with pictures of the Irish stars in action – there's Holland, Kilbane, Quinn, Harte, Duff and Robbie Keane – and I check both sides just to see if there's an embarrassing photo of Roy Keane on there, but there isn't. I even check the back, just in case there's a larger-than-life snap of him walking his dog around the streets near his Cheshire home, which would have been a classy joke, but there isn't.

Around six the Irish lads start filtering through the hotel lobby. Mick McCarthy is one of the first, and he hangs around, sorting something out with the hotel manager. He is clutching a paperback in one hand – *The Painted House* by John Grisham, if you're interested – and a mobile phone in the other. When it rings it plays the theme from *Mission: Impossible*, but surely a two-goal win for his team isn't beyond the bounds of possibility tonight.

There are a few watery cheers and some quick snaps taken, and the boys are on their way. They are smaller than I thought they were, apart from Quinn, of course, who's huge.

After seeing the Irish team on their way I head off to the subway. As usual in Japan, finding any station involves nego-tiating the merchandising warrens of the department stores and arcades placed like obstacles in your path hoping to divert you from your journey into buying hand luggage or shoes. A train comes straightaway – naturally – and so I, being used to allowing oodles of extra time for any journey, having spent much of my life at the mercy of Connex trains in south London, get to Shin Yokohama far too early.

About a dozen blokes in green plastic fish costumes bundle past another group in ginger leprechaun beards that would pass muster at an Amish barn raising, so I know I'm in the right place.

The main drag past the station is a six-lane traffic fest, with Irish fans spilling off the pavements on either side. It is impossible to move freely so I wander off to make my way towards the stadium along a quieter parallel route, and suddenly all is calm. The buildings are tall, dark and looming in the twilight except one, a little way off, that is lit up like a Christmas tree. It seems to be calling to me. I have time to kill so I go to see what it is.

DREAM ECHO, the big illuminated sign on the front says.

It's a karaoke venue. And how. It's not like at home, where karaoke exists as an occasional speciality event in the back room of a pub. This is an eight-storey, seventy-two-room shrine dedicated to karaoke.

I love karaoke. I had karaoke at my last birthday party but one, and for every friend who said, 'If you make me do anything I'll stab you to death with a small fruit knife,' there were three or four who couldn't wait to share their version of *That's Life* or *It's Not Unusual*. It's about showing off, really, more than anything, and knowing how much I enjoy it is the only thing that makes me feel faintly guilty about slagging off Darius off of *Pop Idol*.

The word karaoke is derived from the Japanese words for 'empty' and 'orchestra', and the phenomenon first emerged in Japan in the seventies, possibly invented by a record-store manager in Osaka. The first machines were big square eight-track tape players, and salarymen in smoky bars would howl away into heavy-duty microphones while following the lyrics off a song sheet. Nowadays the technology is more sophisticated, and the words appear on a TV screen accompanied by a little video that usually has little or nothing at all to do with the song being massacred – a couple in soft focus stroll hand in hand along a beach, for example, while some frustrated accountant screams: *'Finish wiv my woman cuz she cudden help me wiv my mine . . .'*

A range of echoing effects designed to flatter the singer and subtly take the edge off for the listener have also been incorporated, leading to the karaoke machine acquiring the nickname 'the electronic geisha'.

Here in the land where football supporters feel the need to practise their chanting for fear of getting something wrong in public, it should perhaps not come as a surprise to find that not only are there karaoke bars in Japan, but there are also karaoke booths, karaoke boxes, karaoke kiosks, and karaoke private rooms. Small venues where an apprehensive karaokeant can practise on his own, check out that unexpected or long-forgotten middle eight, or just let rip without fear of being seen by anyone from work. And these are what Dream Echo is all about.

The only thing that gives me a moment's pause as I cross the threshold is that it looks and feels exactly like a brothel (I saw in a film once), and there is something uncomfortably masturbatory about solo karaoke. The place is run, naturally, by a big madame who is smoking nonchalantly and won't meet my eye.

'English?' I ask tentatively.

She nods: 'We do English here,' and I suddenly have the strong impression that I have asked for some particular kind of perversion, perhaps involving a bowler hat and a cricket bat.

I am given a book to flick through, and although it has an almost entirely nude lady on the cover, thankfully it is full of song titles. At this point I am not a hundred per cent certain that I am going to indulge – after all, it's half past seven now and the game kicks off at half past eight. Then I spot *Only Yesterday* by The Carpenters in the book – they know how to hook a punter in this place – and I've got my money out and booked myself into a solo karaoke box for an hour before I could stop myself.

The madame tucks my large-amount-of-yen note into her cleavage – really, she does – and then, a somewhat bizarre touch, she rings a little bell, whereupon a subservient little hunchback appears and, with a series of grunts and nudges, shows me to my private karaoketorium.

The room is a bit like a living room in a council flat. There's a rather battered old sofa, a coffee table, a picture of a waterfall on the wall, a rack full of slippers which, as usual, are all far too small for my great flat feet, and there, at the end of the room, the karaoke console. I kind of miss the audience element, but at least you don't have to wait your turn with this set-up. I experiment with the remote control, and *All By Myself* by Eric Carmen, an appropriate number to begin with, I think, kicks off.

Next I muck it up, and get five minutes of some execrable jappo-pop with hieroglyphic lyrics. It is unbearable, and I'm on my hands and knees on the point of ripping the plug out of the electric socket when it mercifully comes to an end.

I find that I don't know *South of the Border* or *I Write the Songs* quite as well as I thought I did, but *Don't Let the Sun Go Down on Me, Without You* and, of course, *Only Yesterday* slip by enjoyably, and I'm just doing the guitar solo at the end of *Goodbye to Love*, making the 'neeeeyow!!' noise with my mouth – which is something you absolutely can't get away with in a karaoke bar – when the phone goes.

It suddenly occurs to me that this would be quite a bad time to have to do a piece for talkSPORT, but I scrabble around and find a mute button, and anyway it is David. He's inside the stadium, in his seat, and he wants to know where I am so he can look for me.

'I'm . . . on my way,' I say, suddenly realising just how fine I am cutting it. I have to leave without looking back in anger, which is what I was about to be doing, and run to the Yokohama International Stadium up the road.

Most of the 65,000 crowd are already inside, so I make it through the security checks and smiley welcomes from people in yellow waterproofs pretty quickly, and find my way into Green Block just as the game is kicking off.

Yokohama is not the best stadium for watching football, not by a long chalk. There is a running track all round it for a start, which has been cunningly disguised by covering it in

朝日新聞　速報号外　2002FIFAワールドカップ™

朝日新聞 ご購読のお申し込みは フリーダイヤル 0120·33·0843

64のドラマ刻んだ

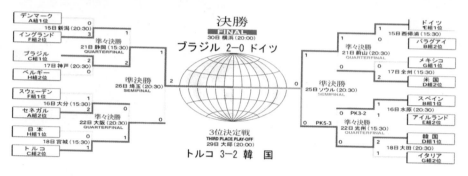

決勝 FINAL
30日 横浜 (20:00)
ブラジル 2-0 ドイツ

3位決定戦 THIRD PLACE PLAY-OFF
29日 大邱 (20:00)
トルコ 3-2 韓 国

左側（上から）:
- デンマーク A組1位 ── 15日 新潟 (20:30) 0
- イングランド F組2位 ── 3
- 準々決勝 21日 静岡 (15:30) QUARTERFINAL
- ブラジル C組1位 ── 17日 神戸 (20:30) 2
- ベルギー H組2位 ── 1
- 準決勝 26日 埼玉 (20:30) SEMIFINAL
- スウェーデン F組1位 ── 16日 大分 (15:30) 1
- セネガル A組2位 ── 2
- 準々決勝 22日 大阪 (20:30) QUARTERFINAL
- 日 本 H組1位 ── 18日 宮城 (15:30) 0
- トルコ C組2位 ── 1

右側（上から）:
- ドイツ E組1位 ── 15日 西帰浦 (15:30) 1
- パラグアイ B組2位 ── 0
- 準々決勝 21日 蔚山 (20:30) QUARTERFINAL
- メキシコ G組1位 ── 17日 全州 (15:30) 0
- 米 国 D組2位 ── 2
- 準決勝 25日 ソウル (20:30) SEMIFINAL
- スペイン B組1位 ── 16日 水原 (20:30) PK3-2
- アイルランド E組2位 ──
- 準々決勝 22日 光州 (15:30) QUARTERFINAL PK5-3
- 韓 国 D組1位 ── 18日 大田 (15:30)
- イタリア G組2位 ──

決勝トーナメント

90分間で同点の場合は前後半15分ずつのゴールデンゴール（Vゴール）方式による延長。それでも勝敗が決まらなければPK戦

大荒れ1次リーグ　相次ぎ強豪敗退

上位2チームが決勝トーナメント進出。勝ち点で順位を決め、勝利は3、引き分け1、敗戦0点。延長はない。勝ち点が同じなら①得失点差②総得点③当該チームの試合の勝ち点④同得失点差⑤同総得点の優先度で順位を決め、それでも同じ場合は抽選

背景が赤い国名は決勝トーナメント進出　白は1次リーグ敗退

グループ A

	デンマーク	セネガル	ウルグアイ	フランス	勝点	得点	失点
デンマーク		△1-1 6日 大邱	○2-1 6日 大邱	○2-0 11日 仁川	7	5	2
セネガル	△1-1 6日 大邱		△3-3 11日 水原	④ 31日 ソウル	5	5	4
ウルグアイ	○2-1 6日 大邱	△3-3 11日 水原		○0-0 6日 釜山	2	4	5
フランス	○2-0 11日 仁川	④ 31日 ソウル	○0-0 6日 釜山		1	0	3

グループ B

	スペイン	パラグアイ	南アフリカ	スロベニア	勝点	得点	失点
スペイン		△1-1 7日 全州	○3-2 12日 大田	○3-1 12日 光州	9	9	4
パラグアイ	△1-1 7日 全州		△2-2 2日 釜山	○3-1 12日 西帰浦	4	6	6
南アフリカ	○2-3 12日 大田	△2-2 2日 釜山		○1-0 8日 大邱	4	5	5
スロベニア	○1-3 12日 光州	○1-3 12日 西帰浦	○0-1 8日 大邱		0	2	7

グループ C

	ブラジル	トルコ	コスタリカ	中国	勝点	得点	失点
ブラジル		○2-1 3日 蔚山	○5-2 8日 西帰浦	○4-0 8日 西帰浦	9	11	3
トルコ	●1-2 3日 蔚山		△1-1 9日 仁川	○3-0 13日 ソウル	4	5	3
コスタリカ	○2-5 8日 西帰浦	△1-1 9日 仁川		○2-0 4日 光州	4	5	6
中国	○0-4 8日 西帰浦	○0-3 13日 ソウル	○0-2 4日 光州		0	0	9

グループ D

	韓 国	米 国	ポルトガル	ポーランド	勝点	得点	失点
韓 国		△1-1 10日 大邱	○1-0 14日 仁川	○2-0 4日 釜山	7	4	1
米 国	△1-1 10日 大邱		○1-3 5日 水原	○1-3 14日 大田	4	5	6
ポルトガル	○1-0 14日 仁川	○3-2 5日 水原		○0-4 10日 全州	3	6	4
ポーランド	○0-2 4日 釜山	○3-1 14日 大田	○4-0 10日 全州		3	3	7

グループ E

	ドイツ	アイルランド	カメルーン	サウジアラビア	勝点	得点	失点
ドイツ		△1-1 5日 茨城	○2-0 11日 静岡	○8-0 1日 札幌	7	11	1
アイルランド	△1-1 5日 茨城		△1-1 11日 新潟	○3-0 11日 横浜	5	5	2
カメルーン	○0-2 11日 静岡	△1-1 11日 新潟		○1-0 6日 埼玉	4	2	3
サウジアラビア	○0-8 1日 札幌	○0-3 11日 横浜	○0-1 6日 埼玉		0	0	12

グループ F

	スウェーデン	イングランド	アルゼンチン	ナイジェリア	勝点	得点	失点
スウェーデン		△1-1 2日 埼玉	△1-1 12日 宮城	○2-1 7日 神戸	5	4	3
イングランド	△1-1 2日 埼玉		○1-0 7日 札幌	△0-0 12日 大阪	5	2	1
アルゼンチン	△1-1 12日 宮城	●0-1 7日 札幌		○1-0 2日 茨城	4	2	2
ナイジェリア	○1-2 7日 神戸	△0-0 12日 大阪	○0-1 2日 茨城		1	1	3

グループ G

	メキシコ	イタリア	クロアチア	エクアドル	勝点	得点	失点
メキシコ		△1-1 13日 大分	○1-0 3日 新潟	○2-1 9日 宮城	7	4	2
イタリア	△1-1 13日 大分		○1-2 8日 茨城	○2-0 3日 札幌	4	4	3
クロアチア	○0-1 3日 新潟	○2-1 8日 茨城		○1-0 13日 横浜	3	2	3
エクアドル	○1-2 9日 宮城	○0-2 3日 札幌	○0-1 13日 横浜		3	2	4

グループ H

	日 本	ベルギー	ロシア	チュニジア	勝点	得点	失点
日 本		△2-2 4日 埼玉	○1-0 9日 横浜	○2-0 14日 大阪	7	5	2
ベルギー	△2-2 4日 埼玉		○3-2 14日 静岡	△1-1 10日 大分	5	6	5
ロシア	○0-1 9日 横浜	○2-3 14日 静岡		○2-0 5日 神戸	3	4	4
チュニジア	○0-2 14日 大阪	△1-1 10日 大分	○0-2 5日 神戸		1	1	5

World Cup wallchart, Japanese style

My talkSPOR studio facilit

The headquarters of the Osato Corporation, 'You Only Live Twice'

Saitama, 2 June. Buy World Cup bonsai tree, flag made from origami cranes, cheap shirt from Thailand

Because of football, is no more Buddha . . .

Saitama stadium, three hours to kick off

Campbell scores with his only decent header of the match

Mickey, the ITV Digital monkey and Johnny Vegas (unseen)

WE WANT 2 TICKETS PLEASE!! OWEN HARGREAVES WE LOVE BECKHAM

Some Owen Hargreaves fans

Sapporo, June. The author waits to be beamed aboard the mothership

Odori park, Sapporo

David Beckham's 'better than four years ago' wins Understatement of the World Cup

A tiny struggling actor dressed up as Doraemon, the blue robot cat, lures children to the undersea domain of the Head Morlock

Japanese snack

Osaka: 'a khazi' – Cube

Yokohama, 11 June. R. Keane leaves hotel to go to stadium ...

... where he plans to mount an unsuspecting Damien Duff

Osaka, 12 June. Pelé's Player of the Tournament gets his head down so as not to be distracted by the glare off Nigeria's kit

Niigata, 15 June.
(Top left) Beckham
groupies outside the
team hotel.
(Top right) There he
is, look, over there, near
the middle

Rio gleefully
celebrates the
arrival of some
unpixillated
porn . . .

. . . possibly featuring Snow White and
a couple of zebras, as seen at the Beppu
Sex Museum . . .

. . . or a huge Aso.
. . . ooking down into the cloud maker

Boiling
mud in a
jigoku,
Beppu

The A-bomb memorials in
Nagasaki and Hiroshima

MM, the King of
Comedy, with his
New York subway tie

Loopy Huis
ten Bosch,
with its
windmills and
clog outlets

At the oldest
football ground
in the world, in
front of the
home end

One of the newest football
grounds in the world,
Shizuoka, 21 June

Michael Owen scores the
opening goal …

… but by half time, at 1-1, the
author is fearing the worst …

… and in the second half it happens, as
Seaman decides to keep goal according to
the laws of snooker, with one foot always
on the deck

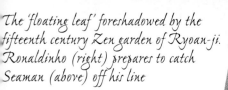

The 'floating leaf' foreshadowed by the
fifteenth century Zen garden of Ryoan-ji.
Ronaldinho (right) prepares to catch
Seaman (above) off his line

Attractions from Theme Park Japan – Todai-ji in
Nara (replica) and Kinkaju-ji in Kyoto (replica,

The bloke next to me
watching Brazil v Turkey
semi-final on a tiny telly
while sitting inside
Saitama stadium where
the match is taking place

SomeMexican

Toasthead
toepokes the
winner

Batistuta
and Kahn
provided some
of the World
Cup's lighter
moments

Yokohama, 30 June. The World Cup. Brazil
won it. Not the Germans (so that's something . . .)

green astroturf, so you are a long way from the action, and you really feel it too. The Irish playing in green, the same green as the pitch, not to mention the surrounding area, doesn't help matters much. Then the rake of the seating is quite shallow, not that anyone was sitting down near me. My seat is smack in the middle of a large and exuberant leprechaun party, as it happens, so I decide to look for David and Tomoko before laying claim to it. David has an empty seat next to him, as he did in Sapporo, coincidentally, so I can join him rather than having to answer embarrassing questions about my lack of a little ginger beard and a pixie hat.

David is particularly concerned with how the authorities would keep the crowds in touch with events in Shizuoka at the Cameroon v Germany game, now that matches are being played simultaneously. There is a big screen here – surely they could put the latest score up from time to time with the tiniest amount of forethought and planning.

I remember going to a match in Florence between Austria and USA at exactly this stage of Italia 90. Italy were playing Czechoslovakia the same night, and nearly all of the crowd in Florence had come with little transistor radios to keep in touch with that game. When Roberto Baggio scored one of the goals of the tournament, the huge cheer and Mexican Wave dwarfed anything that happened in response to the game in front of us all night.

The game kicks off, and for the first few minutes it's all Robbie Keane. He's winning a free kick on the left, he's setting up a chance for Kevin Kilbane, he's barging around in the penalty box. We are in the far distance behind the goal which Ireland are attacking, and after six minutes Keane sticks the ball into the back of it. A high looping cross comes in from Gary Kelly on the right, and Keane keeps his eye on it all the way and nails the volley under the keeper from the edge of the box. He's changed his goal celebration – he's not a cartwheeling gunslinger any more, now he's Robin Hood.

Funnily enough the goal is so early that I feel a bit cheated. I've come for some good old-fashioned nail biting, and this is in danger of becoming a breeze.

Speaking of breezes, there was a weather forecast earlier on. Here in Asia the weather is much bigger than at home. Where in Britain the weather bulletins will draw fine distinctions between the cloudiness of much of northern England and the sunny spells in Cornwall and the West Country, out here we are more often than not looking at satellite pictures of weather systems the size of half of China. Tonight there was a warning about a typhoon coming in from the Pacific, and after about a quarter of an hour of the match it arrives, bringing driving rain and strong blustery wind. There is some cover where we are sitting, but nothing like enough.

You'd think the rain would suit Ireland rather better than Saudi Arabia, who come, after all, from a desert, but after a confident start buoyed by Keane's goal the game begins to drift away from them, and by half time Shay Given has had to make a couple of saves from Al Jahani and Al Yami, and the impressive Nawaf Al Temyat is causing the Irish midfield one or two problems.

During the first half there has been nothing, no word from Shizuoka, and so Tomoko telephones a friend who is watching the other game at home. He tells her that it is still 0–0, and that Carsten Ramelow has been sent off. This is good, as it means that Ireland don't need a second (yet), but if Cameroon can make their one-man advantage tell then Germany could go out.

In the second half Niall Quinn comes on to play up front with Robbie Keane, allowing Damien Duff free rein to play as a left winger. He spends the first few minutes of the half running the Saudi right back ragged. If only he could cross the ball Ireland could be two or three up.

A frisson shivers through the crowd as thousands of text

messages arrive bringing the news that the Germans are one up. A young Irish lad passes this on to us, with a look of raw panic in his eyes, although actually this makes Ireland's position stronger. A Cameroon equaliser, now that would be a problem . . .

Just past what commentators like to refer to as the hour mark Kevin Kilbane is fouled on the left wing. Steve Staunton swings the free kick into the box, where Gary Breen wriggles between two defenders, stretches out his long right leg, and somehow steers the ball into the goal with the outside of his right boot. It is an extremely good finish, provoking the unusual thought that I haven't seen a goal quite like it before. Breen is the only player at the tournament not on the books of a professional club at the moment – his performances here won't do him any harm finding a new job.

So now it's 2–0, and it's all right for us to want Cameroon to come back in Shizuoka. Next time we hear anything from Tomoko's friend, though, it's more bad news. First Patrick Suffo has been sent off, his favourite way of making the headlines – he was centrally involved in the shambles at Sheffield United last season where Neil Warnock tried to get a game abandoned after the Blades had three sent off by withdrawing a couple more players 'injured'. Then, a couple of minutes later, Klose scores his fifth goal of the tournament and virtually seals Germany's place at the top of the Group E table. This, oddly, means Klose is the leader in the race for the Golden Boot without having used his boots to score any of his goals, apart from to stand up in while he heads them home. He may not win the boot, but surely the Golden Forehead is his for the taking.

Saudi Arabia bring on a sub with an impossibly fat arse for an international footballer – I'm sorry, but there it is; it puts me in mind of that bloke on Esther Rantzen's *The Big Time* who got to play in Tommy Smith's testimonial – as though they've decided, 'Oh well, we've been knocked out, let's give our fat fan a game just for the hell of it.' Or perhaps he's a member of the Royal Family . . .

Four minutes from time Mark Kinsella sends Damien Duff through on the Saudi goal. His shot is straight at Mohammed Al Daeyea, but it squirms through the keeper's hands ('a great shot-stopper' – T. Gubba) and plops into the net. Duff bows graciously – when in Rome – and Al Daeyea kicks the net in frustration and embarrassment. He has become the most-capped player in international football tonight (171), and his stated ambition (naturally) is to play for Manchester United. He shouldn't give up all hope – after all, Massimo Taibi got a couple of games for them.

Three–nil, and it's been a straightforward job of work in the end. Duff and Keane have been a constant threat, and Duff in particular looks an absolute star in the making. He's strong, he's fast, and he beats opponents with gleeful ease. Roy who . . . ?

David selflessly throws himself into a group of dancing Irish fans so that Tomoko can get a photo for the *Evening Standard*, and then we make our way out. As at Saitama, all the exits seem to lead to one path, and the ten-minute walk back to Shin Yokohama station takes well over an hour of tightly packed shuffling and inching along. There is one brief moment of interest as a small earth tremor rumbles underfoot and people look at one another and say: 'Did you feel that? Or was it just me?'

And then I lose touch with David and Tomoko. Very slowly. One moment they're right next to me, next thing I know they're about five feet away . . .

Late at night I see the highlights of the Germany v Cameroon encounter. Salomon Olembe should have scored in the first half, but the monster Oliver Kahn just terrified him into fluffing the chance. Ironically, it was Cameroon boss Winfried Schafer who gave the young Oliver Kahn his break while coach at Karlsruhe years ago. It looks as though the big keeper has been reading his own clippings and he's becoming annoyingly arrogant. His cocksure attempt to catch Olembe's second effort one-handed almost backfired as he palmed it towards the goal, and then he punched a free kick which he should have caught and it hit an astonished Christophe Metzelder smack in the face. It would be nice to see him get his come-uppance some time soon.

The German goals were quite good ones. Miroslav Klose attracted four defenders to him in midfield, and then threaded a ball through to Marco Bode, racing through unnoticed, and he just passed it into the corner. Then Klose demonstrated his uncanny ability to lose markers, as he scored his fifth completely unchallenged headed goal in three games from a couple of yards out, getting on the end of a Michael Ballack cross.

The Spanish ref A.L. Nieto established a new World Cup record by flashing the yellow card sixteen times, with Ramelow and Suffo seeing it twice. The previous record of twelve had stood since about quarter past five, when the Dutch ref J. Wegereef blew time on the card-littered Senegal v Uruguay game thinking he'd secured his place in football history for ever. Before that? It was a game at USA 94 between Mexico and Bulgaria which harvested a measly ten.

13
Osaka

'I don't usually sunbathe in that kind of heat,
let alone play football.'
– Rio Ferdinand

12 JUNE

Up at dawn to get the Shinkansen from Shin Yokohama to Shin Osaka. You're supposed to be able to see Mount Fuji from this train, but it's too cloudy and I only get a glimpse of the lower slopes and not the trademark cone. Still, plenty of time for that.

When I get to the hotel it's too early for them to have got a room ready and so I go off to have some breakfast with Nick, who is waiting for me in the lobby. I am a little surprised to see him sitting there, and he explains that he is monumentally bored.

'I was hoping some interesting things might have happened to you and I could live them vicariously,' he says.

The Cube, when he appears shortly after, is also unimpressed with Japan's second city. 'Osaka is a khazi,' he mutters with all his customary charm.

Nick has dragged The Cube off for a spot of fishing during their stay here, in what sounds like a deeply unattractive venue – a canal on an industrial estate. There is a famous 'Fishing Bridge' nearby – *Ebisu-bashi* – but it turns out that it is a place where trendy young blokes try to snare girls in mini-skirts rather than any actual fish. This is where hundreds of Japanese fans leapt into the Dotonborigawa river to celebrate the win over Russia the other day. The Russians, less pleased, rioted outside the Kremlin, eight thousand of them, setting fire to cars, and two people were killed.

Nick and Cube have also, to their great glee, bumped into the Sheffield Wednesday-stroke-England band in the street.

'Which one of you lot has got the scarf?' Nick demanded, and when they produced their 'Tebbit test' for his inspection he and Cube took them through their mistakes one by one in careful detail.

In the papers a fevered build-up is under way to Japan's third game, against Tunisia here in Osaka the day after tomorrow. Kazuyuki Toda is required to insist that his bright red mohican is not inspired by David Beckham.

'I just wanted to look a bit tough,' he says. Yeah, like Lulu, mate . . .

Early afternoon Nick, Cube and I go down by subway to Nagai and climb out into the baking sunshine. Temperatures are in the mid-nineties, apparently, and there are an awful lot of bare torsos on display. We were led to believe that this was something that would shock the locals to the very core of their being, but all the Osakans I can see are remarkably unconcerned.

Two young Japanese girls pass by sporting the full England fashion set. They have white England shirts, the cross of St George painted on their faces, hats, flags, the works. And on their sleeves are little enamel badges featuring the club crest of Stoke City FC.

We get into the great heaving queue for the beer stall, where the vendors are fighting a losing battle trying to keep cans cool. They have big bins full of ice, but the demand is so great that they have no sooner plunged a load more cans into the bins than they are having to pick them out again, still tepid, and sell them.

Under a tree nearby, Nick and Cube run into a bunch of lads from Stoke that they know. Nick introduces me to a great hairy bloke called Animal, and before I have time to wonder whether he behaves like one or just looks like one, Animal has grasped my hand and shaken it enthusiastically, saying earnestly, 'How are you doing? *Very* pleased to meet you.'

Whatever sort of animal he's meant to be, it's a very polite one. I tell Animal about the Japanese girls I have just seen with Stoke City FC badges on. He gives me a great wink, and pulls out a plastic bag full of these badges which he has brought with him.

'Just spreading the word,' he says.

The same girls come past a few minutes later and get Animal to write 7 BECKHAM on their forearms with a red felt pen.

Eggy, a policeman back home, is telling a story about how he and a gang of Stoke lads found themselves drinking in a bar until eight in the morning after the Argentina game in Sapporo with the former England captain Terry Butcher.

'Reno went into the toilet, wrapped bog paper all round his head, covered himself with tomato ketchup, and then came running out screaming, "Caged tigers! Caged tigers!" We all pissed ourselves.'

David rings up. He and Tomoko have just arrived at Nagai station and are somewhere in the milling throng. I tell him I'm standing under a tree next to a bloke called Animal. He finds us really easily.

We discuss the various rumours that we've both heard (so they must be true). Apparently the Nigerians have given up, they've stopped training altogether, they're treating their last few days in Japan as one big holiday, they've all been out shopping, and the Nigerian FA have flown in crates of Nigerian beer for them. Also, for good measure, Rio Ferdinand is going to Manchester United for 35 million quid . . .

As we walk to the ground we pass the now-familiar clutch of sponsors' displays, the inflatable McDonald's, and that idiotic

Hyundai test-your-strength fairground thing. I turn to point it out scornfully to David, and he's running over to have a go on it. It's a bit of a naff scam, really. Bash it with the hammer, and if it lights up all the way to the top then you win this gleaming Hyundai car which the two pretty girls are sitting on, is what it looks like. David lights up all the lights and wins a carrier bag with a baseball cap and a Hyundai catalogue in it.

Inside the Nagai Stadium it is mortally hot. I have climbed one flight of stairs and I feel as if I need to lie down for half an hour. Of course, I am not in the first flush of youth nor the absolute peak of physical fitness, but even so, I wouldn't like to have to play ninety minutes out there. Dom is in his seat already, and we are facing right into the blinding, boiling-hot sun.

'They're going absolutely mental back home, you know, about the World Cup,' Dom says. 'Parties in the street, people skiving off work, the lot.'

Susan told me that Peter and John are being allowed to come into school late – or early if they want to watch it in the school hall.

Amazingly it appears that Dom has heard the one about the Nigerians going shopping and having crates of beer flown in as well. I can't help thinking that people have been making up the rumours that they want to hear.

The two teams appear, England in red, Nigeria in an unbelievably retina-busting fluorescent green kit. It's a lot easier to see than the Irish green last night, and I shouldn't think any of their fans are going to be hit by traffic on the way home. In the bright sunshine they seem to leave after-images as they walk along.

Sven has stayed with the same side that played most of the game in Sapporo. Owen Hargreaves is not fit, and Trevor Sinclair – his substitute last time – starts in his place. Emile Heskey has recovered from his knock, and so Teddy Sheringham returns to the dugout.

Nigeria make five changes, including bringing in a nineteen-year-old keeper, Vincent Enyeama, and a centre back whom I've seen playing against Oldham for Macclesfield Town in Efetobore Sodje – he scored the winner that day, as well, bandanna and all.

Nigeria kick off, and play keep ball for a while. Jay-Jay Okocha shows us his trademark bit of skill straightaway, rolling his studs over the top of the ball and shimmying Sinclair and Heskey after his shadow before knocking a long crossfield ball out to the left wing from inside his own half. Moments later Okocha has it again, this time on the edge of the England area, probing for an opening. His attempted through pass goes astray and Ashley Cole becomes the first Englishman to touch the ball. After a minute.

That first minute sets the pattern for the first twenty or so. England pull everyone behind the ball and allow Nigeria to pass it around in midfield. Okocha is pulling the strings, although there is one very enjoyable moment when he tries his stud-rolling trick on Sinclair again, and the West Ham man sees it coming and tackles him so hard that the ball flies high into the back of the stand.

Nigeria look relaxed and competent, England tentative and hesitant. We watch Nigeria hold the ball and knock it around, but whenever we get it we 'try to hit the front men early', which is manager-speak for punting it hopefully forwards, and give possession away. Julius Aghahowa is seeing way too much of the ball for my liking, mostly on the right wing, and Ashley Cole seems to be staying very close to Sol Campbell for some reason, only darting out to left back when danger threatens.

Gradually one or two more hopeful signs emerge. England get a couple of corners, both of which cause the young Nigerian keeper to flap helplessly, and then finally a long ball from Butt finds its mark, Mills on the overlap. The resulting low cross is toe-poked goalwards by Heskey, and young Enyeama makes a decent save. Beckham then skips and turns on the edge of the area, but his shot curls straight at the keeper.

The band crank into life over to our left, to much eye-rolling and tutting from the crowd around us, who are too busy biting their nails to join in with the bloody Self-Preservation Society. I fear for the health of one bald man in front of us, who is determinedly wearing his woollen England scarf, and who seems to have heat haze coming up off his head.

It must be hellish out there on the pitch. At one point Aghahowa goes down under a challenge from Campbell and stays down. Nicky Butt sportingly boots the ball into the crowd, and to a man the England team gallop over to the dugout to get bottles of water or isotonic whatsit to rehydrate with.

After an increasingly tense half hour Udeze attacks the left edge of our area, steps on the ball, and kicks Nicky Butt on the knee as he falls. Incredibly the referee gives Nigeria a free kick for this – maybe the heat is melting his eyeballs – and Okocha whips the ball to Seaman's right-hand post. Muffing set pieces is something of a speciality of the pony-tailed one, as we know, and he drops this one at Aghahowa's feet while crashing into the woodwork, but mercifully we are spared having to watch the acrobatic flick-flack celebration as the Shakhtar Donetsk man pokes the free gift wide.

Towards half time England seem to be getting on top. Rio Ferdinand starts to look like a man who is getting the measure of Aghahowa, Nigeria's most dangerous attacker, and he's not only taking care of his own business but he's sweeping up behind the sluggish Campbell as well. Sinclair is coming into more central areas to link up with Scholes and Butt, and Michael Owen is beginning to make the Nigerian back line look panicky.

At one point he picks up the ball in space in midfield, turns with it, drops a shoulder and Joseph Yobo in the same movement, and races into the area with the bright green defenders trailing in his wake. Just as he pulls the trigger, though, Isaac Okoronwo makes a desperate last-ditch lunge that deflects the ball out. It looked as if it would have been a goal – we don't even get the corner.

Just before half time England come closest to opening the scoring. Our best spell of pressure around the Nigerian box culminates in Paul Scholes picking up a short pass from Butt and unleashing a fantastic swerving shot towards the top right-hand corner. It looks a goal all the way, but somehow the dodgy young keeper gets his left hand to it and turns it onto the post. Terrific shot, amazing save.

Half time, and Dom and I are tense, wound up tight. We agree that the Nigerian keeper looks terrible under high crosses, and can't understand why England haven't got more of them in. All Ashley Cole's deliveries have been low and cut out by the first defender, and even Beckham's have been disappointing. And Cole seems to be concerned about protecting the lumbering Campbell and exposing our left wing for some reason.

We retreat to the sanctuary of the shade under the stand, and sample the refreshment options – cold beer (warm) and hot dogs (freezing cold).

The rumour rippling around from conversation to conversation is that Sweden v Argentina is also 0–0, and that Claudio Caniggia has been sent off. This is astonishing news, as all the team talk has centred on whether Gabriel Batistuta or Hernan Crespo would play up front, and no one has even considered the possibility that Marcelo Bielsa might plump for the 35-year-old shot-kneed Italia 90 veteran for such a crucial game. Well, well . . .

Back into the cauldron, and the heat is like a wall across the end of the access tunnel. There's a bloke in a full-sized furry lion costume – I shouldn't think he'll be conscious much longer.

The second half gets under way, and England start to press Nigeria back into their shell. Scholes and Butt are neat and tidy in the middle, Owen and Sinclair are working hard. The

Africans are reduced to the occasional breakaway, always it seems by Julius Aghahowa, and each time Rio Ferdinand picks his pocket and brings the ball clear.

After about ten minutes the bloody band start up again with *England Till I Die.*

'Sooner the better,' Dom mutters.

Then suddenly their ghastly racket is being drowned out by a rising chorus of 'One Nil to the Sweden, One Nil to the Sweden . . .' but whether this is news from Miyagi or wishful thinking is not clear.

The players seem momentarily to shake off the torpor that this game is slipping into, and first Aghahowa has a chance, which Rio snuffs out, and then England have a good opening. Heskey has the ball down by the corner flag with Okoronkwo at his back. As usual, Emile is trying to wrestle the ball under control under his feet, then suddenly, with great expertise, he uses his big arse to steer the defender away, turns, and whips a low cross along the six-yard line which the lunging Owen just fails to connect with. Shortly after this Heskey makes way, as usual, for Teddy Sheringham.

Ashley Cole begins to come into the game more and more as an attacking force down the left, and he finally makes Sodje look like a Crewe player, dumping him on his backside and whipping in his first decent cross of the match. Owen is so surprised he can't react in time, and the ball bounces off his thighs to Sheringham, who scoops a great chance into orbit from eight yards out.

Owen makes way now for Darius Vassell, and England retreat into a 4–5–1 with Teddy on his own up front. Vassell tries to run at the Nigerians, but his team mates are all spent and no one can keep up to support him. After that he just tucks in on the right.

The last ten minutes are tense, because anything might yet happen, but in truth it never really looks as if it's going to. Wayne Bridge comes on to shore up the defence, and England have clearly settled for the draw. There is a sudden buzz that Argentina have equalised, but as long as we don't concede one it doesn't really affect us. The Nigerians start to show off some of their fancy footwork, standing on the ball, stepping over, but all in the centre circle rather than the six-yard box, so let them. Okocha tries to put one over on Paul Scholes, who has seen the trick before and thumps the ball away.

And then, rather anti-climactically, it's over, it's a 0–0 draw, and for the second time in two days I've been to see a potentially exciting inter-continental World Cup encounter that has turned out to be just a job of work for the players.

England will now play Denmark in Niigata, and it's easy to see why this would suit England better than meeting the unpredictable Senegalese in Oita. It will be an evening kick-off, and Niigata is in the cooler north, whereas if we had topped the group we'd be playing in possibly the hottest of the World Cup venues in the middle of the afternoon against the most impressive of the African nations. The experience of playing in this afternoon's 94 degree cauldron did not look like one they will be over-keen to repeat.

As Dom and I make our way out some people are already making their arrangements for Niigata. A smug fat bloke next to us is on the mobile phone, bellowing at the top of his voice, not because the connection is bad, but because he wants everyone to know just how sorted he is.

'Yeah . . . category 2, OK, yeah . . . six hundred dollars . . . ? Yeah, that is a done deal, my friend . . .'

And then – I'm not sure how – the news spreads that Sweden v Argentina has finished 1–1, and the rather subdued procession towards Nagai station turns into a party after all:

You can stick your Batistuta up your arse!
You can stick your Batistuta up your arse!

You can stick your Batistuta, stick your Batistuta,
Stick your Batistuta up your arse!

Etc . . .

In the warren of little back streets behind our hotel Nick has located a perfect bar for the evening. It's long, and thin, and has a row of large plasma television sets all along one wall, some of which will be showing Spain v South Africa, and some Paraguay v Slovenia. And even though there's only room for about a dozen people in there, it's not a problem, because he has been down there already and reserved about half the bar stools in the place. He's turning Japanese, I think he's turning Japanese. I really think so . . .

Nick, Cube and I get down there in time for the start, and David joins us too, as does Theo with his Palm Pilot. During the second half this turns out to be an essential piece of equipment. It's not a great name for a gadget, though, is it? I'm constantly reminded of a friend of mine who used to describe his own habit of watching pornography by himself as 'sitting in the pilot's chair', and maybe that does actually tell you something about the Palm Pilot's target market.

David keeps looking at his phone to check it's still working.

'I was sitting with Norman and Zoe,' he explains. 'You know, Fatboy and Zoe Ball? They took my number and said they were going to call. We'll probably end up going out somewhere later . . .'

Spain are top of the group with six points, and are definitely through to the last sixteen. The only way that they can be pushed into second place is if South Africa beat them tonight. Jomo Sono's team currently have four points, while Paraguay have only one, so a draw will be enough for Bafana Bafana. If they lose, however, and Paraguay win, then it will be down to goal difference. Slovenia, with their tearful coach and their star player sent home, are already out of it.

Spain score first, through Raul on four minutes, when Andre Arendse embarrassingly spills an overhit Mendieta through ball at the feet of the Real forward. This opens the door for Paraguay, but things aren't going well for Cesare Maldini's men, for whom Carlos Paredes is sent off after twenty-two minutes for flooring Milenko Acimovic.

Benni McCarthy hooks in a volleyed equaliser for South Africa to theoretically give them the point they need after half an hour, and then, on the stroke of half time, Paraguay's barmy keeper Jose Luis Chilavert deflects Acimovic's low cross into his own goal, nutmegging himself in the process, to put Slovenia one up.

At this point the mathematics are firmly in South Africa's favour, even when Gaizka Mendieta restores Spain's advantage direct from a free kick, also right on half time.

The familiar figure of Lucas Radebe, incredibly playing after missing the whole season injured for Leeds United, nods South Africa level again from a corner in the fifty-third minute, and it's looking good for big Jomo.

Then, however, the tide turns. In Seogwipo, Cesare 'Cancer Man' Maldini brings on Jorge Campos and plays with three up front. Then, in Daejeon, Raul pops up at the back post to head home a superb Joaquin cross and it's 3–2 to Spain.

Maldini chucks on yet another striker, Nelson Cuevas, in a desperate attempt to turn things round, and within a few minutes the River Plate man has scored an equaliser, twisting his way into the area from the right wing and squeezing a left-foot shot in at the near post. Minutes later Campos, the other sub, hammers in a raking low shot from long range, and Paraguay are 2–1 ahead.

Now Theo's Palm Pilot is working overtime, and he determines that another goal for Spain – which seems quite likely – would put Paraguay and South Africa level on points and with identical goals-for-and-against records, both 5–6. The game between the two countries finished 2–2, so they would have to be separated by lots.

Has this ever happened before? When teams finished level in earlier World Cups, before television schedules and the like, the organisers would have the elbow room to set up extra play-off matches. There were three of these in 1958, for example, with quarter-final places at stake, in which Northern Ireland beat Czechoslovakia, Wales beat Hungary, and England lost to the Soviet Union. Since lots became an option, though, I don't know of an occasion when they have actually been called into use.

I remember being in Italy in 1990 with a group of Scottish friends. We'd been at the desperately unlucky 1–0 defeat by Brazil in Turin the day before, and were watching Uruguay play South Korea in their last group game. In that tournament the best four of the six teams placed third in their group tables would go through to the second phase, and as the game trundled towards a 0–0 draw it dawned on us that if that was the final score then Uruguay, Scotland and Austria would all be level pegging for the last available qualification place. We started singing:

> *We're going in the hat,*
> *We're going in the hat,*
> *We're going in,*
> *We're going in the hat . . .*

Which was all very enjoyable, the more so when Moray suddenly said: 'Maybe it's not a hat, maybe it's a pouch.'

> *We're going in the pouch,*
> *We're going in the pouch,*
> *We're going in,*
> *We're going in the pouch . . .*

I suspect that even as we sang, deep down we knew two things.

One: that, as it was Scotland, it just wasn't meant to be, and sure enough, in the last minute, Daniel Fonseca scored a winner for Uruguay that took them through. The other: that it would almost certainly not have been a hat or a pouch, but would have been an improbably large brandy glass with plastic balls in. Not so easy to sing about.

Now, in Osaka, it looks as though the big brandy glass may finally need polishing for action. Having been deprived of any excitement to speak of this afternoon, we become enthusiastic supporters of Lots, banging the handles of our cutlery on the bar:

Lots! Lots! Lots! Lots . . . !

It's a much more nervy last fifteen than we endured at the Nagai earlier. On the left screen Albert Luque has a shot well saved, then Luis Enrique misses an open goal. That could have been it . . . !

Lots! Lots! Lots! Lots . . . !

On the right, Chilavert punches out a Doni Novak shot, then takes a brilliant thirty-six-yard swinging free kick which is tipped onto the bar by Mladen Dabanovic. Phew!

Lots! Lots! Lots! Lots . . . !

With six minutes to go, Cuevas again cuts in from the right for Paraguay and lashes a stunning left-foot shot from the edge of the area in off the underside of the bar. Goal! It's straight back to the Palm Pilot – what does this mean? What do we need to have happen so we can get good old Lots back on track? Sadly it looks as if we still need Spain to score again, and now South Africa too. Oh well.

At the end, Paraguay have nicked it on goal difference, and they will play Germany, while Spain will take on Ireland in Suwon.

Before we go back to the hotel, Nick, Cube, Theo and David all insist that I go to the toilet and won't tell me why. When I do I find not only the standard Japanese crapper with as many push button controls as your average Mini Metro but also a television set sunk into the floor under a glass panel, surrounded with fairy lights, and showing the football, so you can carry on watching between your own feet while you're completing your business. This bloody country, really . . .

David comes with us for a nightcap. Fatboy and Zoe haven't called . . .

13 JUNE

A horror story from Seoul in the *Daily Yomiuri* about parents having their children's tongues operated on to facilitate the better pronunciation of English, in order, in effect, to eradicate Benny Hill syndrome. It's just 'a simple cut in the frenulum', it seems, and then the child can miraculously say 'rice' rather than 'lice'. Or 'frenulum' rather than 'flenurum'. Or a phrase such as: 'That's really rather cruel . . .'

I've now seen highlights of yesterday's Sweden v Argentina game. It looked as though Pablo Aimar and Ariel Ortega were running things in the first half, Claudio Lopez came close to scoring with a couple of angled shots, and an Argentina goal seemed inevitable.

In the second half, though, Sweden came out of their shell. Anders Svensson of Southampton lashed a brilliant free kick over the wall, through the floppy wrist of the diving Cavallero, and inside the left-hand post to put Sweden one up.

Argentina's equaliser, two minutes from time, came from a penalty, won by the theatrical Ortega with a tiny amount of help from the leg hair of Mattias Jonson. Ortega took the kick himself and Hedman made an excellent save, but Hernan Crespo, following up, slid the ball home. Actually it should never have been allowed to stand, as Crespo had encroached so far that he was virtually level with Ortega when the kick was taken, in serious danger of being offside.

At full time, the Swedes piled on top of each other, while Batistuta crouched in front of the dugout, crying like a baby in the ugliest televised snotfest since Juliet Stevenson's performance in *Truly Madly Deeply*. Crespo, too, was helped from the pitch in tears, but it was difficult to have any sympathy with this mob.

Batistuta reckoned that Argentina were the better side against England and that England had done nothing except score the goal. Presumably his girly hair had obscured his view of Owen hitting the post, of Sheringham's fantastic volley, of Scholes's terrific long shot . . .

Caniggia, whose hair is, if anything, even more impossibly girly and especially unattractive on one so very old, thought Argentina had been the better side in all three of their games. His sending off, it turned out, was for swearing at the referee from the substitutes' bench – calling him a 'son of a bitch', apparently – thus reducing his team to eleven men.

Coach Marcelo Bielsa maintained the most fabulous blinkered arrogance right to the end. He had announced his team for Sapporo a full two days in advance, effectively saying, 'Here they are – you'll never stop them.' His summary of his nation's campaign was: 'We were unlucky – it was just a penalty kick and a free kick.'

Neglecting to mention, firstly, that penalty kicks and free kicks count as goals just the same as getting the ball in the net any other way, and secondly, that Argentina's two goals were a set piece – the corner against Nigeria, and a penalty which was missed and then followed up with the blatant disregard for the rules for which his nation's footballers have become justly infamous. So how impressive was that, Marcelo?

Nick takes me to the pachinko parlour, the scene of his big win the other day. I've seen these places everywhere, especially from the windows of trains, little neon-bright mini-Vegases. Pinocchios, The Cube calls them.

The pachinko machine is an upright glorified bagatelle that looks not unlike a fruit machine. They are arranged in rows, tightly packed together, with a fixed plastic bucket seat in front, and each one is subtly different from its neighbour. The pins that the steel ball bearings jiggle through are in a slightly different arrangement, or the cartoon character that pops up in the middle to tell you your score is a rabbit rather than a moose. To play you have to acquire a big plastic box full of ball bearings to feed the beast with, and then you control the speed with which they are fed into play by manipulating a handle. There's very little actual skill involved, and thirty people all playing at once makes a noise like the end of the world.

Nick buys a half-sized shopping basket of ball bearings and sits down in front of one of the machines.

'This looks like a good one,' he says confidently, because he is an expert now, of course. This is his second go.

Along the row from us half a dozen zombies, locked into their games, pay us not one iota of attention. The racket is horrible, and makes me grind my back teeth together. Nick shovels his ball bearings into the maw of the machine, and it starts. I watch him changing the speed at which the balls spew out at the top, and if one of the balls falls into a winning slot some more little silver balls trickle out of the bottom.

After about twelve seconds I'm thinking: 'Yeah? So what . . . ?'

'Here,' says Nick. 'You have a go.'

I slip into the seat, and start fiddling with the handle. The balls fly out at the top, trickle down, some come out the bottom, a large neon number clicks over in the middle.

After about eight more seconds I'm still thinking: 'Yeah? So what . . . ?'

One of the attractions for the Japanese, it seems to me, is that you cannot possibly do this socially, so there's really no etiquette to consider. It is the most anti-social, solitary pastime, just you against the machine, with the real world blotted out by the most tremendous mind-numbing racket. A good number of the most popular leisure activities here seem to be games you play solo.

Take the karaoke, for instance, which is supposedly the fourth most popular way to pass your free time in Japan, after the bland beauty pageant trio of dining out, travelling, and driving a car. Back home this is something enjoyed by gregarious show-offs in large bars, by hen parties, by office staff on a night out, and while that's true here to a certain extent, karaoke has also evolved into an entirely solo activity in private booths in places like Dream Echo.

Golf – *gorruf* – is massively popular in Japan, but I've travelled two-thirds of the length of the country now and not seen a single actual *gorruf* course. They exist, obviously, I just haven't seen them. What I have seen, though, and literally every half a mile or so alongside the Shinkansen tracks, are huge netting contraptions, dwarfing the surrounding buildings. These are the ubiquitous driving ranges, practice facilities, where you play solo *gorruf* to your heart's content without ever having to meet, play with or talk to anybody else.

And this is the home of the computer game, the birthplace of the gameboy. Say no more.

A big win, like the one Nick had the first time he came in here, means that silver balls crash out of the bottom of your machine at a fantastic rate, and you have to collect them in the little shopping baskets. Most of the hardcore zombies in here have a little stack of baskets alongside their positions. One big time Charlie has more than a dozen – he's like the man who broke the bank at Halfords.

You don't leave the premises with these winnings, of course, you convert them for prizes, and although it is technically illegal for pachinko parlours to exchange a big win for cash, there is usually a way, a little shady booth nearby, to which the authorities turn a blind eye. And a deaf ear, if they have spent more than a couple of minutes in here.

Like all forms of gambling – which is essentially what pachinko is – the odds are firmly stacked in the parlours' favour, and Japan's 18,000 or so rake in something like 27 trillion yen a year, a sum equivalent to the combined national gross domestic product of Denmark, Finland and Norway.

'Yeah? So what?' I say.

'Well, so there,' they say.

I can't stand the noise in there, and after about five minutes Nick and I up sticks and vacate the premises. For many pachinko enthusiasts, though, I suspect the noise is part of the attraction. The parlours are especially busy during the lunch hour, when harassed salarymen will grab a sandwich and spend their break blinkered and mesmerised in front of the twinkling, clattering pachinko beast, having their cares and problems and pressures simply blattered into oblivion.

Tomorrow Osaka is hosting the crucial Japan v Tunisia clash. Such is the fervour that the last game generated, with the wild scenes in Roppongi and the like, that the Japanese police are out in force, nailing barbed wire around the telegraph poles and lamp posts to stop people climbing up them, putting out pedestrian control barriers, and generally preparing for a riot. The really interesting thing about this is that it is happening the day *after* an England match in the city.

In the afternoon David and I find a long thin bar, full of tellies and Brazilians. It's up a dark staircase, and we have to join something and pay a membership fee before they'll let us in. It's strange, to say the least, to feel that watching the World Cup in the host nation is such a clandestine activity, and we almost feel as if we need a password or a secret knock.

The place is not too packed, and we can keep up with both games by nipping along a little corridor. We quickly find that we can't drag ourselves away from Brazil against Costa Rica, though, because it's a sensational open game with both sides creating an absolute hatful of chances. Brazil, of course, are already through, and perhaps some of their defending is a little on the relaxed side, but even so it's a thrilling match to watch, once the camera gives up its relentless scouring of the Brazilian sections of the crowd for good-looking women in skimpy tops.

First of all, though, along the corridor, Turkey take a two-goal lead inside ten minutes against China in Seoul. First Hasan Sas bundles past two defenders and lashes an unstoppable shot past Jiang Jin. Then a looping header from Bulent Korkmaz sails over the stranded Chinese keeper. This should ease the pressure on manager Gunes, who has been flayed in the Turkish media after their first two games.

Thereafter, it's all about the game in Suwon, on a pitch that is half bathed in dazzling sunlight, and half patchwork-shaded by the semi-translucent roof of the stand. Ronaldo opens the scoring on ten minutes. Edilson crosses low from the left and the Inter Milan star, with two defenders hanging off the back of his shirt, steers it in off the shin of one of them. Three minutes later he receives a Rivaldo corner low to the left of goal, turns, nudges, flicks, and squeezes a shot between his three markers to go in at the near post for 2–0.

For the rest of the half Brazil charge forward at every opportunity, while leaving some horrible gaps at the back. Walter Centeno slices Costa Rica's best chance wide, but they have several more before Edmilson makes it 3–0 with one of the best goals of the tournament. The centre back gallops upfield and into the penalty area to join in the attacking fun, and finds a deflected cross sailing behind his shoulder six yards out. He launches himself at it and hooks a brilliant overhead kick into the roof of the net.

Costa Rica pull one back immediately, Paolo Wanchope finishing neatly after a deft one-two with Mauricio Wright, and both teams now look as if they are going to score every time they attack.

Early in the second half Turkey still haven't added to their two early goals, and so Costa Rica can sneak ahead of them on goals scored if they can get the scoreline back to 2–3. On fifty-six minutes they deservedly do this, Ronald Gomez ramming in Bryce's lovely cross with a flying header, and for a brief heady period it seems as though both of these great attacking sides will be in the last sixteen.

Just past the hour mark, though, Brazil give Costa Rica a mountain to climb with two more well-taken goals. First Rivaldo turns in a hard, low Junior cross with casual aplomb, and then Junior himself races onto a long through ball, and waits for keeper Erick Lonnis to commit himself before lashing it in at the near post for 5–2.

Costa Rica don't give up. They continue to flick, backheel, and one-two their way through the Brazilian defence. Wanchope, at the top of his game, hits the post, hits the bar, Rolando Fonseca has a great shot just wide, then Ronaldo hits the post too. It is a breathless, open, brilliant match, and you can't take your eyes off it for a moment – except to nip along the corridor to see the replay of Umit Davala's late volleyed third for Turkey, which the AC Milan star with the airstrip hairdo smashes home from a terrific Hasan Sas cross.

Turkey win 3–0 and join the Brazilians in the next round. Costa Rica go out with a bang – if only they'd scored a few more against China . . .

I pop into a convenience store on the way back to the hotel. These convenience stores are everywhere – it's ever so convenient. I've been living off sandwiches, which are uniformly fresh and delicious. If you buy pre-packed sandwiches back home you are entering a kind of lottery, never knowing which end of the sarnie scale you are going to find yourself. It could be 'just like I made them myself' or 'just like an old tramp who got sacked from working in the buffet cars on Virgin railways made them about nine days ago and has kept changing the date labels ever since'. Here, though, they are always the same, soft white bread with the crusts cut off, cheap, tasty, excellent. Add a carton of Blendy, the sweet white iced coffee, and there's your lunch right there.

Or, if you like, there is a soft drink in Japan called Pocari Sweat. It comes in a blue bottle or can, and it just looks wrong every time I see it. Sweat for sale. Nonetheless, I have to try it – the listeners of talkSPORT require no less of me. I just hope Pocari means something along the lines of: 'Doesn't-smell-or-taste-anything-like- . . .' and isn't the name of a well-known Sumo wrestler or his loincloth.

Actually it is one of those electrolyte replacing concoctions, and not at all bad, although its main rival, Love Body, sounds a lot more appetising.

Each convenience store, whether it's a Lawson's, a Seven-Eleven, a Just Stop, or a Family Mart, has a decent-sized newspaper and magazine stand, and I have noticed that it is quite common to find half a dozen adolescent lads just standing and browsing there. The shop assistants seem remarkably tolerant of this, although I imagine that from time to time a senior manager comes in and bellows at them, Benny Hill-style: 'Hey! What you think? This ribarary?'

They are flicking through comics, big thick affairs, and when I have glanced at them myself they mostly seem to be concerned with grinning villains in long dark leather coats threatening small doe-eyed idealised girls, and then having the shit kicked out of them by heroic young boys.

Manga, Japanese comics and cartoons, are a multi-billion yen business, and they account for something like a third of all publishing here in Japan. They're not just entertainment – although many many are – they can be used as a teaching tool for high school students, or to explain complex current affairs issues in a palatable form for really quite grown-up people.

At its best, *manga* is more than a big business, it is a recognised and highly collectable art form, and the best artists are respected all over the world. Some cross into the world of *anime*, Japan's sophisticated cartoon film industry. Since it is easy to dub English language versions of animated films, *anime* are probably Japan's biggest international cinema and television successes. We see things like *Pokemon* and *Digimon* on our televisions, but there is also a much more adult output, tremendously imaginative melting pots of violent science-fiction, martial arts, samurai and vampires. The number one grossing film in Japan in recent years was the animated *Mononoke-hime*, which was dubbed into English using the voices of Billy Bob Thornton and Minnie Driver, amongst others, as *Princess Mononoke*, and was a big breakthrough hit in the USA.

I have on my to-do list searching out a *manga* character called Captain Tsubasa, who is the star of a football strip in the vein of *Roy of the Rovers*.

Manga hero Tsubasa Ozora has been around since the mid-seventies, but like Roy Race himself, he has aged fantastically slowly. Unlike Race, he has not had his playing career curtailed by amputation following a helicopter crash. Not yet, anyway. Originally he was a schoolboy football star – more *Billy's Boots* than *Roy of the Rovers* – which was the upper limit of his Japanese readership's footballing dreams at that time.

In the nineties, though, the scale of Captain Tsubasa's ambitions multiplied. The start of the JLeague launched him on an aspirational career in pro football, and he developed the all-important desire to lead Japan to the World Cup, first in 1998 and then in the current tournament. To service this dream he felt he had to make the heartbreaking decision to leave his homeland and become a star fit to rub shoulders with the best in the world by playing overseas. Hidetoshi Nakata, of course, currently Japan's biggest star, made his name in Italy, at Perugia, Roma and Parma. His predecessor, and Tsubasa's role model, was Kazu Miura, who went to play his football in Brazil, which is viewed as the absolute apex here. Captain Tsubasa followed in Miura's illustrious real-life footsteps, and his struggles for acceptance and his ultimate capture of the number 10 shirt at Sao Paolo FC have inspired a generation of Japanese boy footballers.

Imagine my delight, then, when I glance over the shoulder of one of the browsing boys at the magazine rack, and see he is flicking through what is obviously a football cartoon strip. I quickly note which one the lad is reading and buy a copy.

As I munch my lunch I turn to the first story in the mag, which is at the back, since the pages turn the other way. All the explanatory captions and dialogue bubbles are in Japanese, of course, and so I am not sure whether what I've got hold of is in fact a Captain Tsubasa, but one of the titles is in English – 'Road to 2002' – and I think I've seen enough footy strips down the years to get the hang of what's going on.

The main character is a football star, and he is drawn in the same Japanese style as the boy in *Pokemon*, for example. Big, round, happy, babyish face, huge round eyes, little snub nose. We see our boy training with his team mates, and he seems to be having a disagreement with one of them, who is similarly round-featured and childlike, although the artist has managed to make these simple features sneer at the hero.

Then it's a match, and a pretty, idealised girlfriend is wishing the footballer good luck with a chaste peck on the cheek. He runs out onto the field, his powerful thigh muscles rippling and looking like they really belong to a much older man in a different cartoon.

Once the game sequence is under way it is all very familiar, and I think I can make a stab at translating some of these captions. The one running alongside some swerving speed lines as the ball hurtles into the top corner – that probably means something like 'Whooosh!!!'

Then the speech bubble from the baffled Hispanic defender who has just been nutmegged, I reckon that's 'What the . . . ?' or possibly 'How did you . . . ?'

And the crowd cheering behind the goal net, they're most likely shouting 'Hooray!', although it could be 'Gird yourself and eviscerate these sons of goats.'

Our boyish boy's brilliant play wins the game for his side, which I take to be Japan in one of the build-up games to the World Cup, and he gets a hug from his delighted manager. Next he's having a joke with a team mate in the shower, and then he's driving away from the stadium in an open-topped sports car with the lovely doe-eyed girlfriend.

Well, I think, what a charming, innocent little tale of sporting excellence and the benefits it can bring. I turn the page . . .

. . . and spew egg sandwich and Blendy all over the bed-spread.

There, in the very next frame, is the lovely doe-eyed girl-friend, on her back, stark naked, legs in the air, tits like chapel hat pegs, doe-eyes become eloquent slits of ecstasy, and our lad's tousled head is buried between her thighs. *Pokemon* boy is having sex.

All sorts of jokes tumble over each other in their rush to get out, including:

He's lethal in the box.

Going down, going down, going down . . .

He could be booked for diving like that. (Or perhaps she's the one who's simulating.)

He's scored.

My favourite way of relaxing after a big match? I'd have to say eating out.

Something about this is really disturbing. I think it's because the cartoon characters look so much like children. Or perhaps it's the flash of understanding of why all those adolescent boys spend so much time hanging out in convenience stores – yet another pastime for the Japanese to play solo.

The Japanese have an interesting attitude towards pornography. On the one hand it's absolutely everywhere, as I've just discovered, but on the other you never actually see anything. The cartoon characters have little black letter boxes over their groins, but it's quite clear what they are up to. Each hotel I've stayed in so far has offered some kind of porn channel, sometimes more than one, on the television, and you see couples banging away unashamedly – at least until your free thirty seconds runs out. It's not the soft porn style, either, with lots of moaning and shots of people's ears – it's full-length, all-action stuff. Any hint, any glimpse of genitalia, however, is completely pixillated out, so that the bloke's tadger always looks exactly like a cowboy plumber on *House of Horrors*.

Dom told me yesterday, incidentally, that Rio Ferdinand had lodged an official complaint with the FA about the pixillation ruining the pornography on his hotel telly – I hope that's true.

Come the evening, Nick, The Cube and I head back to the bar where the toilet has a telly in the floor to watch tonight's Group G games – Mexico v Italy and Croatia v Ecuador.

It's The Cube's last night in Japan, and you'd think he'd be pleased to be going home after the amount of moaning he's been doing about Osaka, but he keeps returning to this theme like a scratched record: 'I bet you'll all have a bloody great time once I've gone. You will, you'll have the time of your bloody lives without me . . .'

It's a pity Fatboy never turned up – he could have set it to music.

A draw will do for Mexico in Oita, but Italy must win to be certain of progressing, and could conceivably find themselves disputing first place in the group on goal difference with Croatia.

Early on Filippo Inzaghi has a goal disallowed for offside. This is a particularly sensitive issue for the Italians after the

Croatia game, and Inzaghi, here starting for the first time at this World Cup, looks close to tears. Nonetheless, he, Christian Vieri and Francesco Totti take the game to the Mexicans for the first half an hour, and the three of them create several decent openings with some delightful inter-passing, at one point wriggling through the Mexican back line doing keepy-uppies between themselves.

Gradually, though, the Mexicans begin to assert themselves, and after thirty-four minutes a long period of Mexican possession culminates in a gorgeous chipped through ball by Cuahtemoc Blanco. Jared Borgetti sprints clear of the struggling Paolo Maldini and twists in mid air to send a looping reverse header over the helpless Gianluigi Buffon to open the scoring. Italy promptly go to pieces for the rest of the half, while Blanco and Gerrado Torrado start to find acres of space in midfield.

Mickey is at Croatia v Ecuador in Yokohama tonight, which is a 65,000 sellout. I have seen a handful of Croatians knocking about, it's true, and even the occasional Ecuador supporter, but most of the crowd, like Mickey, are Japanese fans who have been fobbed off with this match by the FIFA ticketing helpline while trying to get tickets for Japan, Brazil or England games.

Both teams need to win, and Ecuador need a big victory coupled with a defeat for Italy to have a chance of going through, but there is only a single chance for Alen Boksic in the whole first half there. Early in the second half, though, Agustin Delgado nods a right-wing cross down and back for Edison Mendez to expertly half volley under Pletikosa's body, and Ecuador have a surprise lead. Thereafter we wait in vain for the sprightly Croatian side that took the game to Italy in their last game to emerge, but the bronze medallists of France 98 seem to be subsiding without putting up much of a fight.

David turns up, and says: 'Tomoko's on her way over with my pants,' causing, it has to be said, the odd raised eyebrow. 'The *Evening Standard* wants a photo of them, and it has to be tonight,' he explains, not making things much better.

David is utterly at sea in his attempts to guide Tomoko to the bar to join us. In the end he hands his mobile phone to the guy behind the bar and asks him to talk her in, which seems to be how things are done in this country. She arrives shortly afterwards, smiling as ever, and she has indeed got David's pants with her. These, you see, are David's lucky pants, as described in the article he has written about the Nigeria game yesterday. Or rather they aren't, because he left the really lucky ones, the ones with a cross of St George emblazoned proudly on each buttock, in 'a safe place' in the chest of drawers in his Sapporo hotel room after the Argentina game. These pants are in fact a botched-up attempt to recreate the magic of the lucky pants, which he has done himself using ordinary white pants and a red felt-tip pen. He discovered yesterday afternoon that they are nothing like as lucky as the lucky lucky pants, which is rather the point of his article, which is why Tomoko needs a photo of them. Poor Tomoko, this really must be her dream job.

David holds up the pants in the bar, but I suggest he might get a better picture over the road in front of a sign for a nightclub which reads 'BIG MEMBERS', and he and Tomoko duly trot off outside.

Meanwhile in the second half at the Big Eye in Oita the Mexicans are passing the ball fluently and smoothly, and Italy can't get back into the game. Arellano's underhit shot is hooked off the line, Morales has a shot, Rodriguez comes close, and Mexico should really be two up. As the final whistle approaches, Italy are absolutely on pins. Trapattoni clearly knows that Croatia are losing, and that as things stand Italy will go through, but a late Croatian goal would change everything. When Montella hooks a bouncing cross into the box and Alessandro Del Piero, on as a substitute, glances it in for the equaliser, the relief looks almost life-threatening.

Confirmation of Ecuador's win filters through to the men on the pitch, and they all play out the injury time as a non-contact sport, with Mexico keeping the ball for fifty-four consecutive passes before Carlos Simon, the Brazilian referee, ends the ordeal. Trapattoni promptly takes out a little phial of holy water and sprinkles it on the floor of the dugout.

Mexico top the group, and second-placed Italy will need to improve significantly if they are to justify their position as third favourites (after Brazil and Spain). Mind you, as France and Argentina know, you have to be in it to win it.

Tomoko was telling me earlier that a lot of big British and American stars do adverts over here, thinking that it is so far away that it can't possibly damage their credibility. They reckoned without the World Cup, I suppose. Hence Ewan McGregor's smiling features promote an English language college, Jodie Foster tells of the joys of cooking bacon, and good old Pele is still banging on about his faulty hydraulics.

Shinji Ono, the Japanese star who plays for Feyenoord, is featured in a car advert that is on all the time, while Nakata crops up in sleek mobile phone and computer campaigns. Ono is shown doing keepy-uppies in a Dutch supermarket, and speaking in Dutch to a small fan, before driving off in his flash car. We can tell he's in Holland because he drives past a windmill.

Out of the window of my hotel room, many storeys up, the expressway looks like a Scalextric set. Late at night a couple of boy racers loop around at tremendous speed, with utter disregard for everyone else on the road, as if remote-controlled by a pair of gigantic Godzilla-like hyperactive children.

14
The Streak

'Portugal were telling us that with a draw we
could both go through.'
–Ahn Jung Hwan, South Korea

14 JUNE

Ever have one of those days where nothing seems to work out
quite as you want it to? Not huge disasters, just little niggly
things you could have done without, all just adding up? Today
starts out a little bit like that.

Nick and I travel on the Shinkansen up to Tokyo, where we'll
change to go up to Niigata, which is a port on the northern/west-
ern coast of Honshu. Just as we are waiting to get on the train,
David rings up about the hotel we are all heading to tonight.

Nick has managed to find us some accommodation in
Niigata through his travel agent friend James back in Stoke.
The city is booked solid at the moment, apparently, by French
fans and journalists confidently expecting that France were
going to top Group A, so there'll be plenty of empty rooms
but it will be impossible to get them. Nonetheless, James has
managed to get hold of a number for a decent Niigata hotel
with a few vacancies, and last night David got Tomoko to ring
up and book it for us all. Now he rings up to say: 'This hotel,
apparently, it's not exactly in Niigata.'

'What do you mean, not in Niigata?'

'Well, it's in Niigata *prefecture*, that's the thing, but it's not
in Niigata city, and Niigata prefecture is the size of Wales.'

'So how far outside the city is it?'

'About a hundred kilometres. Apparently it's in a place called Echigo Yuzawa . . .'

Great.

Then there's talkSPORT to worry about. Ordinarily they will put me on the air about 3.50, when I'll be on the train to Niigata. Now the mobile phone works all right on the Shinkansen, and so this should be OK, I'm thinking, until I start reading about Niigata in the guide book.

It seems that the Shinkansen line across country from Tokyo to Niigata was the brainchild of Tanaka Kakuei, the MP for Niigata who was Prime Minister of Japan between 1972 and 1974. He made it his personal crusade to transform Niigata from a backwater into one of Japan's major cities, and forced through the plan to drive a Shinkansen link across some of the most inhospitable countryside imaginable for rail engineering – mountains, volcanoes, you name it. The line took eleven years to build, was completed in 1982, and cost 1.7 trillion yen, which means – naturally – that it is the most expensive railway line anywhere in the world.

More than a third of its length is through tunnels, which will of course be hopeless for the mobile phone, so it looks as though I might have to wait in Tokyo and catch a much later train, which is a real drag.

Then there's the worry about tickets for the game tomorrow. We are reasonably confident that we will get in, but we'd rather have it sorted out than have to hang around Niigata all day tomorrow haggling with cockneys.

Nick buys us both a *bento* box lunch. You see these for sale everywhere, especially at stations, all wrapped up to look like a presentation box of biscuits. I'm hungry, but not hungry enough to struggle with chopsticks on a moving train beyond a couple of cold mouthfuls.

And out of the window it's cloudy and hazy again, so yet another chance to spot Mount Fuji passes me by.

All in all, I arrive in the capital just a bit fed up. Not hugely pissed off, just a bit weighed down and stressed. We meet up with Theo in Tokyo station – he's coming up to Niigata with us – and I nip off (sorry) to call London. I get through to Gary, the producer of *The Sports Breakfast*, and explain to him about the tunnels, and that I can either wait for a later train or go on the air later in the show. He says, 'No, you're all right, mate, you get your train, we'll have you on tomorrow instead.'

Later on, I will look back at this moment as the point the day turned into a different sort of day altogether.

'Oh, by the way,' Gary goes on, 'we hear there's been quite an earthquake out there – did you feel it?'

I didn't, but once we are on the train to Niigata Theo tells us that he did.

'I was in my hotel room on the thirtieth floor,' he says, 'and the whole place starts shaking around, and for about fifteen, twenty seconds I'm thinking "Hey! An earthquake! That's cool!" but then I'm like "OK, that's enough now, you can stop now . . ." and it just kept on and on for another forty seconds. By the end my life was flashing before my eyes.'

Nick, Theo and I have the carriage to ourselves, apart from one English chap opposite buried in some paperwork. We start to go through the practicalities. This train goes to Niigata. It also stops at Echigo Yuzawa, about an hour earlier. The thought is that we should perhaps go all the way into Niigata and see if we can find alternative accommodation for the next two nights, as it looks as if it will be very difficult to get back to Echigo Yuzawa after the game tomorrow evening, especially if it goes to penalties, which it very well might.

Theo suggests we could go into Niigata tomorrow morning and hire a car, which would mean we could drive back to the hotel tomorrow night. It's not a great plan, but enough to make us decide to get off this train at Echigo Yuzawa.

The English chap opposite shuts his briefcase and stands up.

'Can you watch my case for me, lads, while I go to the toilet?'

His case has a big blue sticker on the lid which says 'FIFA' in big letters. When he's halfway along the carriage I say in a loud voice:

'Quick, let's see what he's got in there!'

And he shoots us a grin, a grin that knows we won't look in his briefcase but also knows that we would be interested in what's in there. Intriguing . . .

When he comes back Nick buys him a coffee from the trolley that happens to be passing and starts to chat to him.

Our new pal is called Ged, and he seems a thoroughly nice and friendly bloke who just hasn't had anyone to talk to for a while. He works, he tells us, for the Manchester company that FIFA have entrusted with organising the ticketing for the World Cup. He's a marketing man, basically, and he has found himself rather beleaguered in the last few weeks as the media have looked for a scapegoat for all the things that have gone wrong.

There have been any number of stories in the past few days about empty seats at supposedly sold-out games, and Ged tells us about one photograph that appeared in a newspaper, purportedly showing one lone Polish fan in the middle of a huge empty block of seats, with the implication being that some huge cock-up had occurred. If you look closely, though, you can see the stadium clock, and the picture was taken a full ninety minutes before kick-off.

It does sound rather as though Ged has been hung out to dry by FIFA, who are wanting to distance themselves from the various ticketing fiascos and blame the British printers. He's been on the television a lot, trying to explain in as calm and polite a way as possible that all tickets would first of all be printed in time, and then distributed in time. He does this in English, of course, and then the Japanese television news puts up a translation as subtitles. What he's only found out later, thanks to a Japanese friend who happened to be watching, was that the subtitle to his eminently reasonable, lengthy and positive explanation read: 'I don't know.'

Worse, there are several ways of saying 'I don't know' in Japan, where they hate to give an outright negative, some of which carry the meaning: 'I'm not going to tell you.' So all the while he's been trying to put an upbeat spin on the situation, Japanese television has been showing him no-commenting away like the most abjectly guilty of politicians.

The most frustrating aspect for Ged seems to be that all of the problems there have been stem from the fact that the organisers were months late in getting the plans of the various stadia to the ticketing people. The stadia were almost all new and purpose-built, of course, and hadn't been used before. This meant that in Manchester they couldn't get on with printing or distributing tickets because they simply didn't know where all the seats were going to end up being put. Ged, however, is strictly forbidden from mentioning any of this, for fear that FIFA will offend the host nations by appearing to blame them. It seems then that he has taken on the role of official Aunt Sally for the World Cup, so we can hardly blame him for feeling somewhat friendless just at the moment.

'So have you lads got your tickets sorted for tomorrow?' Ged asks.

'Not yet,' Nick says, looking pretty worried about it all. 'I suppose we're just going to have to get there early and hustle on the streets, see what we can pick up. It'll probably break the bank, but what else can we do . . . ?'

I've never seen Nick fishing, but I begin to realise that it must be a bit like this.

Ged whistles through his teeth. 'Japan's no place to be hustling on the streets,' he says. Next thing we know he's on his mobile phone, arranging for us to get Category 1 tickets at face value, which we can pick up from the FIFA office in Niigata tomorrow at our leisure. Excellent man.

'You can come and sit with me,' Ged says. 'It'll be nice to be with some chums for a change.'

I have a sudden ghastly vision of what it must have been like for him in Japan so far, going to all the games, but having to sit with FIFA executives who all blame him personally for messing up their World Cup.

Nick, Theo and I get off the train at Echigo Yuzawa in buoyant mood, naturally enough, and things continue to go almost supernaturally well from this point on. Ever have one of those days where things just start dropping into your lap? (Half days, anyway . . . ?)

Echigo Yuzawa is a lovely little resort village up in the mountains, with wooden chalet-style buildings and a rather Alpine feel to it. We have absolutely no idea how to get to our hotel, but straight outside the station is a blue minibus with the name of the hotel painted on the side. Excellent.

We arrive at the hotel, which is huge and luxurious, looking at our watches, and itching to get checked in so we can see the second half of Japan v Tunisia, and right here in the lobby is a huge telly showing the match. Excellent.

Despite the fact that Tunisia need to win by two, the first half has been something of a non-event, according to one of the guys on reception, apart from one moment where the reckless red-headed Toda clattered Trabelsi in the area, and the referee somehow managed not to spot it. For the second half, Phillippe Troussier – already being linked with the France job – demonstrates his managerial acumen by bringing on Hiroaki Morishima and Daisuke Ichikawa. Within three minutes Morishima has scored, latching on to a loose ball in the area and finishing with aplomb. Then with fifteen minutes to go Ichikawa bamboozles his Tunisian marker and pings a great cross to the far post, where superstar Hidetoshi Nakata dives and heads the ball under Ali Boumnijel. Excellent.

After the game has finished and we've dumped our bags in

the most enormous rooms I think I've ever stayed in anywhere, the three of us go for a stroll back down into the village. It's quiet, the mountain air is fresh and crisp, which is a great change from the concrete jungle and overhead cable spaghetti of Osaka. Excellent.

We have a drink of some kind of local beer in a small bar by the station. It is delicious, and on the wall is a bright yellow poster which says, in English:

DRINK BEER – IT'S GOOD FOR YOU.

We're starting to giggle now about how well things are working out. I stroll over the road into the station to find out about trains back from Niigata after the game tomorrow, and find that special Shinkansens have been laid on and will be stopping here every ten minutes between midnight and 2 a.m. Excellent.

Down the deserted main street – it's well out of season for Echigo Yuzawa, it seems – we come across a shooting gallery, like something from an English seaside pier in the sixties. The guns are long-barrelled pop guns, which fire little corks at matchbox targets on shelves behind the counter. The little old lady who runs the place cackles hysterically whenever one of us hits something, encouraging us to lean over the counter as far as we like, and we cause corking matchbox mayhem, winning our pick of strange prizes from a cardboard box full of cheap crap. What could be more fun than this?

We stroll a little further, and just as we start to think we'd quite like something to eat – why, there's a place right here. They serve beer, and cook chicken, beef, pork and lamb on skewers. The first half of Portugal v South Korea is on the telly in the corner, and a little Japanese child is laughing his head off, squirming on the floor, while his dad tickles his tummy. You have to laugh.

Although all eyes are on South Korea v Portugal, the first

twists in the Group D story happen in Daejeon. Emmanuel Olisadebe, Poland's Nigerian-born striking hero, thrashes in a loose ball from a corner off the underside of the bar after three minutes. Landon Donovan has an immediate reply disallowed for a push on the keeper, then Pawel Krysalowicz makes it 2–0 to Poland with a sharp finish at the near post and there's still less than five minutes on the clock. The USA's campaign is imploding, and only the excellence of Brad Friedel prevents matters from getting even worse.

Meanwhile, South Korea, driven on by a hysterical crowd in Inchon, are just edging the first twenty minutes or so. Then Joao Pinto assaults Park Ji Sung, an awful foul, wrapping both his legs around Park's left leg and crumpling it under their falling bodies, the sort of challenge that can end a career. The Argentinian referee, Angel Sanchez, pulls out the red card, and Portugal go spare. Fernando Couto remonstrates with Sanchez, holding the ref's head in both hands, and Pinto actually punches the official in the ribs, but then he can hardly be sent off twice.

Nick gives the laughing child his prizes from the shooting gallery, and we stroll back to the hotel under a clear starlit night sky to watch the second half. There's no telly in the bar, but just along the corridor from our vast rooms there is a vending machine selling cans of beer. A mechanised off licence twenty yards from my bed. Excellent.

My chief concern now is that we have somehow slipped into the Twilight Zone. We'll try to head out in the morning, and find that the seraphically happy stationmaster won't let us.

'Oh no, sir, there are no trains out of Echigo Yuzawa. Why would anyone ever want to leave such a beautiful place?'

Then, in a flash, we'll realise that in fact there is no best-hotel-in-the-world, there was no FIFA ticketing man on the train, no cackling old lady in a time-warp shooting gallery, and in fact we all died in Theo's earthquake in Tokyo . . . No-o-o-o-ooo!

Portugal's ten men calmly and competently take the sting out of the frenzied South Korean players and fans in the second half, and with the USA losing a draw will see both these teams qualify. South Korea can't relax, though, and the drums and the squeals drive Guus Hiddink's team on in a series of fluent and quick-footed attacks.

After sixty-six minutes in Daejeon Marcin Zewlakov powers in a Marek Kozminski cross, and shortly after this Brad Friedel makes a good low save to his left to keep out a Maciej Zurawski penalty.

Now surely Portugal and South Korea will just play out time, we think, but then Beto picks up a second yellow card, so Oliveira's team are down to nine, and before they can really regroup South Korea win a corner.

Lee Young Pyo's first ball in is headed back to him; his second reaches Park Ji Sung at the far post. He traps the ball on his chest, feints to shoot with his right, convincing Sergio Conceicao to turn his back, but instead dinks a little volley to his left and half volleys the dropping ball through Baia's legs for a really neat goal.

The crowd go mental, including the President, who waves his little red baseball cap in front of his fixed grin. Portugal have to pull something out of the bag now, and for the last ten minutes the nine men peg the eleven back. Luis Figo, looking tired and drawn, bears an uncanny resemblance, suddenly, to Judd Hirsch in *Taxi*. His free kick whistles over the wall and just past the post. Nuno Gomez rushes onto a through pass but in his anxiety his leg lands on top of the ball, stopping it dead rather than nudging it past Lee Woon Jae. Conceicao hits the post with a brilliant scissor kick, and then skins the full back twice before shooting straight at the keeper.

It is terrifically exciting, but they can't break through, and at the final whistle Antonio Oliveira lurches glumly off on his crutches, presumably planning to brain Joao Pinto with one of them.

In Daejeon, Landon Donovan has sidefoot-volleyed home a late consolation for the States, but they are dejected, knowing they haven't picked up the point that they needed. Then the news from Inchon comes through, and they have sneaked into the last sixteen after all to play Mexico. South Korea, for whom joy is unconfined both inside the ground and amongst the red millions watching in the main square in Seoul, march on to meet Italy.

While Japan were beating Tunisia this afternoon, Belgium needed to win the other Group H game, as any other result would see Russia go through. Johan Walem flipped a brilliant free kick over the Russian wall and into the top corner after only seven minutes, and Bestchastnykh equalised early in the second half. It looked good for Russia, then, until twelve minutes from the end, when Wesley Sonck nodded in a Walem corner. The excellent Marc Wilmots gave Belgium a two-goal cushion four minutes later, and although Sychev pulled one back, Belgium held on and go through to play Brazil in Kobe, where I for one wish them luck.

Down in the bar of the best-hotel-in-the-world there is a small but perfectly formed karaoke night in progress. Theo and I rub our hands together with glee, but Nick needs convincing.

A large group of middle-aged Japanese men loaf around a table, wearing hotel *yukatas* and slippers, very relaxed – in fact, relaxed as newts by the look of some of them. One is on stage, growling tunelessly along to some dirge, and one of the younger members of the group perches on the edge of his seat, clearly itching for it to be his turn.

We sit at a table on the opposite side of the room, get some drinks in, and Theo and I start thumbing through the song books. The growler winds up, and we carefully give him our enthusiastic applause – good karaoke etiquette. The singer doesn't leave the stage at once, though, he picks up a glass and makes an elaborate toast to the elderly gentleman in the centre of the group, bowing obsequiously the while. Sucking up to the boss, presumably.

Next up it's the keen young upstart, who is more of a performer than his growling mate. He gives us a bit of Japanese Elvis, and his colleagues laugh their heads off – clearly this lad is the office clown. Theo and I are down to do songs by now, but Nick looks as if he would rather have his fingernails pulled out than get on stage.

We ooze patiently through another growler, and he too toasts the senior fellow at their table before vacating the performing arena, and then Theo is up. He's gone for *My Funny Valentine*, and there are two complications to this plan. One is that he has in mind the Elvis Costello version, and the music is Sinatra's – the other is that the lyrics appear on the screen in Japanese. Still, he gamely bashes through it from memory in a very decent impression of old Declan's style, and draws warm and indulgent applause from the other table. They are ever so slightly less impressed, though, when the next song to come up is Theo doing *My Funny Valentine* again, with the lyrics in English this time.

Now I discover the true value of the karaoke box that I visited a few days ago. I am utterly confident that I can manage *All By Myself*, which I do, and then straight on to *Only Yesterday*. At this, Japanese Elvis leaps up and cries out, 'Ah so, the music of Richard Carpenter!'

Which I wasn't expecting. Nor was I anticipating that he would leap up on stage alongside me, grab a second microphone, and do all the harmonies (and there are a fair few). I return to our table, where Nick is beaming. He is still refusing to take part himself, but Theo and I can see his performing instincts coming to the surface, and before long all three of us are giving it 'Nah, nah, nah nananana!' as Japanese Elvis bellows out *Hey Jude*, and then Nick is strutting around to the strains of *Paint it Black* having a whale of a time.

At some point, maybe when Theo was doing *California Dreaming*, or possibly when I was in the middle of *From Russia with Love*, the *yukata* party opposite began to break up, and the slippers flip-flopped up the stairway towards the lifts. I got the faint impression that we might have pissed them off, muscling in on their evening, but what the hell.

I am a football fan, so naturally I am prone to superstition. I've never, unlike David for instance, noticed that any of my pants are particularly fortunate. For me the thing is magpies. One for sorrow, two for joy . . . (Once you get up to ten, of course, that means Susan Stranks and Mick Robertson showing you how to make stuff out of old bogrolls and Sellotape.)

I see a single magpie on the way to the game, Oldham will lose. I see a pair, Oldham will win. I am always amazed at how reliable an indicator this seems to be, although with the benefit of hindsight a pair with a little bit of space between them looks very like two singles, and two singletons several miles apart could have been a pair who were temporarily lost. How do the magpies know, though, and why do they expend so much time and effort getting into just the right place to spoil games for me?

I am also a great believer in The Streak. Once a run gets going where things are going unusually well, this will carry on to include the match and your team will win. The reverse, of course, is also true. Since Tokyo station this afternoon we have been on one of the best streaks I've ever seen – if only it carries on tomorrow we'll have nothing to worry about.

Echoing in my head as I make my own way to bed later is The Cube's plaintive and, as it turned out, prophetic lament: 'I bet you'll all have a bloody great time once I've gone. You will, you'll have the time of your bloody lives without me . . .'

15
Niigata

'Beckham will take the free kick and he's a world-
class bender.'
– German television commentator

15 JUNE

Echigo Yuzawa is, it turns out, an *onsen* resort, and our hotel
has its own hot spa bath – naturally, as it's the best hotel in
the world. Already ensconced when we turn up in the morning
are the 'businessmen' we annoyed last night by hogging the
karaoke. It's difficult not to notice, in this social situation,
that all of them, especially the senior chap that everyone
was so particularly deferential to yesterday, have a number
of tattoos. Now at home this would mean they were football
fans, perhaps, or builders, or possibly gentlemen of a naval
persuasion. In Japan, though, tattoos can mean only one thing.
We've pissed off the *yakuza*.

This ranks with an incident at France 98, when Nick and
I went to see Iran play the USA in Lyons, and Nick told a
noisy bunch of Iranians near by to sit down and shut up,
whereupon the bloke sitting next to him grabbed his arm
and hissed: 'These are the Mujaheddin!'

All the while we've been in Japan, Nick has been lugging
around a variety of fishing equipment. For a fisherman, it
seems, it doesn't matter whether or not there's anywhere
to fish handy, as long as there's a fishing-tackle shop to
go to, and stuff to buy just in case the opportunity should

suddenly arise. At the last count Nick had picked up some little red wellies (always handy), a fishing hat (stylish), and a big bamboo contraption like a large lacrosse bat. Also never far away from his grasp is his fishing book, acquired out here and entirely in Japanese, which he likes to stick under the nose of hotel receptionists and ask: 'Are any of these places anywhere near here?'

This is how he, Theo and I find ourselves in a cab on our way to Yuzawa fishing village this morning. I'm not greatly interested myself, and find a picnic table nearby at which I can write this diary. Nick and Theo, though, are buying bait, and hiring rods, and tramping off up the bank of the little river. Theo has the hat, Nick the little red wellies.

A little later I go and find them, and Nick, as a proper serious angler, is a little put out. It seems the fish are being farmed, fed on exactly the same stuff that is being sold as bait, and then dumped in the river upstream by the hundred, and so there's precious little in the way of real sport to be had here. In fact it looks virtually impossible not to just catch a great big pile of fish really really quickly. Just along the bank two surely teenagers are whipping fish out of there as fast as they can bait their lines. One of them isn't even looking, he's casting backwards over his shoulder with a fag hanging out of the corner of his mouth. They are sitting by a pool, formed by a kink in the river, which seems to be more fish than river, and every time a bit of bait plops in there the fish think it's feeding time again. You may as well just tip them all into a barrel, give these youths a shotgun and have done with it.

So, not exactly what Nick had in mind, but then one of the great attractions of fishing, I'm told, is the grounding it gives in learning to live with life's disappointments.

Onto the Shinkansen, which is heaving with England fans on their way up from Tokyo. Niigata is cool and overcast, and there are a few spots of rain, so it looks as though Eriksson's meteorological masterplan might be working. Our first port of call is the FIFA office, at which we bump into Ged and pick up our tickets. There is a sort of festival of football going on outside, which for some reason involves some Covent Garden-style unicycling – never all that entertaining, I find. A rather earnest English chap thrusts a magazine into my hand – it is a kind of glossy fanzine called *Free Lions*.

'Thanks,' I say. 'How much?'

'Free. Free Lions, see, mate? Free. It's free. *Free Lions*. Coh!'

OK, mate, calm down. I was joking.

Then we need some lunch, preferably somewhere where we will be able to check out Germany v Paraguay, which is due to start soon over in Seogwipo. We have heard that Hotel Niigata will fit the bill, so we get in a cab and head over there.

When we arrive we find the police have cordoned off the street. A vast crowd of squealing girls are barely being held back by ropes and barriers, and harassed policemen are rushing up and down trying to fill in gaps where the girlies might burst through. Some of them look as if they've been crying – others as if they have been shouting 'Ringo!', or possibly 'Donny!', for the last few hours and are ready to be carted off by St John's Ambulance people.

What the hell is happening here?

One thing is for certain. When faced by a top-quality security operation dedicated to keeping the public at arm's length, the thing to do is to arrive by taxi. We are beckoned through, and are driven right up to reception, where we wave to the fans – they deserve no less – and disappear inside.

It's only the gaff where the England squad are staying, isn't it? All the fuss outside is because of Beckham. They're all waiting for a brief glimpse of his scruffy blond hair-ridge and a shy wave from behind the tinted window, before the sudden cold-shower shock of catching sight of Paul Scowls in the seat behind as the coach eases round the corner and away.

Sadly the bars and restaurants here are depressingly footy-free, but we grab some lunch anyway. Nick bumps into an old friend who is producing some television segments here, and while he's off chatting to her, Theo and I find ourselves talking with one of her presenters. She tells us remarkable tales of blithely walking into games without any tickets at all. It seems that if you are an accredited journalist you have to apply for tickets to sit at the consoles in the media section, but to get to the place where you go to find out if your application has been successful you have to go actually inside the ground through where all the commentators sit, so she's been getting that far, no trouble at all, and just plonking herself at an empty position.

Inspired by her chutzpah, I suggest to Theo that what we should do is find a room somewhere in the Hotel Niigata that is being cleaned, go in as if it is our room, and ask the maid to come back a bit later. Then we could just switch the telly on, watch Germany v Paraguay, and Robert is your father's brother . . . For a heady minute or two we are steeling ourselves to do this, but then we bottle it and go off to another hotel round the corner – we'll meet up with Nick again later on.

On the way we run the gauntlet of the screaming Beckha-maniacs, and pass a barber shop in which a Japanese man is actually, at that very moment, having a David Beckham haircut. And in the paper this morning an Australian government minister called Warren Truss has leapt to the defence of Beckham and his kangaroo-skin boots, assuring animal rights campaigners that the kangaroos are killed humanely with big guns before being made into the boots. Surely Becks has a reasonable claim, now, to being the most famous man in the whole world? Well, if not him then who? The Pope? Michael Jackson? Muhammad Ali . . . ?

The next hotel we come to is much more obliging on the World Cup front. There is a big television showing the game in the lobby, and a dozen or so England fans, mostly in the white shirts, lounge around on the comfy chairs watching it go by, every now and then strolling over to a beer vending machine in the corner. Theo and I sidle over and join them.

It's Germany nil Paraguay nil at the moment, and a truly terrible game – definitely not worth risking the hotel-room scam for. Miroslav Klose looks off his game – apparently he was bothered by suspiciously Spanish-sounding nuisance calls throughout the night. The England gang keep up a loud and boisterous conversation, and Theo and I quickly develop a tacit understanding that we aren't going to be contributing much to this. They are swapping war stories of 'rumbles' past, and I begin idly to wonder whether any of them have come over from Thailand on inflatable boats.

'You see, the thing about Charleroi is that none of that need ever have happened. We was just minding our own business, but then they come in giving it this and we can't let that stand, can we? So the tables go flying, and I'm sat on this geezer's head. Next thing we know they've brought this fackin' water cannon in an' everyone's on the fackin' news . . .'

'Yeah, Marseilles, same fing, we're all walkin' along the side of the road, when all these fackin' Tunisians turn up an' start chuckin' bricks at us, shoutin' your mother's this an' your mother's that. We was just goin' to have a drink, but we can't have that. So I get hold of one an' I'm givin' him a right spankin', an' then it's what? Riot police, TV, the lot, you name it . . .'

Theo and I keep our heads down and concentrate on the game. Paraguay have had a couple of half-decent chances from long range, but Oliver Kahn is stopping everything at the moment. One of the lads changes the subject.

'Hey, you know these Jap school uniforms? I reckon they're really sexy . . .'

'Yaaaaagh!'

'I do! I've only been and got one for the fackin' wife, the

whole kit, the white blouse, the navy blue skirt, the socks, and the special glue for 'em an' all . . .'

There always seem to be flocks of twittering schoolgirls on the streets. Hundreds of them are waiting for Beckham to smile at them just around the corner from here. They wear these big white woolly socks, and the fashion is to have them all crumpled and baggy, so they all look somewhat like Nora Batty auditioning for *Fame*. This style is called *rusu sokkusu* – loose socks, just try saying it quickly – and it wasn't especially noticeable in Tokyo, where it is considered passé, but it was definitely de rigueur in Sapporo, and here too. In order to achieve just the right level of studied rumpliness in the sockage, the schoolgirls evidently glue the tops to their calves, using special glue which is provided in school uniform shops.

'How do you know you've got the right size?'

'They only let me go round the shop trying to find an assistant with the same size arse as my wife.'

'What, they let you feel all their arses?'

'Yeah, they seemed to enjoy it . . .'

Another lad comes in from a ticket recce. 'Any joy?'

'Yeah, you can get 'em, but they're about three-fifty at the moment, that's the going rate.'

'They'll come down,' says one, the voice of experience. 'Stand on me . . .'

Theo and I try to shrink a little further into our seats, but it's no good. We've been spotted.

'You're a right pair of fackin' miserable barstards, encha? Come on, cheer up!'

'Not while Germany are still in,' Theo growls, which is a very good answer. It makes us sound even more hard line than they are, without us having to invent any stories about beating people up. After this, our dourness is treated with more respect.

Two minutes from time Bernd Schneider is in behind Julio Cesar Caceres down the right touchline. His cross is low and hard and coincides exactly with a brilliantly timed run by Oliver Neuville. How many times have we seen this? The Germans looking vulnerable, looking as if they could be in trouble, but then pulling something out at the last. It's Groundhog Day.

Still, at least we're spared extra time in what must surely be the worst game of the whole tournament so far, and Theo and I leave to go and find Nick in another bar in another hotel overlooking the river. As we walk we hear the distant screams as the England team coach leaves for the stadium.

When we get there I glance through *Free Lions*. More power to them, actually. It's nicely presented and bang up to date – stuff about the matches so far, and about nightlife in Japan. Anyway, they are running a competition for fans to get a picture published of themselves standing next to a celebrity of some kind out here. The current winner – surprise surprise – is standing next to Chris 'Course you can, yeah!' Kamara.

Nick, funnily enough, has just passed some blokes who've cornered John Motson, and they ask him to take their picture for them, so maybe he'll get a picture credit in the next edition. (If there is one, I think hurriedly, not wanting to tempt fate.)

Theo is trying to work out how to phrase the suggestion to the mother of his two-week-old baby that Daddy should stay a bit longer in Japan. His best plan is to say: 'Why don't you come and join me out here?' in a wistful sort of voice, trusting that his wife will not be able to face a fourteen-hour-long plane journey while breastfeeding a small child. 'You're sure? Oh well, it was a nice idea . . .'

On the next table to us another gang of Englishmen have gathered. Once they start to inflict their conversation on us at top volume, they turn out to be an incredibly posh bunch of braying rugger buggers. It doesn't take long for them to set our teeth on edge.

'Do you know this will be my first-ever professional footer game?' one of them barks. 'I wonder what it will be like . . .'

Theo is reminded of a woman sitting near him at the 1994 World Cup final in Pasadena, saying to her son: 'And you mean to tell me that none of these guys can pick the ball up with their hands?'

'No, Mom . . .'

'Well, what about that guy then?' (pointing at the referee putting the ball on the ground for a free kick).

'Oh *Mo-om*!'

You just think of all the people who would have loved to be there that day, or here today, and these are the ones who actually make it. The rugger buggers can't sustain a conversation about 'footer' for more than half a minute, and soon they're braying stuff like: 'Jonathan Davies was a thing of splendour!' and 'I once knew a chap had eight brothers, and they all played for the same rugger team, so it was "Thrum to Thrum, to Thrum, to Thrum, to Jones, back to Thrum, to Thrum . . ."'

Theo and I would really like to introduce these people to the boys we watched the Germany game with.

Back outside Niigata station is the departure point for the shuttle buses to the Big Swan stadium. There is a massive heaving crowd waiting there, and each bus that inches away, a *bento* box full of meat, has faces squashed up against the windows, surrounded by stray arms and legs that belong to torsos packed somewhere inside. The only time I've seen a vehicle so packed to bursting before was the car that used to carry the Ant Hill Mob in *Wacky Races*. We decide to get a cab.

We meet up briefly with David and Tomoko before getting in separate taxis and losing them again. He says, by the way, that his latest article in the *Evening Standard* was accompanied by Tomoko's picture of me and him together at Ireland v Saudi Arabia. In the early edition, anyway. Later in the day I was apparently replaced by the picture of him and his lucky pants outside BIG MEMBERS.

And this isn't the only time I've been done down by the press without my knowing it on this trip. I discover that there was a mention of the Ferrero Rocher amusement at the embassy in Tokyo in the *Sun*, of all places. One of the footballing MPs, trying desperately to spin some positive publicity out of the PR fiasco that was their Japan junket, related the gag as one of the highpoints. Except that in his version David did it.

The Big Swan – called Swan because the curving main stands resemble a swan's wings folded on its back as it swims along, and Big because of all the comparatively little swans that live on the neighbouring lake – is on the outskirts of the city in an area of open flat land, which means we can watch its bright lights getting closer from quite a way off as we approach in our taxi. It's another alien spacecraft, this one, drawing humans helplessly, hypnotically, towards its beams.

I'm allowing the excitement to get to me as we half walk, half run under a concrete underpass, past the stupid Hyundai fairground thing, towards the security check-ins. This is knock-out stuff, now. No 'a boring draw will do us'; it's a duel to extinction. This could be extra time, this could be penalties. The rumour going round is that Eriksson has picked his five penalty takers already, and they are Becks, Owen, Teddy, Scholesy and Rio. Not bad, although I'm not sure I've ever seen Rio take one before. And it will be a blow to Emile Heskey's hopes of getting a full ninety minutes in for once, knowing that Sven is already planning to have Sheringham on by the end.

Inside we all queue up for cold hot dog and drink, dutifully obeying the one-beer-each instruction. The bloke next to me, though, asks for four.

'Sorry. One beer per person.'

'Yeah, I know. I've got three mates.'

'Oh. OK, then, four beer . . .'

There is already a huge but orderly queue for the bogs, but the wait is enlivened by some impromptu street entertainment, provided by a fabulously drunk man who is trying to get his passport into his pants.

Ged is waiting for us at our seats, our – it has to be said, Ged – excellent seats. Thanks to him we have the luxury of having our own names printed on our tickets. This was supposedly the security measure that would prevent touting and forgery altogether but of course it is utterly unenforceable, and FIFA admitted as much just before the tournament started. For the first three games I'd have had to borrow Jim's passport to get in, and for Ireland v Saudi I'd have been masquerading as a member of the Football Association of the Seychelles.

Ged is thrilled, too, by the occasion, and this would be a dream gig for him, no doubt about it, if it wasn't for the fact that he was spending large parts of every day being slagged off by the world's media.

The teams come out – without Dom's inside track this time I'm trying to spot any changes, checking the numbers on their backs. It looks the same starting line-up as for Nigeria, three days ago – Seaman, Mills, Cole, Ferdinand, Campbell, Butt, Sinclair, Beckham, Scholes, Owen and Heskey. Despite the stories coming out over the last day or two, Denmark have both Tomasson and Tofting – nickname, 'the little lawnmower' – as well as the recalled striking star, Ebbe Sand, in their eleven for the national anthems.

Again we are given the trick second verse to deal with. This time a young Japanese fan in the row in front, outstandingly well prepared, shows us his mobile phone on which the lyrics to this verse are displayed, so while all the English people in the place are tutting, humming or reprising verse one, this chap is giving it 'confound her enemies' like a champion.

So. Which England is going to turn up today? The compact, competent, effective side that outplayed Argentina, or the hoof-it-and-hope merchants that crumpled in the second half against Sweden . . . ?

The first signs are that England are going to try to hit the front men early, as Rio Ferdinand finds Emile Heskey with a good ball into space on the right, but the big galoot shins it into touch and then falls flat on his face. Then Nicky Butt tries something of a hit-and-hope towards Michael Owen, and Martin Laursen nervously and unnecessarily heads it out for a corner from twenty-five yards out, clearly concerned about Owen nipping past him and doing him for pace.

Beckham takes the kick from the England left, to the usual accompaniment of hundreds of flashbulbs going off. Thomas Sorensen comes off his line to claim it, but the ball sails over his head to Rio Ferdinand, who has made a late run in beyond the far post. He nods it square, looking for Owen lurking in the middle of the goal, but Sorensen blocks with his chest, and for a micro-second that seems to be that, but then the ball squirms away from the Danish keeper, he swipes at it a couple of times, but can't stop it bobbling over the line. He swats it out, too late, and Heskey smashes it back into the roof of the net in any case. Five minutes on the clock – 1-0 to England.

A couple of days ago Rio Ferdinand complained that England were lagging behind the other countries when it came to goal celebrations – actually when it came to goals, too, come to that – but now that push has come to shove he himself doesn't seem to have much to offer. Maybe he's not sure he'll be allowed to have the goal, it was so obviously an own goal by Sorensen.

Worse news for Denmark: Thomas Helveg, Laursen's AC Milan colleague, seems to have run into the goal stanchion after his forlorn attempt to stop Ferdinand reaching the ball, and he's being carted away by stretcher bearers. Morten Olsen has to reorganise his defence – he brings on Kasper Bogelund, another baldy, which doesn't make the game any easier to follow.

The early goal seems to throw both teams out of their stride for a few minutes. England sit back and let Tofting and Gravesen have acres of space in midfield, but when the ball goes out wide Danny Mills and Ashley Cole are keeping a very tight rein on the dangerous wingers, Jesper Gronkjaer and Dennis Rommedahl, and Denmark's attacking moves are coming to nothing.

When England do begin to exert some pressure they nearly put together a tremendous goal. David Beckham is being forced away from goal at the edge of the area, when he suddenly turns and dinks a perfect flighted pass which clears both centre halves and drops for Owen to volley, but sadly for the scrapbooks he doesn't get hold of it properly.

The pattern the game settles into is one where England hold possession and stroll around slowly, until someone will crack and look for the killer long ball. When Denmark have possession they immediately try to up the tempo and catch England napping. Gronkjaer, Rommedahl, Tomasson and Tofting all have chances to put in decent crosses, but all of them are overhit.

On twenty-two minutes, England rouse themselves, and put together a sweeping passing move covering virtually the whole playing area. Trevor Sinclair has the ball on halfway, on the left wing. He lays it back to Cole, who plays it infield to Paul Scholes. The little ginger nut unleashes a piercing crossfield ball to Beckham on the right wing, who is closed down by Niclas Jensen, and forced back towards his own half. The captain plays back to Ferdinand, who quickly knocks the ball forward to Heskey. He touches it into Butt's path, and it's swept out to the left wing for Sinclair again, now on the edge of the box. His low square ball finds Butt again, who deftly flicks it forward, via Gravesen's thigh, for Owen, suddenly free, six yards out. His first touch kills the ball, his second sweeps it past Sorensen.

I'm on my feet, fists in the air, just like thousands of others all around me. I can hardly believe what I'm seeing. England two up, and what's more they're ripping apart a Denmark team that a few short days ago made the World Champions look ordinary.

I'm quickly back to earth, though, being as I've said of that cursed generation too young to remember 1966 but old enough to be traumatised by events in Leon in 1970. Two-goal leads can still be 3-2 defeats, that's the hard, hard lesson we learned that day, and here there're still golden goals and penalties to think about.

As if to bring this message home, Tofting plays Ebbe Sand in on the right. He makes to shoot, but then twists inside. Both Ferdinand and Campbell, worryingly, buy into the dummy wholeheartedly, but Sand drags his shot just wide. It's a wake-up call, boys. Not that anyone could sleep, with the racket that cretinous band are making.

The pattern reasserts itself. England seem muted, somehow, squandering possession almost casually, and Denmark have a lot of the ball without being able to penetrate. Butt is in charge, really, and there is a calmness about him, a serenity almost, that I haven't seen before. Then every now and again Sven's boys turn it on and pierce the Danish defence, sending panic shivering into the red lines. Ferdinand curls a beauty down the line to Beckham, who whips in a first-time cross to Heskey, who is just muscled out of it by Laursen, but the Danes are looking at each other, wondering where the next shaft of sudden brilliance will come from.

It starts to really tank it down towards half time. We're under cover, though, and in sufficiently buoyant mood to think that even the weather is on our side.

Suddenly there is a moment of complete silence. It's eerie how it happens. One moment there's noise, cheering, hubbub, the next we can quite clearly hear the players shouting to one another on the field, as though we were watching a Sunday park game. You'd swear you could hear birdsong. I'm wondering why, and then it dawns on me. The bloody band have stopped, that's what it is. It's taken everybody by surprise. They've been making their relentlessly wretched, half-witted, dreary, mind-numbing, no-talent row since the kick-off, and everyone else has just forgotten to make any sound. What a blessed relief that's over, particularly that skull-rattling, brain-perishing drum. Perhaps they've finally got the message. Perhaps someone has snapped, and strangled one of them with their bloody stupid 'Tebbit test' scarf. If they could just pack it in, now, then maybe . . .

BLAM! BLAM! BLAM! BLAM! BLAM! BLAM! BLAM! BLAM!

ENGLAND TILL I DIE! I AM ENGLAND TILL I DIE!
Too much to hope for.

Coming towards half time there is some movement on the England bench. Robbie Fowler, yet to kick a ball in the tournament, strips off his tracksuit, comes out onto the running track, gets wet, goes back, puts his tracksuit top back on again, sits down. What does that mean? Owen injured?

Tomasson skins Ferdinand, that's a bit of a shock, but his cross goes nowhere. I'm just saying to Ged that we need to hold on another couple of minutes till half time, it's vital to go in two up, when this happens: Mills takes a quick throw-in down the right, which Jensen back-heads into Beckham's chest. Beckham rolls it inside into Heskey's path, and the big forward runs onto it and bashes it joyfully under Sorensen's body and in for three. The Danish keeper seems to be beaten by the prodigious swerve, and the ball cannons off his elbow, down into the ground and up into the roof of the net.

England 3 Denmark 0.

In the remaining minute of the half, Gravesen finally gives up on trying to break down the massed white ranks with clever build-up play, and just wellies one from thirty-five yards, which David Seaman tips over the bar.

Half time, and we can't believe our luck. All around, England fans are smirking at one another, and giggling at how brilliantly, unexpectedly well everything is going. We've expected a nerve-shredding, all-the-way-to-the-wire experience, but surely it's a piece of cake now, and we'll be in the quarter final on Friday against Brazil (or Belgium).

I chat briefly with a Denmark fan, who is staring up at the floodlights on the curved front of the stand roof.

'It's not a three-nil game,' I say, trying to cheer him up. 'Denmark have had loads of possession, they don't deserve to be three down.'

'Actually,' he says, 'I'm going home tomorrow anyway, come what may, so really in a way I'm quite pleased.'

Quite pleased?

The second half is rather like watching a friendly. I'm sure everyone is still taking it seriously, especially Mills who gets booked for clattering Henriksen. But the steam has gone out of it. Eriksson makes substitutions, as is his wont in friendlies, with Fowler replacing Owen and Kieron Dyer coming on for Scholes, and these two put themselves about, having something to prove to the boss. I presume Beckham will move infield and Dyer will play out on the right, but in fact Eriksson seems to be having a look at Dyer alongside Butt.

Beckham is again prominent, trying one swerving shot that Sorensen has to tip over, but England concentrate on keeping things tight and making themselves difficult to break down. Denmark huff and puff but can't really make anything happen – there's a chance for Tomasson when Campbell slips but the linesman flags him offside, and Sand nearly twists his way through, but mostly they are resorting to long shots from Gravesen and Claus Jensen.

The crowd sing:

> *We're not going home,*
> *We're not going home,*
> *We're not going, we're not going,*
> *We're not going home . . .*

And a great long conga starts in the aisles, blokes who've paid God-only-knows-what to be here, not watching the game any more, just larking about in the walkways, with little Japanese children balancing on their shoulders, having a whale of a time. Hey, because of football, no more Buddha.

Gronkjaer and Rommedahl swap wings, but Mills and Cole still have their measure. Sheringham comes on, which must give the Danes a glimmer of hope as Sven clearly still believes it's going to penalties.

Long before the end, though, we've started thinking about Brazil (or Belgium), about the sumptuous samba-style flair of the Three Rs (or the doggedness of Marc Wilmots), the play-acting of Rivaldo (or Gert Verheyen). And at the end the players look relaxed and confident, there's no extravagant celebrating, just the feeling of a job well done. Only Robbie Fowler looks a bit downcast – he's not had the chance to show much in the second half, and he's got that nasty racehorse allergy to worry about.

Nick shoos me and Theo out of the exits at the end, but not before we've primed Ged for a call about tickets for the quarter final. We get to the cab ranks before the main crush of people are out of the stadium, and join a reasonable-sized queue. Nick is in extravagant mood, totally made up about the result, and the performance too, and the only real downer is the prospect of the journey ahead, crawling into town, then the inevitable ungodly crush at the station.

He suddenly says, 'Hey. Why don't we get a cab to take us all the way back to Echigo Yuzawa?'

Well, because it's at least an hour away on the fastest train in the civilised world never mind by car, and it will cost a fortune.

'I'll pay,' Nick says. 'I don't want to muck about all night trying to squeeze onto trains that are all packed. I don't want to spoil tonight, it's a great night. I'll pay.'

Theo and I decide to let him.

Our driver, when we reach the front of the extremely orderly queue, is an elderly gent with something of the air of a retired admiral. He has a white nautical-looking cap and a smart dark blazer, and he looks as if he's come straight here in his cab from a yacht. Maybe he has. With the cab fares in this country I imagine most of the yachts are owned by taxi drivers.

He pulls out into the slow-moving stream of traffic, and we head slowly towards a major junction a little way ahead. I can see that a left turn there will take us into the gridlock that is building on the road into Niigata, with the first motorised *bento* boxes full of fans just beginning to inch their way out of the car parks, while a right turn will lead us straight onto the expressway south, and freedom. I can see the lights of traffic moving freely on the flyover just beyond the junction, and the perfect getaway is in sight. We have until that junction to explain to the driver where we want to go.

At first it goes reasonably well.

'We go,' I say carefully, 'to Echigo Yuzawa.'

'*Hai*, Echigo Yuzawa!' the admiral nods.

'Echigo Yuzawa, hotel New Otani.'

Nope, the admiral is not with us any more. I try just repeating this a few times, and then remember the Japanese word for hotel. It is *hoteru*.

'Hoteru New Otani, Echigo Yuzawa.' The admiral nods happily. He understands that this is where we are staying. So far so good.

'You drive? You drive to Hoteru New Otani, Echigo Yuzawa?'

It's fortunate that we are in a line of stationary traffic as this goes in. The admiral turns to stare at us, a look of the frankest astonishment on his face. Over and over again we reassure him that this is what we want, and he pushes his cap back, scratches his head, giggles, it's the craziest thing he's ever heard.

We get him to write down how much it will cost on his notepad – it's a lot, but Nick waves it away nonchalantly – we say OK, let's go.

The admiral chuckles away to himself, shaking his head, and he inches forwards in the line of cars and buses. Every ten seconds or so he turns round to check that he's got it right, and we don't want to go to the station like everybody else.

'Hoteru New Otani?'

'Yes please.'

'Hoteru New Otani, Echigo Yuzawa?'

'Yes, that's right.'

'Hee hee hee hee hee!' The admiral takes his hat off, shakes his head in continued disbelief, scratches his crown, and puts his hat back on. We're all laughing along with him, now, but it looks as if we're on our way. As we get close to the junction, though, the point of no return, the admiral has a sudden crisis of confidence. With a squeal of brakes and a parp of complaint from the cab behind, he wrenches us over onto the hard shoulder.

We have no idea what he's up to now. This would be a truly horrible place to be thrown out of his cab – we'd have to walk back to the stadium and join the queues at the end, it'd take bloody hours to get away.

The admiral is radioing his head office, just to check that it's all right for him to take us all the way to Echigo Yuzawa. This is very frustrating, as we are now stopped, and all the traffic is really beginning to pile up.

'Drive!' we shout at him, but he holds his hand up for us to wait. 'Do this while you're driving!' – but he's now deep in a yammered conversation with his supervisor.

Eventually it appears that his boss wants to call ahead to the Hotel New Otani in Echigo Yuzawa just to check that we are really staying there, and aren't going to biff the admiral on the napper as soon as we get into open country. Fair enough, I suppose. The admiral turns to me.

'You!' he says, jabbing his horny forefinger in my face. 'You! Name?!'

Oh, here we go.

263

'England,' I say.
'Eng-u-ran?'
'England.'
'Eng-u-ran?'
'Yes. Me. Name. England.'
'Ah. Name. Eng-u-ran.'
'Yes.'

Finally the light dawns, but now the admiral has to sell this to his mate down the radio. We hear his end: 'Yada yada yada Eng-u-ran san . . . *Hai* . . . *Hai* . . . Eng-u-ran . . . *Hai* . . . Eng-u-ran . . . Yada yada yada yada . . . Eng-u-ran yada yada . . .'

Then he turns to me again. I think: 'At last we have sorted this out.'

He says, 'You! Name?!'

Oh hell.

'England. Me. Name. England England England!'

All the while we are helpless on the hard shoulder, with the roads ahead getting busier and busier and busier, all the advantage of our nifty exit trickling away into the night.

The admiral tells his boss for the umpteenth time that my name is England, but he's not buying it, and he's clearly undermining the old man's trust in me. When he turns back to me after a lengthy and increasingly heated debate down the radio, and says, 'You! Name?!' I give up.

'Listen,' I say. 'Forget it, forget my name.' In any case, it suddenly occurs to me, the hotel rooms are booked in Nick's name. 'Never mind about my name. His name . . . Hancock.'

I am anticipating this making everything go much more smoothly, but if anything the admiral is even more baffled.

'Han-cock-ooh?'
'Hancock.'
'Han-cock-ooh?'
'Hancock.'

'Han-cock-ooh?'

Oh dear God. Will to live oozing away . . .

'You. Name. Eng-u-ran? You. Name. Han-cock-ooh?'

There you go.

Now the admiral is very game, but this additional information seems to make the head of the man at the other end of the radio connection go pop in a big way. Back and forward the chatter goes, always the same.

'Yada yada yada Han-cock-ooh . . . Han-cock-ooh . . . *Hai* . . . Eng-u-ran . . . *Hai* . . . Han-cock-ooh . . . Han-cock-ooh.'

Then back to us.

'You? Han-cock-ooh? You Eng-u-ran? Han-cock-ooh? Eng-u-ran . . . ?'

We could have walked to bloody Echigo Yuzawa by now. Any minute I'm expecting to see the stadium lights go off and a night watchman strolling around the deserted car parks.

At last – *at last* – the man in the taxi office calls the hotel, and after another few minutes in which another bout of 'Han-cock-ooh? Eng-u-ran?' is going on between him and the hotel reception – which mercifully we are not privy to – the admiral gets the all-clear to go. We are round the corner, and up onto the expressway within two minutes.

I can't understand what went on just now. I am used to my name causing great merriment and confusion all around the world, but once we gave them Nick's name everything should have been much easier, shouldn't it? Oh well.

At the hotel, when we finally get there – and Nick has given the admiral a wedge of cash the size of a house brick – we are in different rooms to last night. The Western-style rooms we vacated this morning were already spoken for, and now Nick and I are sharing a Japanese-style room.

This is pleasant enough accommodation. The floor is covered in a soft rush matting that feels slightly padded underneath, and there are no beds, as such, but there is a cupboard stuffed with bedding. There's a low table in the centre of the room, surrounded by chairs with no legs so you can squat round and take tea, presumably.

I am dog tired, but when I stretch out on the floor to try to sleep, I think: 'Oh dear me no, this isn't going to work, not at all . . .'

Next thing I know it's four in the morning, and Nick has gone, driven into Theo's room next door by my contented snoring.

16
Hot Hot Hot

———

'We weren't lucky. It's the Irish who've got flowers
in their arses.'
– Jose Antonio Camacho, coach of Spain

16 JUNE

At this point in the trip I have planned to spend a few days
in Kyushu, the south-westernmost of Japan's main islands. Of
course, if England had topped the Group of Death they'd be
playing in Oita this afternoon, and the whole plan would have
made a bit more sense. With Cube back in England and Theo's
plans uncertain, Nick has decided to tag along with me, and
in the morning we go by train and courtesy bus to the airport
where we catch a shuttle flight south.

Travelling down to Fukuoka from Niigata, our luggage
makes perhaps the most offensive journey in world aviation,
labelled as it is 'NIG to FUK'.

Next to me on the plane is a Brazilian journalist from Globo
TV, the South American broadcasting giant. I ask him about
Brazil's open and attractive style of play, given that we had
been led to believe that Scolari had made them into a bunch
of dour and defensive underachievers.

'I am not surprised how they are playing,' he says. 'Nobody
in Brazil is surprised. If they had come to the World Cup and
played how they played in the qualifying competition Scolari
would have been lynched. It must be beautiful football for
Brazil, that is the most important thing. We want to win, of

course, but most important is to play beautiful football.'

In the row in front is a garrulous English man, the sort of chap who has everything sorted out, and he bangs on about what a great deal he got on flights, and how the hotels he booked made a mistake with his reservation so he got everything for free. He arrived in Japan with no match tickets, but that's no problem to the likes of him.

'This guy from JAWOC, the organising committee, came up to me out of the blue in the airport as soon as we arrived, and gave me Prestige Silver hospitality packages for all the games, just like that, absolutely free. And he's been taking me to the games in his silver Mercedes, and he gave me a digital camera . . .'

Kyushu has a reputation for being a relaxed and uncomplicated place. We pick up a small and cheap hire car from a rental place near the airport – a Nissan Matchbox, I think it is. The only thing that stops us setting off and heading out is that the car hire people have no maps of the island. Nick trots off round the corner, where he has spotted a specialist map shop. This place has maps of anywhere you might want to go – Tokyo, London, Australia, even one or two imaginary places. But none of Kyushu. All of which is nicely relaxed, right enough, but does tend to make driving around the place more complicated.

In the end we find a half-decent drawing of the surrounding streets at least in the car hire company brochure, and this is good enough to get us up onto the toll expressway, where we can follow our noses. And some great big signs. We are heading for a resort on the east coast called Beppu, which is actually the next big place up from Oita, where Sweden play Senegal this afternoon.

After lunch in a service station called 'Hello Square', one of a chain which was presumably founded in the sixties by sarcastic hippies, we belt along the Yamanami Highway, which carves a scenic route towards the sea through rolling green hills, and is relatively traffic-free. This is a surprise, given the stories I've read in advance about Japan's gridlock, but when we reach the tollbooth at the far end and find out how much we have to pay we realise why.

Ultimately we find ourselves coming down a big slope towards both Beppu and Oita in bright and gorgeous sunshine just as the Sweden v Senegal match is kicking off. It is the last to be played at the Big Eye, and as we pass a special road sign put up by the World Cup organisers giving directions how to get there we see that five workmen are already swarming all over it, dismantling it. Very efficient.

Beppu is spread up the hillsides surrounding a very attractive bay. As you drive down into it you can't help noticing that steam is pouring up all over the place, through tall thin metal chimneys, up from behind buildings, or just up from cracks in the ground, and the town seems to be quietly hissing. From above, it looks a bit as if Beppu is hosting a large traction engine rally, but of course it is the volcanic activity for which Kyushu is renowned.

The Suginoi hotel in Beppu, when we eventually find it, is a vast resort place perched halfway up a mountain overlooking the bay, dedicated more or less entirely to bathing.

Two huge and rather garish *onsens* are the main attraction, with pools of all shapes and sizes set in giant hothouses so you can make believe you are having your hot spa bath in the middle of a jungle. One has waterfalls and slides, the other a statue of Kannon, the Buddhist goddess of mercy, revolving slowly on top of a big fish tank. The whole place is pretty much what you might expect if the subtle and ancient art of the Japanese bath had been taken over by the people who run Center Parcs.

There are also things like a baseball machine, a bowling alley, loads of restaurants and fancy gift shops, but these are things you are supposed to use just to fill in the hours between baths, while you wait for the wrinkles in your fingers and toes to flatten out again.

It's practically empty, though, and we are really rattling around in here with a super-abundance of bored-looking staff. It feels wrong, somehow, for a place like this to be out of season in the middle of June on a baking hot day like today, but Japan's big holiday times are April and October, apparently. This is supposed to be the rainy season.

We don't have to make the choice between a Western-style room and a Japanese-style room, not this time, because our rooms are Western-style with a complete Japanese-style room in the middle of it. With a deft rearrangement of some sliding wood-and-paper shutters you can choose between sleeping on the floor, in the traditional way, or in a big luxurious double bed in the decadent European fashion.

Well, you know the old saying, that begins: 'When in Rome . . .'? I have my own old saying, which goes: 'When in Rome, try to get your hands on as many home comforts as you possibly can.' Big bed for me, I think. But thanks for asking . . .

I nip (sorry) next door into Nick's room to watch Sweden v Senegal, which is already under way.

The Swedes draw first blood, which is perhaps just as well for them, given the probability that Senegal will last better in the heat. A straightforward corner is swung in from the left, and Henrik Larsson, unmarked, simply drifts in front of Tony Sylva and nods it firmly down and into the net.

I find myself pondering again whether Sven deliberately avoided topping Group F so as to play in Niigata rather than having to deal with this tricky game against the Africans in mid-afternoon.

'It looks really hot there,' I say.

'Well, you know, it's really hot here and we're only about five miles away,' Nick says. Good point, well made.

It's an even sort of a game, and Senegal just about deserve to draw level when they get a goal out of nothing. A pretty random header by Diouf falls to Henri Camara on the edge of the area, right of centre. He brings it down on his chest, and big blond Johan Mjallby ambles out to close him down. A step over, and a jink to one side, and Camara has suddenly created half a yard of space and raked a low shot past Hedman into the bottom corner for 1–1.

The two teams slow down to strolling pace in the second half, and begin to cancel one another out. The best chance falls to substitute Zlatan Ibrahimovic – good old Nordic name, that one – but the twenty-year-old Ajax wonderkid selfishly shoots rather than squaring to Larsson who would have had a tap in.

The urgency returns, though, when this becomes the first game in the tournament to move into golden goal extra time. I don't approve of it myself – just think of the classic 1970 semi between Italy and West Germany that finished 4–3 to Italy, with five goals in extra time. That would have been 2–1 under these playing conditions. To West Germany. I have to admit, though, golden goal can be heart-stoppingly exciting. And this game very nearly produces a goal as golden as any we've yet seen in the tournament.

Larsson hooks a high ball into the Senegal box, looking for Ibrahimovic. Coly nicks it away from under the striker's feet, and it rolls out to Anders Svensson standing fourteen yards out. As Lamine Diatta goes to close him down, Svensson starts to turn his back on goal, drags the ball back with first one foot then the other leaving Diatta flailing, spins right round through 360 degrees and curls a sumptuous right-foot shot round the on-rushing Coly. It smacks against the post and away. Svensson holds his head in anguish, knowing that Sweden's quarter-final place and a really great crack at Goal of the Tournament were both just six inches away.

Just before the mid point of extra time, Pape Thiaw runs diagonally across the midfield, going nowhere in particular, and show-off-backheels the ball to Henri Camara in more or less exactly the spot from which he scored in the first half.

Four defenders move to crowd him out, but Camara drops a shoulder and bursts through them, and his mishit left-foot shot fools Hedman, who is expecting more power, and scuttles just inside the post.

Senegal are through, and they rip off their shirts in delight and go into their little kicking dance. They're the first African nation into a quarter final since Cameroon in 1990, and who's to say they won't go even further. Henrik Larsson's international retirement announcement comes so quickly at full time that he must have given it out in envelopes to all the commentators, saying, 'If we lose, you can open this.'

I'll remember this match, though, for the Svensson Spin.

Nick and I drive down into Beppu for a look around, and come across Takegawara *onsen*, which is inside a big old wooden building in the backstreets near the sea front. It's Meiji era, apparently, and while I'm not altogether sure when that was I think I can safely say that this is one of the few buildings I've seen in Japan so far that dates from a time before the Beatles.

As well as the hot hot hot spring baths that we've seen elsewhere, this place also boasts a bath in hot volcanic sand, and I decide to give this a try. Nick, not having to do an offbeat daily piece about life in Japan for talkSPORT or anything, is not so bothered, but comes in anyway.

The woman in the kiosk takes our money and hands over a couple of little towels with which to preserve our modesty. Even though she must do this all day every day, this still gives her a fit of the giggles, and she can't look us in the eye. There's really no excuse for such mirth, unless the whole thing is some elaborate hoax.

Inside, once we've shoved our valuables into a locker and hidden our other valuables behind the free towel – which is really far too small – we get our first look at the sand bath. A long steaming mound of black sand fills most of the lower level of a large room, divided in the middle by a tall screen. Behind this screen is the ladies' sand bath – they get two little towels, apparently. The steaming sand is being shovelled around, constantly on the move, by two elderly ladies in overalls, who look like a couple of school dinner ladies. A couple of disembodied heads, pink and also steaming, stick up above the surface of the sand, their eyes fixed on a big clock on the far wall.

The dinner ladies pause in their shovelling for a moment to indicate, using the international language of mime, that Nick and I should wash ourselves in the small bathing pool before coming on down so the real fun can start. Now this seems a bit much to me. I can understand why it would be considered necessary to cleanse yourself thoroughly before sharing a nude bath of hot water with a bunch of strangers, it's only polite. To go to the trouble of washing yourself in front of a captive, if steaming, audience just so that you're clean for a couple of seconds before they bury you alive in hot black filth – well, that's making a fetish of cleanliness, to my way of thinking. That's not healthy.

Still, I do as I'm told, and then trot down to the sand tray, where a dinner lady has made a shallow little sand coffin for me. I lie down, to find I am sloping at an angle of around forty-five degrees, I arrange my little towel just so, and then she begins to slop the black muck all over me, with the same nonchalant carelessness a real dinner lady might exhibit while doling out mushy peas. When only my head is showing, she leans over, points at the clock, and says, 'Ten minute, OK?' I nod tinily.

A little way off, Nick's head is sticking out of the sand, like David Bowie's at the end of *Merry Christmas Mr Lawrence*. Perhaps this is where they got the idea for that bit.

It is a curious experience. I can feel the heat building along my spine, from the sloping mass of black sand beneath, and before long I am suffering the exquisite torture of sweat running down from my hair and into my ears, without being able to do anything about it, because my hands are buried and I can't move my head.

Apart from this, though, it is quite comfortable, until it starts to get just that little bit hotter, and then hotter still. I glance up the clock – barely five of my ten minutes are up. When I was about ten my family lived in New Zealand for a while, and I have a vivid childhood memory of being taken to a Maori feast where the food was cooked by burying it in the ground with a bunch of hot rocks. I think they were hot from a fire rather than volcanic activity, although I can't be sure. Anyway, the feast – meats, vegetables, sweet potatoes – had been underground for hours before we arrived for the digging up and eating part, as it was a very long and slow process. Here, though, I have the feeling that I'm cooking rather quickly, and my sweet potatoes are just about done.

At ten minutes I wriggle clumsily out of the clinging sand, as Nick is doing a little further along. *Merry Christmas Mr Lawrence* turns into *Night of the Living Dead*. Of course, we have to wash ourselves again before we're allowed to go and wash ourselves in the public bath. Nick opts out of the last bit, presumably feeling that it's only possible to get so clean. I go into the *onsen*, which is old and wooden and brown. Three or four Japanese gents are squatting by the edge, washing themselves by dipping a wooden bucket in, but no one is actually venturing bodily into the water. When I step in myself I realise why. It is bloody unbearably hot, that's why. I leap out again like Tom when Jerry has put his tail in the toaster.

While I'm getting dry and dressed I find I am looking absent-mindedly out of a window at the convenience store over the road. The sand bath is supposed to be invigorating, but that's not quite the word I'd use. I'd go for gritty, I think, if pushed . . . I suddenly realise that the window is open to the street, it is full length down to the floor, and I haven't got any clothes on. All of a sudden that convenience store looks a damn sight too convenient.

Before the Ireland v Spain match starts, Nick and I look around the hotel for something to eat. There are plenty of restaurants in the complex, but they are all now shut. At eight in the evening. A poster catches our eye. 'World Cup Bar' it says, 'open throughout the 2002 World Cup. Food drink football'. That sounds more like it. It's on the top floor, and we head up there, but as we step out of the lifts it is suspiciously quiet. There is a low background of jazzy muzak, but otherwise no sign of human life. There is a bar, a classy, relaxed place with lots of black leather furniture and smoked-glass tables, all empty. There is a fantastic view over Beppu harbour, and more large potted plants than you could shake a stick at, but no TV. This must be the wrong place. We turn to leave, and a smart waitress appears.

'Ah, hello,' Nick says. 'World Cup Bar?'

'Yes, sir, this is World Cup Bar. What would you like to drink?'

'But . . . you don't have a television, with the World Cup on it, anywhere?'

'Oh no, sir.'

'So, in what sense is this the *World Cup* Bar?'

The waitress smiles vacantly. She is baffled by this question, and frankly so are we. We go down to Nick's room instead, and raid the World Cup minibar.

After eight minutes Spain catch Ireland napping. Puyol takes a quick throw-in on the right wing and gets the ball straight back from Luis Enrique. With Kilbane struggling to get to him, Puyol whips in a near-post cross, which sails over Ian Harte and is glanced in by Fernando Morientes. Spain 1 Ireland 0.

Ireland come back at them. The crowd noise surges as Damien Duff gets the ball, and he takes the Spanish defence on, but he finds himself expertly steered into a cul de sac by the imposing Fernando Hierro.

One rather Irish touch I haven't noticed before. On the back of his white number 10 shirt Robbie Keane has not just his surname but also his initial – R. KEANE. This is to distinguish him from who, exactly?

Spain are sitting back, confident that they have the measure of the Irish attack, and they are happy to concede the bulk of the possession. Ireland are finding that their forward thrusts are being picked off, and the midfielders Matt Holland and Kevin Kilbane often seem to be stuck for a forward ball to play. Spain, meanwhile, are streaming forward on the counter-attack, and their three clever forwards, Raul, Morientes and Luis Enrique, are moving skilfully and dangerously. Mick McCarthy has clearly decided that his back line will play an offside trap, and time and time again one of the three Spanish stars gets caught out by the linesman's flag. In the dugout, McCarthy himself is throwing his arm up in the air like Tony Adams in his heyday, appealing for each one.

A bout of head tennis in the Irish area sees Luis Enrique poach the loose ball and stick it away, but his aeroplane celebration is cut short by the linesman, and then Morientes too has a goal, lobbed over the on-rushing Given, chalked off. Really quite a close call, that one. The coach, Camacho, is getting quite agitated about all the offsides – by half time there have been nine – and unbelievably no one has yet suggested to him that he should wear dark tops. He flashes his sweaty pits, like dark dinner plates on his sky-blue shirt, as he berates the officials from the technical area – he could hardly perspire more if he were buried up to his neck in volcanic black sand.

Just before the break Ireland have their best chance so far, when Holland dinks a through ball to Keane. Unfortunately, though, the ball gets big on the Leeds man, and in the end he can only toe-end it over Iker Casillas and also the crossbar.

As the teams troop off, though, it seems that Spain have been relatively comfortable, and Ireland need to change something in the second half if they are to break them down.

Nick and I, meanwhile, are starving. We run out to the car and drive down the main drag into Beppu to try to get a bite, quickly, but the whole place is shut. Like Blackpool in November, without the lights (as turned on by Keith Harris and/or Orville). We scuttle back, stomachs still audibly rumbling, just in time for the restart, having achieved precisely nothing.

Gary Kelly has looked more and more like a right back playing out of position on the right wing, and he puts in two poor crosses in quick succession just before McCarthy hauls him off and brings on Niall Quinn. This means Damien Duff moving out to the right, and straightaway he begins to torment Juanfran, while Quinn gives Hierro a very different opponent to deal with. Soon Quinn is winning the ball in the air, and dumping the Spanish captain on the turf in the process.

Spain still look in control of things. On the hour, though, Duff gets the ball on the right, and sells a dummy which is comprehensively bought by three Spanish defenders before pinging in a dangerous cross. This is a taster for what is to come for Spain, as a minute later he surges into the area and is tripped by the out-paced Juanfran to give Ireland a penalty.

Ian Harte, the Leeds dead-ball specialist, takes it. He blows hard, concentrating, feeling the pressure, and plays it waist high to the left. Casillas has gone the right way, and almost dives too far, but he manages to block the ball back into play. Kilbane, following up, has the whole goal gaping in front of him and unbelievably shins it wide. Harte, Holland, Kelly, McCarthy – the hands go to the heads in disbelief.

Raul almost rubs salt into the wound by stabbing home a Baraja through ball on the turn, but yet again Spain have the goal disallowed for offside. Ireland are playing a dangerous game here – Sweaty Camacho, a member of the Spain side which lost to Northern Ireland in 1982, is beside himself.

In Beppu we have the bilingual facility on our television, and so we are able to hear Barry Davies go through an inexplicable phase of referring to Duff, easily Ireland's best player now, as 'Dunn'.

Ten minutes to go. Camacho's settled for 1–0, and has taken off both strikers, Raul and Morientes. Spanish ambition has drained away completely now with the finishing line in sight, and they are resorting to fouling and time-wasting. Baraja gets booked for booting the ball away, Casillas clatters Keane but gets away with it, and then Mendieta stops an advance down the right with his elbow.

There're two minutes left now. Steve Finnan hoofs a high ball into the mixer, and suddenly Anders Frisk, the excellent Swedish referee, is pointing to the spot and showing a yellow card to Hierro. Spanish players are protesting, but Hierro isn't one of them – he knows what he's done. On the replay it looks positively comical. As the ball comes in he's got two handfuls of the back of Quinn's shirt, and has lifted them right above the big Sunderland striker's head. What on earth was he thinking of?

Keane must score, and slams it low and left past the rooted Casillas. Harte's face on the bench is a picture of delight and relief, and the cry goes up all round the Suwon stadium: *You'll never beat the Irish!*

Duff weaves his magic one more time before we go into golden goal time, and Ireland are looking the stronger team all of a sudden.

Nick and I are chomping our way through a very small packet of minibar nuts, and we have to postpone our quest for more food a little longer . . .

In the breather before it all starts again, McCarthy moves amongst his men, embracing, cajoling, stirring up. The spirit he has inspired in this team, after the potentially catastrophic shenanigans with Roy Keane, has been a credit to him.

The earlier golden goal game between Sweden and Senegal was breathlessly exciting. When this extra period begins, however, it becomes clear that Spain have shot their bolt. Camacho has removed their strikers, trying to sit on a 1-0 lead, and now they are toothless up front. They are also a man down. Having used all three substitutes, Camacho finds that David Albelde cannot continue as he has a twisted testicle – amazing, that there should be a football injury that I've never heard of. The Spaniards clearly think the whole world is against them and they are snapping at one another and contesting every decision. In short, they are there for the taking.

And, to be sure, Ireland are all over them. Duff, in particular, is having the time of his life out on the right wing. Time and time again he bundles his way past three, four Spanish defenders, stumbling to the floor, picking himself up, finding he still has the ball, nutmegging the next man. Spain are reduced to hoofing long balls up to Luque, isolated up front on his own with no support at all. On the bench, Raul and Morientes, despair etched on their faces, can hardly bear to watch.

Baraja has a good shot beaten out by Given. Seconds later David Connolly drills a shot achingly just wide with Casillas flailing. For the last few minutes Spain exert a little pressure, but it is clear that they are playing for penalties and just trying to contain Ireland further up the field. There is time for Duff to have one more mazy run past the right back, but his pull back fails to find Keane.

And then Anders Frisk brings on the penalty shoot-out.

McCarthy gathers his men into a huddle, and he's giving them a blood-and-thunder speech, jabbing his hand emphatically. He's proud of them, they've done the country proud, whatever happens now.

The Irish line up on the touchline, all the players, all the subs, all the backroom staff. Each man has his arms round the bloke on either side of him. The players are wearing bright orange bibs, the colour of the hair of half the people in the crowd. We're in this together, this gesture says. Now can the spirit that has got them this far take them one small step further . . . ?

The Spanish drift around, in contrast, squeezing water from yellow bottles down their necks. Raul and Morientes have cheered up, despite the fact that Spain have an undistinguished record in big shoot-outs. They lost to Belgium in 1986, and England in Euro 96, when Stuart Pearce went just that little bit mental in front of the nation. Now, though, their mood is better than Ireland's, I think. They are relieved. Ireland feel they should have won it already.

First up it's Robbie Keane, who's been terrific, against Iker Casillas. He runs up quite slowly, waiting for the keeper to go. He put one low and left just over half an hour ago – now he goes . . . high, hard and in.

For Spain: Fernando Hierro, captain, regular spot-kick taker, who has scored two penalties in the tournament already. Has Given been watching the tapes? Hierro also runs up slowly. Given can't wait, and dives to his left, Hierro thumps the ball the other way. 1–1.

Next it's Matt Holland for Ireland. He's had a really good World Cup, but doesn't look as if he's relishing this. He doesn't look at the keeper, goes high, and hits the bar.

Ruben Baraja licks his lips, and sidefoots in for 2–1 to Spain.

Then David Connolly trots up, places the ball, then places it again. When Frisk's whistle sounds, he runs up as fast as he can and blams it down the middle. Casillas parries it easily. Poor penalty. Poor Connolly.

Juanfran steps up next for Spain. His penalty sends Given the wrong way, and the ball too, banging into the red JVC hoarding alongside the goal.

Now Ireland have a chance to put a bit of pressure on, if

only Kevin Kilbane can stick his away. It's another shocker, though, on a plate for Casillas, diving to his left.

Valeron stands ready, lips clamped together, looking doomed. The little stop in the run-up does for Given, but the kick grazes the post on its way towards the photographers. Still 2–1. Perhaps no one else is ever going to score another one.

Steve Finnan is up for Ireland. If he misses it's all over. Casillas guesses wrong, and the Fulham full back whacks the ball in, top right, clenches his fist, still a chance.

Gaizka Mendieta walks to the gallows, puts the ball on the spot, walks backwards, a long straight run-up. Then he puts up his hand like a traffic cop, and walks forwards to place the ball again, ever so just so. Nails are being bitten, hands are on heads, over eyes. The Irish Tiller Girl line holds firm, and they all have to watch – their hands are all on each other's shoulders. Mendieta jogs up . . . and slides it in just where Given was standing a split second before he guessed right, which was wrong. 3–2 to Spain, and Mick's boys are out.

A pile of Spaniards suddenly materialises on the penalty spot. Mendieta is at the bottom of it somewhere, and it is not only jubilation but also relief on those faces. Jose Antonio Camacho, particularly, will know he's got out of jail.

Ireland have had a fantastic ride, and deserve better. At the end, though, the luck of the Irish simply deserted them. The replay of Mendieta's decisive penalty, incredibly, shows the ball heading straight for Shay Given's outstretched leg, until it hits the six-yard line in a puff of white paint and kicks up an unexpected and crucial extra couple of inches.

Nick and I finally manage to get a bit of pizza in the self-styled World Cup Bar on the top floor, overlooking Beppu's twinkling nightscape. It tastes good, but it could have tasted so much better . . .

17
Active My Aso

'You are filth and you smell of manure.'
– Robert Waseige, coach of Belgium, to the Belgian
press contingent

17 JUNE

Nick and I go on an expedition today, and learn about a couple
more aspects of Japanese politeness, particularly their horror
of disappointing or inconveniencing us in any way.

Rather than hang about in Beppu (which is closed), we
pack up our tiny hire car with all the fishing gear that Nick
has been acquiring, and which now seems to inhabit a large
khaki-coloured canvas bag that I haven't seen before, and set
off into the middle of Kyushu.

I fancy taking a look at the active volcano, Mount Aso, in
the middle of the Aso-Kuju National Park (spectacular scenery
promised). Nick has been pestering the hotel receptionists with
his Japanese fishing directory, and one of them has assured him
that one of the places where fine fishing is to be had might be
quite near to Aso.

We avoid the toll expressway, and take a winding road
through lush green forests. It's the sort of road on which
in Derbyshire, say, I'd inevitably come up behind some Mr
Magoo pootling along at nineteen miles an hour with no
prospect of passing him before the following Tuesday. Here in
Japan it's a little different. The back end of a white hatchback
with an extremely careful driver tooling along at a much more

282

gentle pace than mine hoves into view, and I sigh inwardly, fall into line, and change down a gear, preparing to watch a small convoy building up in my mirror for the next little while. No sooner has the motorist in front caught sight of me, though, than he (or she) has pulled right off the road and stopped to let me by. I think at first that they are having some kind of medical emergency, but no, when I look behind me I see the white car easing back onto the road and continuing on its merry way.

A few minutes later it happens again, a van this time, struggling up a slight hill. I come up behind it, and it virtually leaps off the road for fear of holding me up.

Well, this is a right result, and with seventeen years of London driving on my CV I leave a trail of other people's skidmarks all over the grass verges of Kyushu, as cars, vans, buses, tractors, and on one occasion a horse, all make way for the Brit in a hurry. All this politeness is a little unnerving at first – I am worried that they are bowing as they drive, taking their eyes off the road ahead for crucial seconds, and that if they bow too enthusiastically to me they might set off their airbags with their foreheads – but I soon get used to it.

Our twisty one-lane road climbs up a heavily forested mountain. I am presuming, for a while, that this is a foothill of the great volcano, but we start going downhill again, and emerge on a great plain, stretching flatly on for miles in front of us, the road becoming arrow straight as it heads off into the haze.

Eventually, after a couple of hours of driving, we reach the town of Aso, which is at the foot of the volcano itself. We stop for a coffee in the railway station, which has a small tourist information centre. When we ask about the fishing, and Nick shows the lady his fishing directory, we discover that the man at our Beppu hotel reception was being excessively encouraging when he said that it was near here, desperate not to disappoint us, and in fact it's up Mount Aso and down the other side, a good hour further on.

I say what the hell, we've come this far, I'll take Nick fishing, leave him there, and come back to look at the volcano by myself. So I drive all the way up Mount Aso, all the way down the far side, and then we optimistically start looking for signs of a river. After at least half an hour we spot another local information centre, and Nick trots in with his fishing directory. It turns out that the lady in the first information centre was just being polite, hoping not to disappoint us, and in fact it's another half an hour further on. Back into the car, and off into the hills.

Forty-five, fifty minutes later it dawns on us that the lady in the second information centre was being extremely optimistic in her estimate, out of politeness no doubt and a desire not to disappoint us. We can see where we are on the map, and we aren't lost, just excessively encouraged. Finally we see a sign with a happy cartoon fish on it, pointing down a side road – 'Fishing 1 kilometre'. Hoorah!

Four kilometres later we realise that the sign was only being polite, not wanting us to get downhearted, but we do eventually actually find the place. I leave Nick there, wrangling over rod hire and bait and the like, and pulling on his little red Japanese wellies.

I then retrace my steps back up the slope of Mount Aso. The Aso Caldera is an ancient crater – the world's largest, as the Japanese are excited to tell you – formed by the collapse, around 100,000 years ago, of what must have been the world's largest volcano. It's fifteen miles from north to south, and over eleven east to west, and lava thrown out by the ancient beast is said to cover two-thirds of the island of Kyushu. It is thought that after the volcano's collapse a lake formed in the crater, but the volcanic activity continued and thrust up a handful of peaks in the centre, which today are collectively known as Aso-san – the *san* a mark of respect for the volcano – or the Aso Gogaku. The lake drained away, leaving a flat plain which is now inhabited by over 70,000 people who work the rich volcanic soil – and for all I know have invigorating and gritty baths in it too.

Aso-san's five main peaks line up across the caldera, stepping up in height west to east. Taka-dake, at 1,592 metres high, is the biggest, and Naka-dake, which butts onto the side of it, is the one that is still active, and consequently the one to see. Another, smaller than the main five, is called Komezuka, and it's a perfect little cone, like a little pet volcano. It's known as the 'hill of rice', the story going that the god Takawatsu-no-mikoto scooped a giant handful off the top to feed his starving people, thus creating the distinctive bowl-shaped indentation.

Before you get to the steep winding road which leads up Naka-dake, there's a large and fancy gift shop, because, who knows, you might want to commemorate your trip to the top of an active volcano by buying a glass dolphin or a cuckoo clock. A museum shows dramatic views of the eruptions at Mount Aso in the recent past, and other volcanoes around the world, and also, naturally, an exhibition of antique European music boxes. What else would you expect there to be?

There is a ropeway which takes visitors almost to the summit, but I feel it will be more dramatic to make my way up under my own steam.

It has turned into a dark and brooding afternoon. A heavy layer of grey cloud is sitting just above the peaks, and it is starting to rain as I climb, and getting cold, too. Near the top the grassland which covers most of the slopes gives way to volcanic rocks in a whole range of browns and oranges, some of them colours that rocks usually aren't. The top ropeway station, like the gift shop below, is deserted, this being the off-season for all Japanese tourist destinations, and so when I walk up the last slope to the rim of the crater, it's just me and the volcano.

I walk gingerly up to the edge and peer over.

The inside of the crater slopes away from my vantage point,

great scratches in the sides that look like the work of giant fingernails. The rocks scattered loosely here have a yellowish, sulphurous tinge, and if you tried to walk down you'd soon be scrabbling, sliding, breaking your own nails trying to stop yourself. Down at the bottom, almost obscured by clouds of grey-white steam but occasionally coming into clear view, is a lake, a hissing boiling plate of striking pale blue. To the side of this, round the corner so you can't actually see its point of origin, a constant plume of steam is rushing out with tremendous force, not straight upwards but kind of diagonally as if out of the spout of a great kettle, and there is an incredible roaring sound like a blast furnace. The white-grey steam gushes up, spreading wider and wider as it rises, and then it meets and mingles with the clouds only a few feet above my head.

It is as though I have found the place where the clouds come from.

I am fascinated by this sight, and stay up here by myself for a long while, wandering around the bizarre striated moonscape, watching the clouds hanging just overhead being fuelled by the great belching cavern below, the boiling hotline to the centre of the earth.

The time arrives for my slot on talkSPORT, so I call them and tell Gary, the producer, that I am on top of an active volcano called Mount Aso, and I go straight on air with Mike and Alan. They are fascinated, naturally, by the pronunciation of the volcano's name, and it has to be said that in the information centre it was definitely being pronounced Arse-o. The sulphurous fumes now emanating from the lake below really clinch that particular deal.

I describe the scene for them, and Alan says, 'It sounds like something out of a Bond movie.' He's thinking of *You Only Live Twice* – clearly he's done the same research for this World Cup as I have.

I go on to talk of related volcanic activities, the *onsens* and the hot black sand baths, and in return they tell me that the USA are leading Mexico 1–0.

Once I'm finished with talkSPORT I speak to Susan on the phone. I just have time to tell her I am on top of a volcano, and then the phone cuts out in a great cloud of interference. That puts the wind up her for a moment or two until I get reception back. It's breakfast time at home, and it feels decidedly odd to hear about Peter cutting his head on the shower – no stitches required, apparently – while staring into the pale blue eye of the bowels of the earth. Michael the baby, too, has been in the wars (he fell off a guitar).

I can hardly drag myself away from this view, it's so dramatic and elemental, but gradually I find I'm getting short of breath and my hands have come out in a red rash all of a sudden. I've been up here too long. Down below a sign warns you not to approach if you suffer from asthma, so God knows what poisons are being chucked into the air all around.

Down to the car, and off to fetch Nick. He, too, has had a satisfying afternoon. The fishing place, like the one at Echigo Yuzawa, is heavily stocked by a farm upstream, but Nick was able to wander off on his own and use his own flies rather than the bait supplied, which meant, as I understand it, that he could use a certain amount of skill and didn't have to kill absolutely everything he caught, so he was feeling pretty pleased with himself.

On the way back we pass a vantage point from which the five peaks of the Aso Gogaku take on the aspect of the Buddha in repose. If, one day, the skyline was changed by a massive eruption, would that mean no more Buddha . . . ?

Back in Beppu we switch on the game which will decide England's quarter-final opponents on Friday. Shades of Moore and Pele, Banks and Jairzinho, Astle and Tostao jostle with one another, along with – in the background, barely noticed – the single more recent snapshot of Platt's last-gasp winner against Preud'homme in Italia 90. Belgium's odds are 9–1 in this two-horse race, such is the excitement generated by the Three Rs. They are reunited this evening, as Ronaldinho comes back into the side, along with the fourth R – Roberto Carlos.

It is an open game, and both sides make chances. First a sweeping Belgian move finds Mbo Mpenza outside the box, and he almost catches Marcos out with a floated lob to the back post. Then van Buyten blocks a Ronaldo shot, accidentally bashing the striker in the mouth. Van Buyten wants to be careful – those teeth could have his arm off.

Brazil's defence looks pretty rocky – or Roque junior, strictly speaking. Verheyen, Wilmots, and Mpenza all win the ball too easily in the air in quick succession, and right back Cafu is more likely to be found between his own front men than tracking back.

The camera roves the crowd relentlessly, on its eternal and faintly depressing search for Brazilian girls with big breasts. It reveals a surprising number of Argentinian supporters mingling with the Brazilians doing the samba. I don't think you'd have seen a similar picture at any previous tournament, but here, at this World Cup, perhaps it really is a case of no more Buddha.

Jacky Peeters drifts a high ball right to left towards the back post. Marc Wilmots challenges Roque junior, but the Brazilian has misjudged the flight totally, and the Belgian captain climbs and heads home comfortably, confidently, to give Belgium a shock lead. Wilmots wheels away, only to find, to his and everyone else's utter disbelief, that referee Peter Prendergast has disallowed the goal, seemingly believing that it is impossible for an international defender to make as feeble an effort as Roque junior's without being impeded in some way.

Half time arrives with the game goalless. Ronaldo has had a number of decent chances, and looks powerful and fast, back to his best. Ronaldinho has twice found himself marked by four Belgians, and just twisted and turned his way through them to make a chance for a team mate. Roberto Carlos has scorched one free kick just over the bar, but Belgium have had a perfectly good opener chalked off. Honours even.

Belgium start the second half strongly, with Wilmots in particular proving a real handful. He turns away from Edmilson and sends a shot just inside the post, but Marcos is able to scramble it away. Then Marcos blocks Mpenza, and Verheyen air-kicks when unmarked three yards out. At one point, Wilmots backheels a through ball to Johan Walem – it's just like watching Brazil. Against Brazil.

Then, on sixty-seven minutes, with Brazil coming back into it a little, Denilson has a breakaway down the left. The hopeless showboater wastes the opportunity for a quick attack, though, choosing to come to a standstill in front of two Belgian defenders, and by the time he does lay it off Belgium have everyone behind the ball. Gilberto Silva plays it right to Cafu, who moves it on to Ronaldinho. All the options are closed down, now, seemingly, but the little magician flick-curls a pass with the outside of his right foot to the edge of the D where Rivaldo chests it down, takes a touch to tee himself up, and then lashes the ball goalwards. Timmy Simons can only get a stud in the way, and unluckily deflects the shot past De Vlieger. Rivaldo peels off his shirt to reveal a yellow vest underneath, in another vote of confidence for the new shirt technology on this, one of the most humid nights of the tournament so far.

Robert Waseige, the Belgian coach, chews his gum as though it has suddenly turned to gall in his mouth. Brazil still look shaky at the back, though, and Bart Goor almost glances in a header to equalise with Marcos stranded. Sonck has a shot, so does Vanderhaeghe, and Belgium press Brazil right back.

Then, with three minutes to go, Brazil strike like lightning. Klebersen belts down the right, and his perfect low cross is struck home through the keeper by the rampaging Ronaldo, and that's that. 2–0 to Brazil.

It's exciting, of course, to be playing them next, but I have the uneasy feeling that they can't defend quite as badly again as they have done tonight, and Ronaldo, Rivaldo, and especially Ronaldinho all look on top form. Still, bring it on . . .

This afternoon the USA beat a Mexico side that was unrecognisable from the one which outplayed Italy just a few days ago. Evidently, George W. Bush called the USA team before the game, saying he wasn't really a soccer fan but had been watching some of their games, which must have done their morale no end of good. 'Get 'em on first base and then nuke 'em second down,' was the advice of the most powerful man in the world. Stirring stuff.

The first goal, on eight minutes, was started by a quick Brian McBride free kick in midfield which sent Claudio Reyna away down the right. He beat two men and crossed low to the near post where Josh Wolff laid it back cleverly to McBride who picked his spot.

Mexico rarely threatened to equalise, although they should have had a penalty when John O'Brien brazenly punched a corner off Cuahtemoc Blanco's head.

Midway through the second half, O'Brien found Lewis in space on the left. The Fulham man raced for the bye-line, got in behind the full back, and put a superb cross to the back post where Donovan met it at full tilt and headed emphatically in to make it 2–0 to the States.

Or, as a US sports website put it:

Two soccer points to no score. Eddie Lewis makes a crosspitch play from the left zone finding Landon Donovan alone in the danger area. He top-bodies the sphere into the score bag, and Mexico have a double negative stat.

Blanco and the boys never looked likely to get back in the

game, as the US team turned out to be a great deal more effective at keeping out Mexicans than the US immigration department. Luis Hernandez was booked for the most laughable of dives in the area, and captain Rafael Marquez was dismissed for a dreadful assault on American sub Cobi Jones, he of the dreadlocks and the brief stint at Coventry City. Jones jumped for a high ball, and Marquez jumped for him, kicking him up the arse and headbutting him on the ear simultaneously. The American number 13 had clearly said something out of turn, as the Mexicans spent the remaining minutes kicking lumps out of him. Arellano also went for the backside, Mercado raked him with his studs, and Jones, miraculously still able to walk, nearly got his own back with a great run and cross which Donovan hoofed over an open goal in the last minute.

I had high hopes for Mexico, too, since I'm desperate for someone to beat the Germans. The draw looks in serious danger of disintegrating in their path at every stage. Still, there should be either Spain or Italy waiting for them in the semi . . .

Nick has had a call from Theo, who is heading back to the UK. His determination to stay for the quarter final wavered when he spoke to his two-year-old child late last night – I didn't even realise he had a two-year-old as well as a new-born – and evaporated altogether when he found himself all alone in Echigo Yuzawa in the morning.

18 JUNE

This morning I wake up to find that I have written a note to myself. 'Go to hell,' it says.

Actually there are eight hells in Beppu, or *jigoku*, to give them their local name, and the name of the equivalent of hell in Buddhism. Each one is a small volcanic attraction, slightly different from the last. Bozu jigoku is a lovely little Japanese garden, beautifully tended, and dotted around between the neatly trimmed shrubbery there are pools of glooping grey-brown boiling mud. Umi jigoku has a cobalt-blue steaming pool in it, in which a little wooden see-saw contraption dunks a basket of eggs to hard-boil them every half an hour. Not altogether sure why.

Another hell is set in a zoo, for no readily understandable reason, and various animals – lions, monkeys, an elephant – swelter away in their own personal hells as needless decoration, as though they'd go anywhere near a boiling pool of mud if left to their own devices.

Then there's one in a kind of crocodile farm.

'The force of the steam is so strong here that about one and a half train cars can be pulled by its pressure and it creates ideal conditions for breeding crocodiles . . .' reads a sign.

There's no train car in sight, nor even half a train car, so presumably this message is theoretical rather than advertising an actual attraction. Unless it sank. And I imagine they discovered that crocodiles breed in scalding water when they tried to boil a mating pair alive, since that's how the Japanese like to deal with things they are going to try to eat.

Then there's a red hell, which is like the others except the water in the pool is red, and a waterspout hell, in which a geyser shoots twenty metres up into the sky every twenty-five minutes, absolutely on the dot (well, this is Japan).

The one typical formation that all these volcanic attractions have in common is a large gift shop, at which you can buy samples of cold mud and allegedly health-giving minerals, but also toy trains – which you can imagine being jigoku-powered, if you are a very dull little boy – and some rather dusty World Cup memorabilia, which is neither volcanic in any way nor actually even to do with the World Cup which is currently under way in this country.

The first one, Bozu jigoku, was the most interesting, since it reminded me of Blofeld's garden of death in the book of *You Only Live Twice*. All the plants in his garden were deadly, and together with the boiling mud pools provided an abundance of ways for folk to top themselves, so that it became a sort of mecca for suicidal Japanese. I don't think it was part of a plan to take over the world – it was more a hobby.

Over the road from a couple of the hells I catch sight of a building decorated with statues of naked women. Beppu is supposed to have 'bawdy pleasures' to offer, according to the guide book, so I nip (sorry) over to see what it is. Beppu Hihokan, it's called, and it's nothing more nor less than a museum of erotica, worth a thousand yen of anybody's money.

The exhibition begins in quite an academic way, and it looks as though the whole business of sex is going to be treated in a serious archaeological and anthropological fashion. There are long glass cases filled with statues from Shinto shrines, and unearthed at ancient historical sites. OK, they are all either of blokes with their knobs out or just of giant knobs, but it seems to be attempting some sort of historical contextualising, and perhaps a statement about how all the civilisations of the world have been phallo-centric.

The biggest and oldest stone phallus – or *ukiyo-e* – has a little group of coins perched on the top, a gesture intended to bring good fortune to someone who perhaps wants a baby or maybe a duvet tent every now and again. Maybe Pele was just here . . .

Round the first corner, though, things begin to slide. There, one whole wall is occupied with a display of two enormous zebras having it off. Real zebras. Stuffed and mounted. And mounted.

And then it's downhill all the way. There's a bizarre and really quite off-putting exhibition of animal genitalia, at which you are invited to match the tackle to the photo of the beast. There's a little cinema showing a suspiciously seventies-style sex education film, very much in the spirit of *The Joy of Sex*, demonstrating a number of different positions in which to copulate. It is being watched – not for the first time, I suspect – by a little old man with a walking stick. And very thick glasses.

Then you come to the tableaux – shop mannequins arranged in a variety of really not very appetising sex acts and supposedly erotic gear. One female waxwork in a mesh of leather straps hangs from a wooden contraption, another is wearing a negligee which is lifted up by a wind machine if you press a button on the front of the glass case, and a third is becoming very attached to an Alsatian dog.

These are small beer compared to the *pièce de résistance*, though – a tableau in which Snow White has it off with the Seven Dwarfs. Inside the little house in the middle of the woods we can see the bed which our seven homuncular chums share. On her back, legs akimbo, is Snow White herself, modesty preserved by the fall of her big skirt. The dwarfs are arranged around the place in a state of casual readiness.

Until you press the button, and then hi-ho, hi-ho, it's off to work they go.

Up goes the skirt, down come the midget keks, and one little chap – difficult to tell which, if you really want to know I should check the small print of the Disney lawsuit – buries his chubby little chops between Snow White's legs, while her head lolls back in waxy ecstasy. Doc and Bashful slide over to watch, and both are furiously cracking one off. Dopey, meanwhile, has Snow White's knickers, and is giving them a good old sniff. It is unbelievably tacky and awful, and tatty too – I can't help noticing, for example, that Bashful's knob has fallen off – what in God's name is this all for?

Upstairs there is another attempt to operate at a more intellectual level, and there are some old-looking scrolls of pornographic artwork laid out, under glass, for inspection. Like the Playboy channel on the hotel telly, this has had the genitalia blurred out, which has been done by covering the scrolls with a sheet of glass, inside the cabinet, with the appropriate areas scratched into opacity. This sheet hovers a couple of inches above the pictures, though, and by changing your viewpoint to – oh, I don't know – the angle from which a child might look at them, then nothing is left to the imagination.

The scroll seems to tell a story, and it is of woman's sexual voraciousness. At the start the man is unmistakably enthusiastic, if you know what I mean, but by the last picture he seems to be reaching desperately for a reviving cup of green tea, his life force ebbing away.

One more exhibit just knocks the Snow White thing off the top of the chart, for me. It's a peephole thing. You put your eye to the eyehole, to see a female mannequin arranged with her legs spread. You press the button, and she urinates at you. Right in your eye. And they say the Japanese have no sense of humour.

It's one of the strangest places I have ever been, and all the way back to the hotel to check out I'm trying to decide how to describe it on the radio later. One thing I am sure of, though – you'd never drag Rio Ferdinand out of there.

18
Going Dutch

'I have no intention of paying a salary to someone who has
ruined Italian football.'
– Perugia president Luciano Gaucci

18 JUNE (STILL)

Around lunchtime Nick and I set off to drive across Kyushu
to the west coast, where we are going to spend a couple of
days, once again taking the toll expressway, the Yamanami
Highway, up to Saga and then down around the finger of land
on which the city of Nagasaki sits.

Nagasaki is a port, bustling, busy, and its narrow roads make
it difficult to drive into. The name of the place is so resonant, so
charged with its history of a moment of utter catastrophe, that I
seem to feel a dark hand grasp my vital organs as we work our
way towards the centre through the suburbs, and I find myself
imagining the bomb is imminent rather than fifty-seven years in
the past, imagining all this life about to be wiped out in an instant.

Our hotel is different to all the others we have stayed in so
far. It feels Mediterranean, Spanish, maybe, with its decorative tiling, its terracotta flagstone floors and its dark wood
furnishings. We have barely checked in when I get the call
from talkSPORT.

'Where are you today, Chris?' Alan Brazil asks when I get on
the air.

'I've come to Nagasaki,' I tell him.

'God, what's that like? I mean, what are the buildings like?'

296

I start to say that naturally they are all pretty modern, but in that Nagasaki is much like any Japanese city. Tokyo, for instance, was flattened by American bombing during the war, and many old wooden buildings there were either destroyed by incendiary bombing or pulled down to prevent them spreading fires, so the capital has few buildings left standing dating from before the great building boom of the sixties. As I talk I'm looking out of my hotel-room window to find some buildings to describe, and to my surprise I am faced by some distinctively European-style houses, and what's more many that are clearly well over a hundred years old. Like Alan, I have the mythology of the bomb locked into my head, that it destroyed everything in the city, all the buildings, all the people, everything, and yet here is a whole part of the city which must have survived unscathed. I change the subject – clearly not qualified to talk about Nagasaki with any authority.

Much of the traffic we were caught in on the way to the city centre seems to have been people rushing home to see Japan's last-sixteen match against Turkey, as outside now the place looks really quiet. A couple of weeks ago Japan had never won a World Cup finals match – now they are looking ahead to a quarter final against Senegal, and dreaming of a semi against Brazil or England, which would be the biggest thing imaginable.

That shiny dream bubble bursts as early as the twelfth minute in rain-sodden Miyagi. Koji Nakata at left back for Japan inexplicably plays a pass straight to the lurking Hakan Sukur. The veteran forward displays the dodgy touch he has shown throughout the tournament so far and muffs his pass to Hasan Sas, allowing Nakata to tackle back and retrieve his mistake, but the ball skids out on the wet turf and Turkey have a corner.

Ergun, it is, who swings the ball in, and Japan have all eleven players back in the box defending, while Turkey have ventured just five attackers forward. The keeper, Seigo Narazaki, comes out to catch, realises he isn't going to make it, and begins stumbling backwards. Shinji Ono, guarding the post, suddenly goes walkabout. None of the other nine Japanese players seems to be marking anybody. Umit Davala rises utterly unchallenged eight yards out and plants a firm header just where Ono was standing moments ago, as the Japanese blink at one another in total disarray.

Phillippe Troussier's men now put their trust in the high-energy approach which has stood them in good stead during their triumphant march through Group H, but Turkey play much the same way, and are ideally suited to snuffing them out. Japan's best moments come from the young naturalised Brazilian, Alessandro Santos – 'Alex'. He forges one chance for himself down the left, and then has a free kick that rebounds off the corner of post and bar with Rustu nowhere.

Astonishingly, at half time, Troussier takes Alex off, and Inamoto too. Alex has looked their best player, and Inamoto is capable of turning a game, but the Frenchman has something in mind, and on come Takayuki Suzuki and Daisuke Ichigawa. Turkey remain in control throughout the second half. With Sukur off the pace, their main goal threat comes from the shooting power of Basturk and Sas. Japan, meanwhile, become increasingly agitated as the half wears on, and they seem unwilling to try shots on goal, always wanting to take one pass more, to get that little bit closer, which plays into Turkey's smothering plans.

The end comes with a tearful whimper rather than a bang, with the tough and violent Toda in particular looking unexpectedly moist. The Miyagi stadium, even on the television, seems eerily quiet, racked with the occasional massed sob. Troussier comes in for plenty of stick for his use of substitutions, and stands down almost immediately: 'Aujourd'hui je quitte le football japonais . . .'

Nick and I wander out around the backstreets near by in the

early evening. We are not far from Chinatown – in fact we are not all that far from China.

Nagasaki is a cosmopolitan little place, thanks to more than two centuries of continuous contact with the outside world while the rest of Japan was closed to foreigners. Its position at the extreme west of the country meant that it was the first point of arrival for Chinese traders, and for European adventurers making their way past India and Malaya and up the Chinese coast. The Portuguese were the first Westerners to establish a foothold here, in the sixteenth century, and Nagasaki remains to this day Japan's centre of Christianity, despite periodic persecutions down the years. One of these ejected the Portuguese traders, who had been confined to a tiny enclave called Dejima, and their place was taken by Dutch merchants, who provided Japan's only contact with the West until restrictions began to be relaxed in the middle of the nineteenth century. Nagasaki's foreign community expanded then to include the British, who established a diplomatic mission, and the Americans, who stationed military personnel here.

Puccini's *Madame Butterfly*, written in the early twentieth century, tells the story of an American lieutenant stationed in Nagasaki who marries a Japanese woman. It was common for Western men to 'marry' geisha girls, in order to ensure their faithfulness, but these marriages were not taken too seriously on the men's part. Madame Butterfly, however, has given up her religion and her family to marry her Lieutenant Pinkerton, and is heartbroken when he returns to the United States. She bears his son, unbeknownst to him, and when he returns three years later he has an American wife with him. He offers to adopt the child, and Butterfly kills herself. A cheerful little tale of everyday Nagasaki folk.

The years of trading in and out of the port explain the wide range of architectural styles here, from the Chinese district with its fancy Confucian shrine, to its nineteenth-century tea-exporters' houses, with their verandahs, their stables, and their servants' blocks. It doesn't explain why they are still standing, though.

In a Kinko's I try to show Nick, a computer illiterate, some of the benefits of the internet. We discover that the BBC beat ITV by 13.2 million viewers to 3.6 in their head-to-head coverage of the Denmark game: this despite the presence on their panel of Ian Wright, a man whose credibility is surely still in tatters after his attempt at a Val Doonican-style Christmas special in a big fake snowbound house – to date, I think, the single worst programme ever broadcast on British television.

Then I try to find out the latest test score from Old Trafford where England have been playing Sri Lanka. The game was petering out to a draw when Ashley Giles took the last couple of wickets in consecutive balls, and Marcus Trescothick and Michael Vaughan found themselves with six overs to get fifty and got them in five. It takes a minute or two to find all this out, and Nick, with the attention span of the average goldfish, has wandered off to the other end of the shop.

'Hey, Nick,' I call to him. 'Guess what, England—'

'Won by ten wickets,' he says. 'I know. I couldn't wait so I called James. Come on, let's go . . .'

Later it's time for the hosts of the other World Cup to see if they can top the efforts of the hosts of ours.

A banner in the crowd as the teams come out reads: 'AGAIN 1966'. This, an admirable sentiment in so many ways, is, I think, a reference to Italy's shock Ayresome Park defeat by North Korea at the equivalent stage of the 1966 tournament. Despite the fact that the South is technically still at war with the North, and that whatever happens here this evening in Daejeon is unlikely to be reported on the other side of the 38th parallel, the South Korean fans clearly feel that football renders such distinctions irrelevant, and that for a short while at least, because of football, there's no more Buddha.

The crowd are, as we have now come to expect, absolutely frantic, and their high-pitched squealing reaches a previously unmatched volume when Ecuadorean referee Byron Moreno awards the hosts a fourth-minute penalty. Christian Panucci and Francesco Coco have both, it seems, decided not to wait until full time before swapping shirts with Seol Ki Hyeon and Yoo Sang Chul respectively.

Pin-up boy Ahn Jung Hwan – of Perugia, in Italy – takes the kick, almost obscured by the nine players encroaching alongside him, and Gianluigi Buffon, diving low to his right, makes an excellent save. It is the fifth missed penalty of the eighteen so far in this tournament.

There is a perceptible dip in the noise of the crowd, which lasts for maybe four seconds, until a drum starts up and the encouragement cranks back up to near the top of the human vocal register.

Italy try to break the game up, prevent South Korea getting into their pacy swarming game. Their main tactic seems to be throwing themselves to the floor at every opportunity, however slight the contact made by the puny Asians. When they take the lead, on eighteenth minutes, this game plan eases into overdrive.

It is a Francesco Totti corner from the left which does the damage. Christian Vieri charges in at the near post and manages to duck in front of both his marker and the keeper to slam the ball in.

This game doesn't have the option of an English commentary – that seems to be only games that are live on the BBC – so we sit listening to the Japanese guys at work. As the opening minutes are played out, we start to notice that the commentary is featuring a word which sounds remarkably like 'Hancock' – or more particularly 'Han-cock-ooh!' – over and over again. It dawns on us that this is the Japanese word for South Korea, and suddenly the conversation we had back in Niigata with our taxi driver, the admiral, began to make sense.

You can understand his bafflement once you realise that

after several minutes of trying to persuade him that my name was England – yes, that's right, the same as the country – I'd started saying to him: 'Never mind, forget that, forget that my name is England. We'll use his name, OK? What's his name? It's . . . The People's Republic of South Korea.'

He must have thought he was on *Beadle's About*.

Italy are killing the game, sitting back, content with 1–0. They occasionally rouse themselves, and Lee Woon Jae, South Korea's stocky and excellent keeper, has to make one top-class reflex save from Vieri, but Buffon, at the other end, could be doing his nails and chatting to the photographers for all the work he's having to put in.

Nick is excited, distracted, can't keep his mind on the football. As soon as we arrived, of course, he had shown his fishing directory to the receptionist to see if there was any angling fun to be had. The bloke on the desk, a young chap with a round face, speaks perfect English with an American accent, and was extremely helpful. Thanks to him, Nick was lined up to leave the hotel at four-thirty in the morning to go out in a small boat into the East China Sea with a grizzled old Japanese sea captain who doesn't speak any English. I'd be a little wary of this if I were him – I think there's a decent chance he'll find himself going after a whale.

Two minutes to go and Italy have almost stifled their way through. Then Sun Hong Hwang sends a pass into the Italian area which Panucci haplessly fails to clear properly with his thigh and maybe even his hand. It falls to Seol Ki Hyeon, whose left-foot shot beats Buffon and sends the red thousands in Daejeon and millions more in the big square in Seoul into a shocked frenzy.

The Italians shake their heads in disbelief, and demonstrate how easily they could have made the game safe by immediately creating the best chance of the ninety minutes. Damiano Tommasi's cross finds Vieri all on his own, and he inexplicably blasts the ball over the bar from maybe five yards out.

Into golden goal extra time, and a game that was dying a slow and tortured death has suddenly sprung into vibrant life.

Nick's phone goes off, making its distinctive tinny rendition of the theme from *Merry Christmas Mr Lawrence*. It's James, his travel agent friend from Stoke, concerned about an air traffic controllers' strike in Europe on Wednesday. This won't affect us, of course, but it will affect Nick's wife, Shari, who is meant to be flying out here on that day, and James is gallantly trying to get her onto a flight a day early. This will mean Nick having to cancel his sea expedition so he can head to Tokyo to meet her rather than out to sea, and for the rest of the evening he is getting bulletins about her flight, and his to Haneda.

Italy, in Daejeon, seem to be embarrassed that their game plan has come unstuck, and they are pouring forwards. Gennaro Gattuso brings a remarkable save out of Lee Woon Jae. Then Totti, who has been a disappointingly peripheral figure, steps into centre stage with a flimsy dive under a half-hearted challenge by Song Chung Gug. The Italian looks up to see Byron Moreno brandishing his second yellow, for simulating, and he has to walk the walk.

Even with ten men, though, Italy are on top. Their sense of grievance, still bubbling near the surface after the two disallowed goals against Croatia, erupts after Tommasi runs onto the ball from an onside position to score the golden goal, only to find that he has been flagged offside. Trapattoni thumps on the glass wall of his dugout, gesticulating at a FIFA official, who shrugs helplessly.

Italian sphincters will be clenched, with four minutes to go and a shoot-out looming. They have gone out of the last three World Cups on penalties – in 1998 (to France, in the quarters), 1994 (to Brazil, in the final), 1990 (to Argentina, in the semi). Then Lee Young Pyo sends in a long high ball from deep on the left, and Ahn Jung Hwan leaps in front of the leaden-footed Maldini and glances in the golden goal.

Pandemonium. The red hordes squeal, the banners wave, the

players hold hands and all dive on their bellies in the goalmouth in what is either an elaborate tribute to Jurgen Klinsmann or a cruel piss-take of Francesco Totti, the TV cuts away to the scenes in Seoul where somehow people seem to avoid being hurt in the frantic crushing celebrations, the waxy president beams his unearthly fixed smile, and the adventure goes on for the South Koreans.

It's good news too for Italian greengrocers, who will be rubbing their hands together with glee: 'After all I will be able to sell these over-ripe tomatoes and other dodgy vegetables and fruit – the Italian team is coming home in disgrace!'

19 JUNE

I get the hire car out from the hotel car park – or rather, our little American-speaking chum gets it for me, since the car park is in the tiny basement and involves the guests' cars sliding around on a motorised rack like a giant-sized brain teaser. He moves one across, another one down, another one up, then the next three across until he has mine pointing at the door, and then I can drive it out.

Before I return it to the car hire office I need to fill up the tank, so I pull onto the forecourt of a petrol station. Immediately five young men come running out from all directions, all dressed in red uniforms, and all shouting '*Hai! Hai! Hai!*' like some demented petrol-company-sponsored circus act. They don't do a human pyramid, which did seem on the cards at first, but they set to with a manic frenzy on the car. Each has a specified task to perform, like when Michael Schumacher pulls into the pits and he can change all his wheels, fill his tank and buy a packet of Rolos inside nine seconds. One lad whips off the petrol cap, and another shoves the nozzle in – is this a Job Creation scheme or what? One wipes the windscreen and the wing mirrors, one gets my bill ready, and the fifth one, some kind of supervisor, is off shouting '*Hai! Hai! Hai!*' at another car, to which four *more* identically dressed youths are already attending. It's all happening in a blur – they've finished in seconds and I haven't said a word to them yet.

'Actually,' I say, 'I only wanted to use the toilet . . .'

At the railway station I have a few minutes to wait for my train, and I have a wander around. There is a large World Cup memorabilia shop on the concourse, several stalls of T-shirts, mascots, replikits, bath towels, key rings and so on. Japan went out of the tournament yesterday, though, and now each stall is covered with heavy black cloth, as if it were in mourning for lost opportunities, sporting and commercial.

I am going to a place one hour outside Nagasaki called Huis ten Bosch.

The Japanese are great tourists. It's one of their most readily identifiable comedy characteristics. Turn up at any major landmark, any day, anywhere in the world, and the chances are a group of hardy individuals from these islands will be taking a photograph of each other standing in front of it. And, since it's a comedy characteristic we're talking about, they'll more than likely be saying something like: 'Ah so, Reaning Tower of Pisa!' or 'Rook! Acloporis!'

These, though, are the bold ones. Many of their countrymen and women are too apprehensive about the outside world to ever leave Japan's shores. However daunting the language difficulties are for me coming here, they must be multiplied hundreds of times over for a timid Japanese tourist overseas. After all, he's never going to find signposts in his language in a foreign country, is he?

Then there's crime to worry about. The crime rate is so low in Japan that people have got used to not even considering it a problem, but they have all heard terrifying horror stories about rampant street crime in the Western world, muggings, rapes, carjackings, drive-by shootings – you name it, they are scared of it.

And of course we Europeans are all riddled with disease

because of our appalling hygiene habits. There's one sure-fire way to get a seat to yourself on a Japanese subway train, and that's to be foreign. Japanese people will stand, preferably in the next carriage, rather than take an empty seat next to you. Imagine what torment it would be for them if they had to visit a place where there were more of us than them on the trains.

The timid Japanese tourist would love to see (and photograph) exotic and different places, but he simply daren't leave his homeland. Fortunately for him, though, he is catered for. A variety of different 'worlds' have been created in Japan by canny entrepreneurs, theme parks and resorts where you can go to sample the atmosphere, the architecture, and the cuisine of foreign lands without ever having to get yourself mugged, beaten, or infected. Or a passport.

There's Canada World in Hokkaido, for example, all big forests, lumberjacks, and people saying 'aboot' when they mean 'about'. There's an English theme park near Tokyo called Shakespeare Country where you can take English tea at four in the afternoon, and see extracts from *Hamret* and *King Rear*.

And down here in Kyushu there's Huis ten Bosch, a meticulously engineered and lovingly recreated tribute to all things Dutch. I think I am fairly safe in saying that it is one of the nuttiest places in the whole world.

Huis ten Bosch – 'the house in the woods' – has huge coach parks for all the hundreds and thousands of visitors they are expecting, but today it's practically deserted. I take my pick of the dozen ticket kiosks, pay my money, go through the entrance, and suddenly there're windmills everywhere. And tulips.

As you walk into the park, you gradually become aware of the massive scale of the project. There are picturesque canals, bridges, museums, streets with vintage cars pootling along them, and more windmills, of course, all in a cute lid-of-a-jigsaw-box style, stretching away for hundreds of yards into the distance.

They have taken care to make sure that it is very flat, but the surrounding countryside is actually quite mountainous, great green forested hills, larger than any in Holland, I'm sure. It is as though the whole of Europe has become compacted, and Huis ten Bosch has ended up right next door to Bavaria World.

Amongst the attractions – which include windmills, did I mention? – you will find the Domtoren, a 105-metre-high replica of a tower from Utrecht. From here you can look down on the whole place, and it comes to me where I've seen something like this before. This place is like the Village in *The Prisoner*. Brightly coloured umbrellas, strange eclectic out-of-place European architecture, a little harbour, people walking around just a little too serenely, bright and cheery announcements over a tannoy, preceded by a little 'bing bong'. The gift shop even sells maps, which end at the edge of the Village, like the ones which so frustrated Patrick McGoohan.

There is a porcelain museum and any number of canalside cafés. They should perhaps consider opening a pornography museum and some cannabis cafés – it would be no less Dutch but a hell of a lot more interesting.

No shortage here of places to eat, though – House of Chocolate, Bikken Bikken (if you like biscuits), The Batavian Kitchen – and if you go for a meal here the waitresses absolutely insist that you and whoever you're eating with share the bill.

And everywhere you turn there's a gift shop, selling items with a strongly tulip-related theme – tulip-shaped fridge magnets, tulip-shaped clothes pegs, tulip-shaped table mats, tulip-shaped umbrellas, tulip-shaped pens, tulip-shaped wooden fake tulips in a tulip-shaped vase. After a few minutes I can't even think of the word tulip any more, it's gone wrong in my head, it's stopped making sense. Edam cheeses, of course, and Pompenkoek – a cake – are also available, while a couple of cans of imported Grolsch or Oranjeboom will set you back around twenty quid.

There seems to be no evidence here in Huis ten Bosch of

a liberal attitude towards homosexuality, or, for that matter, prostitution. I was expecting at least one bored housewifely figure in a basque sitting in a shop window somewhere.

In the little harbour there are replicas of two of the tall ships with which the Dutch, great explorers, of course, in their day, opened up trade routes all around the world. They are not full-size replicas, so strictly speaking they are not tall ships, they're medium-sized ships, but I dare say they are seaworthy enough. I wonder whether there's any danger that one day explorers from Huis ten Bosch will set out across the bay and discover Surinam World or a Dutch East Indies Resort Park.

For me the main important thing about Holland is that it's the land of Cruyff and Kluivert, of Neeskens and van Basten, of total football. Here in Huis ten Bosch there is a total absence of football. Still, I suppose if you had been wandering around the real Holland for the last few weeks you'd have found plenty of people going 'World Cup? What World Cup?'

I pass a bewildered Japanese gentleman trying on a pair of wooden clogs in one of the shops. He snorts with bemused laughter and shrugs, as if to say: 'I don't get it, what is the point of these?'

I feel that way about the whole bizarre place.

At the far end is the *pièce de résistance*. Paleis Huis ten Bosch is a replica of the Dutch royal palace, which sits there looking vaguely grand but utterly pointless.

Huis ten Bosch is built on reclaimed land. It cost 250 billion yen, and as well as the theme park it contains an exclusive residential area; the long-term target is to have it set up as a fully functioning town in its own right. I can't imagine living here, though – I'd go bonkers within a day.

19
King of Comedy

'Well, what do you know. God isn't an Argentinian.'
– *Olé*, Argentinian tabloid newspaper

One thing I wanted to get my head around whilst in Japan was Japanese comedy. I thought I'd seen some Japanese comedians in action on the television, but it was difficult to be quite certain. One pair certainly seemed to be doing a double-act routine at a microphone the other day, and they were strongly reminiscent of Mike and Bernie Winters – one big goofy bloke in a loud checked jacket, and one smooth smiley one, neither of them looking at one another as they worked through their gags. They weren't getting any laughs at all, though – as I say, strongly reminiscent of Mike and Bernie Winters.

David told me that the *Evening Standard* wanted Tomoko to send photographs in a different format to the way she was used to working, and she said she couldn't. When David asked couldn't she just do it the other way, just for this one job, she replied, 'I don't ask you to be like a Japanese comedian and tell stories about princesses.'

A small but valuable insight there into the world of Japanese comedy, I think.

Nick said the other day: 'I keep thinking I'm watching a comedy show, and then the presenter will turn to a weather map or bring out a plate of food . . .'

One man who is definitely a comic, and he's on everything, it seems to me, is a big goofy chap with phenomenal white teeth. Samma Akashiya is his name, and he looks as though he's put in two sets of Dick Emery's comedy vicar choppers, top and bottom. He appears on the football magazine show, and also crops up hosting a thing called *Much Ado About Love*, where he seems to have the licence to dress up as a frogman and bash women on the head with a big foam hammer. He gets tremendous laughs doing this, and I honestly believe this could be the format that revives the career of Lennie Bennett (so for God's sake don't tell anyone about it).

I really thought I shouldn't leave Japan without having made some attempt to understand the Japanese sense of humour. I know they're laughing at something, I've seen them. Hoping to shed a little light on the subject I looked up one of the contact numbers that my friend Hugh – who worked out here for the BBC – gave me.

Masumi Muramatsu – 'MM' – is the director of the Tokyo chapter of the Japan Society for Humour Studies. 'He speaks pretty good English, he's full of energy, and he loves telling terrible jokes,' Hugh had written. 'He lives in Yokohama, but doesn't need much encouragement to come up to Tokyo.' He sounded just the ticket.

I called him at six one evening, while I was in Tokyo, and it turned out that as luck would have it he was in Tokyo too, and not only that, he was giving a lecture, in English, on the Use of Humour in Simultaneous Translation. It was being sponsored by the United Nations, and it started at seven on the other side of town. He put me on the guest list – I got my skates on.

I had been doing so much walking in Japan that the soles of my shoes were falling to bits. There was no chance of finding a shoe shop in Japan that sold shoes in anything like my size so I was walking them to death. If you were to turn them over you would have seen that I had worn through the sole in places to a layer of little square air compartments, and in wet weather – it was absolutely slashing it down on this day – these had been filling up and making the most fantastically loud squirty squelching noises as I walked along. So when I arrived at MM's lecture about fifteen minutes after it had started, there was no chance of my making a discreet entrance. The only available seat was down at the front, and my attempt to tiptoe to it unnoticed was badly undermined by my misbehaving footwear.

Squirt, squelch, squirt, squelch . . .

I presumed the speaker – a little elderly bald chap almost completely hidden behind a wooden podium with a microphone on it – was MM himself, and he stopped to allow me to settle before he carried on. This meant that the entire room full of people, maybe two hundred Japanese people, now turned and watched me make my way down the aisle.

Squirt, squelch, squirt, squelch . . . Sorry . . . Squirt, squelch, squirt, squelch . . .

Finally I reached my seat and smiled a watery smile. MM nodded courteously to me, and then turned and carried on with his lecture.

I gathered that he founded Japan's biggest simultaneous translation company, and that he has had a long career working for Japanese politicians and diplomats at the United Nations. The audience was made up mostly of people who aspired to follow in his illustrious footsteps. His theme for the evening was that humour can be used to break down national barriers and oil the wheels of diplomacy, and he himself had the manner, bearing and delivery of the stand-up comedian he'd clearly always yearned to be.

'Now then, ladies and gentlemen. What do you think is the language most commonly spoken at the United Nations?' he asked them.

There was silence.

'Come along, somebody guess.'

A voice from the front row said: 'Broken English!'

MM ignored this, even though there was a little polite sniggering.

'Nobody? Well, I will tell you. The language most commonly spoken at the United Nations is . . . Broken English!'

Ouch! The heckler heckled him with his own punchline. Still MM pressed on and completed his joke regardless, and you have to admire that in a comic. The audience, though seated, all bowed, as if to acknowledge that a joke had passed, but no one laughed.

I sensed a little unease in the room, and I think the heckler was genuinely mortified, and had only been trying to help. MM himself, though, was completely untroubled, and embarked on a routine containing many and varied anecdotes from his life as a simultaneous translator for the great and good.

Ronald Reagan was a favourite, and MM told of Reagan's humour when dealing with the Russians. 'I find Mr Gorbachev ... disarming,' was the tagline to this one. The audience, perfectly synchronised, bowed to acknowledge the fact that a humorous story had been delivered, but there was still no laughter. MM provided his own punctuation, baring his teeth in a huge smile, and saying, 'Ha HA!'

On with another tale, about Nikita Khrushchev this time, who once bellowed, 'We shall bury you!' at his Western antagonists at the UN – meaning that Communism would outlast capitalism, not that he was going to kill them. Evidently Nikita was keen to ram the point home, so he took off his shoe and banged it on the podium for emphasis, whereupon his simultaneous translator also removed his own shoe and banged it on his desk. A neat little story, worthy of a laugh, but again the Japanese audience bowed as one, as if spotting the joke and paying it respect, but making no audible response.

'Ha HA!' grinned MM.

The evening went on like this, with MM pulling out all the stops, giving them his best material, and every time he would tell them a joke, his audience would silently show him the tops of their heads, he would grin and shout 'Ha HA!', and move on to the next thing. Tough room.

I did think at first that he was dying a death up there, but gradually I realised that this is what a Japanese comedy turn sounds like when it's going really really well.

I did a film once, years ago, with a bunch of American stand-up comedians. One of them – a very witty guy, actually, to talk to, and good company – would never ever laugh at anything anyone else said. The absolute apex of response you could get with a gag or a funny remark was to have him point his little finger at you while narrowing his eyes to admiring slits and saying, nodding gently, 'That's funny . . .'

And this was what MM's act was getting by way of feedback. Two hundred people bowing at his gags, effectively pointing their little fingers at him and saying, 'That's funny . . .' I actually thought he was funny, and I'd have liked to give him a laugh or two, but people would have stared.

MM began to work the room.

'I like movies, you like movies, lady?' he addressed one matronly Japanese woman near the front. She bowed.

'I like movie *Full Monty*. You like this movie, lady, you like this movie very much. All men take pants off! Ha HA!'

Everyone was highly amused by the matronly lady's embarrassment at being singled out for attention. They all indicated this by bowing, silently, in approval.

Encouraged, MM's eyes swept the audience, and he caught sight of me.

'Aha, this is the gentleman from England who telephone me one hour ago to say he want to learn about Japanese humour. That's right, isn't it?'

'That's right.'

'What is your name my friend?'

'England.'

MM executed a faultless Peter Glaze double-take, as trademarked by the late *Crackerjack* comic of the sixties and seventies, whereby the performer begins to repeat what his sidekick has just said, and its meaning only dawns on him halfway through.

'Engla . . . huh?'

'England.'

'Yes, I know your country is England, but what is your name?'

'England.'

'So your name is England and your country is England?'

The audience had all turned to stare at me again. Maybe I prepared the ground for this little routine with my comical squelching shoes, but there was now, building slowly but definitely there, the unmistakable sound of laughter. Actual laughter, not bowing and nodding and silent acknowledgement, but one or two real guffaws, and folk nudging their neighbours in a bid to share glee.

MM is not a man to let an opportunity like this pass him by.

'Wait a moment, I am confused. So you say you are from England, and your name is England.'

'Yes,' said the stooge, yours truly.

'*Mister* England? Your name is *Mister* England?'

I know that you will find this hard to credit, but the mirth in the room was reaching quite staggering proportions. I was keeping quite deadpan, trying to work out whether they were laughing with me or at me.

'Well, this is a remarkable thing! Does anybody here know of anybody in our country called Mister Nippon?'

People were trying to bow and laugh at the same time now, and some of them appeared to be literally holding their sides. MM was having the time of his life.

'Ha HAAAA!' he cried, waiting for the merriment to subside. 'Ha HAAAA!'

Now I've seen people take this name-the-same-as-the-country thing big before – one German youth hostel manager I met in my backpacking youth turned purple and I thought he was going to pass out – but never anything like this.

MM actually had to hold both hands up to get the crowd

to settle down, and there were still hankies being dabbed to eyes as he moved on. And this was an audience that, only a minute or two earlier, had been listening in absolute silence to his very best stuff.

Then, with the audience thoroughly warmed up, the evening took an even more bizarre turn. MM introduced another speaker, Siegfried, a tall elderly Austrian gentleman from Hawaii who was one of the pioneers of simultaneous translation, and he got up to the podium and began to tell his amusing anecdotes about the Nuremburg trials.

Siegfried was very interesting, actually. It appears that simultaneous translation was used as a tool for the first time at Nuremburg, which would have been impossibly cumbersome and unwieldy without it, and all the subsequent war crime trials have used it as a template, the ones here in Tokyo after the war, and in Rwanda and Yugoslavia more recently.

As a twenty-two-year-old, Siegfried found himself responsible for taking testimony from Goering and von Ribbentrop, amongst others, and found that the senior Germans tried to use the language differences between themselves and their accusers to obfuscate and backtrack. At one point, for example, they seemed to have admitted to seizing the population of Poland, using the word 'erfassen', which means 'to seize'. It can also mean 'to register', though, and when this supposed confession was brought up in court they claimed that all they had admitted to was carrying out some kind of census.

He and MM took questions, every one prefixed by a lengthy and elaborate compliment to each of them, through which MM bowed modestly. He was itching to return to his theme, which is that humour is a vital part of the translator's art.

'A joke, if told properly and without pain . . .' (always best, I've found) 'can make people laugh, and when they laugh they wake up, they listen to what you are saying. You never see anybody laughing and asleep at the same time, do you?'

Eager to recapture the magic of our earlier double-act routine, he suddenly turned to me and said, 'Mister England from England, what do you think? Do Japanese people have a sense of humour?'

'Well, I, er . . .'

'Come up onto the stage and tell us.'

Ah. Seeing no way to politely refuse, I got up and walked to the podium, accompanied by a deal of respectful applause, and: squirt, squelch, squirt, squelch . . .

I stood in front of the microphone with MM, and he said, 'Tell us all what you think of Japan. Have you found the language difficult?'

I looked out at a sea of earnest Japanese faces. They were all keen students of English, but even so, it is daunting to try to make people laugh in a language that is not their first. Suddenly, from up there, it seemed to me that MM had been doing exceedingly well to get as many silent bows and nods as he had.

What could I possibly tell them? Did I have any tales of linguistic amusement to share with a bunch of simultaneous translators? Actually, it occurred to me that I had. I told them about no more Buddha, and the bright young lad who wants to work, like them, for the United Nations. This went very well indeed.

I suddenly remembered that an Italian friend of mine in London, Daniela, works as a simultaneous translator, and she told me one horror story which I decided to pass on. She was in a conference with some British businessmen who were attempting to do business with an extremely fiery Italian gentleman, who was getting very worked up, pacing the room, shouting at the top of his voice. She was having to translate his outpourings, and it quickly became clear to her that the Italian was connected to the Mafia.

'You pigs! You sons of whores!' he was screaming in Italian. 'You offal! If you do not change your pitiful minds I will have you shot! I will come to your houses and burn them, and I will burn your wives and your cars!'

'Ahem . . . Signor Facchetti is most anxious to see the deal completed as soon as possible,' Daniela said.

'Did you tell them? Did you tell them I will shoot them?'

'Er . . . yes, I told them.'

'You dogs! You shits! Why do you treat me like this? I will shoot you in the knees, I will do it myself! And your children, your children's knees!'

'Ahem . . . Signor Facchetti is really very angry, and really would like to see some progress . . .'

'You are not telling them what I say! Look what I have to deal with! Look at this wretched whore they have given me to translate my words! What use is she? Well, I will burn down her house too, and shoot her family, and burn her car . . . ! Tell them! Tell them what I will do!'

And so poor Daniela found herself having to translate violent threats being made against herself and her family by this raving madman. To an audience of people who aspire to this career themselves this was naturally an eye-opener, and this bit also went down extremely well.

Then I told about the taxi ride after the England v Denmark match in Niigata. The 'Mister England from England' stuff is, as I have already discovered, a sure-fire hit, but when I revealed that I had been travelling around Japan with a name as downright hysterical as mine is, and with a travelling companion whose name is The People's Republic of South Korea, well, the house came down. There was actual weeping. The previously earnest crowd of Japanese interpreters before me turned into those helpless cackling aliens in the old 'For Mash, Get Smash' adverts.

I left 'em wanting more, like the old trouper I am, and left the stage, and the applause was so loud I couldn't even hear my shoes. And that is how I ended up doing stand-up comedy in Japan.

After the show I went out for a meal round the corner with Siegfried and MM, who made sure to order Japanese dishes, so that I could say I had tried as many as possible. A simple dish of porridgey rice mixed with green tea I had a go at, and some big slabs of tofu, which I really didn't see the point of. It was a hundred per cent texture, no taste at all, even when drowned in sauce.

I discovered how MM met my friend Hugh. It was when the BBC were making a documentary about the end of the war and the subsequent American occupation of Japan. MM, fifteen when his country surrendered, was interviewed for this project, and told a tale of getting together with a group of friends of the same age, and vowing to kill as many of the occupying Americans as they could with whatever weapons they could get their hands on. They knew that they would inevitably be caught, but were burning with the shame of their nation's defeat, and counted their lives as worthless. Then the Americans arrived in their jeeps and personnel carriers, and they were all smiling and waving, and leaning out of their trucks to give sweets and gum to the boys' younger brothers. The Americans, it seems, unwittingly disarmed their teenage rebellion by simply being too friendly to kill.

MM was very keen to exchange jokes. I struggled to think of any that aren't over-dependent on puns or idiom. One of my favourites, which I tried, for example, is a joke about an anteater who goes into a pub, orders a pint of beer and sits in the corner. The landlord comes over and asks, 'Everything OK?'

The anteater says, 'Yes, fine thanks.'

'Not too cold?' says the landlord. 'I can put the fire on . . .'

'No, I'm fine.'

'Is the beer all right? Doesn't taste funny?'

'No, it's fine.'

'You hungry? Want something to eat?'

'No, really,' says the anteater. 'Everything is absolutely fine.'

And the landlord says, 'So why the long face?'

And neither MM nor Siegfried had heard the expression in their fifty-plus years of translating, so that went for absolutely nothing.

In return, MM told me this:

'A Frenchman will laugh when a joke is half told. The Englishman will wait until the end of the joke and laugh. The German will philosophise all night and laugh the next morning. And the Japanese will smile and say, "*Hai! Hai! Hai!*" but won't understand it at all. The only guy who doesn't laugh is the American, who says, "Yeah, that's an old joke and you don't tell it right."'

Ha HAAAA!

I made my farewells and headed off into the night, still flushed with my evening of comedic triumph. I had, without any preparation, taken on an entirely Japanese audience and had them eating out of the palm of my hand, when all good old MM had managed to get for his pains, bless him, was rows of polite bows and . . . then it struck me like a slap in the face. Of course! They were only being polite! They gave MM exactly the response that he was expecting of them, and then they did precisely the same for me. They saw that I really wanted them to laugh, and I was a guest, and they couldn't bear to disappoint me. Well, now they had . . .

20
About the Bomb

'I like Butt.'
– Pele

After the loopiness of Huis ten Bosch, a quite different experience this afternoon, as I make my way up to the northern part of the city, to Urakami, to take a look at the A-bomb site.

There is a small and sober park there now, at the Hypocentre, it's called, which is the point on the ground directly beneath where the bomb was exploded in mid air. A stark black marble monument marks the exact spot, and it is decorated with splashes of colour by daily visitors – not flowers, but elaborate chains of origami cranes. As the traffic thunders by fifty yards away a few people sit here in quiet contemplation, apart from one young bloke who is using the paths to do wheelies on his bike.

I go into the Atomic Bomb Museum, where the first corridor is filled with huge enlargements of photographs of Nagasaki before the explosion, and the doom-laden ticking of a clock, counting down the seconds to the end of life as the people in the pictures knew it.

It was eleven in the morning, and a B-29 bomber nicknamed 'Bockscar' was returning to its base in the Pacific. The intention had been to unload the plutonium bomb it was carrying on the city of Kokura, near Fukuoka, where there was a Japanese army arsenal, but cloud and smoke made it impossible to see the place and so after circling three times they abandoned that attack and headed home by way of Nagasaki, the secondary target. Here too the cloud was heavy and impenetrable, and they were running out of fuel, so they were just about to abort the mission entirely when a chance break in the clouds revealed a playing field below, and the plutonium bomb, 'Fat Boy', was dropped. It exploded 500 metres above the ground, searing the name of Nagasaki into the pages of history.

A three-dimensional model of the city shows how it is spread around the inlets and up the hillsides of a natural harbour that is meant to resemble a crane in flight. Suspended above the model, a red light bulb demonstrates the pattern of the initial heat flash and shock wave, and shows how the hills protected the southern part of Nagasaki from the destruction that was wrought in the north, although many buildings there were destroyed by fire in the subsequent hours as all the city's fire stations and fire-fighting personnel were casualties in that first instant.

Seventy-three thousand are reckoned to have died in the first few seconds after 'Fat Boy' exploded, and the figure had risen to 140,000 by 1950 when radiation sickness and burn injuries took their further toll. The museum is a harrowing place, given over to the stories of survivors, like one, sheltered by a fluke, who saw her whole family go up in red flames and be reduced to ashes in seconds, or the boy, five years old like one of my boys, whose awful cry, 'Take me back to the past, just once more. Oh! I want Mother! I want Father! I want my brother! I want my sisters . . . !' is translated here.

A big ugly black replica of 'Fat Boy' itself, ten feet tall and five feet wide, lurks around the corner, and there is a horrible fascination in the mechanics of the event. The surface temperature reached 3,000 degrees centigrade, and burned the shadow of one man and his ladder onto the wall he was standing next to. This happened because the tar on the wall burned away instantly in the heat flash, but the tar that was shielded in that moment by his body and his ladder remained in the shape of their shadow.

Japan has come in for a great deal of criticism since the war ended for not taking any responsibility for the catastrophe which befell it here and in Hiroshima, depicting itself as the guiltless victim of an unspeakable atrocity. There is a timeline of the war on the wall here, and other events, such as the bombing of Pearl Harbor, do come across in a different sort of way, as though they are saying: 'Look, this is how a war is done, a civilised sequence of each side doing stuff to the other, but then the Americans went and did *this* . . .'

The Atomic Bomb Museum in Nagasaki is not a place for military apologists, though. Its message is a wholeheartedly pacifist one, as the latter part of the exhibition takes the form of a sorrowful enumeration of the escalation of the nuclear arms race in the years since the Second World War ended, to all intents and purposes, in the sky overhead. A terrible thing happened here, is the message, whatever you think of the rights and wrongs of why it happened, and every effort must be made to ensure that nothing like it ever happens again.

Especially depressing, then, to read in the *Japan Times* that India and Pakistan are still posturing on the brink of war, and that George W. Bush has ordered the CIA to conduct a covert operation inside Iraq to topple Saddam Hussein, using 'lethal force' if necessary – he's taken care of the title of the movie, if nothing else. Just how covert can an operation be that is plastered all over the front of the world's papers . . . ?

There are no World Cup games today, after nineteen consecutive match days. I flick on the telly anyway this evening and stumble across a riotous football panel show, being chaired by Samma Akashiya, the Japanese comedian and game-show presenter with the enormous and supernaturally white teeth. The boisterous panel includes Arsene Wenger and his interpreter, and Junichi Inamoto, who also has an interpreter, as the discussion is switching between Japanese and English. The two former Arsenal colleagues sit rather stiffly, almost blanking one another, and their interpreters don't seem to be on speaking terms either. There is another foreigner, who I think is Zico, and then there is a bank of rowdy reporters, each specialising in following a particular team. The England one looks like Eddie the Eagle, with big thick specs and a jaw like a cash register, and he has had a Beckham haircut.

A very brave face is being put on Japan's exit yesterday, and there is no mistaking the fact that the whole show – and, from the look of their voxpops, the whole nation – has swung behind England now. Samma himself is wearing a red England top, the 1966 version, as is Eddie the Eagle, and when I join them they are all cheerfully dissing Ronaldo. That's five-goal Ronaldo.

As the show progresses it is remarkable to see a side to Arsene Wenger that he keeps hidden from the British public, for whom he has now spent five years carefully cultivating the impression that he is a super-intelligent and cultured man. Here, though, he struggles to maintain any kind of dignity whatsoever. The whole panel starts taking the piss out of his book, to begin with, to much red-faced hilarity from the Gunners' supremo.

Next it's a montage of all those shots that football directors love to do where they rove the crowd looking for particularly photogenic women. There's an Argentinian, a Swede, some Italians, any number of samba-style senoritas from Brazil, and Arsene Wenger is asked to say which bird he fancies the most. Astonishing stuff – imagine Lineker or Lynam trying to pull this off; they'd never present again. Still more astonishing is that Wenger – whom I've watched carefully judging every non-committal remark for the last five years on British telly – actually picks one, the French girl, stopping just short of going 'Phwoooarr!' and making a rude gesture with his fist.

All the while Inamoto sits there stone faced in the midst of all this mirth.

Having established that Wenger is game for a laugh they try to tap him up for the Japan job, now that Troussier has fallen on his samurai sword. A frisson of alarm crosses Inamoto's face, and Zico begins to shift uncomfortably too – perhaps he fancies it . . . ?

In the course of this show I do pick up one or two little World Cup gems. Michael Owen and Paul Scholes are injured, apparently, but are expected to be all right for the Brazil game, as is Owen Hargreaves, who seems unlikely to unseat Nicky Butt, though, now.

Now that he has, amazingly, been nominated by Pele, no less, as his player of the tournament so far. Yes, that's right, Nicky Butt, like Scholesy a former Boundary Park junior. Pele goes on to give honourable mentions to a few others, namely Ferdinand and Campbell, Ronaldo and Ronaldinho, Hasan Sas, Ballack, Metzelder, O'Brien and Donovan. But the cream of the crop? 'Well, I like Butt . . .'

Giovanni Trapattoni has blasted the World Cup referees, surprise surprise, and says that he won't quit. Remarkably his country seems to be with him on this one, and there doesn't seem to have been any fruit pelting going on at all.

They show some astonishing shots of a remarkable impromptu street party in Seoul enjoyed by three million people – three million! – and a hilarious piece of film of a bus in Shanghai with a telly mounted behind the driver's seat on which all the passengers are watching a World Cup game. The bus stops at a red light, and the driver gets out of his seat and comes round to join them, scooting back up front when the lights change. The most important football story of all, though – Becks is said to be thinking about a new hairstyle.

Meanwhile, CNN runs an item about Sepp Blatter going on

about refereeing standards. The service features a running text
in the top left of the screen, clearly being typed out on the spot
by someone listening to the reports live, and this can lead to the
odd entertaining inaccuracy. Tonight the transliterator pauses
at the name of the FIFA supremo, before deciding, gloriously,
to write it as 'A STEP LADDER'.

Outside my room it is absolutely tanking it down.

20 JUNE

A long journey on the Shinkansen today as I make my way
up the country to Kyoto. Breakfast is a tin of coffee brought
by a smiley stewardess, and it's hot.

'Black Blend', it says on the side of the can. 'This coffee is
the very delicious coffee which a deep taste and a rich smell
have. Let's spend the wonderful days to drink every day.'

Indeed.

As Kyushu flashes by the window I get to have a good look
at it for the first time, having been concentrating on the road
up till now. Many of the buildings down this end of Japan have
a more Chinese feel, with the distinctive upturned ski-jump
shape to the tiled roofs. As in the rest of Japan, though,
there are no hilltops unforested, no skyline unmolested with
overhead cabling, no meadows unpaddied.

Just as we head back onto the main island, one of my fellow
travellers, suffering from hay fever by the sound of him, takes
it upon himself to mark the transition.

'KYUSHU!' he snorts, and then, after a moment, '. . . *HON-
SHU!*'

Pele, never short of opinions to share with the world, now
says that England v Brazil is a game worthy of being the
final. The complexities of organising a co-hosted competition
meant that was never a possibility, though, however the group
games panned out. And don't let Senegal and the USA hear
you talking like that, Edson . . .

Something you see almost everywhere is the 'PuriKura' machine. I had a go in one at Huis ten Bosch. It is like a photo-me booth, and the name comes from the words 'Print Club' – *purintu kurab*. You first select from a variety of backgrounds, then choose a cartoon character to accompany you, and then have your snap taken, and when, four minutes later, your sheet of pictures comes out it is in the form of a page of small stickers. These were all the rage a while ago, apparently, and people would exchange them like business cards, or stick them onto business cards, or into albums of all their chums, or on phones, or jackets, or briefcases, or foreheads, or whatever you like, really. The effect is extremely cute – apart from the fact that my stickers have a picture of me on them – and it's a rather sickly sweet, super-friendly little trend that I can't really see catching on in the UK ever. You never know, though, we went for those *Pokemon* things . . .

I wonder as I ride along: just how fit is Gary Neville at the moment? His metatarsal injury was a couple of weeks after Beckham's, so is he now where Beckham was a couple of weeks ago (the day before the Argentina game)? If Sven had known we were going to get this far it might have been worth bringing him, because poor old Wes Brown is just a passenger. And what about Steven Gerrard – could he have been fit by now?

I'm having a deal of trouble suppressing the dream – it wants to pop out of my head at every opportunity. If – *if* – we beat Brazil, then it could be Senegal in Saitama, and who . . . ? Spain? Or Germany . . . in the final? I see a black-and-white bird, that could be a magpie, and then another. Now was that two for joy? Or two one-for-sorrows? I guess I'll find out tomorrow.

Hay fever man is honking a particularly disgusting lump of phlegm around his sinuses. If he tries for 'Hokkaido' next I'm afraid I might catch it in the neck.

I am also still rather preoccupied by my visit to the Atomic Bomb Museum yesterday, and when the train pulls into Hiroshima I decide to stop for a couple of hours and have a look around there.

An old-fashioned street car brings me through the main shopping streets of this thriving modem city to the Peace Park. At the northern end is the A-bomb Dome, a mangled, twisted shell of a building with the half-melted metal skeleton of the dome which once sat on top of it now rusting and open to the sky. This was once a relatively undistinguished government building, built in 1914, but as just about the only thing still standing in a circle of devastation with a three-kilometre diameter after the uranium bomb explosion, it has been left as it is as a monument to the terrible event of 6 August 1945.

The Peace Memorial Museum is just as harrowing as its Nagasaki counterpart. It is set in a much wider open space, and the traffic and bustle of the city are kept much more at arm's length so the atmosphere is rather more contemplative and reverent. During the war Hiroshima was a garrison town, and as such an obvious target for Allied attacks, but it had been spared in the months leading up to the A-bomb. There is speculation that this was deliberate, the intention being to highlight the effects of the new weapon so that there would be no way to blur its impact through propaganda.

Two models of Hiroshima, before and after, are particularly chilling. A great red billard ball hangs over the toy city, representing the point at which 'Little Boy' was exploded 580 metres above our heads after dropping from the belly of *Enola Gay*. Because the area is quite flat, quite unlike the layout of Nagasaki, the devastation was all but total in a circular area consumed in less than a second by a radioactive fireball.

The horror of the aftermath is depicted in vivid details, in photographs and by really disturbing wax models with the burning flesh falling from their arms and faces, but the build-up to war and the militarism which took hold of Japan in the thirties and forties are also explained and nowadays shoulder their share of the blame.

Eighty thousand people were killed instantly, with something like 60,000 more succumbing to the after-effects in the ensuing years. It is worth remembering, though, that over 200,000 died in a single night of conventional Allied bombing of Tokyo, and that the atomic explosion paradoxically brought a thankfully premature end to that kind of destruction, as well as, in the words of Harry S. Truman, 'saving the lives of thousands and thousands of young Americans'.

Hiroshima has assumed a great symbolic importance since the war ended, and the very name of the place is almost now a unit of destructive force – earthquakes, or volcanoes, being described as 'unleashing the power of X Hiroshimas'. The nightmare of the sudden sunburst obliterating huge numbers of people in the blink of an eye is one that mankind has had to live with for the last fifty-seven years, and it has coloured the world's politics ever since. Even now, with the Cold War and the nuclear arms race supposedly long over, world leaders are constantly exercised at the thought of the power of even one single Hiroshima falling into the hands of an Osama bin Laden, or a Saddam Hussein. It's a strange thought, but arguably I am standing at the point where the modern era began.

The Shinkansen passes a couple of notable landmarks on its way up to Kyoto. There's Himeji, which is probably Japan's most impressive castle, a white feudal-era fortress with great white pagoda-style battlements with curly brown tiled roofs that looms above the trees and the surrounding countryside. It was where James Bond trained to be a ninja with Tiger Tanaka's men in *You Only Live Twice*.

Then there's the port city of Kobe, shattered by a major earthquake in 1995, which is where my talkSPORT chum Dom is staying, so as to have easy access to the England training camp on Awaji island nearby. It is also where Bond and Aki came to investigate the Osato Corporation tanker that they've seen on the microdot in *You Only Live Twice*.

I give Dom a ring to see if we might meet up, but he's already moved up to Shizuoka with the England squad. He tells me, though, of a press conference given by Paul Scholes at which the England midfielder was asked to name his favourite players of all time, and – as he did in 1998 – he went for Andy Ritchie and Frankie Bunn. Top man. Scholes was also asked a question, apparently, by the largely incomprehensible Garth Crooks, which the BBC man began with: 'Now then, Nicky . . .'

To which Scholes replied, 'And you are . . . ?'

They should really let Scholes do press conferences more often, I think.

In Kyoto, once I've checked into yet another new big city hotel, I go in search of an internet place recommended by the desk clerk. Two blocks away I find it, and it's free. I think it's a university library – excellent. I check the e-mail and find that talkSPORT have paid me, so I can tell Susan that we have enough money to pay the mortgage – excellent too. And it's raining, which is exactly what we want in Shizuoka tomorrow. Maybe I can get another streak going . . .

Susan e-mails me, incidentally, that it is boiling hot in the UK, and that Railtrack's rails have buckled in the heat bringing the trains to a standstill. The wrong kind of sun now . . . And she reports that she saw a white van in the street in London without a flag of St George on it. Must have fallen off. A cockney on the news, apparently, claims that he went into the flag business eight weeks ago and has since sold six million of them.

As it's free, I also check out the Oldham site, not really expecting that we will have bought Ilhan Mansiz or Anders Svensson – perpetrators of the best bits of skill so far, for me –

but it turns out there is some news. Iain Dowie is the manager now, by the look of things, and I have to scroll back through three weeks to find where Mick Wadsworth was sacked owing to 'disagreements with the direction the club was taking' with our thrusting young chairman.

Later I see the World Cup programme on the box – it's all England v Brazil, barely a mention of USA v Germany. It's being billed as the best defence in the World Cup against the best attack. Big Phil Scolari is said to be concentrating on defence – good news, because they were shit at that. What we don't want is him concentrating on attack, that would be terrifying.

Perugia have terminated the contract of Ahn Jung Hwan, the South Korean striker whose golden goal knocked Italy out of the cup. Amazingly this is actually being given as the reason.

Perugia's owner says: 'Those who down Italy cannot expect to come back here.'

So that's Byron Moreno's holiday in Tuscany ruined, as well.

I speak to Jim on the phone. He says that London has gone absolutely insane for the World Cup this week. If England win tomorrow, apparently, talkSPORT are going to come over and do the *Sports Breakfast* from Tokyo. If they lose, they're going to throw everything behind the Brazilians, and do next week's shows from Rio, on the Copacabana beach, no less. I can tell that Jim is seriously torn, now, about the result. On the one hand he'd love England to win, of course he would, but on the other Tokyo is such a pit, whereas at the Copa, Copacabana, I think you'll find that music and passion were always the fashion . . .

21

Shizuoka

'The last time the World Cup was played in an island
nation with a constitutional monarchy where the public
drive on the left, England won . . .'
– Bulgarian journalist to Robbie Fowler

21 JUNE

I haven't slept.

The day has dawned – I saw it – overcast and gloomy. Kyoto
is being pelted with driving rain, and – although in a way I hate
to say it – there is a definite nip in the air. This is excellent –
exactly what Doctor Eriksson ordered. Let the Brazilians see
how they like English weather. I suppose this will increase
Juninho's chances of starting, with his experience of Teesside
in February. Unless Kleberson comes from old-fashioned rain
forest country . . .

I breakfast in the self-styled 'Restaurant at the Top of Kyoto',
which is actually the restaurant at the top of my hotel, looking
out over a big black pagoda and the railway station, with the
Shinkansens easing smoothly in and out. I'm eating, and I'm
looking, but I'm not really concentrating. I can barely stand the
tension already, and the game is still several hours away. If it goes
to golden goal I am seriously concerned that I may die. I shove a
half-finished plate of cholesterol to one side just in case.

On the train to Shizuoka I find myself still going over and
over the possibility that the game will go to golden goal, which
would be awful, or penalties, which would be unspeakable. The

coaches, the players, the pundits, the experts all say that it is impossible to prepare psychologically for a penalty shoot-out. The England players have been practising, I'm told, by walking from the centre circle with all their team mates watching, but it still isn't possible to be fully prepared for the emotional burden of it all. And if they can't prepare, how am I supposed to? It's the quarter final of the World Cup, against Brazil. I can hardly breathe with the momentousness of it all.

Two Irish journalists in the row behind me take my mind off the game for a while. They are extremely smug because a World Cup tournament director called Junji Ogura has declared that the Irish fans have been the best.

'They taught Japan the joy of watching football,' apparently, according to Ogura.

God, they'll all be insufferable now. If these two are anything to go by, anyway.

We start talking about cricket, which seems like something that happens on another planet a hundred million miles away. Alistair Brown of Surrey has hit 268 not out in a one-day game against Glamorgan, surpassing the previous best one-day innings – one by Graeme Pollock in South Africa in 1974 – by no less than 46 runs. England have announced their one-day squad – Brown is not in it.

I borrow their paper to try to take my mind off the game for a while, and flick through today's World Cup tales. Luciano Gaucci of Perugia is still banging on about Ahn Jung Hwan: 'I do not want to see him in Perugia again. I do not want to.'

Italy are taking their defeat very badly indeed. Their press are accusing FIFA of deliberately orchestrating the Azzurri's demise – though small matters such as 'why' and 'how' are not clear – and FIFA have had 400,000 e-mails of protest from people who really should have taken the time to go to the airport and sling some rotten fruit at Trapattoni and the boys. It would have got them out of the house and allowed them to let off a bit of steam, instead of bottling it all up stuck in front of the computer.

Panini have withdrawn their World Cup stickers from sale in Italy – where sales were all set to go through the roof – in protest at the manner of Italy's ejection, 'which went against the spirit of clean football we have promoted for so long', according to Umberto Leone, one of their directors.

Bruno Metsu of Senegal is trying to persuade his team not to indulge in any superstitious hexes. 'If they worked,' he says, 'then we'd have won the African Nations Cup.'

Fabien Barthez is refusing to watch any of the World Cup games on the box – thank heavens some intrepid investigative journalist has finally got to the bottom of *that* story.

Cesare Maldini has quit Paraguay, and is currently under investigation for tax evasion – that sounds like one of those tie-up-the-loose-ends captions at the end of a film. And Paraguayans have been celebrating their national fiesta by burning hundreds of little effigies of their former manager.

At this crucial point in the tournament, Sepp Blatter has decided to take it upon himself to condemn the referees. 'It is better to award an offside goal than to disallow a good goal,' he says.

I overhear someone saying that tickets were changing hands for 900 dollars last night – I thank my lucky stars again that we met Ged on the train to Niigata.

I look up from the paper to see that the rain has stopped, and that between the grey clouds there is enough blue sky, to coin a phrase, to make Jose Antonio Camacho a couple of his trademark sweaty shirts. Still mostly cloudy, though.

The Shizuoka stadium is not in Shizuoka city. Rather like discovering that our hotel last weekend was in the prefecture of Niigata, the ground turns out to be in the prefecture of Shizuoka, but fifty kilometres from the city itself. Happily, though, the Shinkansen between Kyoto and Tokyo stops handily for it at a station called Kakegawa, according to my World Cup information booklet. I am alarmed then to see about five hundred bucolic Englishmen in the shirts and the flags and what have you piling off the train at Hamamatsu station, the one before Kakegawa, and pouring along the platform. Is this the stop? I grab my stuff and start making for the door . . .

Suddenly their boisterous march stops and breaks up, and all of them turn and rush back onto the train just before it pulls away. One person got off too soon, that's what happened, and everyone else on the whole train followed him.

At Kakegawa station I join the mob piling along the walkways and then onto a little local train heading for Fukuroi City, which is where the stadium is. It seems a real pity, given the solidarity of the Irish attitude behind manager Mick McCarthy when Keane walked out, that they never got to play here. Here there are station staff with white gloves shoving people into the trains, just as there are legendarily supposed to be every rush hour in Tokyo. The English are good-natured about this – it's all part of the experience – and no one turns and shoves back.

Outside the station when we reach journey's end there are hundreds of fans milling around in the fans' village, a now familiar assortment of stalls and promotions. The stadium itself is at the end of a long curving uphill pathway, glinting away amongst the trees in the brilliant, dazzling sunshine. The weather has well and truly broken, now, and it's turning into a real scorcher. That wasn't part of the plan, not at all.

The mix of yellow Brazilian shirts and the white or red of the English is relatively even by the look of things, and for once we are not going to have it all our own way. The Brazilian community of around 200,000 is Japan's third-largest foreign ethnic grouping – after the Koreans and the Chinese – and Shizuoka is the centre of this population. You will find Portuguese quite widely spoken in the city, and it looks as if all the staff of the Restaurante Sao Paolo have been given the day off. England are going to have plenty of support, too, by the looks of things, but it's going to be like a home match for Brazil.

I stop and watch a television crew interviewing a young Brazilian babe, the sort who'll be too busy flashing her navel at the world's media to watch the actual football. She says: 'I very very happy today. But I would like to have tits.'

It's very early still, as once again my London Transport training has led me to allow far too much time to get here, so I wander around looking at the stalls. There are beer and burger stalls, and scarf and shirt outlets, all very busy, but one or two other oddities. One, staffed by four young girls in kimonos, is offering 'View of Mt Fuji', something I have to admit I still haven't sampled yet. I presume they're from a travel and tours company, but I suppose they may just have a big pair of binoculars in there. A little further along there is 'Free Green Tea Service', and a dozen or so Japanese people can be glimpsed sitting behind rush mats having a tea ceremony.

I drift into Fukuroi World Square and watch a display of drumming for a few minutes, but I'm too on edge to stay, and decide to walk up to the stadium.

If you visit a shrine in Japan – and God knows there are plenty of them – you will more often than not find that the path leading up to the entrance is decorated, every few feet or so, by red flags. And this is what the path to Shizuoka stadium looks like, red banners shimmering in the baking sun, fluttering in the slight breeze, showing the way to the shrine of football. They are advertising Coca-Cola, as it happens, but still it looks very evocative.

Of course I can't go in until Ged gets here with the tickets, so once I get to the first security check I have to wander back to wait for him.

He arrives amidst a crowd who all emerge from the station realising that they have worn too many clothes. People are removing sweatshirts and waterproofs left, right and centre and stuffing them into backpacks, as it's really starting to get hot now. Ged is wearing a smart and tweedy jacket – he's English, so he keeps it on – and his white shirt turns out to be an old-fashioned, seventies-style replica Mansfield Town top.

Ged has work to do. FIFA have responded, finally, to criticism of their ludicrous system of selling tickets over the internet, and are going to make extra tickets for the Saitama semi available to buy at a ticket office in Tokyo – if England win. Ged has a press statement about this, which is embargoed until after the match, and he's due to be interviewed by Rob Bonnet for the BBC. I give Dom a call – it turns out he's near by – and we can get Ged's statement onto talkSPORT as well, so I am able to do him a small good turn.

Ged is happy to have some good news to spread around for a change, having spent most of his time out here making excuses for other people's cock-ups. His face darkens with worry at one point when we see a bloke holding up a sign reading: 'Eight thousand miles and no ticket – thanks Adam!' Then we work out that the guy means Adam Crozier, and not some employee of Byrom's who has let him down.

We go through the security checks and up to the forecourt of the stadium, and while Ged waits for Dom to sort out his satellite phone link I stand looking down the hill at the yellow-and-white wave surging up towards me, and breaking either side. Suddenly a little clutch of dark FA blazers appears in front of me, and Howard Wilkinson goes one side, and David Platt the other.

Nick and Shari arrive from Tokyo, and we head on up and into the stadium. Shari is remarkably unperturbed by having had to drop her life at a moment's notice and come out a day early to avoid the air traffic controllers' strike.

An England flag is draped over a balcony, facing outwards for some reason. Across the middle, where you would normally expect to see the legend Bristol Rovers or Nuneaton, is written the single word 'KNOCKERS'. They should try to get together with the Brazilian girl I saw earlier – they have priorities in common.

We pass a bloke shouting: 'Any tickets? Buying or selling . . .'

He's the most incompetent ticket tout I've ever seen. He's actually standing about two hundred yards beyond the security barriers, where everyone who passes him must have a ticket already or they couldn't be here, and if anybody had spares they would naturally have unloaded them before coming in.

Inside the ground we find our seats staring straight into the glaring sun, and retreat back into the shade under the stand. Shari heads for the refreshment stand and comes back with an improbable mountain of food, hot dogs, cold burgers, plastic boxes of stuff, cans of drink.

'It's just in case anybody wants it,' she says. I relieve her of a hot dog or two, just so she hasn't got so much to lug around. And a drink. And some crisps.

The teams emerge to the sound of a drum beating out:

Bang, bang, bangbangbang, bangbangbangbang . . . England!

They stride forward behind the Mexican referee and his officials through a phalanx of photographers, who are all wearing bright red security tops.

England are in white, and Brazil in their blue, almost purple, second strip, which is a slight disappointment. White and yellow isn't a clash, is it? It wasn't in 1970, anyway, and most people had black-and-white tellies in those days.

On the big screen we get a shot of Prince Andrew, and he doesn't know the words to the second verse of the national anthem any more than we do. If you had to pick a word for the Brazilian national anthem, then I think it would have to be 'twirly'. It sounds a bit like the theme to *Bilko*.

England have the first attack, Scholes flicking the ball with the outside of his right foot to set Cole away overlapping on the left past Lucio, and Edmilson comes across to give away a corner. Beckham trots over to take it, and his kick is flighted deep, looking to find Ferdinand as he did early on against Denmark, but Marcos punches clear.

When Brazil have their first bit of possession it's noticeable that they want to try to run at England. Edmilson tries to bring the ball out from the back, but Heskey stays close to him and ends up giving away a free kick. Next it's Gilberto Silva, who takes on Scholes, and Rivaldo nutmegs Nicky Butt, but can't pick up the ball on the other side. England are closing down tightly, but when they get the ball they seem to be happy to simply hoof it away. First Mills, then Ferdinand, then Mills again launches the ball upfield to nobody in particular, allowing the Brazil back three to pick it up and bring it back.

Sinclair and Cole are doubling up on Ronaldinho. Cafu wants to get forward, but there is no space for him. Rivaldo finds a yard for a snap shot but he's thirty-five yards out and it bobbles harmlessly wide.

Brazil ping the ball about on the edge of England's area, but it's sewn up tight as a gnat's chuff. Roberto Carlos tries to go past Mills, but can't. Then Ronaldinho comes inside Cole and finds a chink of light, but Campbell closes it down.

Beckham, who has been quietly tracking Ronaldo, robs Roberto Carlos and bursts away down the right. His early diagonal cross finds Heskey, but Cafu takes the ball off him before he can control it.

Ronaldo, starved of the ball, starts lurking around the left back position. Beckham takes a free kick onto Heskey's chest, and then flicks the return forward for Scholes. For a moment it looks like a good shooting chance, but Edmilson blocks with his backside.

Brazil inch down the field, playing triangles, Cafu to Edmilson, to Gilberto Silva, to Ronaldinho. England are not giving them any space, but we're not seeing too much of the ball.

Scholes goes in late on Ronaldinho, and Brazil have their first free kick in a dangerous place, on the right, twenty-five yards out. Rivaldo, Roberto Carlos and Ronaldinho stand over it, and you wouldn't want any one of them to take it. Doesn't

Lucio fancy a go? In the end, Rivaldo and Ronaldinho do a crappy little tappy-tap to one another, and Roberto Carlos can only whack it against Heskey and away for a corner.

Seaman, worryingly, comes for Rivaldo's corner but doesn't get it. Campbell, leaning back, does well to head it away from the advancing Lucio. Shortly after this Rivaldo does a nasty two-footed studs-up challenge on Mills as the Leeds full back is belting the ball upfield again, and the ref, Mr Ramos Riza, doesn't even book him.

It's a tight, congested game, with both teams squeezing the space, and both Ronaldo and Owen are looking for the ball around the centre circle rather than where they can do real damage. Brazil have Kleberson and Gilberto Silva holding the centre of midfield in front of their back three, Lucio, Edmilson and Roque Junior. Cafu and Roberto Carlos are reined in at the moment, and their set-up is much more defensive than it was against Belgium or in the Group C games. Ronaldo is a lone front man, with Ronaldinho and Rivaldo doing their work deep.

It's really very hot, even hotter than Osaka. I can feel my forearms burning, and withdraw them inside my T-shirt, but this is the sort of thing you do on a cold day, and I'm hotter than ever. Shari lends me a pullover to cover them. Then the guy in front turns round and hands me some sunscreen in a spray.

'There you go,' he says, 'Factor 35. It's like wearing a duffel coat.'

Ronaldo has a first burst through, with the England defence unsure whether he is about to pass to the offside Rivaldo, and Campbell comes across, Rio-like, and snuffs out the threat. Then Ronaldo plays a neat one-two around the box with Rivaldo, and gets a good shot away but it's straight at Seaman.

Scholes brings it out, shimmying beautifully past both Rivaldo and Ronaldinho, drawing a cheer from the England fans. He feeds Mills on the right, who for once looks up and plays a pass rather than trying to kick it as far as he can.

Heskey has time to control and turn, and plays a through ball towards Owen. It's too close to Lucio, though, but in an instant the Leverkusen defender has let it get away from him and suddenly Owen is racing through with the ball. Marcos comes out to smother, but Owen wills him to dive right and deftly lifts the ball over him . . .

Time slows almost to a standstill as the ball spins inevitably, gorgeously, dreamily into the middle of the goal, and the net cushions it welcomingly, as though it knew, it just knew it was coming.

1–0.

I am standing, staring up into the blue sky, roaring. The last few days have been a constant struggle to keep the dream in the bottle, but the cork's out now. Don't think about it, don't even think about it . . . But here it comes, spilling out, tempting fate . . . a semi-final against Senegal, or maybe Turkey, and Spain, probably, in the final, or it could be Germany. Beckham sitting on red-shirted shoulders in front of a blue sky, smiling, holding up the World Cup, Scholesy doing a little Nobby Stiles jig . . .

England are bossing the game now, no doubt about it. Brazil are having the lion's share of the ball, but they are always faced with eight, nine, snapping eager white-shirted men, and they are beginning to get frustrated.

Beckham in particular is everywhere, nicking the ball away from Ronaldo, and ending up on the deck for his trouble. Brazil seem to look for Cafu wide on the right at every opportunity, but Ashley Cole is marking him out of the game.

England get the ball and begin to play a bit. Scholes works the ball to Beckham, then it moves on via Owen to Mills, and his high ball into the box is headed goalwards by Heskey, just dropping onto the top of the netting to Marcos's relief. Heskey is having a good game – as against Argentina he is hustling the opposition centre backs when they bring the ball out of defence, closing them down. He has a spin and run of his own

340

from the centre circle which frightens the life out of them. Then a good move which begins with Sinclair and Cole on the left, ends with Beckham sending Heskey to the bye-line, and his good low cross is gathered by Marcos just ahead of the predatory Owen.

The blue shirts are reduced to potshots from range, which are invariably cannoning to safety off the massed ranks of the English defence. When one of these Kleberson efforts ricochets to Ronaldo, and there seems the ghost of a chance for a split second, Mills appears and boots the ball away. More and more Brazil are getting cross and heated. Lucio fouls Ashley Cole, as does Cafu, who is lucky not to get booked for his Sunday League hack.

England are calm, composed, confident. Scholes, Butt and Beckham are running the game, and Brazil have barely had a chance worthy of the name. If we can just keep them out till half time . . .

Then, just before the break, Seaman comes out to catch a hopeful punt forward by Gilberto Silva that has ricocheted up off Ferdinand, and falls awkwardly over Campbell's shoulders. The physio is on for some time massaging the big keeper's back, and shortly after this we hear that there will be four minutes of injury time, most of which are due to this one incident.

These are nearly up, when a high volleyed clearance down the right wing by Ferdinand falls out of the blue sky towards Beckham and Gilberto, who both make a half-hearted jump for it, and both miss it. It bounces high into the air, and both of them go for it again – this time it skews out towards the touchline off the back of Gilberto's head. Beckham trots after it, and it seems to be going out for the throw-in, so when Roberto Carlos and Roque Junior both come in to sandwich him, the England captain, boxing clever he thinks, leaps into the air to protect his recently broken foot.

The ball doesn't go out, though, and Roque Junior comes away with it. Mills comes to challenge for it, and Roque Junior plays it inside towards Kleberson. It's too close to Scholes, though, and he rides Kleberson's sliding tackle, but Ronaldinho nicks the loose ball before the England midfielder can turn, and suddenly he's racing through the middle straight at the heart of the English defence. Mills and Beckham are stranded upfield, leaving England's right exposed, and Ronaldo makes a run wide left to take advantage. Rivaldo, meanwhile, makes the opposite run, into acres of space on the England left.

Ashley Cole confronts Ronaldinho forty yards from goal – a step over, right and left, and the little Brazilian is through. Now he has Ferdinand and Campbell in front of him, but Ferdinand is half watching Ronaldo, outside him to the right, and Campbell has an eye on Rivaldo, on his left. One of them has to go and meet the threat, but which one? Ferdinand comes over, risking everything, and meets Ronaldinho on the edge of the area just as he dinks the ball with the outside of his right foot to Rivaldo. Campbell should have this covered, but he has been drawn too far away from the Barcelona star into no man's land, and a brilliantly precise left-foot shot across goal into the bottom corner beats the ailing Seaman, and it's 1–1.

The half-time whistle blows a matter of seconds after the restart, and the teams troop off into the shade, and so do I, taking refuge under the stand from the fierce sun. Seaman seemed to be holding his back – maybe he won't come out for the second half.

We so nearly held on, we deserved to hold on, actually, and what a difference that might have made. Brazil would have been down just now, apprehensive, and they must know they've been brilliantly handled for the first forty-seven minutes. Now they'll be up, though, and they'll come at us hard at the start of the second half.

Sven has to say the right things. What they are, though, I couldn't tell you.

For the first few minutes after the restart there seems to be a little more space for both teams. Cafu finds a bit of room down the right wing for the first time in the match, but runs offside, and then Mills advances into acres down our right, and finds Heskey on the corner of the box where Roque Junior dumps the Liverpool man on his enormous backside. Beckham trots over to take the kick, and Roberto Carlos delays and delays, complaining that the kick is in the wrong place. When it is eventually taken a desperate Brazilian head gets in front of the lurking Owen, but a foul elsewhere would have ruled the effort out in any case.

Then Cafu takes a throw-in down the Brazilian right flank. He finds Kleberson, and Scholes is quickly on him, but fouls him as he turns inside. Brazil try to take it quick and short, but the referee wants Kleberson back on his feet first and they have to bring the ball back. It's thirty-one, thirty-two yards out, judging by the pattern of the mowed grass, and Ronaldinho is taking it.

I'm sitting right in line with the jostling for position in the England box. Five Brazilians are in there – Ronaldo, Rivaldo, Gilberto Silva, Edmilson, Roque Junior – watched by eight Englishmen. As Ronaldinho runs up the England line holds, hoping for an offside, and then Ferdinand and Mills drop in towards the goal line. The ball loops towards the goal, and the Brazilian forwards stop, seemingly realising that the cross is terribly overhit. One or two hands go up in scorn, and they are already turning to berate Ronaldinho. From the vantage point I have, the ball looks to be sailing way over the bar, and I'm thinking: 'Well, that's just rubbish . . .'

At the last instant it starts to drop, losing pace, and Seaman, who has come out to meet what he thinks will be a cross, is back-pedalling. His arm goes up, but it doesn't look like a serious attempt to touch it, just shepherding the ball over, and then, incredibly, it falls over his head and into the net.

I can't believe what I've just seen, and neither can the Brazilians. There is a stunned moment as those in the penalty box take it in, and then they rush to little Ronaldinho, who by now is chicken-strutting with glee along the running track.

No way he meant that, no way. Not even if he's spent the last week watching David Seaman's showreel.

England hold the ball for a while, trying to get their heads together. Owen almost gets on the end of a long Scholes pass, but it unluckily gets away from him under a Roque Junior challenge. If only it had been Lucio again . . .

Brazil are peacocking it now, backheeling and dribbling, cocksure and cock-a-hoop. England, shaking their heads, shocked, start to press them back.

Mills comes down the right again, and his cross finds Heskey on the left of a crowded box. He gets half a yard on Cafu and crosses low and hard into the box, where a last-ditch Brazilian boot nicks it out for a corner in front of Owen. Beckham's corner is headed out with the keeper flapping, and almost immediately Roberto Carlos fouls Scholes on the right of the box. Beckham again causes panic with his free kick, but neither Ferdinand nor Cole can get their shots on goal.

Roberto Carlos takes a free kick on the left, about as far out as Ronaldinho's for the goal. Incredibly, Seaman starts wandering off his line again, and all around me England fans scream at him to get back. The shot, as it turns out, is deflected away by a Brazilian heel.

Kieron Dyer comes on for Sinclair, who has had a quiet time on the left, and his first touch is to hold the ball too long in the centre circle and ruin the chance of a quick England break. Brazil surge forward with Rivaldo. He squares to Ronaldinho, who is having the time of his life. Mills half wins it, and then tackles again, and suddenly he's on the floor holding his shin and like lightning the referee has a red card out. I'm level with this action and have a decent view of it, and my first thought is that he's sent Mills off, but after a long spell in which things are not quite clear, it seems that Ronaldinho is on his way.

The little number 11 is holding his head, a huge incredulous grin on his face, and seven Brazilians cluster round the referee. Ronaldinho is laughing, he's actually laughing – is it all going to turn out to be a mistake? It's taking ages to sort out – was it a yellow after all . . . ?

No, he's off. He must have shown Mills his studs, it's the only explanation. This is, after all, the same ref who sent off Thierry Henry for that very offence. We don't get a replay here, thanks to a FIFA instruction which prevents anything remotely controversial being shown, in the ludicrous fear of igniting an incident, so all we know for sure is that Brazil's best player today, who's made one and scored one, is leaving with 'Off! Off! Off!' ringing in his ears, and we will be playing ten men for the last half an hour. Scolari hugs Ronaldinho as he finally reaches the dugout, and the Paris St Germain striker is *still* smiling.

It takes the best part of three minutes to resume the game, and then it turns into a photo-negative of much of the first half, with Brazil lumping it forwards out of danger, and England working it back, playing possession football around the edge of a packed area, with Scholes and Dyer shots being charged down.

Scholes lofts a ball over the top to Beckham in the area, and Gilberto Silva just clips the England captain's heel as he goes to run onto it and sends him sprawling. The referee isn't interested in further controversy just at the moment, though, and Beckham slaps the turf in frustration.

Ronaldo shows us a flash of his best form, having had a quiet match. He drives powerfully at the England back line, tries a step over, but Ferdinand and Mills combine to shut him down. A minute later he's joined his similarly orthodontically challenged team mate on the bench and Edilson is on.

The one remaining R shows how he is planning to approach the last twenty minutes. He volleys an ungainly clearance out into touch from inside his own box, and goes down, arching his back in agony, holding his ankle. The referee wants none of it, and so Rivaldo just gets up and jogs away. Then Campbell is astonished to find Rivaldo crumpling to a heap at his feet before he's even started to make a tackle, and minutes later the Brazilian is on the floor again, having been lightly brushed by the very tip of Sol's finger.

Then a Beckham throw finds Butt. He shoves it low in to Mills, well advanced on the edge of the area. He is tightly marked by Cafu but turns him superbly, like a forward, muscles his way into the box with the Brazilian captain hanging onto a fistful of his shirt, and unleashes a powerful left-foot shot, which is on target, but deflected over by Roque Junior's thigh. Unlucky Danny . . .

Campbell rises to meet Beckham's corner, but he's climbing on Lucio, and anyway his header was miles wide. Rivaldo has flung himself to the ground again, this time getting Paul Scholes booked, and wasting a bit more time.

Quarter of an hour to go. Scholes beats his man and plays it out to Mills. In it goes to Beckham's feet, and he's down again, and again it's not a penalty.

Brazil keep the ball. They work it gradually up to Edilson on the edge of England's area, then slowly all the way back to Marcos. When we have it we are finding the Brazilian box is packed. We need a change, and ideally someone who can create a little bit of magic, beat a man with the ball to find a bit of extra space. Joe Cole, I'm thinking, it could be made for Joe Cole . . .

Sven brings Owen off, and on comes Darius Vassell. This seems to be like-for-like, to me. Maybe Owen is feeling his injury, but Vassell just doesn't seem the right move.

Then Teddy comes on for Ashley Cole. That's all three subs now, and so this is Sven's last throw. It looks like we are looking for headers now, when we really could do with a bit of individual flair to break down these massed blue ranks.

Roque Junior pulls Vassell down and it's a free kick to England. Roberto Carlos runs over, picks up the ball, and runs away with it. When he has dropped it, and it's booted back for the free kick, Roque Junior kicks it away. It's placed again and Edilson toe-pokes it into touch. None of these players is booked or even spoken to. That's *jogo bonito* for you – the beautiful game.

Scholes is played neatly through the middle, and unceremoniously crunched to the deck in Beckham territory, but the referee is still embarrassed by sending off Ronaldinho and is trying to make it up to the ten men. This one's an absolute shocker, if you ask me . . .

Four minutes left – where did all that time go . . . ? England can't get the ball, even with their extra man. Brazil break away, three on two, but Cafu would rather waste time than try to extend the lead, and off he goes to the corner flag.

Butt heads a Beckham corner just wide, challenged by Rivaldo. Rio, up for the corner, stays up as a centre forward for the four minutes of injury time.

Rivaldo crumples at the feet of Campbell, who stands over him, shouting, and waving at him to get to his feet and play football. This urgency is somehow lacking in England's play, though, as they move the ball across the Brazilian box, without a clue how to get in there. Hopeful balls forward bobble out for goal kicks, which take for ever to be taken, and England's World Cup campaign gently subsides.

One more last long ball, and the referee blows for full time before it lands.

I am stunned. Numb. Stunned, numb and very hot. Not as hot as Osaka, perhaps, but close. Maybe the heat partly explains how England ran out of steam in the second half, but we should have made a couple of chances against ten men, shouldn't we?

Brazil are ecstatic, as well they might be, embracing one another. Seaman wanders around, lost in misery, and his team mates go up to him one by one and put their arms around him. They'll be telling him it wasn't his fault. I don't know. It seems to me that he only had three saves to make in the whole game, and he didn't make two of them.

Ged has passes to some sort of hospitality reception, but it's at a hotel back at Fukuroi City somewhere, and anyway I'm not in the mood. I don't think he is, really, either.

I walk down to the station in a daze. Somewhere in the crush outside I lose track of Nick and Shari, and find myself filing along with dozens of England supporters, all of us stupefied with heat and disappointment. Dozens of Brazilian fans have lined up alongside the path and are flaunting their exuberance, taunting us, sticking their tongues out, shouting: 'Bye bye England! Bye bye!' It's not colourful, it's not joyous, it's not the samba-style señors of South American soccer having their bit of fun, it's just nasty. I want to kill them all. To everyone's credit, no one leaps over the barrier and starts smashing their faces in. I am not a violent person, not at all, but I wouldn't like to promise that I wouldn't have joined in.

Stuck on a slow train to Hamamatsu I call David, who was there somewhere, but there's not much to say.

'We hardly had a shot,' is about the extent of our analysis.

At Hamamatsu I shuffle, zombie-like, up to the Shinkansen platform. As I go up the stairs the middle-aged English man behind me treads on my heel, and then, moments later, he does it again, really quite painfully. I make an inarticulate complaining noise, and he mumbles an apology. He too is preoccupied, stumbling around, lost in thoughts of what might have been. As he passes by me I see that it's Howard Wilkinson.

On the train to Kyoto depression, torpor, disappointment, futility of life, four more years of hurt all begin to catch up with me, and it's all I can do to haul my sorry frame back to my hotel room, where for the second night running I utterly fail to sleep.

22
Theme Park Japan

'a last-gasp hand-job on the line there . . .'
– David Pleat, watching Germany v USA

Well. I asked for football that felt as if it really meant something. I asked for that all-absorbing, mind-filling, heart-stopping feeling back once again, and I got it. We should be careful what we ask for.

Now that England's adventure was done the vast majority of the travelling support was heading home just as soon as they could get a flight. I was staying, though, till the bitter end, and spent the next couple of days wandering around Kyoto and Nara like a zombie, unable to clear the mental image of that ludicrous free kick floating into the top corner.

One of the places of interest I hauled my miserable carcass to was a fifteenth-century dry Zen garden set in the grounds of Ryoan-ji on the outskirts of Kyoto.

The garden consists of a long rectangular area of painstakingly raked grey-white gravel surrounded by a low earthen wall on three sides and a wooden temple with a viewing verandah on the fourth. Visitors sit here and try to plumb the hidden depths of meaning expressed in the arrangement of fifteen larger stones, arranged in five groups amongst the gravel.

I looked at this ancient layout and it gradually revealed its wisdom to me. That large lump there, look, at the far end, it's too far from the back wall. That smaller stone to the right only has to give that little round stone enough air and the big rock

349

will never get back in time to cover it. The big rock even had a bit of a spur jutting out, like a ponytail, and looked older than all the others. It certainly had a deal more moss on it.

Ronaldinho, cocky, claimed he meant it. He said that Cafu alerted him to Seaman's tendency to wander too far from his line, and the Brazilian captain should know – he was in the Real Zaragoza side when Nayim beat Seaman from the halfway line in the 1995 European Cup Winners' Cup final in Paris.

Rio Ferdinand said this: 'It was a freak goal. I was in the drug-testing area with him after the game and I asked him whether he meant it and he just started laughing.'

This didn't strike me as conclusive evidence one way or the other. After all, Ronaldinho was sent off for next to nothing and looked as if he was laughing his head off. He could play the Joker in *Batman*.

Seriously, though. There is, I'm told, a genuine Brazilian technique called 'The Floating Leaf'. The weight of the kick is judged so nicely that it runs out of steam and begins to drop suddenly rather than carrying on in the expected parabola. It's tricky and risky, and it has to be just so or else it looks like the worst kick ever as it plops gently into the hands of the keeper. Maybe Ronaldinho simply got this just right.

Anyway, the issue was not whether Seaman was too far off his line – clearly he wasn't, clearly he had to cover the cross everyone in the stadium was expecting. The problem was his inability to track backwards from the position he had taken up and leap high enough. Shouldn't the man beaten by Nayim have heard the alarm bells sooner than anyone? Did the knock to the back he took in the first half impair his ability to deal with this surprising eventuality, not to mention the Rivaldo goal, and if that was the case, why didn't he say to the management at half time that he could not/should not carry on?

Japan seemed to go into mourning once the England team were knocked out, even more so than after the demise of their own team, and a sorrowful item about Beckham and the boys checking out of Awaji and heading for the airport was the lead item on the national news, ahead of looming war in India and Bush's latest pronouncements on Iraq.

The rest of the World Cup quarter finals trundled along, virtually unnoticed.

Germany, predictably enough, beat the USA 1–0, the goal a Michael Ballack header that Brad Friedel should probably have stopped. The match was notable for the refereeing of Hugh 'Crybaby' Dallas, who missed a blatant handball on the goal line by Torsten Frings, and fell for any number of obvious dives by Oliver Neuville, who seemed to have embarked on a personal mission to get as many Americans booked as possible.

Beckenbauer wasn't impressed. He said: 'If you were to put all the outfield players in a sack, shake it about, and punch it, whoever you hit would deserve it.'

Spain and South Korea battled out a goalless draw in Gwangju. Joaquin, Spain's youngest player, was the star, running the hyperactive Koreans ragged throughout. His free kick was headed in by either Ruben Baraja or the 'man in the mask', Kim Tae Young, but the goal was disallowed for some argy bargy in the area. Then in golden goal time Joaquin hit the bye-line and pulled back a cross for Morientes to score, but the linesman was flagging that the ball had gone out of play so that was disallowed too.

It went to penalties. Hwang Sun Hong, Hierro, Park Ji Sung, Baraja, Seol Ki Hyeon, Xavi, and Ahn Jung Hwan all scored theirs to make it 4–3. Then, sadly, it was young Joaquin – man of the match by a country mile – who missed for Spain. He did a little stop in his run-up which allowed Lee Woon Jae to charge out at him, and by the time he actually kicked the ball the Korean keeper seemed to be almost halfway out to meet it. Hong Myung Bo then clinched South Korea's semi-final place with a tremendous penalty kick, for which he seemed able to turn his foot so that it was almost pointing backwards as it struck the ball.

Jose Antonio Camacho was beside himself at the end, again sporting his trademark sweaty armpits. He must be after some kind of deodorant endorsement, I reckon. The anti-perspirant that can claim to have tamed his rampant glands would just fly from *supermercado* shelves all over Spain.

And it should be said that once it went to penalties South Korea had a distinct advantage. Any K-League game that ends in a draw is decided by a penalty shoot-out, and goalkeeper Lee Woon Jae was involved in seven with his club, Suwon Blue Wings, last season. His record? Won seven, lost none. President Kim Dae Jung hailed this as 'the greatest day since Dangun' – a reference to the god-king who founded Korea 5,000 years ago. And we hark back to 1966 . . .

Senegal were slight favourites for the fourth quarter final against Turkey. They had disposed of France and Sweden, while the Turks had only played one difficult game, against Brazil, and they lost that. The Africans had the better of the early exchanges, but Turkey gradually got on top, creating chance after chance for veteran striker Hakan Sukur, who managed to miss them all. As the match wore on Basturk and Sas seemed to be trying to bypass Sukur altogether, and eventually manager Gunes got the message and took him off. With Ilhan Mansiz, his replacement, in attack Turkey looked much more dangerous, and the top-knot pony-tailed playboy grabbed the golden goal winner shortly after the match went into extra time, deftly turning home Umit Davala's cross.

It was noticeable that when his team mates gathered to gee themselves up for the extra period Hakan Sukur, the captain, stood alone to one side, not speaking to anyone.

As I made my way around some of Japan's finest tourist attractions over the next few days, for all the undeniably fabulous array of splendid photo opportunities in this part of the world, one nagging disappointment kept cropping up.

Take the Golden Pavilion, Kinkaju-ji, for example. This is an absolutely gorgeous building set in a perfectly maintained Japanese lake garden, with ponds and gravel paths and wonderfully manicured little trees. The first sight of the gilded pavilion peeping through the trees, and then spectacularly reflected in the Mirror Pond, is breathtaking. Originally part of a retirement villa built for a fourteenth-century Shogun, a fabulous display of his wealth, refinement and power, it was converted into a Zen temple on his death, and has stood on this site for six centuries.

Or has it? You read the literature with your mouth open at the thought of all this ancient gold surviving for hundreds of years, until you get to the bottom and find that the pavilion was in fact burned to the ground by a crazy monk in 1950. This replica took five years to build – the giveaway is the phoenix motif on the roof gable – and was regilded at enormous expense in 1987.

Then there's the great temple of Todai-ji, which I travelled down to Nara to visit. A vast wooden hall houses Japan's largest bronze statue, a huge black Buddha, fifteen metres tall. The temple was founded by the Emperor Shomu in 745, you are told, its grandeur intended to cement his shaky hold over the nation. The main hall is the world's largest wooden building, apparently, and they are right to be thrilled about that, of course, although many other countries in the world have built much larger things out of bricks. I strolled around gawping at the big Buddha, round his big black back and out the other side, and was duly impressed. Imagine this having stood here for twelve and a half centuries, this great awe-inspiring statue and this monumental dark wooden hall . . .

And then I read that this wooden building, while still the world's largest, is a replica built in 1709, two-thirds the size of the ancient original, and that the Buddha's original head fell off in a ninth-century earthquake, and then his hand burned off in a fire in 1167, and more of him was destroyed by an act of God – some other God, presumably – in the sixteenth century, and so on and so on, until now only tiny fragments of the great Buddha remain, and it's impossible to work out which bits they are.

In Nikko, an hour to the north of Tokyo, you can visit a World Heritage site that has been sacred to both Buddhism and Shintoism for a thousand years. Walking up from Nikko station to the main sightseeing area, you pass one of the town's most well-known landmarks – Shin-kyo bridge, a red wooden arched structure dating back to 1636, which commemorates an eighth-century legend concerning a priest being helped across the river here by two obliging snakes who made themselves into a bridge for him. It is completely covered by corrugated sheet metal at the moment, although there is a picture of what the bridge would look like if you could see it displayed on the side. The original bridge is, of course, being completely rebuilt – not preserved or restored, you understand, but replaced with a red wooden replica.

From a tourist's point of view, Japan is an amazing place. It is as though old buildings falling into disrepair and ruin is not seen as a natural part of things at all, and they are quite as happy to look at a replica of how things used to be as they would be looking at the actual thing. It feels a bit as if Japan, the whole country, is a massive Huis ten Bosch. Theme Park Japan, featuring reconstructions and two-thirds size replicas of everything that has ever been burned or bombed or smashed or pulled down.

I did enjoy visiting these places, but there was just something vaguely unsatisfactory about it all, as though it was cheating, and not proper tourism somehow. It made me wonder about all the Japanese that come over to Europe with their digital cameras and their bumbags. Perhaps their awe at looking at the

Colisseum, for example, comes from their sheer disbelief that
the Italians could have left it like that and not rebuilt it again
in concrete right up to the top, and put seats in, and maybe
some holographic lions. And how irritating is that Stonehenge
thing? Look, two blokes with a couple of forklift trucks could
have that good as new in a weekend . . .

Maybe if you live in a nation where the ground could
suddenly start shaking violently at any moment, or molten
lava could come raining down out of the sky, you tend to
value the permanence of things slightly differently. If you're
used to having to rebuild everything every few decades, why
not rebuild all your historic monuments while you're at it?

I did see some authentic Edo-period architecture at one
point, but it was at a place called the Toei Movieland Theme
Park, and was the set for a Japanese sitcom called *The Edo
Period*.

While on a day trip back to Osaka, only half an hour away
from Kyoto, I had it in mind to visit Osaka-jo, a castle that is
Japan's most-visited tourist attraction, even outdoing Himeji,
which is Japan's most spectacular fortress. Then I read that
Osaka-jo has had a seven billion yen facelift, and that much of
it has been reconstructed using concrete, and that while some
seventeenth-century towers and gates remain, it is all but a
modern replica of the ancient landmark that has dominated
Osaka for centuries. I decided to go to the aquarium instead.

The aquarium trip was just because I was missing my
children. Peter and John love visiting the aquarium in London,
and any other smaller ones we come across on family trips,
and they absolutely hoover up underwater programmes like
The Blue Planet, so I went there, rang them up and described
it to them over their distant British breakfast.

The outside is decorated with a colourful fish mosaic,
which makes it look like the largest sushi restaurant in the
world. There were many Japanese visitors inside, a significant
number of whom seemed to me to be tapping on the glass

tanks and saying things like: 'That one please, waiter,' and, 'Ooh look, my favourite! And still alive, too, just how I like it! Yum yum!'

The Great Buddha of Nara at Todai-ji is an awe-inspiring sight, however little of it is authentic, original, unburned, unloosened and unreplaced. It sits blackly in the dark, seemingly on the point of standing and bursting through the roof of the building. One hand is raised, with the middle finger leaning forward, as though the Buddha has been captured in the middle of daintily pressing a doorbell.

The Japanese will bow to no one in their readiness to exploit their holy monuments commercially. Todai-ji is set in a deer park, and the deer will come right up and eat biscuits from your hand. You can buy special deer-feeding biscuits for this purpose from pavement vendors, and all the gift shops and stalls have a vast array of deer-related souvenirs for you to unbuckle your yen on – cuddly deer, china deer, plastic deer, deer-patterned lampshades, deer wind chimes, and a variety of brightly coloured inflatable deer with red noses who look suspiciously as if they have been designed to pull an inflatable Santa on an inflatable sleigh.

At Nikko the main attraction is a spectacular seventeenth-century blue-and-gold mausoleum for the shogun Tokegawa Ieyasu, competed by his grandson in 1617. You reach it through the Sun Blaze gate, having passed a large red-and-green pagoda (built: 1650; burned down and rebuilt: nineteenth century) and the sacred stables. These are decorated by one of the most renowned wood-carvings in Japan. It depicts the three monkeys that traditionally illustrate the phrase 'See no evil, hear no evil, speak no evil', representing the three major principles of Tendai Buddhism, and also the opportunity to make a monkey-themed trinket killing at the commercial outlets down the hill. The gift shop here is not so much a gift shop, more a gift supermarket. Folk were wheeling huge trolleys crammed with monkey lanterns, cuddly monkeys, bronze monkeys, wooden monkeys, monkey key-rings, monkey candles, monkey wallets, monkey hatstands, monkey umbrellas, inflatable monkeys, you name it (and stick the word 'monkey' in front of it), out to their cars and coming back for more. I bought a monkey ocarina for my sister, who is a music teacher.

All the shrines here – and I visited plenty – have little gift shops, staffed by bald and bored-looking monks, who presumably thought they were getting into the shrine business for some sort of spiritual reason rather than as a Saturday job. You can buy little tokens with which to ask for all sorts of benefits from the gods – success in exams, in your driving test, in love, in your search for a new job, the usual secular preoccupations of the modern world.

At Rinno-ji, a Buddhist temple established in the eighth century on the site at Nikko, three huge gilded statues – of the thousand-handed Kannon, the Amida Buddha, and the fearsome horse-headed Kannon – lurk in the dark of the red-painted wooden hall, Sanbutsu-do.

I strolled round the back of the three Buddhas, and was almost outside, when I passed the obligatory gift stall, with votive offerings, incense, and little Buddha statues for sale. This was staffed by a young shaven-headed monk, in his robes, and just then he had no customers. I looked at him, and he had his feet up on the table, he was chewing gum, and reading a comic book which I could see, even from where I was standing, featured drawings of naked women. Bad monk. Bad, bad monk. He glanced up at me surlily, as if to say: 'Yeah? You want a prayer stick or not, you mother? If you don't, just get out of my face and stop wasting my time . . .'

He didn't seem overly spiritual, this youth. I wondered if he really was a monk. Maybe in Theme Park Japan none of the monks is real, they're all just kids with a crap holiday job, the local equivalent of the Puerto Ricans who bumble around Disneyland dressed as Goofy or Donald Duck.

'Two pound fifty an hour I'm getting for this, *and* I had to shave my head.'

The day after England went out of the World Cup I wandered around Kiyomizu-dera (founded: 778; completely rebuilt: 1630), a wooden temple complex on the side of a hill which afforded great views over Kyoto. I'd almost put the game out of my mind, and then I came across a gift kiosk selling particularly poignant votive offerings, which merely said: 'For Victory'. Too late . . .

It was hot, and I was thirsty, so I popped into a shop and bought a bottle of Coke. The shop was still selling special World Cup promotion bottles, and the shopkeeper fumbled below the counter for the little red paper packet containing my gift. Outside I ripped it open and it was a model, about an inch and a half high . . . of Rivaldo. My fucking favourite.

A minute or two later I found myself at the top end of the oldest streets in Kyoto, or some such thing. There're two of them, Sannen-zaka and Ninen-zaka, the 'three-year slope' and the 'two-year slope'.

Apparently it is very bad luck to stumble on their cobbled stones – and not just because you might graze your knee or get an irritating hole in your trousers, it's a bona fide traditional superstition. I put little Rivaldo on the ground and booted him down the hill, and he bounced and stumbled and rolled until he came to a grubby halt in the gutter. Ha! No Golden Boot for you, you great gangly cheat.

My brain did get clogged up after a day or two with shrine overload, and I found that I was beginning to mutter to myself: 'No more Buddha . . .' My favourite shrine, though, was well worth the trip.

In Nara I was having some lunch – a sort of deep-fried sweet potato that I bought from a street vendor thinking it was chips – flicking through a leaflet from the Nara tourist information office. Shrine, shrine, temple, shrine, hot spring, temple, temple with a hot spring in it, shrine, shrine, temple, shrine was about the gist of it. Then something about the very last one in the booklet caught my eye.

Tanzan shrine, framed by the forest of Mt Tonomine, offers a rich variety of scenic delights year-round. The elegant and colourful pageant of the Ball-Kicking Festival, held here each fall, adds further zest to the beauty of the autumn mountains . . .

Ball-Kicking Festival?

I hurried along to the tourist information desk at Nara station to see if I could find out more. Now although, according to the literature, the Ball-Kicking Festival takes place in what our American friends are pleased to call 'the fall', don't go booking your flights just yet because the lady on the tourist information desk at Nara station said it happens every 29 April.

Either way it looked as if I wasn't going to see any Ball-Kicking action today – which would make a change on this trip – but a pilgrimage to a shrine of football, well, that had to be worth doing.

First I needed to take a thirty-minute train journey on the Kintetsu line to a station called Sakurai, a pleasingly evocative blend of the words 'soccer' and 'samurai', it seemed to me, so already the pilgrimage was going well.

Another heartening feature of the journey was that the train was taking me away from the well-trodden tourist routes and out into the heart of the Japanese countryside. At Sakurai station I found myself, for the first time, in a place where there were no signs in English at all, which was rather refreshing, and I looked forward to living by my wits for a while.

When I tried to make head or tail of the bus timetable, though, the lack of any English stopped being refreshing and started to be a bit of a nuisance, and I realised how much I had been spoiled up to this point. I decided to take a *takeshi*, and as the driver took me higher and higher into the thickly wooded mountains, and I watched the meter ticking over furiously, I consoled myself with the thought that this journey would have taken hours on the bus, even if I could have worked out which one to get.

We pulled up a steep track and then stopped.

'Tanzan Jinjiya,' the driver said, his first words for about half an hour. He must have been absolutely bursting to tell me what was wrong with the government or what famous people he'd had in the back of his cab, but that's the language barrier for you. Sometimes it works in your favour.

Above the lush canopy of green I could see a striking black pagoda poking up into the sky, thirteen storeys high. The steep path led me up the side of the hill and round the back to the shrine itself, a low building with an extravagantly curving roof supported by narrow red-and-gold pillars. Ornate black incense burners hung on chains from the ceiling, and beautifully carved lanterns, and the whole place, nestling in the forest halfway up a mountain, was really quiet and peaceful. After the tourist crush and gift frenzy at the other shrines I had visited, this finally felt like the real deal. I was alone apart from one young priest, who was just finishing a small individual ceremony of some kind, and as he came out he bowed and indicated that I could go in if I liked, so I kicked off my shoes and climbed the steps.

The cushioned tatami matting gave pleasantly under my feet as I walked around the small, low shrine, the only noise the breeze in the trees and the tinkling of a wind chime. This place enshrines a seventh-century aristocrat called Fujiwara no Kamatari, who joined forces with the soon-to-be Emperor Tenchi to plot the overthrow of the ruler Soga no Iruka, and his sons commemorated his great deeds here by establishing this mountain shrine in 701.

An intricately detailed mural around the walls tells the story of this civil war, and our seventh-century hero is portrayed visiting a great deal of graphic violence upon his enemies, repulsing attacks on the village below and sending arms, legs, heads, and guts flying with his swishing curved samurai blade.

So far, so atmospheric. Then, under a glass display case, I spotted an ancient scroll, depicting what seemed to be a ball lodged in a branch of a tree. Further along there was a photograph of the Ball-Kicking Festival, and an example of the sort of ball that is used. It was about half the size of a modern football, and made from pale deerskin stuffed with sawdust. Also, rather incongruously in this venerable place, there were a couple of flags on show, one from the Japan Football Federation, and another from the Confederación Sudamericana de Fútbol, giving this corner of the shrine the feel of a clubhouse.

The ball-kicking game is called *kemari*. It is played by eight sumptuously robed participants on a three-metre-square playing field, the *kakari*, which has a cherry tree, a maple tree, a willow tree and a pine tree as its cornerposts. After a ceremony to purify the arena, the ball is presented lodged in a branch – as depicted in the scroll – and blessed.

The players stand in a circle, and then try to keep the ball off the ground for as long as possible using only their right feet. Using the left has traditionally always been considered impolite, and left-handedness is trained out of Japanese children to this day. And in case the players feel like heading, they have to wear big black hats tied to their heads with rope. The flowing and brilliantly coloured robes they wear can't be much of a help in this glorified game of keepy-uppie, and I dread to think of the opprobrium that would have been heaped upon the new boy who got his left foot caught in his long right sleeve and took himself out of the play.

Kemari was established here to commemorate 'a historical incident', is all the clue we are given, but looking at the bloodthirsty cartoons around the walls it's difficult to avoid the impression that the incident, whatever it was, probably involved a decapitation. It would originally have been played by members of the imperial court, powdered, scented, highly cultured sophisticates taking a short break from the haiku-composing or the moon-gazing which otherwise filled their days. And they were good, too. One emperor was so delighted when he and his lads kept the ball aloft for over 1,000 kicks that he retired the ball and ennobled it.

Back outside the shrine again, you could buy little wooden prayer tokens – like bookmarks – on which you write your request for the gods to consider. I bought one, scribbled on it 'Oldham to win Nationwide Div 2 please', and added it to the little pile. There was a sweet and odd little note stuck on the wall just above saying in Japanese and English that the gods would not be considering any new prayer requests until at least next Friday. They must have quite a lot on, what with the World Cup and everything.

It seemed appropriate to ask for a football favour in this place, and just now I was seriously wishing I'd come here before the Brazil game. Judging by the flag inside, maybe some Brazilian fan was here only last week . . .

I strolled down the hill by a different path, which took me down past the dark pagoda and round to the top of a wide stone staircase. Down below was a square open space, with a flat gravelled floor. Two matching wooden temples with verandahs on the front stood facing each other to the right and left, while the fourth side was open and afforded a view across the wooded valley. In each corner there was a tree – a cherry, a maple, a willow and a pine.

In a flash I realised what this place was – it was nothing more nor less than an ancient football ground. I was on the terrace at the home end, the grandstands were to either side, and the open end with the most rudimentary facilities was for the visitors, of course. And the ornamental lanterns strung along the roofs' edge? Well, floodlights, of course.

I have been to lots of football grounds in my time. There used to be – maybe there still is – an organisation called 'The 92 Club', which you could join if you had seen a match at all of the grounds in the English Football League. This was in the days before clubs embarked on the recent rash of new ground building, and before automatic promotion from the Conference, so the 92 was a much more constant sort of proposition than it is nowadays. As things stand I am coming up on the century, and there are still eight clubs I haven't visited at all, while some – Brighton, Stoke, Wigan, Reading, Millwall, Northampton – I have done twice.

Here in Japan I have already attended fixtures at six of the newest venues in world football, and now here I was, standing on the site of a football game that dated back to 701. Older than England v Scotland, older than that game between the two Derbyshire villages where hundreds of people kick the shit out of each other all day and the score is always o–o, older than cricket, than the plague, than the Magna Carta, than William the Conqueror, than Alfred the Great. Older even than Notts County.

And unless you can provide me with documentary evidence that the Romans used to play keepy-uppie with the heads of decapitated Christians at the Colisseum, I think it's fair to claim that Tanzan Jinjiya is the oldest football ground in the world. As befits a non-league facility, I can reveal that it has a famous sloping pitch, and like the newest purpose-built stadia in this country, all its exits lead out to one unavoidable bottle-neck down by the car park, so the Japanese have, it seems, learned precious little about stadium access in the last 1,300 years.

23
Arigato and Sayonara

'Sex could never be as rewarding as winning the World
Cup. It's not that sex isn't great, just that the World Cup
is only every four years.'
– Ronaldo

I was back in Tokyo by the time the semi-finals came round,
and made my way to Roppongi to watch the first of them,
between Germany and South Korea. There is a large South
Korean population in this part of Tokyo, and I was hoping to
find some of the exuberant red-shirted support that I've seen
so much of in pictures from Seoul. The Japanese fans, too, had
been encouraged to throw their support behind South Korea
now, in the interests of Asian soccer. This suggestion wilfully
ignored centuries of intractable enmity, however, not only on
the football field but also on the battle variety.

After a bit of searching the back alleys – and rejecting
the chance to spend the evening in a German bar munching
knackwurst – I came across the Tokyo Sports Bar. It was
a tenner or more to get in, but you got one free drink
– which can easily be worth a tenner in this country –
and a little stamp on the back of your hand as if it were
a sixth-form disco. Plenty of tellies of various sizes were
spread around the big open bar, but already it was standing room only. That was normal, though, in Japan, where
every decent seat would have been carefully reserved back in
February. The walls were decorated with scarves and flags
of football clubs from around the world – Juventus, West

Ham, Celtic, Kaiserslautern, Ajax, Liverpool, and many many more.

I stood at the bar with my free pint, and got chatting with the bloke next to me. Alexander, his name was, a lawyer from Glasgow who recently reached the age of thirty and decided to jack in his career and set off on his travels around the world.

'Well, I must say I envy you, Alexander,' I said.

'What, you mean you'd like to set off round the world too?'

'No, I mean I wish I'd recently reached thirty . . .'

He was paying his way by selling the pairs of sunglasses which were hanging round his neck, out of his pockets, and spilling out of the top of his rucksack, all with the lenses painted in the designs of flags of the participating countries – these were amongst the 'must-buy' accessories at this World Cup despite the fact that sunglasses, like tattoos, are firmly associated in the Japanese psyche with the *yakuza*.

Alexander reckoned he'd shifted about four thousand during the World Cup. His stock of 500 England specs went very quickly, apparently, mostly to locals, and so did his load of Irelands. The big miscalculation he made was to order three thousand Japans. For one thing, the Japanese have not been buying, preferring to get behind foreign teams, and for another the red spot on the white background made them look like a horror costume accessory, like lurgy eyes. Alexander was a resourceful chap, though, and he worked out that with a few strokes of a permanent marker he could transform his surplus Japan stock into South Koreas, which were not quite so off-puttingly zombie-like.

The bar filled up to bursting point, but there were no red South Korean shirts on show. The mood in the room was very pro-German indeed, not at all what I was expecting, especially with a perfectly good German bar just up the road that they could go to, and as the teams appeared on the screens a full, room-filling chant began, of:

Kahn-ee! Kahn-ee! Kahn-ee!

It said something for the nondescript character of the German team that the player who most captured the imagination was the big ugly keeper, and he didn't let his supporters down in this match. Early on he blocked a cross shot from Lee that looked destined for the bottom corner, then he scooped up a bouncing shot from Song Chung Gug making it look more difficult than it was. Even when he seemed to lose the flight of a cross and flapped it behind for a corner the room was still with him.

Kahn-ee! Kahn-ee! Kahn-ee!

It looked very much as though the only people in the entire bar supporting South Korea were myself and Alexander, who thought he would be able to shift his entire stock of doctored Japan specs if the co-hosts could make it to Yokohama on Sunday.

The Germans were composed and tough while the South Koreans buzzed around them like flies. In the second half Lee Chun Soo, South Korea's most lively player, ran at the German defence, twisting past Torsten Frings and a comically useless challenge by Ramelow before being cynically chopped down from behind by Michael Ballack, who was booked and would thus miss the final, and also the chance to be a runner-up in a fourth tournament this season after the German League, the German Cup and the Champions League.

It was beginning to look like a definite 0–0. Then Schneider sent Neuville scooting away down the right from the halfway line. His low ball into the box looked easy to clear but the South Korean defenders seemed to leave it to one another, and it reached Bierhoff, who suddenly stepped aside to allow the on-rushing Ballack to shoot at full tilt. His right-footed effort was blocked by Lee Woon Jae, but the rebound fell back to him and he stuck it in with his left. 1–0 to Germany, the scoreline by which they have won their last two games, and it was time to shut up the Geschäft.

The South Korean adventure was at an end, to tumultuous applause at the stadium, and exuberant cheering in the Tokyo Sports Bar in Roppongi. They just ran out of steam in the end, despite seeming to have more steam than anyone else in the tournament.

And it was Groundhog Day again – an ordinary German side had made the most of a soft draw which fell apart in front of them and they were in the final, while better-fancied and more attractive sides were watching at home with their under-employed feet up.

Alexander shrugged, and put all his unsold home-made South Korea sunglasses back in his rucksack.

'I suppose I'll have to think of something else,' he said, resignedly.

The next day I went to Saitama to see Brazil play Turkey, courtesy of one of the tickets Nick wangled in payment for the job he did for one of the Official Partners of the World Cup©. I was a little worried about getting a train back into Tokyo if the match overran, but my mind was put at rest by an illuminated sign alongside the walkway to the stadium which was flash-displaying the message:

If the match extend to an extra inning, it will be left on the train to Ichigaya at 01.24.

Phew, that was all right then.

I was high up, level with the goal line at Marcos's end for the first half. The two seats to my right were empty until just after kick-off, when a dark-suited, middle-aged salaryman arrived with an excessively made-up and very giggly young woman.

She had been carefully primed for this trip, because as soon as Turkey's little number 11 got the ball she leapt to her feet, pointing and screaming: 'Hasan Sas! Hasan Sas!'

I find it hard to believe that young women react this way

spontaneously to the tiny Galatasaray forward, unless it's at a police line-up. Although he did have a good World Cup, it's true.

Next to me, the salaryman took out a tiny portable television, pulled up a little aerial, and watched the game on there, chuckling away to himself at his own off-the-wall take on things.

Brazil took a long time to get going and Turkey made all the early running. They looked bright, lively and inventive, and Yildiray Basturk and Hasan Sas were buzzing around the midfield, probing, playing little one-twos. If only they'd had a decent cutting edge Brazil could have been in trouble, but Hakan Sukur again looked cumbersome and off his game.

Alpay had one good chance after about twenty minutes, a glancing header that Marcos dived to shovel clear, and this seemed to spur Brazil into life. Suddenly we had the best game of the tournament on our hands.

Rivaldo and Ronaldo began to combine, and Rustu Recber, sporting his distinctive warpaint on his cheeks – an American invention called Eye Black, apparently, which reduces glare from floodlights – made some brilliant saves from both of them and also Cafu and Edilson. The way Brazil surged forward left plenty of room for Turkey to counter-attack, and it was amazing that the game reached half time goalless.

As the teams went off down the tunnel Ronaldo seemed to be involved in a scrap with about half the Turkish team. I tried to squint and see a replay on my neighbour's tiny telly, but no luck. Perhaps someone had taken the piss out of his new hairdo, which makes him look as though he has half a slice of wholemeal bread stuck on his forehead.

Down in front there were three Mexicans, in the full clobber, the ponchos, the sombreros, the cowboy boots, and the green Mexico replikit shirts. They didn't seem bothered by the match, and after about twenty minutes or so they became bored. One of them stood up and shouted: '*Una! Dos! Tres!*'

and the three of them tried to start a Mexican Wave, all by themselves.

A handful of Japanese fans who didn't know any better joined in, but all around there was a murmuring of discontent.

'*Una! Dos! Tres!*'

Finally someone snapped and shouted: 'Sit down, you fucking silly bastards. There's a World Cup semi-final on down there, you know.' I say 'someone' . . .

Four minutes into the second half Ergun Penbe played the ball down the left to Hasan Sas, who twisted outside two Brazilian defenders and pinged a cross towards and over Hakan Sukur. Roberto Carlos confidently chested the ball back to Marcos, and as the recriminations started across the Turkish front line Gilberto Silva embarked on a leggy breakaway down the Brazilian left wing, riding one tackle, and playing Ronaldo in about thirty yards out. As usual in this match he was faced by three defenders, but he turned past one, and dragged them all with him into the area. He seemed to be looking for a square ball, but then he suddenly took them all by surprise, jabbing out his right foot and toe-ending a snap shot past Rustu, who got a hand on it but couldn't stop it bobbling in for the opening goal.

Turkey finally – *finally* – played their ace, bringing on Ilhan Mansiz. This time, though, it was Emre who made way, and Hakan Sukur got to finish the match. The young playboy striker put the wind up Brazil straightaway. Within a minute of coming on he'd skinned Roberto Carlos, who crunched him from behind for his presumption. Then he tried a cross-cum-shot from the left wing which was drifting under the bar until Marcos fingertipped it away.

The Mexicans started up again.

'*Una! Dos! Tres!*'

This time the salaryman and his child girlfriend stood and

joined in, holding the little telly above their heads as they shouted: 'Wooooh!'

I was in a fucking madhouse. I made horse blinkers with my hands and tried to concentrate on the play.

Turkey's best chance of getting back into the game fell to Hakan Sukur eight minutes from time. A Hasan Sas free kick drifted over everyone and Sukur, on the corner of the six-yard box, let it drop over his shoulder, before swivelling, David Platt-style, to hook the ball goalwards. Marcos was equal to it, though.

Full time, and yet another 1–0 scoreline, the sixth in the fourteen knock-out games. Brazil went through to their seventh final, equalling the new record which Germany established yesterday. Amazingly the two giants have never before met in a World Cup game.

As I left the stadium, two things of note happened. The salaryman and his girl stayed where they were and watched a cookery programme, and I managed to surreptitiously kick a Mexican shin.

For the last week I was in Tokyo I stayed in a hotel which hasn't featured in any Bond films, as far as I know. As usual, the bathroom fittings were irritatingly small. Everywhere I went the shower head was aimed squarely at my sternum, and the baths were the size of those walk-in baths you see advertised during *Countdown*.

Here, though, there was a new development, an added extra, to the space age push-button toilet. It had a little heater in the seat to keep it warm, with a wire leading out from under, and there are a number of things that I didn't like about this. One: it gave you that authentic 'I'm using this toilet within seconds of somebody else finishing a great long dump' feeling. Two: I was deeply concerned about the dangers of electrocution. I am sure thousands of Japanese are perishing every year in mid-dump electrical accidents, all found face down on the lino like Elvis, and it's all being hushed up by the manufacturers. Three: there was a notice on the toilet lid warning of the dangers of receiving a 'low temperature burn' if you sat on the throne too long, so reading the paper was right out.

On the other hand, though, it kept my coffee warm while I was sitting (bolt upright) in the bath.

Also staying in our hotel, we discovered, was Diego Maradona, who had finally been allowed into the country for the tail end of the tournament despite his many drug convictions. It turned out he was in the next room to Nick, who admitted he'd pushed a glass up against the wall to try to hear whether or not the butterball Argentine superstar was watching the pixillated porn channels.

'I thought the Hand of God might be in action,' Nick said.

Turkey won the third place play-off, beating South Korea 3–2. Whenever Becks or Rio said in an interview, as they did more or less every day, that 'the spirit in the England camp was magnificent', you couldn't help thinking that that was a good thing. But was it? Turkey finished third, and their squad could hardly have been more bitterly divided.

The captain, Hakan Sukur, is a devout Muslim, and he was the leader of a group of thirteen out of the twenty-three players who insisted on the whole team praying together, invited an imam to their base at Ulsan to supervise their religious well-being, and succeeded in overturning a Turkish FA decision to allow wives and girlfriends to stay at the team base. This inflexible approach irritated the hell out of the likes of Yildiray Basturk, who plays his football in Germany, and the young playboy pretender to Sukur's striking role, Ilhan Mansiz.

The manager, Senol Gunes, bowed to Sukur's influence over the Muslim faction, and so the veteran started every game even though he was clearly out of touch. He and Mansiz only started one game together, this last play-off, and they showed what might have been by combining to create a goal, Sukur's first of the tournament, after only 10.8 seconds. Mansiz went on to notch a couple more, with Sukur involved in the build-up both times, and pulled off another cocky Ardiles flick for good measure.

South Korea's goals, an early equaliser from Lee Eul Young and a last-minute consolation from Song Chung Gug, were not quite enough to end their remarkable run on a high note. Hiddink's men were, I thought, just about the most entertaining side of the lot, just buzzing from start to finish every match in a high-energy style which paid big dividends for them.

I watched the game in yet another sports bar with Mickey Watanabe, and asked him what he'd thought of the World Cup. Had it been a good one?

'I am very happy because my country win games, first time,' he said. 'But also I am disappointed. This World Cup my big chance. Big chance to see great players, best players in the world. But France, Argentina, Italy, Portugal, all of them go home too quick, and here we are watching South Korea play Turkey.' And he shrugged eloquently.

YOKOHAMA. 30 JUNE

Nick had tickets for the final but we needed an extra one for Cube, who managed to wangle a business trip to Tokyo that weekend. It was a tough assignment, picking up a World Cup final ticket just like that, especially now Ged was back in the UK, but Nick managed it. Strolling along the corridor in the hotel he came across a young mum at the end of her tether with a small child, and volunteered to play with him for a while to give her a break. By sheer coincidence it turned out she, too, worked for Byrom, and she gratefully fixed it for Nick to buy final tickets at face value. He got a bit carried away at this point, and decided to get us better tickets even though we already had some, which meant that we set off for Yokohama with his original tickets burning a hole in his wallet, hoping to sell them on the street.

There were a number of stories in the papers during the tournament about European ticket touts being arrested trying to sell tickets to undercover policemen, being made an example of, and landing sentences measured out in hard labour, so we were very wary and took a long time spying out the lie of the land.

The streets outside Shin Yokohama station were heaving – plenty more yellow shirts than white, which, in this clash of footballing philosophies, was how it should be. Incredibly, many of the white shirts weren't even German, but were the England ones with 'BECKHAM' across the shoulders, selling well even here at a World Cup final between two other teams a week after the boy has gone home.

We hung about near the shirt sellers for a while, muttering 'Tickets . . . who wants tickets . . . ?' out of the corners of our mouths, but no one would come near the price we needed to just break even. One or two people passed us holding 'I Need Ticket' signs, but they all seemed to be banking on the Japanese tradition of gift-giving rather than actually being prepared to pay any money.

Still, we had some of the most sought-after tickets in the history of sport – how naff did that make us if we couldn't shift them? Two superpowers of the world's most popular sport, meeting in its premier competition for the first time in itsseventy-two-yearhistory.Imean,we'dbetheworsttickettoutsin history.

An hour to kick-off. The Cube had had no joy at all, which was making him a little fed up, especially seeing as he is a professional salesman. We compared notes briefly, and it turned out that, owing to a slight currency miscalculation, he'd been asking people for the equivalent of ten thousand quid.

I wandered back up to the forecourt of the main Shinkansen

station, where there was a large open square, with shops and restaurants all around, and . . . aha! This was where the ticket action was. Dozens of people sat on the low walls around the flower beds holding up signs written on big pieces of card – 'I Need Tickets!', '2 Tickets Please!', 'I Need Category 3 Ticket'. My favourite was a young lad whose sign read: 'Please yield me, supposing your ticket is free.'

He scored so many points here, for me. His politeness, his ambitious use of the conditional tense, his punctuation, his decision to go with a whole sentence rather than the simple and brutal 'I Need . . .' form favoured by his competitors. I almost gave him a ticket on the spot.

Nick joined me and we strolled around, stopping to speak to some of the hopeful punters. No one would go to the price we needed, but one or two were thinking about it, and Nick was confident that it was going to happen.

A big American in a peach T-shirt and Bermuda shorts went up to one of the lads with a cardboard sign, and they had a brief conversation, after which the American stomped away, his eyes scanning the crowd. I was new at this, but I reckoned he was buying, so I sidled after him and muttered out of the side of my mouth: 'Looking for tickets, mate?'

He turned and looked at me, the gum zipping from side to side between his huge and orthodontically perfect American teeth.

'Whatcha gat, buddy?' he brayed, loud enough for the whole block to hear.

'Category 2s,' I murmured, trying to get him to keep his voice down.

'Nat interested.'

I was relieved, in fact, as embarking on an actual negotiation with this foghorn could have brought the whole Yokohama police department down on me. I turned to look for other possibilities, but straightaway he was back at me.

'Hey! How much?' he yelled.

'Hundred twenty thousand yen.'

'Jeeesus H. Christ!'

Just shut up will you, for crying out loud . . . I had a sudden vision of the big rock that I would be spending the next six months trying to break with a little toffee hammer. Nick, a little way off, was trying to make himself as inconspicuous as possible until this voice storm passed.

'I need five together, you got five together?'

'Ssssh . . . I've got three.'

'Well, listen, sonny . . .' I *was* listening, and so was everyone else within a half-kilometre radius. 'You come and see me when your price comes down, OK, boy? Hundred twenty thousand yen . . . Holy shit!'

'That's what they cost, mate,' I said, sidling away and planning to hide somewhere for at least a quarter of an hour.

'Like hell! You'll come down.'

'I won't.'

'Sure you will.'

'No, I won't.' Even though I'd nearly escaped from this nightmare, I couldn't bear to let him have the last word.

'You'll be back!' he sneered from across the square. 'Believe me, *I* know. You'll be back . . . !'

'I fucking won't . . .' I muttered to myself, trotting round the corner and out of sight. I passed two policemen who gave me a curious look, and I decided to put my new career on hold for a while.

Half an hour to go, and we were fifteen minutes' walk from the stadium. The crowds had thinned down to the forlorn throng who had not had anyone yield them, supposing their tickets were free, and people who weren't even planning to go to the match. And the sparser the crowd, of course, the easier it was for the police to see what we were up to. The tension cranked up a notch. Nick and I conferred, and I said perhaps we should bring our asking price down, but Nick was still confident.

'I think it's going to happen,' he said. 'I feel it.'

We grabbed a burger, time ticking by, and it was beginning to look as if we could have five tickets for the World Cup final between two of us and still miss the damn game.

Then, all of a sudden, it began. Out of nowhere a Japanese guy came up and asked if we were selling. We tried to disguise our eagerness, and play it casual, but he still got bits of burger spat onto his shirt front. Twenty minutes to kick-off, and we were now the only ticket game in town. Others saw us sell our first – thankfully no one in a blue uniform – and sidled up to us out of the shadows. We shifted the other two tickets in a couple of minutes, and – pausing only to go 'Woohoo!' like Homer J. Simpson – set off at a run down the road to the World Cup final. We'd played chicken with the world, and won.

We reached the first ticket barriers spread across the broad walkway, still elated.

Having seen the world's worst ticket tout at Shizuoka we now saw the world's feeblest gatecrasher. He came galloping towards us, away from the game, wringing his hands, wailing: 'Fuck! They're checking tickets! They're checking tickets . . . !'

Just before we went through, I saw a familiar peach-coloured T-shirt and heard a foghorn-leghorn voice. It was the American guy from earlier on.

'Five tickets together!' he was still barking. 'I need five tickets together!' He caught sight of me and came lolloping over to grab my arm.

'Hey, buddy! Good to see ya! You still got three Category 2s? I'll take 'em . . .'

'No, mate, sold 'em, sorry . . .' I grinned.

'For hundred twenty thousand yen? Get outa here.'

'That's right,' I said. 'I told you that was what they were going for.'

'Shit!' he shouted at top volume – actually I think his voice was permanently stuck on eleven. 'Shit! Shit!! SHIT!!!'

I couldn't have been more pleased with this development.

Inside, the stadium was swathed in yellow, yellow, yellow as far as the eye could see. Once a lengthy line-up of Emperors, Prime Ministers, Presidents and Step Ladders had been introduced to the two teams, the anthems got under way, the Germans' a sombre classic, the Brazilians' a tiddly-pom nonsense.

Brazil had the same side as for the semi-final, except that Ronaldinho was back for Edilson after his suspension. They lined up 3–4–2–1, with Marcos in goal, Lucio, Roque Junior and Edmilson as the back trio, Cafu and Roberto Carlos as attacking wing backs flanking Gilberto Silva and Kleberson, and then Ronaldinho and Rivaldo behind the spearhead, Ronaldo.

Germany had to reshuffle since the impressive Ballack was suspended, and in the opening few minutes we saw what their master plan looked like. Kahn in goal, three at the back – Linke, Metzelder and Ramelow – with Frings and Bode as wing backs. The rangy Hamann and his little thug sidekick Jeremies were sitting in front of the defence, and Klose and Neuville were the strikers, leaving the burden of creating the play to fall onto the shoulders of Schneider. The Bayer Leverkusen midfielder had been playing wide on the right while Ballack was in the team, but tonight he seemed to have a free role behind the strikers.

The other aspect of Voller's tactics became apparent equally quickly – the Germans planned to get as many set-pieces as they could around the box, and with Neuville and Klose in their side Collina would have to be on top of his game. Worryingly for Brazil, Neuville ran into Roque Junior on the halfway line after only five minutes and went flying, and the Italian was reaching for the first yellow card of the final.

The Germans lumbered up for the free kick – Bode, Hamann, Metzelder, Klose, Ramelow . . . they were an *enormous* team. The Brazilians were going frantic, trying to pick them up, but the free kick cleverly played on their concern as it was rolled square for Neuville to have a pop from twenty yards – the last thing they were expecting. It hit Metzelder on the heel and was cleared, as it happens, but the Germans had clearly turned up with some definite plans in mind, while Brazil were hoping to be allowed to play their natural game.

The first real chances fell to Germany – Schneider twice finding Klose in the area but first Edmilson then Lucio were able to hack the ball off the big striker's toes. Germany were well on top to start with, and Hamann in particular was keeping the Three Rs nice and quiet, and sending them deeper and deeper in search of a way into the game. On eighteen minutes, though, I suddenly noticed Ronaldinho for the first time. He picked up the ball twenty-five yards out, strode forward, and suddenly stabbed the ball into the heart of the German penalty area. Ronaldo sprung the offside trap and had only Kahn to beat, but his attempt to pass the ball into the goal with the outside of his left boot skewed wide.

We were seeing a lot more of Frings and Bode attacking down the flanks than we were of Cafu and Roberto Carlos, and Brazil could hardly get out of their own half. Suddenly, though, Ronaldinho, the little magician, again sprung the German back line to let Ronaldo in one-on-one with Kahn, but he miscontrolled off his knee, tried to toe-poke it, and the big German stopper smothered the chance, a little luckily, truth to tell.

The game settled into a rather dour midfield battle, with both teams cancelling each other out. Rivaldo – oh look, he *was* playing after all – slid in to rob Schneider, whose foot landed in the Brazilian's chest as he tried to elude the challenge. Rivaldo, unsurprisingly, saw this as a good enough reason to roll about holding his face for a minute or two. Once he got to his feet he almost contrived a neat one-two with Ronaldo but Hamann read it, stepped in, blocked it, came away with the ball.

Five minutes to the break and Brazil sparked into life, starting to find the odd chink in the German armour. Kleberson, suddenly haring in on goal, dragged his shot wide. Then Ronaldinho wriggled forward on the left. Hamann barred his way, and the little forward slipped the ball inside to Kleberson, and this time his shot slapped back off the crossbar with Kahn nowhere.

And then in injury time Roberto Carlos banged a low hard shot in from wide and deep on the left, and it cannoned into the shins of Ronaldo by the penalty spot. It bobbled back off Metzelder to the Brazilian, who swivelled and fired in a powerful left-footed effort, which Kahn stopped with his legs.

Half time. Kahn slung his towel over his shoulder and strutted off for his tea. Germany had had the bulk of the possession and a few half chances, with Hamann and Schneider outstanding in the midfield. Nonetheless, Brazil had four more-than-decent sights of goal.

Early in the second half Germany won a corner on their left. Neuville swung it in, and Brazil anxiously watched all the huge Germans who flooded their area. They left little Jeremies all unmarked, and his diving header thumped into Edmilson's shin, otherwise it would have been a goal, with Marcos leaping out of the way for some reason.

Then Schneider won a free kick with a gangling sprawl under the lightest of challenges. Judging by the pattern of the mowing it was thirty-six yards out. Schneider stood over it, but it was Neuville who hit it after a great big long run-up. It was a cracker, swerving round the three-man wall, and Marcos somehow managed to tip it onto the post. Great shot, great save.

Brazil had a corner. Gilberto Silva suddenly popped up behind Rivaldo to power the ball down towards the goal line. Kahn half saved, and then shovelled the loose ball away from Gilberto, who seemed to step accidentally on the keeper's hand.

Bode charged down the left, and squared to the on-rushing Hamann. His first-time shot fizzed just over the bar from twenty-odd yards out. While the play was up the other end Kahn took his right glove off and inspected his hand.

I was just writing in my notes: 'Hamann – man of the match?' when Ramelow tidied up a loose ball and gave it to the Liverpool man thirty yards out from Kahn's goal. It got stuck under his feet, though, and Ronaldo picked his pocket, quickly laying a short ball to Rivaldo, who of course had a shot. His left footer should have been easy for Kahn, but he spilled it off his big paddles and his huge chin into the path of Ronaldo, who'd carried on his run in the forlorn hope of ever getting a return pass off Rivaldo. His blind optimism paid off, and he sidefooted the ball in past the despairing Kahn. Sixty-seven minutes gone: 1–0 to Brazil.

Now the drums were going, and the yellow-shirted hordes were bobbing up and down all around the stadium. Germany forced a couple of corners, but they needed to change things if they were to break through. Oliver Bierhoff replaced Klose, and Gerald Asamoah came on for Jeremies, which gave them a more attacking formation. Voller's men continued to have a lot of the ball, but this Brazilian side can defend a lead, as we knew only too well from Shizuoka.

They can extend one, too, as they proved with eleven minutes to go. Kleberson attacked down the right, cut inside, and laid the ball across to Rivaldo. He stepped over it, which took Linke out of the game, and left Ronaldo with time to take a touch and pass it into the bottom corner out of Kahn's reach. It was a neat move, a clinical finish that actually shaved the inside of the post on its way in. 2–0 for Brazil and the Golden Boot for eight-goal Ronaldo.

Germany took a minute or two to recover from that blow, but suddenly Bierhoff had a sight of the target. He swivelled and shot, but Marcos dived to save brilliantly to his left. Before this game Oliver Kahn was awarded the Lev Yashin prize as the best keeper in this World Cup – I don't even think he was the best keeper in this match.

Ronaldo left before the end to a tremendous ovation, and Geoff Hurst would be breathing a sigh of relief somewhere, his unique hat-trick record intact. Ziege had a go in injury time, but the Germans had shot their bolt, and when Collina finally blew for full time Ronaldo came running back on draped in a Brazil flag.

The story of this World Cup final was his. Four years ago he was a walking shadow, his mystery illness diminishing him and demoralising his team as France walked away with the trophy. Now, incredibly, he was back at the summit of the world game despite hardly having played any football in the intervening time because of his terrible knee injuries. He'd scored more goals in this tournament than anyone else, and more than anyone in any World Cup since Gerd Muller in 1970. So what if he looked as if he'd stuck part of his breakfast on his head for safe-keeping – he was the best footballer in the world.

I stayed to watch the celebrations. Brazil's players leapt over the hoardings and rushed over to the crowd, but they were swamped by photographers and press who weren't allowed on the pitch, so many quickly hopped back onto the grass again. One or two of them were defacing their yellow shirts with messages in black felt pen, and others removed them to reveal T-shirts with I Heart Jesus slogans.

Kahn was inconsolable. His gloves hit the back of the net, and so did his water bottle, and he sat with his back to the post, brooding on his misfortune. Collina walked over to have a word, but he's not Kahn's favourite referee by a long chalk, having also presided over England's 5–1 win in Munich and Manchester United's European Cup triumph in 1999.

A podium was erected in the middle of the pitch, and it was groaning under the weight of world soccer's top dignitaries. Beckenbauer and Pele, football's two biggest rent-a-gobs, were up there applauding. Franz leaned over to say something to Pele with a big smirk on his face, but Pele didn't laugh.

'So, Pele,' it looked very much like. 'I hear you've been having trouble with the old hydraulics. Not me – I knocked up the club secretary at the Christmas party, did you hear? Plenty of lead in my *Bleistift*, old mate . . .'

The Germans slouched up, drenched in misery, to collect their silver medals. The entire Brazilian party – the players, the staff, the medics, the trainers, the coach, the coach driver for all I know – knelt holding hands in a big circle, waiting their turn.

Then, one by one, the new world champions went up to get their medals, their flowers, and their hug from Pele. Cafu, their mighty captain, brought up the rear. He had just played his last international, and become the only man to play in three World Cup finals. Sepp Blatter and Pele had hold of the cup, and seemed to be engaged in an informal tug-o'-war to determine which of them was the most important man in football. The stand that the cup was resting on was empty, and Cafu tested it to see if it would hold his weight, before springing to the top of it, and lifting the World Cup over his head.

Fireworks went off all around the podium, and hundreds, thousands, millions of brightly coloured origami cranes tumbled down from the roof in a magical shower that must have taken weeks of preparation. They lodged in our hair, our pockets, and quickly piled up ankle deep on the walkways, and still they came down.

The barriers outside were lined with stadium staff, all smiling and bowing as people left, and saying: 'Thank you for coming to Japan!', and it suddenly hit me – it was all over, all finished, the World Cup was done, it was history.

I looked forward to getting back, and was already picturing my little boys' faces meeting me at the airport. Football might not be coming home, but I was.

24
Afterthoughts

'. . . the players got carried away, over-acting, over-
running, running all over the place, from right to left,
diagonals, I don't know where. It was like . . . they were
like chickens . . .'
– Guus Hiddink, coach of South Korea

So that was the 2002 World Cup. Undeniably exciting and
refreshingly unpredictable it was, as big gun after big gun
went tumbling out in the early stages. Anyone who was
seeded to get in Germany's way at all seemed especially
vulnerable. This did mean, though – as my friend Mickey
lamented – that the tournament was almost entirely bereft
of big showpiece matches between the world's top teams.
South Korea had knocked them all out, that's why. There
was England against Brazil, of course – a big game whatever
you think of England's standing in the world game – and a
first-ever clash between Brazil and Germany in the final, but
otherwise the climactic knock-out stages were littered with
bog-ordinary games you would expect to see making up the
numbers in the group stages.

How did this come about? Well, first of all the conditions
were harder than anyone had predicted. The pre-tournament
concerns about matches being drenched by the region's rainy
season never really materialised, but some of the European
teams who asked to play in mid-afternoon in the hotter
venues such as Oita and Daegu were visibly suffering after
ten or fifteen minutes. I'm thinking particularly of Denmark,

Belgium and Sweden here, and one of the most vivid images burned onto my mind's eye by the boiling hot sun was of all ten England outfield players scuttling over to the bench to rehydrate early in the Nigeria game in Osaka, when temperatures were in the mid-nineties. This levelled the playing field – metaphorically – and created an environment in which shocks were always on the cards.

The rainy season – and it was *really* rainy – got under way just twenty-four hours too late for England's purposes. I spent the day after the scorcher in Shizuoka dodging the lethal pointy umbrellas being wielded everywhere I went by shoppers mostly at least a foot shorter than me, and it was nothing short of a miracle that I returned home with my eyes ungouged.

Fear of the tournament being ruined by torrential downpours meant that FIFA started it as early as they dared, which created its own set of problems. European teams, and others, such as Argentina, who relied heavily on European-based players, found that stars who had given their all in a protracted club season – which finished a bare fortnight before the World Cup in some cases – had very little left in the tank. Fatigue took its toll, exaggerated by the conditions, and it was noticeable that England faded in the second half of all their matches – indeed, all of their goals came before half time. There was a feeling that top players simply play too much football, which leaves them prone to niggly injuries. The broken metatarsals of Beckham, Neville and Murphy were put down to the stresses of overwork on the players' frames, and a couple of weeks off before leaving for the Far East could have made a huge difference to the performances of players like Zidane and Figo, say, and made the tournament a little more representative of the perceived hierarchy of the world game. Funny though it was to see France and Argentina slink off early.

The conditions and fatigue combined to make the top European players vulnerable, then, and this weakness was compounded and skilfully taken advantage of by the high-energy approach of teams such as Japan, South Korea and the United States in particular. These teams all spent lengthy pre-tournament spells with their coaches – six whole months in South Korea's case – and used the time to develop a hyperactive pressing and tackling game which knocked arguably more sophisticated teams out of their stride. It is unlikely to be so hot and humid in Germany in 2006, and it will be interesting to see how these teams fare then, and also whether this supremely athletic style catches on elsewhere in the meantime. Sven-Goran Eriksson already places a high value on players who can run all day, such as Mills, Sinclair and Butt, and the day of the strolling midfield playmaker may have passed for ever.

Eriksson's tactical approach was defined, I believe, after a Damascus moment in Munich in September 2001. It was then that he thought he saw how to get the best out of the bunch of players he was dealing with. Aware of the English disease, which is an inability to hold the ball against high-class international opponents – and also Albania – he set his team up to allow the opposition to have the ball, to absorb pressure and hit the Germans on the break. Like the rest of us, he watched open-mouthed as the raking long passes of Gerrard, Beckham and Scholes tore gaping holes in the German back line for Owen and Heskey to race through, and that night the master plan was born.

Ever since, England have been a back-foot team. Sometimes it works – as against Argentina, and, for the first half at any rate, against Brazil. When England need to force the game, however, this approach suddenly seems over-cautious and inflexible.

It is entertaining to think that now we have finally got ourselves a foreign coach we have picked one who is so rigidly wedded to playing in a 4–4–2 formation, that most English of systems. Against Argentina the two lines of four provided an impressively impregnable barrier which the tournament favourites never looked like breaking down, but too often the four men at the back find themselves marking one or two opposition strikers, and we are constantly out-manned in the centre of the park, which is where games are won and lost.

My main quibble with a rigid adherence to 4–4–2 is that it doesn't get the best out of the players Eriksson has at his disposal. Too often Owen is isolated and easy to mark out of the game. Long high balls through to him are never going to be a good option, as he will always find himself up against taller defenders who are better at heading, and the long ball over the top only really troubled Denmark in this World Cup campaign – the other teams we played against just defended a few yards deeper to cope with it. Scholes is a fantastic midfielder, and his ability to provide support to the strikers and arrive unexpectedly in the box should be one of England's most potent weapons. Too often under Eriksson, though, he finds himself the holding player in front of the back four. Say what you like about Kevin Keegan's tactical nous, during his reign Scholes was always scoring goals. Under Sven he's become more Batty than Platty.

And then there's Beckham. All right, he wasn't a hundred per cent fit, or anything like it, but he was still capable of exerting considerable influence on England's performances. He spent far too much time far too deep, though, because England were constantly outnumbered in midfield, and he often found himself releasing Mills on the overlap and then having to stay back to cover for him. Now Mills is an estimable player who had a fine tournament, in my opinion, but he wasn't the player all the other teams were crapping themselves about playing against.

I think, under certain circumstances – especially when we are up against the stronger teams – that 4–4–2 is fine and dandy to start with, but against Sweden, particularly, and Brazil the match situation was crying out for a Plan B, and Sven didn't seem to have one. The teams that did best in this World Cup – the two finalists, for a start – played with three at the back and I think this would have suited England very well in Japan.

Imagine Ferdinand, Campbell and Keown (or Southgate) as the back three. Ashley Cole would become a left wing-back, solving at a stroke the left midfield problem which has dogged England for years, with Sinclair as his right-sided counterpart. Then Butt, Scholes and Beckham as the midfield three, with Scholes and Beckham taking it in turns to be the linkman – in 'the hole' – to the attackers, Owen and Heskey. Oh yeah, and I'd have had Seaman in goal, but only because I wouldn't have known, any more than Sven did, that he'd lost the springs in his heels. I think this is a system in which a team can switch from defence to attack smoothly, and what's more there's a role there for a Joe Cole, who doesn't seem to fit into a 4–4–2 at all.

But then what do I know? I've never even tried ski-jumping and I don't know a single weather girl.

Make no mistake about it, England could have won this World Cup with just a little more luck and a little more nerve. The draw was awful for us – to my way of thinking, England had five difficult games on their way to a quarter-final exit, while Germany had one, the final, which they lost. And Eriksson had Brazil reeling after forty-odd minutes, but after their two goals and the sending off he should have changed England's approach to take the initiative. Bringing on Dyer and trying to hit him over the top was the same game plan with different personnel. He should have let Joe Cole loose to run at the tiring Brazilians with the ball at his feet, but hey ho, it's gone now, and it didn't happen . . .

As for the players, I thought they all acquitted themselves well. Seaman's World Cup began and ended with long-range free kicks catching him out, but he should remember his barrel-chested rearguard action against Sweden. Mills was great, Ashley Cole came of age, and Ferdinand elevated himself to the top rank of defenders in the world. Campbell, for me, was the one disappointment. He seemed to have forgotten how to head the ball, and he seemed to be bailed out time and again by Ferdinand or Cole. Nonetheless when FIFA announced its Team of the Tournament Sol was there and Rio wasn't, which I can only put down to a simple case of mistaken identity.

I have the same nagging suspicion, I must admit, about Pele's selection of Nicky Butt as his player of the tournament. Well though Butt played – and he was a revelation – I can't help thinking that good old Pele saw Butt, saw Scholes, and thought to himself: 'The ginger lad's everywhere, isn't he?' Beckham was unlucky, first in not being quite fit and then in that England didn't apply enough attacking pressure to earn him his trademark free kicks around the opposition penalty area. Sinclair's contribution was mightily impressive, after taking the place of the unfortunate Hargreaves who had looked like making himself a permanent fixture in the first eleven before injuring himself running into a team mate.

Heskey was unfairly maligned up front. I thought his defensive work, particularly against Argentina, was top class, and it's not his fault that the team set-up isolated him and Owen too far from the midfield for them to be consistently threatening. Despite this, both strikers actually looked like scoring in every game, and Sheringham – always used as a sub – provided the single moment which will stay with me the longest, I think. His van Basten-like volley from Scholes's crossfield pass against Argentina would have been the goal of the tournament, no question.

This World Cup had many positive features. One – which I have idiosyncratically characterised in these pages as 'no more Buddha' following my conversation with young Daiju in Saitama – was the sense in which the differences between people from all parts of the world were put aside as everyone came together to celebrate a sporting festival. I have read about this sort of thing before, vaguely, at the Olympics maybe, but never thought to experience this kind of spirit at an international football tournament, having too often stumbled unintentionally across the ugly side of things. I put this down to the Japanese people, who welcomed everyone with equal enthusiasm, and although I never went to a game in South Korea I am sure that the welcome was just as warm there.

One of the most interesting sub-plots of the World Cup was the interest shown by North Koreans in the progress of their southern counterparts. Tapes were smuggled across the border and broadcast illegally in the North – typically, when Step Ladder and his FIFA officials heard about this, they didn't hug themselves with glee at the thought of football breaking down barriers between peoples, but tried to work out how to charge them for rights. Loudspeakers the length of the border, that for years have been used to play music across the 38th parallel to drown out the Communist propaganda being broadcast in the opposite direction, played radio commentary of South Korea's World Cup matches as if to try to involve as many North Koreans as possible in the adventure. And flags at these matches displayed the message 'AGAIN 1966', a reference to the glorious cup run of the North at that long-ago World Cup, where they too defeated Italy in one of the biggest shocks in football history.

Sadly, on the very day that South Korea's World Cup story ended, the spirit of 'no more Buddha' seemed to expire, and five South Korean sailors lost their lives in a naval battle with a Northern gunship.

In Japan, the people could hardly have got more into their half of the World Cup. Visiting supporters at every game were supplemented by thousands of locals, who not only cheered along but also invested en masse in the appropriate replica shirts. It was almost as if the country became caught up in a gigantic fancy-dress competition – 'Hey, my shirt's in the semi-final!' – and the feeling of belonging to first their own team and then whatever other team they adopted after that seemed to be a large part of the appeal for them.

And the Japanese were so helpful. Stories abounded of locals going miles out of their way to help visitors find their hotels or transport, and when I washed a load of clothes in the (tiny) bath of my hotel room in Kyoto only to find no way of hanging them up to dry it caused a veritable service frenzy amongst the staff. No fewer than nine people came to my room to help, some dismantled the shower rail, others redesigned a Corby trouser press to make a rudimentary clothes horse, while the hotel manager himself came to oversee the effort, bowing so often and so low that I half expected to see the weave of the carpet imprinted on his forehead.

I went to Japan hoping to rekindle my passion for football. I have to say that in this respect the trip was only a partial success. Certainly I found that I became utterly absorbed in the 2002 World Cup, and the highs – the final whistle in Sapporo, Michael Owen's goal in Shizuoka – were very high indeed, while the lows – Ronaldinho's floating leaf, in particular – exceedingly low.

Overall, though, the adrenalin rushes of the global footballfest left me casting a tired and jaundiced eye over the upcoming season. I found it virtually impossible to summon up any enthusiasm for the imminent Premiership campaign, and rather than rekindling my passion I feared I might have burned it out. The chances of an interesting race for the title anyway seemed to have diminished with the news that Rio Ferdinand was indeed moving to Old Trafford, and the bloated Champions' League was already stirring into life, getting on with the mean-spirited business of eliminating the champions of any non-telegenic countries.

Even the prospect of a new Oldham campaign was leaving me if not cold exactly then at least tepid. We'd a new untried manager in Iain Dowie, and some new players, but were not expected to make much of an impact. Again.

Perhaps I should go into hibernation for four years, awakening just in time for England's golden generation to achieve their destiny and bring forty years (by then) of hurt to an end.

Mind you, though, if the gods of football get the message I left for them at Tanzan Jinjiya, the beautiful shrine to football in the wooded mountains outside Nara, then maybe I'll wake up a little bit sooner than that . . .

25
Acknowledgements

Sumimasen . . .

I am especially indebted to the support and inventiveness of my wife Susan, who not only endured five weeks of enforced football widowhood while I was in Japan, but also devised dozens of new ways to keep Peter, Johnny and Michael out of the study in the subsequent weeks and months while I put this together.

I must also thank Robert Kirby at Peters, Fraser and Dunlop. At an early point in proceedings when I didn't have access to any tickets for any World Cup matches he pulled out all the stops on my behalf, using his extensive network of contacts in the sporting media world, eventually sending me the little oval bit out of the top of a box of tissues with a 'Win a World Cup Trip of a Lifetime' competition entry form on it. The competition question to be answered, however, remained on the rest of the box.

My thanks, too, to Rupert Lancaster, an endlessly supportive source of constructive suggestions and free books, to Paul Simpkin for all the taping and keeping all those newspapers, to James Bartlam of Downes and Bartlam Travel for sorting out all the flights and hotels, to Jim Brown and talkSPORT for the gig, to Mike Parry and Alan Brazil for having me, to Nick, Paul, Theo and David for your company, and to Yoshiyuki Watanabe for the pictures.

Also to Alison, Hugh and Annie for invaluable tips about slippers.

Hai!

Streatham Common, November 2002